THE CAMBRIDGE COMPA
AND THE ANTI

The Anthropocene is a proposed geological epoch marking humanity's alteration of the Earth: its rock structure, environments, atmosphere. *The Cambridge Companion to Literature and the Anthropocene* offers the most comprehensive survey yet of how literature can address the social, cultural and philosophical questions posed by the Anthropocene. This volume addresses old and new literary forms – from novels, plays, poetry and essays to exciting and evolving genres such as 'cli-fi', experimental poetry, interspecies design, gaming, weird, ecotopian and petro-fiction, and 'new' nature writing. Studies range from the United States to India, from Palestine to Scotland, while addressing numerous global signifiers or consequences of the Anthropocene: catastrophe, extinction, 'fossil capital', warming, politics, ethics, interspecies relations, deep time and Earth. This unique *Companion* offers a compelling account of how to read literature through the Anthropocene and of how literature might yet help us imagine a better world.

JOHN PARHAM is Professor of Environmental Humanities at the University of Worcester. He has authored or co-edited five books including *Green Media and Popular Culture* (Palgrave Macmillan, 2016) and (with Louise Westling) *A Global History of Literature and the Environment* (Cambridge University Press, 2017). He has edited the journal *Green Letters: Studies in Ecocriticism* for nineteen years.

THE CAMBRIDGE COMPANION TO LITERATURE AND THE ANTHROPOCENE

EDITED BY

JOHN PARHAM

University of Worcester

CAMBRIDGE
UNIVERSITY PRESS

CAMBRIDGE
UNIVERSITY PRESS

University Printing House, Cambridge CB2 8BS, United Kingdom

One Liberty Plaza, 20th Floor, New York, NY 10006, USA

477 Williamstown Road, Port Melbourne, VIC 3207, Australia

314–321, 3rd Floor, Plot 3, Splendor Forum, Jasola District Centre, New Delhi – 110025, India

79 Anson Road, #06–04/06, Singapore 079906

Cambridge University Press is part of the University of Cambridge.

It furthers the University's mission by disseminating knowledge in the pursuit of education, learning, and research at the highest international levels of excellence.

www.cambridge.org
Information on this title: www.cambridge.org/9781108498531
DOI: 10.1017/9781108683111

© Cambridge University Press 2021

First published 2021

Printed in the United Kingdom by TJ Books Limited, Padstow Cornwall

A catalogue record for this publication is available from the British Library.

ISBN 978-1-108-49853-1 Hardback
ISBN 978-1-108-72419-7 Paperback

Contents

Figures

Contributors

HEATHER ALBERRO recently completed her PhD on the postanthropo-centric worldviews and ecotopian potentialities of radical environmental activists at Nottingham Trent University's Department of Politics and International Relations. Her work spans a range of disciplines including green utopianism, critical post-human theory, environmental sociology, environmental ethics, ecocriticism and political ecology. Heather also serves as co-convenor for the Political Studies Association's (PSA) environmental politics specialist group and as Chair of the PSA's Early Career Network (ECN).

HANNES BERGTHALLER is a professor at the Department of Foreign Languages and Literatures at National Chung-Hsing University, Taiwan. His work focuses on the literature and cultural history of modern environmentalism, social systems theory and neo-cybernetics, and environmental philosophy. Together with Eva Horn (University of Vienna, Austria), he co-authored *The Anthropocene: Key Issues for the Humanities* (Routledge, 2020).

MANDY BLOOMFIELD is an associate professor of modern and contem-porary literature at the University of Plymouth. Her publications include *Archaeopoetics: Word, Image, History* (University of Alabama Press, 2016) and numerous articles on contemporary eco-poetics in journals such as *Contemporary Literature, Green Letters, Configurations* and *Critical Quarterly*.

ASTRID BRACKE writes on twenty-first-century British fiction and non-fiction, eco-criticism and narratology, climate crisis and floods. Her monograph, *Climate Crisis and the Twenty-First-Century British Novel*, was published by Bloomsbury Academic in 2018. She is an alumna of the Rachel Carson Center for Society and Environment in Munich, and currently works as a lecturer of British literature at HAN University of Applied Sciences, Nijmegen (Netherlands).

BYRON CAMINERO-SANTANGELO is a professor of English and environmental studies at the University of Kansas. His research and teaching interests include African literature and popular environmentalism, post-colonial studies, environmental humanities and environmental ethics and justice. His book *Different Shades of Green: African Literature, Environmental Justice, and Political Ecology* was published by Virginia University Press in 2014. He is also the author of *African Fiction and Joseph Conrad: Reading Postcolonial Intertextuality* (SUNY Press, 2005) and co-edited *Environment at the Margins: Literary and Environmental Studies in Africa* (Ohio University Press, 2011).

ALENDA Y. CHANG is an associate professor in film and media studies at the University of California, Santa Barbara (UCSB), and author of *Playing Nature: Ecology in Video Games* (University of Minnesota Press, 2019). Chang is also a founding co-editor of the open-access journal *Media+Environment* and co-directs the Wireframe media studio at UCSB.

EILEEN CRIST received her Bachelor's in sociology from Haverford College and her PhD, also in sociology with a specialisation in life sciences and society, from Boston University. She is recently retired from Virginia Tech where she taught for twenty-two years. Her work focuses on the extinction crisis and the destruction of wild places, pathways to halt these trends, and inquiries surrounding humanity's relationship with the planet. She is co-editor of a number of books, including *Gaia in Turmoil: Climate Change, Biodepletion, and Earth Ethics in an Age of Crisis* (MIT Press, 2009) and *Keeping the Wild: Against the Domestication of Earth* (Island Press, 2014). She has published many academic papers as well as popular writings, and is associate editor of the online journal *The Ecological Citizen*. Her most recent book, *Abundant Earth: Toward an Ecological Civilization*, was published by University of Chicago Press in 2019.

SEAN CUBITT is a professor of film and television at the University of Melbourne. His publications include *Ecomedia* (Rodopi, 2005), *The Practice of Light: Genealogies of Visual Media* (MIT Press, 2014), *Finite Media: Environmental Implications of Digital Technology* (Duke University Press, 2017) and *Anecdotal Evidence: Ecocritique from Hollywood to the Mass Image* (Oxford University Press, 2020). He is series editor for Leonardo Books at MIT Press.

DAVID HIGGINS is an associate professor of English literature at the University of Leeds. His most recent book is *British Romanticism, Climate Change, and the Anthropocene* (Palgrave Macmillan, 2017). He is currently working on a co-written history of British nature writing and a monograph on climate pessimism.

ANDREAS MALM teaches human ecology at Lund University. He is the author of numerous articles on fossil capital, power, Marx and warming, among other subjects, and author of the books *Fossil Capital: The Rise of Steam Power and the Roots of Global Warming* (Verso, 2016) and *The Progress of This Storm: Nature and Society in a Warming World* (Verso, 2018). His forthcoming book *Corona, Climate, Chronic Emergency* is in press with Verso.

PIPPA MARLAND is a Leverhulme Early Career Fellow at the University of Leeds, exploring the representation of farming in modern British nature writing. She has published widely on ecocriticism, nature writing and eco-poetry and is currently completing a monograph entitled *Ecocriticism and the Island: Readings from the British-Irish Archipelago* for the Rowman and Littlefield 'Rethinking the Island' series.

JOHN PARHAM is a professor of environmental humanities at the University of Worcester. He has authored or co-edited five books including *Green Man Hopkins: Poetry and the Victorian Ecological Imagination* (Rodopi, 2010), *Green Media and Popular Culture* (Palgrave Macmillan, 2016) and (with Louise Westling) *A Global History of Literature and the Environment* (Cambridge University Press, 2017). He is co-editor of the journal *Green Letters: Studies in Ecocriticism* and has published extensively on 'Victorian ecology', contemporary literature and green popular culture, including essays on punk, anime and 'digital cli-fi'.

SABA PIRZADEH is an assistant professor of English and environmental literature at Lahore University of Management Sciences, Pakistan. She completed her PhD in English from Purdue University on a Fulbright fellowship in 2016. Her work has been published in *ISLE: Interdisciplinary Studies in Literature and Environment*, *South Asian Review*, *Parergon*, *South Asian Popular Culture*, *Interventions* and the *Routledge Handbook of Ecocriticism and Environmental Communication*.

STANISLAV ROUDAVSKI is a senior lecturer at the University of Melbourne's Faculty of Architecture, Building and Planning. He designs for animals and plants as well as humans. His experiments contribute to knowledge by using scientific evidence and advanced technologies in concert with cultural, political and historical analyses.

SAM SOLNICK is a senior lecturer in English at the University of Liverpool where he co-directs the Literature and Science Hub. He has published widely in the environmental humanities including the monograph *Poetry and the Anthropocene* (Routledge, 2017).

TESS SOMERVELL is a British Academy postdoctoral fellow at the University of Leeds, working on a project titled 'Georgic Climates: Writing the Weather in Eighteenth-Century Poetry'. Previously, she was a research fellow at Leeds, working with David Higgins on the AHRC-funded project 'British Romantic Writing and Environmental Catastrophe'.

LAURA DASSOW WALLS is the William P. and Hazel B. White Professor of English at the University of Notre Dame, where she teaches nineteenth-century American literature, transcendentalism and the history of ecological thought. Her books include *Henry David Thoreau: A Life* (University of Chicago Press, 2017), *The Passage to Cosmos: Alexander von Humboldt and the Shaping of America* (University of Chicago Press, 2009), *Emerson's Life in Science: The Culture of Truth* (Cornell University Press, 2003) and *Seeing New Worlds: Henry David Thoreau and Nineteenth-Century Natural Science* (University of Wisconsin Press, 1995).

SABINE WILKE is the Joff Hanauer Distinguished Professor in Western Civilization and a professor of German. Her research and teaching interests include modern German literature and culture, intellectual history and theory, cultural and visual studies, and the environmental humanities. With assistance from the Alexander von Humboldt Foundation, Wilke founded a transatlantic research network on the environmental humanities.

ZAINOR IZAT ZAINAL is a senior lecturer in the Department of English at Universiti Putra Malaysia, where she teaches Malaysian literature in English and miscellaneous other subjects related to world literature. Currently, she is vice president of the Association for the Study of Literature and Environment ASEAN (ASLE-ASEAN). Her primary research interest is post-colonial ecocriticism, with particular emphasis on Malaysia.

Acknowledgements

At Cambridge University Press, I would like to thank Ray Ryan for suggesting, commissioning and supporting this book, the following for their support – Edgar Mendez, Sarah Starkey and Raghavi Govindane – and Lori Heaford for excellent and sympathetic copy-editing. Once again, I'd like to thank Alex Diaconescu for a meticulous and well-informed index and acknowledge the support of the University of Worcester's School of Humanities – most especially the Head of School, Michael Bradshaw. I owe thanks to the anonymous referees who provided valuable advice that sharpened the focus and extended the breadth of this *Companion*, to Alexandra Antonopoulou and Jack Zipes for the striking image adorning its cover and to Nerea Calvillo for generously providing the excellent visualisation 'Santiago de Chile In the Air'. I would, of course, like to thank each and every one of the authors. Their contributions to this volume have extended my knowledge considerably and will, I hope, do the same for the book's readers.

This *Companion* was completed during the Covid-19 pandemic. The Anthropocene is equally complex, multifaceted and unsettling. Understanding how literature and culture can help address it – indeed, whether they can do so at all – is a formidable task. We hope that these chapters illuminate how we might live through the Anthropocene, and that this book might serve a more pleasurable purpose as well: that of introducing us to or reacquainting us with the authors and artists discussed in these pages.

Finally, I'd like to thank my partner, Elaine Jones, who was with me as I finished the book during a lockdown: sharing space, sharing meals and sharing the rewards which come from living life – if only temporarily – at a slightly slower pace.

Chronology

This timeline shows the Anthropocene and relevant literary works.

Deep History

4.5 billion (Ga) BCE	Earth believed to have formed from an accretion of dust and gases and the collision of large planetesimals
4.44–4.41 Ga BCE	Water vapour enters the atmosphere, creating oceans (from volcanic gas emissions or ice delivered by comets)
4.37 Ga BCE	Oldest known crystals (zircon), discovered in Western Australia (1999)
4.28 Ga BCE	Oldest known rocks, found in volcanic deposits in Quebec (2001)
3.5 Ga BCE	Evidence of life on Earth, discovered from microfossils of single-celled organisms
3 Ga BCE	Earliest certain presence of viruses
2.4 Ga BCE	Photosynthesis begins – cyanobacteria organisms adapt to use water as an electron donor; the released oxygen accumulates in the atmosphere ('the Great Oxygenation')
2.3 Ga BCE	Possible 'Snowball Earth' (first Ice Age); as the ice melts, more oxygen accumulates in the atmosphere
2 Ga BCE	First supercontinent, Columbia/Nuna

'Explosion' of Life (Cambrian Period)

535 million (Ma) BCE	Likely explosion of life, forms fossilised in sedimentary rocks; first vertebrates begin to appear
500 Ma BCE	Animals may have begun exploring land at this time
	Tectonic shifts create continents including the supercontinent of Gondwana, the present-day 'global South' of Australasia, Antarctica, India, Africa and South America
489 Ma BCE	Second 'explosion' – the Great Ordovician Biodiversification Event – creating many species, especially marine life
465 Ma BCE	Plants begin to colonise the Earth

444 Ma BCE	First mass extinction, with 86 per cent species loss (mainly marine creatures) in a severe Ice Age
420 Ma BCE	Fish evolve
397 Ma BCE	First four-legged animals
386 Ma BCE	Oldest known fossilised tree, found in New York State (2008)
375 Ma BCE	Second mass extinction, possibly owing to plants stirring up the earth and releasing nutrients into the ocean
359–299 Ma BCE	Carboniferous Period of global warmth and lush forests; rich deposits of coal laid in North America and Europe
250 Ma BCE	Third (and greatest) mass extinction; volcanic eruptions in Siberia and methane released by methanosarcina; 96 per cent species loss
200 Ma BCE	Fourth mass extinction opens the way for dinosaurs
200–175 Ma BCE	Supercontinent of Pangaea breaks up, gradually forming the present-day continents
150 Ma BCE	'First bird' – *archaeopteryx* – fossil remains discovered in Bavaria (2010)
130 Ma BCE	Flowering plants and insects evolve together
70 Ma BCE	Grasses evolve
65–66 Ma BCE	Fifth extinction event at the end of the Cretaceous Period owing to asteroid impact; dinosaurs become extinct; mammals diversify
55 Ma BCE	Early primates evolve
	Mountain ranges form – Himalayas, Alps, Andes, Rockies
34 Ma BCE	Antarctica freezes over
4 Ma BCE	*Australopithecines* (early human ancestor) walks on two legs; fossil remains of 'Lucy' (3.2 Ma BCE) discovered in Hadar, Ethiopia (1974)
2.5 Ma BCE	Hominids begin to use stone tools and develop meat-rich diets
1.8–1.5 Ma BCE	*Homo erectus*, first hunter-gatherer, masters fire; existed approximately nine times as long as *homo sapiens*
500,000 BCE	Earliest evidence of purpose-built shelters – wooden huts found near Chichibu, Japan
195,000 BCE	*Homo sapiens*; oldest modern human remains – two skulls – found in Ethiopia (1997)
150–100,000 BCE	Humans begin to develop speech
50,000 BCE	'Great leap forward'; humans survive potential extinction, create more sophisticated tools and hunting techniques, and develop clothing and rituals
44,000 BCE	Oldest known cave art (Indonesia)
25,000 BCE	Dreamtime stories/songlines of indigenous people in Australia/ New Zealand preserve memories of geological events (e.g. volcanic eruptions, changes in sea levels)

The Holocene

11,700 BCE	Last Ice Age ends; Neolithic Revolution; development of human settlement and early agriculture
8000 BCE	Forest clearance begins (Eurasia)
5500 BCE	Transition from Stone to Bronze Age; humans begin smelting and working with copper and tin
5000 BCE	Technological improvements in farming; rice irrigation begins in East Asia
5000–3200 BCE	Writing starts to evolve
4000–3500 BCE	First civilisation, Sumerians (Mesopotamia); c.2100 estimated composition of the Sumerian *Epic of Gilgamesh*.
2100–1700 BCE	Narrative literature created (Egypt)
	Woolly mammoth becomes extinct possibly owing to human activity
1500–1200 BCE	Sanskrit scriptures and hymns passed down orally, including *Aranyakas*, wilderness texts composed by recluses meditating in forests
750 BCE	The *Odyssey* (first transmitted orally; later attributed to Homer)
550 BCE	*Ramayana* (first transmitted orally; authorship attributed to Valmiki)
2 BCE–1558 CE	*Popul Vuh* – K'iche/Maya text – inscribed on pottery, walls, bark paper
77 CE	Pliny the Elder, *Natural History*
222–589	Six Dynasties (China), landscape poetry
13th century	Icelandic Sagas
1492	Columbus arrives in Americas. Great Dying of Indigenous peoples. Last fall in global temperature.
1592	*The Journey to the West* (Chinese folk epic, attributed to Wu Cheng'en)

Modernity

1610	'Columbian exchange' – trade networks link Europe, the Far East, Africa, Asia and the Americas; CO_2 levels (recorded in glacial ice) begin to rise
1669	Nicolaus Steno demonstrates that rock strata signify periods of time
1758	Linnaeus names *Homo sapiens* (and 12,000 other plants and animals)
1778	Georges-Louis Leclerc (Comte de Buffon), *Epochs of Nature*
1784	James Watt invents the steam engine
1785	William Cowper, *The Task*
1788	James Hutton, *Theory of the Earth*
1798	Wordsworth and Coleridge, *Lyrical Ballads*
1800	Human population reaches 1 billion
1815	William Smith – establishment of succession via fossil record allows for more precise dating of Earth
1818	Mary Shelley, *Frankenstein*
1830–3	Charles Lyell, *Principles of Geology*; proposes calling the postglacial era 'Recent'; name amended to the 'Holocene' by French geologist Paul Gervais (1867)

1834	Ralph Waldo Emerson, 'The Relation of Man to the Globe', lecture in Boston
1837	Henry David Thoreau begins to keep a journal
1840s	Fly ash (SCP) starts to accumulate
1845–7	Alexander von Humboldt, *Cosmos*
1850	CO_2 level reaches 285 ppm, the upper limit of Holocene variability (260–285 ppm)
1852–3	Charles Dickens, *Bleak House*
1854	Thomas Jenkyn proposes 'Anthropozoic' to indicate visible human agency on the Earth; adopted by Antonio Stoppani in 1873
1859	Charles Darwin, *On the Origin of Species*
1860	Walt Whitman, 'Kosmos'
1880–1900	Sea levels begin to rise
1895	H. G. Wells, *The Time Machine*
1900	CO_2 reaches 296 ppm, exceeding Holocene variability
1904	Baldomero Lillo, *Sub Terra*
1905	Fritz Haber, German chemist, invents an industrial process for fixing nitrogen from the atmosphere; enables production of chemical fertiliser
1907	Leo Baekeland creates the first synthetic, mass-produced plastic (Bakelite)
1908	Ford's Model T leaves the production line in Detroit
1913	British geologist Arthur Holmes publishes the first geologic timescale
1918	Georg Kaiser, *Gas I: A Play in Five Acts*, performed in Frankfurt (28 November)
1927	Upton Sinclair, *Oil!*
1935	First attempted ice sheet analysis
1936	Tasmanian tiger becomes extinct

The Great Acceleration

1945	Human population reaches 3 billion
	40 million motor vehicles
	Global sea levels risen by 3 inches since 1880
	Commercial production of plastic accelerates
	First atomic bomb test, Alamogordo, New Mexico (16 July); atomic bombs detonated over Hiroshima and Nagasaki (August)
1950	CO_2 reaches 311 ppm
1950s	Wholesale production begins of broiler chicken (bred for meat production)
	Dramatic global increases in SCP accumulation
1953	Jean Giono, *The Man Who Planted Trees*
1954	First nuclear power plant generating domestic energy, Obninsk, Soviet Union
1957	Nevil Shute, *On the Beach*
1957–8	International Geophysical Year – ice core drilling begins

1962	Aldous Huxley, *Island*
	Ghassan Kanafani, *Men in the Sun*
1964	Peak in radionuclides (atoms emitting radiation) found in tree rings (Poland) subsequent to nuclear weapons testing
1970	Air passengers globally reach 310 million
	Jabra Ibrahim Jabra, *The Ship*
1971	Greenpeace founded
1974	J. G. Ballard, *Concrete Island*
1975	Ernest Callenbach, *Ecotopia*
1976	Marge Piercy, *Woman on the Edge of Time*
1977	Global Commission on Stratigraphy establishes GSSP's ('golden spikes') to identify geologic periods
1979	*Earth First!* forms
1984	Bhopal pesticide plant leaks 30 tons of toxic gas – regarded as the world's worst industrial disaster
	Ray Bradbury, 'The Toynbee Convector'
1985	Global production of concrete reaches 1 billion tons
	Ursula K. Le Guin, *Always Coming Home*
1986	Chernobyl nuclear disaster
1990	Kim Stanley Robinson, *Pacific Edge*
	Karen Tei Yamashita, *Through the Arc of the Rainforest*
1991	Mudrooroo adapts Heiner Müller's 'The Task'
1992	Andrew C. Revkin speculates (*Global Warming*) that we are entering an 'Anthrocene', 'a geological age of our own making'
	Formation of ASLE (Association for the Study of Literature and Environment)
	Marwan Darwish, 'The Penultimate Speech of the "Red Indian" to the White Man'
1993	Liyana Badr, *A Balcony over the Fakihani*
1995	First United Nations Framework Convention on Climate Change (UNFCCC) conference, Berlin
	Motor vehicles reach 700 million
1996	Luis Sepúlveda, *The Story of a Seagull and The Cat Who Taught Her to Fly*
1997	UNFCCC adopts Kyoto Protocol – legally binding reductions in greenhouse gas emissions
	First mass-produced electric vehicle (Toyota Prius)
	Yachtsman Charles Moore discovers the Great Pacific Garbage Patch
	Yan Lianke, *The Years, Months, Days*
2000	Paul Crutzen and Eugene Stoermer propose the 'Anthropocene'; possible Global Boundary Stratotype Sections and Points (GSSPs): global dispersal of radiation; atmospheric carbon dioxide; fly ash from burning fossil fuels; nitration and phosphate in soil; species extinction; 'techno-fossils' – plastic, buried concrete, chicken bones
	Human population reaches 6 billion
	Air passengers globally reach 1.674 billion
	Global sea levels risen 7 inches since 1880
	CO_2 369 ppm

Early 2000s	Buen Vivir movement begins, South America
2001	Adam Nicolson, *Sea Room: An Island Life*
2002	Chloe Hooper, *A Child's Book of True Crime*
2003	Margaret Atwood, *Oryx and Crake* (first of the *MaddAddam* trilogy)
2004	*The Day After Tomorrow* (dir. Roland Emmerich)
	Keri Hulme, *Stonefish*
2005	Brenda Hillman, *Pieces of Air in the Epic*
	Michel Houellebecq, *The Possibility of an Island*
	Kathleen Jamie, *Findings*
2006	*An Inconvenient Truth* (dir. Davis Guggenheim)
2007	Sarah Hall, *The Carhullan Army*
	There Will Be Blood (dir. Paul Thomas Anderson)
2009	CO_2 387 ppm.
	Sub-commission on Quaternary Stratigraphy establishes Anthropocene Working Group (AWG) to consider evidence for geological signatures of a new epoch
	UNFCCC (Copenhagen) – proposals for a new global climate agreement are retracted
	Zakaria Ali, *The Dam*
	Margaret Atwood, *The Year of the Flood*
	Keris Mas, *Jungle of Hope*
	Yvonne Reilly, *Styrofoam*
2010	Approximately 121 million tons of nitrogen p.a. fixed from the atmosphere (safe level estimated at 35 million tons)
	Susan Abulhawa, *Mornings in Jenin*
	Gasland (dir. Josh Fox)
	Chuah Guat Eng, *Days of Change*
	Ian McEwan, *Solar*
	Dale Pendell, *The Great Bay: Chronicles of the Collapse*
	Ed Roberson, *To See the Earth Before the End of the World*
2011	An earthquake and a tsunami provoke the Fukushima nuclear disaster
	Fate of the World (Red Redemption)
	Magnus Mills, *Explorers of the New Century*
	A New Beginning (Daedalic Entertainment/Lace Mamba)
2012	Kathleen Jamie, *Sightlines*
	Barbara Kingsolver, *Flight Behaviour*
	Robert Macfarlane, *The Old Ways: A Journey on Foot*
2013	*Queers in Love at the End of the World* (Anna Anthropy)
	Margaret Atwood, *MaddAddam*
	Alexis Wright, *The Swan Book*
2014	Sixth mass extinction and defaunation – massive decline in species and populations, emptying of land and oceans; WWF/Zoological Society of London estimate 50 per cent loss of individual animals since 1970
	Stephen Collis, 'Notes Towards a Manifesto of the Biotariat'
	Chang-rae Lee, *On Such a Full Sea*
	Jeff Vandermeer, 'Southern Reach Trilogy'

2015	*El Botón de Nácar* [*The Pearl Button*] (dir. Patricio Guzmán)
	Antonia Honeywell, *The Ship*
	Clare Morrall, *When the Floods Came*
	Juliana Spahr, 'Dynamic Positioning'
	Submerged (Uppercut Games)
2016	Anthropocene proposal debated at the International Geological Congress
	Amitav Ghosh, *The Great Derangement*
	Jennifer Haigh, *Heat and Light*
	Ella Hickson, *Oil*
	Amy Liptrot, *The Outrun*
	Magnus Mills, *The Field of the Cloth of Gold*
2017	An estimated 75 per cent drop in insects since 1989
	Adam Nicolson, *The Seabird's Cry*
	Osama Siddique, *Snuffing Out the Moon*
2018	Air passengers globally reach 4.233 billion
	Worldwide PC sales at 259.4 million
	Optical fibre production reaches 325 million kilometres
	Estimated 23 billion broiler chickens worldwide
	Extinction Rebellion created
	Natasha Carthew, *All Rivers Run Free*
	Richard Powers, *The Overstory*
2019	AWG affirms Anthropocene proposal by 88 per cent, Cape Town; radiation levels agreed as GSSP
	Scientists in California calculate that plastic deposited in the fossil record has doubled every fifteen years since 1945
	CO_2 415 ppm (May)
	David Gange, *The Frayed Atlantic Edge: A Historian's Journey from Shetland to the Channel*
	Amitav Ghosh, *Gun Island*
	Robert Macfarlane, *Underland – A Deep Time Journey*
	Covid-19 outbreak in China (December)
2020	Covid-19 declared a global pandemic by World Health Organization (11 March)
	Estimated 11,000 fewer air-pollution-related deaths in Europe and global CO_2 emissions decreased by 17 per cent (April)
	Deb Olin Unferth, *Barn 8*
	CO_2 417 ppm (May)

Introduction
With or Without Us: Literature and the Anthropocene
John Parham

'Coming events cast their shadow before', wrote the poet Thomas Campbell in 'Lochiel's Warning' (1802). The Anthropocene is the proposal that we have entered a new geological epoch marked by humanity's indelible alteration of the Earth: its rock strata, ecosystems, atmosphere. This book is about how the Anthropocene presages an altered future for the Earth, animals, plants and humans, and how, if at all, literature might help us live in that future. I am writing now, though, under a different shadow – that cast by Covid-19 on health, everyday life and humanity's social, economic and cultural being.

The Anthropocene was initially proposed in 2000 by atmospheric chemist Paul Crutzen and marine ecologist Eugene Stoermer. At the time of writing it is yet to be ratified,[1] but it was debated at the International Geological Congress in 2016 and affirmed by a majority of 88 per cent when, in May 2019, the Anthropocene Working Group (AWG) met in Cape Town.[2] Both the start date of the Anthropocene and its Global Stratotype Section and Point (GSSP) or 'golden spike' – a 'distinct and measurable signal of human presence in the geological record'[3] that would confirm the new epoch – remain under debate. As highlighted in this book's timeline, perhaps the Anthropocene began 8,000 years ago with forest clearance, human settlement and early agriculture[4]; or corresponds to Modernity – the establishment of global trade links and rising CO_2 levels (from about 1610) or James Watt's invention of the steam engine in 1784[5]; or perhaps, as the AWG seems to have concluded, it began with the post-1945 'great acceleration' – parallel lines of population increase, gross domestic product (GDP), nuclear proliferation, energy, and water use and their seismic consequences: devastation of ecosystems; polluting of land, sea and air; climate change; the extinction of plants, animals, eventually, perhaps, humans. All potentially cataclysmic but nonetheless frequently overshadowed by superficially more significant events – the pandemic or the 2007–8 global financial crisis.

And yet, the configurations of Covid and the Anthropocene are near identical. Both appear to confound human understanding. Like climate change, Covid-19 fills global space but can only be seen in the abstract: maps, graphs, bar charts, spiky visualisations of the virus itself. Both, too, are intimate. Contemporary environmental ailments – asthma, heart failure, bronchitis, premature births – and nineteenth-century industrial diseases – tuberculosis or cholera – are, like Covid-19, incubated by air, overcrowded housing, poor hygiene and poverty. Covid likewise evidences a tension which, for historian Dipesh Chakrabarty, underlies the Anthropocene, between two conceptions of the human: the Latin *homo* and the Greek *anthropos*. *Homo*, the rational individual of humanism, acts purposefully, socially, with a sense of justice. *Anthropos*, the human as *species*, acts blindly, from self-interest and with often ruinous cumulative force.[6] Elements of the pandemic – stockpiling, the occasional flouting of social distancing, denial even – make all too visible the inability of *homo* to rein in *anthropos*. Our corresponding, even greater inability to stop flying, driving or buying needless consumer goods is why climate change, pollution or mass extinction may prove impossible to stop.

Arguably a more specific picture frames both Covid-19 and the Anthropocene: the 'Capitalocene'.[7] One interpretation is that it's not humans per se who have created 'this fragile Earth' but human activity under capitalism: imperialism and global trade; plantations and industrial-scale agriculture; factories and the carbon economy (what Andreas Malm calls 'fossil capital'); the twentieth century's acceleration of consumerism. In *The Mushroom at the End of the World*, Anna Lowenhaupt Tsing tracks the complex commodity chain of the valuable matsutake mushroom into capitalism's dark corners: jungle fighters, industrial forestry, corporate negligence about food sources.[8] If we practised the vigilance of Tsing to trace the origins of Covid, that vigilance would lead us into equivalent recesses: the factory farms and wet markets in which tightly crammed animals most likely incubated and passed on the virus; global merchant banks investing in Chinese poultry farms; the international business travel and holiday cruise ships that carried the virus around the world. Pursuing these correspondences, Covid-19 might highlight likely consequences of climate change too – soil erosion, droughts and floods, water pollution, insect loss. Contact tracing the virus might stop us pretending that the precariousness of food, farming and nature in elongated international supply chains is inconsequential.[9]

'I do not intend to conflate ecological with epidemiological calamities, though of course they can be intimately linked', wrote Anahid Nersessian in 2013.[10] This is underlined in one final convergence. In Tsing's study the matsutake mushroom is both a survivor – of Hiroshima, of commercial logging – and an enabler of alternative lifestyles, for instance, for a community of pickers in Oregon living in coexistence with nature. Covid-19 has allowed us to glimpse hitherto marginal existences and the possibilities of a better life: azure vapourless skies, emptier roads, birdsong. In April 2020, the Centre for Research on Energy and Clean Air reported a 10 per cent monthly reduction in particulate matter pollution and, in Europe, an estimated 11,000 fewer air-pollution-related deaths.[11] Global CO_2 emissions decreased by 17 per cent.[12]

Yet atmospheric CO_2 keeps rising. So, how do we offset the danger 'that the clean air of early [Covid] lockdown will be but a footnote in the narrative of environmental catastrophe'?[13] The Anthropocene is unprecedented. Its future, our future, is unknown. Coupled with the likelihood of human activity having created an ungovernable, catastrophic planet, with earth system feedbacks such as methane release threatening changes where human populations would dwindle, collapse or die[14] – Alan Weisman's *The World without Us*[15] – there is considerable risk of epistemological paralysis. Yet Higgins and Somervell remind us in this volume (Chapter 10) of an alternative etymology, the Greek *katastrophē*: an 'overturning' or 'sudden turn' in individual or cultural consciousness. In that sense, the one upside of Covid-19 implies that the Anthropocene, too, could become the 'Cosmocene' imagined by geographer Jamie Lorimer:

> The Cosmoscene would begin when modern humans became aware of the impossibility of extricating themselves from the earth and started to take responsibility for the world in which they lived—turning to face the future, rather than running from the past, and acknowledging, building, and absenting from relations with all the risky, sustaining, and endearing dimensions of the planet. The Anthropocene would become a staging point, the threshold at which the planet tipped out of the Holocene before embarking upon a post-Natural epoch of multispecies flourishing with its own, perhaps less dramatic, stratigraphy.[16]

The opportunity, writes Kate Rigby, 'for deeper understanding and, potentially, new directions'[17] is why, even pending ratification, the *concept* of the Anthropocene has generated an explosion of interest in the social sciences, humanities and literature. As Hannes Bergthaller (Chapter 12) says in this book, how we think about, write about and 'characterize the Anthropocene and what we believe it to be will change what the Anthropocene *is*'.[18] Taking that opportunity will first require, as Chakrabarty says about history, 'probing the limits' of our discipline.[19]

Flailing

> Cemeteries give a more powerful push toward civilization in a single
> season of scarlet fever than all your dramas, diaries, poetry, pamph-
> lets, orthographic reforms, and propensities do in a year.[20]

Crises engender what Lauren Berlant calls 'genre flailing', a 'mode of crisis
management' that arises when long-standing practices, like literature or
literary criticism, seem useless and become 'disturbed in a way that intrudes
on one's confidence about how to move in it'. Trying not to despair, we
'improvise like crazy' where '"like crazy" is a little too non-metaphorical'.
We throw 'language and gesture and policy and interpretations at a thing
to make it slow or make it stop'.[21] Flailing can be iconoclastic – nullifying
any sense of what literature can do – or defensive. It 'can be fabulously
unimaginative, a litany of lists of things to do, to pay attention to, to say, to
stop saying . . . in the pinch of a crisis we return to normal science or
common sense—whatever offers relief in established clarity'.[22] As lovers of
literature, we may, for example, prove reluctant to let go of established
forms like (say) narrative fiction or lyric poetry. Yet, Berlant sees this
'ambivalence toward opening our objects to a transformation whose effects
are not foreclosed'[23] as beneficial. It makes us better able to hold on to what
remains valuable: 'whenever one is destroying some things in the object
one is also trying to protect something else in it that matters, [and] that
deserves a better world for its circulation'.[24] Together we flail; but together
we defend and adapt our practices towards an 'aspirational co-being' better
suited, one hopes, to altered circumstances.[25]

Underpinned by the chapters in this book, Berlant's advocacy of
a practice that disturbs rather than destroys will be the template, in this
introduction, for how literature can and has adapted to the proposed new
epoch. To get there, however, we first have to confront the fact that the
Anthropocene has eroded confidence in how, and even whether, literature
can move in this new world.

'There's a Scale to This Shit That I Don't Think You're Getting'

Disturbed by the 'shock of the Anthropocene', literature and literary form
have been flailing.[26] This is partly because of a paradox foregrounded in
Richard Powers' multi-layered Anthropocene novel *The Overstory* (2018).
An environmental activist suggests: 'The best arguments in the world
won't change a person's mind. The only thing that can do that is a good

story.' Yet in another passage, describing a married couple reading their way through *The Hundred Greatest Novels of All Time*, it is remarked:

> To be human is to confuse a satisfying story with a meaningful one, and to mistake life for something huge with two legs. No: life is mobilized on a vastly larger scale, and the world is failing precisely because no novel can make the contest for the *world* seem as compelling as the struggles between a few lost people.[27]

This echoes key critiques concerning literature and the Anthropocene. In *The Great Derangement*, Amitav Ghosh argues that dominant literary forms evolved at about the same time as 'the accumulation of carbon in the atmosphere was rewriting the destiny of the earth'. Accordingly, an absence of climate crisis in (specifically) literary fiction implicates literature's 'practices and assumptions', especially those of the novel, in a 'deranged' collective evasion of climate change in social and cultural discourse.[28] Yet, nineteenth-century novels describing the ecological disturbance wrought by cities and industrialisation, post-colonial literature, in the twentieth century, documenting the impact of resource wars on environments and people, and an accelerating number of contemporary 'literary' treatments of ecological crisis all question the extent to which writers have evaded humanity's rising ecological impact.[29]

A more persuasive critique argues that literature is ill-equipped to address a requirement, in the Anthropocene, for human perspective to readjust to vast spatial, temporal and existential scales.[30] Literature is habitually structured to a human scale – households, workplaces, villages, towns or cities.[31] Narratives and perspectives centre on human drama (events happening to individuals, families or communities) and invariably reach humanly meaningful or rewarding conclusions with proportionately little account of environments, other animals or the Earth.[32] The Anthropocene begs fundamental questions, therefore, about literature: how can personal narrative or the notion of the autonomous individual, central to conventions ranging from the novelistic or dramatic protagonist to the essayist, nature writer, gamer or poetic 'I', really help us reflect on the overlapping geological, environmental and interspecies dimensions of humanity's impact on the Earth; or foster the collective ecological consciousness, and activism, required to address that impact?

Fundamental to this assessment has been the 'scale critique' developed by critics such as Timothy Clark and Derek Woods. The Anthropocene is propelled by vast 'Hyperobjects' – the global economy, the Earth system, climate. This might encompass the cumulative agency of *anthropos*, although, as Woods argues, what is actually changing the Earth is not humans but, rather, 'large-scale' assemblages. Composed of 'horizontal patterns of relation among ontologically different entities' (which exist in 'discontinuous scale domains'), assemblages conglomerate human, non-human and technological agency.[33] If the task is to work out which 'mediators' might best capture the scale and complexity of hyperobjects or assemblages,[34] Clark, in particular, seems to have concluded that realities which are 'invisible at the normal levels of perception' and can 'only emerge as one changes the spatial or temporal scale at which the issues are framed'[35] demand non-literary forms of representation. An example might be the Spanish architect Nerea Calvillo's 'In the Air' project, which makes visible how microscopic agents (gases, particles, diseases) react upon cities.[36]

Perhaps, as Clark suggests, cumulative, global 'geological force', human or otherwise, can only be represented 'as a totality . . . in graphs, statistics and computer projections', not in the individualist mode of, for example, the realist novel.[37] Scale critique issues a challenge that any conception of

A 2009 'In the Air' example showing Santiago, http://intheair.es/santiago/.
Architect: Nerea Calvillo; Collaborators: Katha Caceres, Francisco Calvo, Christian Oyarzun and Ricardo Vega; Funding: Video and Media art biennale of Chile BVAM09 and the Spanish Agency of Cooperation and Development (AECID).

literature and the Anthropocene must answer. It is addressed throughout this *Companion* most notably by Sean Cubitt (Chapter 2), Mandy Bloomfield (Chapter 3), Astrid Bracke (Chapter 4), Sam Solnick (Chapter 13) and Pippa Marland (Chapter 17). These – and other, preceding studies – suggest avenues of engagement with scale critique which can lay the foundations for the adaptive, hybrid forms of literature that the Anthropocene will necessitate.

First, the human perspective is all we have. Writing about plastic waste, Richard Kerridge suggests that we seem to be able to 'encounter' things

> at the two extremes of perspective, the panoramic zoom out and the microscopic zoom in, but not, it would seem, in the middle range, the range available to human vision without technological assistance. Yet this middle perspective is the one we need in order to visualise the actions of human individuals or communities.[38]

The elegance of Calvillo's image of Santiago is that it brings invisible assembled agency into dialogue with a recognisably human dimension, the city. Literature must find similar ways to cross scale or assemble together larger 'patterns of relation'.

An analogy can be made with a corresponding preoccupation with scale in ecological science,[39] one motivated by ecology's own mismatch between its study of localised plant communities and the need to factor in large-scale dynamics: evolution, the Earth system science, climate change.[40] Woods argues that ecological science now presupposes differential scale domains,[41] yet, actually some ecologists have found, in scale, grounds for a 'unified ecology'.[42] Jérôme Chave proposes 'dispersal as the fundamental process that bridges across spatial scales'.[43] Nathan et al. define dispersal as 'the movement of individuals from their source location (e.g. birth or breeding site) to another location where they might establish and reproduce'.[44] Their study of the long-distance dispersal of plant seeds supports Chave's conceptualisation of dispersal as a process 'driven' by larger forces such as climate, ocean currents or human migration but which, itself, drives macro-level shifts via, for example, population spread or the colonisation or alteration of unoccupied or existing habitats. Stating that 'the attempt to synthesise timescales, and see how the players contribute to changing their theatre, is a result of foremost importance in ecology',[45] Chave resolves the tension between scale divergence and a unified ecology into a 'global change biology', an assemblage of species and physical processes, each percolating across porous scales and fluid ontological boundaries, to shape and reshape each other.

Correspondence with this 'global change biology' will not be possible where literature is overly solipsistic. Clark makes this point as he jumps from scale effects to scale framing.[46] Discussing the argument that empathy for literary characters – or landscape or animals – can transport us across time and space, Clark insists that it's futile to bring literary form, 'which privileges the realm of personal human experience as the basic reality', to bear on multidimensional scales or complexities that we cannot 'perceive with ordinary human faculties'.[47] Yet, he jumps too quickly in assuming that literature will (or can) only ever prioritise the human scale. For something analogous to scale unity does occur in literature that seeks to diminish or subject the narrative voice or poetic 'I' to (say) geological history. We see, for example, in Marland (Chapter 17), the visibility of deep time and global space in new nature writing. Correspondingly, Bloomfield describes the darting and convoluted syntax by which the poet Ed Roberson attempts to 'yoke together incommensurate scales'. And it is there in texts that unify scale by isolating a 'conjuncture of histories in a uniquely concrete moment', a device central, suggests Sean Cubitt (Chapter 2), to literary and cultural form.

Cubitt distinguishes between 'two regimes of truth'; abstraction and anecdote. The former culls a sense of large-scale dynamics from massive datasets (graphs or computer modelling) while anecdote – for example, storytelling – seizes on instances where historical or ecological forces are experienced by an individual person, family, community, etc. Thom van Dooren has demonstrated how his own photograph of a nesting albatross crystallises the matrix of relations through which we coexist with it: plastic and chemical pollution, habitat disruption, possible extinction.[48] Andreas Malm, in Chapter 14 of this *Companion*, cites Walter Benjamin's *The Arcades Project* to argue that works of art, or even fragments, can be read as an object – 'more precisely, a monad' – 'into which all the forces and interests of history enter on a reduced scale'.[49] Malm's example is Ghassan Kanafani's novella *Men in the Sun* (1962). As three Palestinian men seek new lives in Kuwait's booming oil economy, the forces and interests of the fossil economy (both forced political exile and global warming) converge in a reduced, dramatic scale, on an ultimately tragic journey: 'The lorry, a small world, black as night, made its way across the desert like a heavy drop of oil on a burning sheet of tin.'

Yet, suggests Cubitt (in Chapter 2) because we know that each moment exists in a continuum of other moments, we know too that things can be changed. The conjunctive can become subjunctive; it can signal (he writes) 'the possibility of becoming otherwise'. For example, van Dooren's photograph also instils an ethical demand – it reminds us of 'the long history of life on this planet' (evidenced, too, in this *Companion*'s Chronology) and impresses upon us our accountability to past, present and future multispecies generations.[50] The *Men in the Sun* become, in Chapter 14 (Malm), a trigger for seeing Palestinian literature as a model of resistance to the accelerating, imperialising forces that underlie the Capitalocene.

There remains a danger of overstating the significance or influence of such moments. Possibly Clark's sharpest critique is that the Anthropocene debunks long-standing delusions about the ability of cultural modes – symbolism, imagination or narrative – to determine history and shape human affairs.[51] The lesson from Covid-19, however, arguably undermines both scale critique's scepticism about literature's ability to scale up (or down) and Clark's apparent dismissal of literary agency. As Bruno Latour has said: 'What the virus gets from banal droplets from coughing going from one mouth to another—the halting of the world economy—we can also begin to imagine via our little insignificant gestures put end to end.'[52] Covid shows, likewise, our mistake in thinking of 'the personal and the collective as two distinct levels'.[53] Nonetheless, just as ecology has pushed beyond its own threshold by integrating perspectives and methods from other disciplines,[54] I'd suggest, too, that the endeavour of engaging with the Anthropocene needs to be collective, that is individual acts of literature and literary scholarship should be put alongside ('end to end') equivalent insights, gestures or findings in other disciplines.

Writers in the 'new humanities' frequently argue that a dramatically changing, increasingly complex world – full of escalating risks and new possibilities – requires the innovative configurations of thought that come from converging disciplines.[55] Writing of environmental humanities, Emmett and Nye suggest: 'If one takes seriously this range of [ecological] concepts and the urgent problems that they address, it seems irresponsible to adopt the old-style humanities, working within a single discipline, content to focus on narrowly defined concerns.'[56] The very act of engaging with the Anthropocene, itself a concept grounded between geology and Earth system science, initiates interdisciplinary communion. The two chapters that bookend this *Companion* address, for example, how Emerson and Thoreau in the nineteenth century and British 'new nature writers' in the twenty-first have internalised and adapted to advancements in geology. What constitutes a genre or poem, a game, play or narrative pattern can fundamentally alter, as we shall see, in the light of the Anthropocene.

Nonetheless, even in crisis there are reasons for continuing to attend to discrete areas, modes or specialisms. Those reasons are both pragmatic and, as Berlant says, about retaining what deserves to be preserved in lieu of a 'better world'. Talking of local conservation, Carl Safina writes: 'You dodge despair not by taking the deluge of problems full bore. You focus on what can work, what can help, or what you can do, and you seize it, and then – you don't let go.'[57] Likewise, suggests McKenzie Wark, we prevent discussions and debates about a topic as complex as the Anthropocene becoming overwhelming by working out which knowledge and which practices might 'be useful in a particular domain'.[58]

If the Anthropocene has engendered an inquisition into the value of literature and literary criticism, it also offers an opportunity to reinvigorate both. In the remainder of this chapter, I will argue that literature *can* adapt its unique practices and distinctive facility to, as Ghosh puts it, 'approach the world in a subjunctive mode, to conceive of it, *as if* it were other than it is'.[59] Such adaptation could help effect a cumulative movement in *anthropos* towards an understanding that humans are embedded on the Earth. Supported by the chapters in this *Companion*, I will argue that literature can best do so by adapting and evolving its practice in two ways: by sharing divergent experiences (for different people, even species) of the Anthropocene; and by reconnecting human life with exponentially vaster scales: deep history, the planet Earth, the distant future. I will take each in turn because, as Wark indicates, the ability to develop an aesthetics for imagining and rewriting the Anthropocene rests first on working out which particular knowledges literature holds, and for whom.

State of Interdependence

It may pose a fundamental challenge to literature, yet, as Alexa Weik von Mossner points out,

> the very idea of the Anthropocene—regardless of whether it will become an official geological epoch or not—continues to be immensely productive for storytelling, inspiring artists to look for innovative and more adequate modes and media for conveying what it means—and what it can mean—when humans wield a geological force.[60]

How we write about the Anthropocene will be determined by our interpretation of it. Dating, defining, even naming the epoch matters: 'The event or date chosen as the inception of the Anthropocene will affect the stories people construct about the ongoing development of human societies.'[61] Evidence of a universal heedless *anthropos*, for example, runs deep. Pliny the Elder records, in AD 77:

> The miners gaze as conquerors upon the collapse of Nature. And nevertheless even now there is no gold so far, nor did they positively know there was any when they began to dig; the mere hope of obtaining their coveted object was a sufficient inducement for encountering such great dangers and expenses.[62]

Yet, the Anthropocene is not the same for everyone nor have all people been equally culpable in its evolution.

Demarcating competing conceptions of a generic ('aggregate') and 'divergent' Anthropocene, Rob Nixon makes the point that prevailing narratives have 'neglected immense disparities in human agency, impacts, and vulnerability'.[63] These relate to what he calls, elsewhere, 'slow violence'[64] – a gradual, near invisible destruction of ecosystems, indigenous cultures, and nations in the global South by processes of colonialism, imperialism or globalisation. Twentieth-century post-colonial literature and criticism has teased away at these stratigraphic signifiers of the Anthropocene: diminishing land and material resources; climate change and rising sea levels; increased radiation levels; the offshoring of toxic waste; and associated health consequences, poverty or political instability. Among several related case studies in this book are intimations of lynching and slavery in the African American Ed Roberson's nature poems; dual processes of resource extraction and colonialism impelling migration from Palestine to an unbearably warm Iraq; the role of organised religion and global trade in bringing injustice, rising sea levels and oceanic pollution to the Indian subcontinent; and the reconfiguration of Malaysia by neo-liberal economic development. We better understand the Anthropocene by reading 'through the magnifying glass of other knowledges'.[65]

Eva Horn and Hannes Bergthaller suggest that two ways have been conceived for how rational *homo* might reassume agency from self-willed *anthropos*: *eco-modernism*, postulating that human prosperity on a sustainable planet can be maintained only by technology; and *ecological posthumanism* – we'll survive only by recognising that we are just another species, kin to other animals and non-human nature.[66] Aside from disclosing connections among imperialism, global capitalism and the great acceleration, literature from the global South is, too, a valuable resource for kindling a sense of interspecies being. Researching Chapter 1 in this *Companion*, Laura Dassow Walls found that Alexander von Humboldt – whose *Cosmos* (1845–7) helped instigate human planetary awareness – relished what he called 'sharply indicative' words: Arabic terms to distinguish low-lying valleys from high ones; numerous Persian and Mongolian, Turkish and Chinese words for deserts; words describing 'the properties of vegetation, aspects of atmospheric motion, and the form and grouping of clouds'.[67] In parallel, chapters in this book consider how a land-based environmental ethics partly articulated in fiction has envisaged, for example, an alternative restructuring of Malaysia (Chapter 15); Palestinian literature as modelling resistance to fossil capital (Chapter 14); an indigenous Australian adaptation of German theatre that restates humans' entanglement in deep history and interspecies networks (Chapter 7); and the post-colonial essay's embodiment of that same relationality as an alternative to apocalyptic 'science fiction' (Chapter 6).[68]

Pursuing this last point, Elizabeth DeLoughrey has read Maori cultural tradition through Keri Hulme's collection *Stonefish*, a hybrid work of science fiction, modernism, magical realism and poetry specifically evolved to articulate the complex interweaving of scale and interspecies entanglement that the Anthropocene compels us to imagine.[69] The hybrid form makes sense given the imminence of geological dynamism to Hulme's home town, Okarito, on New Zealand's South Island. However, while contrasting *Stonefish* to end-of-the world stories – unlikely to be as useful, ultimately, as 'being-with-the-world' narratives[70] – DeLoughrey interestingly implies a need for literature to adapt to *all* the circumstances, experiences and responses that a divergent Anthropocene engenders.

For Eileen Crist (Chapter 11), the word 'Anthropocene' carries Promethean connotations that shrink the 'discursive space', for redressing human domination of the biosphere, to technological remedies.[71] Furthermore, as Higgins and Somervell illustrate (Chapter 10), literature causes us to question humans' capacity to manage the 'unruliness of the hyperobject of global environmental change'. Via *Frankenstein*, they suggest that technology, whatever the intention, is always prone to unleash unforeseen, ruinous consequences. Yet, other chapters in this *Companion* suggest that literature could intercede to sponsor the possibilities of beneficial technology. Alenda Chang (Chapter 9) gives examples of where digital games might model positive, even utopian human-technological assemblages. Stanislav Roudavski (Chapter 8) advocates entangling 'agile' eco-engineering with interspecies coexistence, for example, in the design of digitally fabricated owls' nests in Melbourne. Elsewhere, Zainal suggests (Chapter 15), environmental activism premised on traditional beliefs could be supported by information and communication technologies, while Marland (Chapter 17) cites the lovely image with which Amy Liptrot describes the view from her family's farm: 'Out at sea, bobbing on the surface, I can make out wave-energy devices being tested by engineers.'

Whatever one feels about technology, we are compelled nonetheless to think through its possibilities, risks or contradictions. The anthropologist Heather Anne Swanson astutely defines 'The Banality of the Anthropocene'. We have failed to notice its onset because the agents of ecological impact are the very housing developments, offices and agribusinesses, transportation, technology and modified food that constitute routine everyday life.[72] In this context, as DeLoughrey implies, apocalyptical narratives in Hollywood films might communicate quite effectively in countries where, perhaps, viewers need to be sharply jolted from a dependence on or uncritical faith in technology, or from their own unexamined consumerism.[73]

Which particular literature or other culture we turn to will, in other words, depend on how, exactly, each one of us inhabits the Anthropocene: which impacts affect us; our level of culpability as consumers; the historical moment, or social or geographical location, we inhabit; our experiences and cultural taste. There is no one literature *of* the Anthropocene, only literature and the Anthropocene.

Faltering Stories: Literature and the Anthropocene

The rupture that humans have enacted on geological time, and the unknowable future we have most likely created, may well compel, argues Filippo Bertoni, 'stories that will not easily fit together in the ways we are accustomed to'.[74] A related and valuable model of Anthropocene aesthetics is suggested in Anahid Nersessian's essay 'Two Gardens: An Experiment in Calamity Form'. Nersessian begins with Marx. Political economy (or human 'civilisation') deranges form. It goads things to jump out of their material being into something else: commodity form.[75] Attempts to conceive the world other than it is might begin, therefore, by exerting pressure on form. Nersessian's example is Romanticism's response to industrialisation. Experiments in 'language, syntax, and image' denoted, she writes, an intellectual crisis brought on by the period's own sense of impending catastrophe, an unknowable future and 'the uncertain impacts of our actions on it'.[76] Romanticism developed, Nersessian argues, a 'calamity form' which met potential catastrophe by 'assuming unexpected rhetorical postures'. Like the calamities they represent, we do not know the outcome of these postures. Yet, in the act of exerting pressure on external circumstance, the form constitutes 'an adjustment' which could make the calamity bearable or even start repairing it by remaking knowledge and linking that knowledge to action.[77]

Though not Nersessian's intention, this connection between disrupting literary form and reconstructing knowledge could equate ecologically minded literature with avant-garde or experimental form. Recapping what avant-garde means – to envisage futures that might one day become 'normal' – Kerridge argues that ecological crisis is unlikely to afford the luxury of the time required for experimental forms to become common-place. Therefore, lying outside 'the idiom and conventional narrative structure of personal experience', such modes will struggle to elicit affective investment in addressing ecological crisis.[78] Stating, however, that litera-ture evolves to meet the *various* needs, pressures and desires' of any given moment – and that 'different literary forms . . . do different jobs'[79] – Kerridge underscores the argument that literature should adapt to all the contexts and experiences of the Anthropocene. The forms which evolve should encompass both the jolt of 'unexpected rhetorical postures' and a more temperate (but tenacious) disturbance of less experimental modes. Precisely this duality runs through the ways in which three core compo-nents of literature – form, genre and narrative – are adapting and innovat-ing to meet the Anthropocene head on.

Form

Affect theory describes how, for example, aesthetic experiences, ideas or an environment can stimulate body-based sensations. These register as feel-ings and emotions which may, in turn, develop into thought. The relation between 'sensation and sensibility'[80] can encompass awareness of ourselves as ecological beings. Pippa Marland, in an essay on W. G. Sebald, suggests that affective, bodily responses to matter allow 'a sense of human subject-ivity as unstable, fluid, and co-constituted by the nonhuman'. This might prompt a 'recalibration of ethical positions' and 'encourage us to think about history and how we wish to live now'.[81]

Heather Houser argues that literature, too, mediates relays from affect to 'ethical and social dispositions' and that it does so by 'tropes, metaphors, and . . . patterns'.[82] One way, therefore, in which literary texts exert pressure on form is by affective techniques such as shock, derangement or fear. In Chapter 7 of this *Companion*, Sabine Wilke describes how theatre audiences for Georg Kaiser's *Gas I* (1918) physically experience the explosive and catastrophic consequences of humans' misuse of energy; while, in Chapter 13, Sam Solnick details how, a century later, Juliana

Spahr's 'Dynamic Positioning' (2015) disrupts iambic pentameter (and thus the bodily act of reading) to convey a forfeiture of technological control and the disaster of an oil spill. Correspondingly, the affective leverage of incongruity can signify a derangement of human–nonhuman relations: in *Bleak House* (1852–3) – in that most human of forms, the novel – Dickens personifies smoke, smog, water and dust to convey an unsettling 'thing power' menacing nineteenth-century London; just recently, Deb Olin Unferth's *Barn 8* (2020) deploys screwball comedy to spotlight the horrors of battery farming and the adversities of animal liberationist activism. Unexpected emptiness, silence or inactivity might foreground the chilling prospect of a world without us, white space or caesuras in poetry, for example, or the 'creepiness' that Paolo Ruffino finds in forms of gaming operated by nonhumans.[83]

Yet, Ruffino goes on to suggest, nonhuman gaming can also model interspecies companionship. Two books on poetry and the Anthropocene likewise intimate that affective modes could conjure a cosmocene aesthetics. Tom Bristow and Sam Solnick both deploy systems theory to posit ecology, biology, language, feeling and thought acting upon each other. Experiments with sound and space, shifts in rhythm, deployments of tone such as irony, white space or ellipses – each creating interludes in which the word is quelled for, or by, the world – allow us, in a 'play of thought and affect', to feel realities and/or dimensions of time and space that would usually exceed human comprehension or language.[84] Bristow, in particular, finds hope in harnessing poetic affect to check the 'looming darkness' of the Anthropocene. His study of John Kinsella, John Burnside and Alice Oswald emphasises how lyric poetry's encouragement to feel, experience and dwell upon an emotional attachment to place might elicit what he calls 'Anthropocene emotion', a greater sense of connectedness with the Earth's ecology.[85]

Genre

Ghosh complains that climate change has been tackled in literature only within a generic ghetto of science fiction.[86] However, the possibilities that exist in adapting, blending or creating new genres have been acknowledged in discussions of literature and the Anthropocene. Influenced by Berlant, Stephanie LeMenager suggests that crises, like the Anthropocene, threaten 'representational impasse' and precipitate 'genre trouble'. LeMenager calls for 'adaptive' forms: 'artistic genres are fraying, recombining, or otherwise moving outside of our expectations of what they ought to be because life itself is moving outside of our expectations for what it ought to be . . . life itself begins to encourage new representational regimes'.[87] Two approaches have been taken to the Anthropocene genre: adaptation of existing forms; and the evolution of new genres or sub-genres.

The most apparent examples of the former occur in science fiction and crime fiction. Swanson, Bubandt and Tsing propose the Anthropocene as a science-fiction concept. It 'pulls us out of familiar space and time' and makes us 'view our predicaments differently'. It also invites us to appraise our current world, 'to take the view from afar and look at the earth as if we were explorers from the far distant future'.[88] Far from being a ghetto, science fiction, sci-fi, has evolved into climate fiction, cli-fi, and indeed into other forms such as ecotopian or 'weird fiction'. Surveys by Adam Trexler and Adeline Johns-Putra detail cli-fi's increasing popularity across literary fiction – for example, Margaret Atwood, Barbara Kingsolver, Ian McEwan – popular and young adult (YA) fiction, online 'fan' fiction, anime and computer games.[89] Characters returning from the future to address our present world are commonplace. In the narrative computer game *A New Beginning*, visitors from a climate-stricken 2500 return to the 1980s and plead with a scientist to resume his abandoned life's work of developing a sustainable energy source. Conversely, in Ray Bradbury's 1984 short story 'The Toynbee Convector' a traveller (allegedly) returns from 2084 bearing evidence of a utopian society and restored natural environment that, inspired by this, his contemporaries then create. Cli-fi can, therefore, imagine both catastrophe and the ecotopian futures of species coexistence that Heather Alberro describes in Chapter 16 of this volume.

While Ghosh, too, discusses literary cli-fi (citing Kingsolver's *Flight Behavior*), his argument that we must also consider literature set in the present day, and how it details transformations which may haunt the future,[90] has invariably been addressed by crime fiction. Adaptations of the genre, sometimes categorised as 'Anthropocene Noir', address complex questions about our own culpabilities, to suggest, argues Deborah Bird Rose, that 'we, human beings, are all criminals, all detectives, and all victims'.[91] David Farrier, for example, finds elements of this in novels by Margaret Atwood, Alexis Wright, Ghosh himself (discussed in Chapter 5 by Saba Pirzadeh) and, with reference to the 'incalculable' consequences of humans' relation to other animals, in Chloe Hooper's *A Child's Book of True Crime*.[92] Both science fiction and crime fiction have evolved, that is, into Anthropocene fiction by adopting complex interwoven plotlines, ambiguous perspectives and often unresolved conclusions that reflect the dangerous, unknowable, but open futures that the Anthropocene portends.[93]

The evolution of new genres is, arguably, an even more fertile example both of the adaptability of literature to the Anthropocene and of the benefits to be gained from blending literary form with other media and modes of writing. LeMenager envisages cli-fi in terms of new forms of 'interactive and multi-sited authorship' developed in online and digital media.[94] Examples include blogs, social media and, in particular, online non-fictional story sites. One example is 'The Living Archive', a multimedia resource of extinction stories, from around Oceania, created by van Dooren.[95] Another is the Climate Stories Project, 'oral histories' from across the globe in which people video-record experiences of flooding (Malawi), coastal erosion (Senegal), deforestation (Mali), ocean warming and reduced fish stocks (Japan) or climate activism (USA).[96] Converting individual stories into online archives, these platforms shape a cumulative human imagination of and response to the Anthropocene. They unite data's accumulation of knowledge with anecdote's power to imagine and co-experience ecological impacts, while also sharing messages of resistance and hope.

Narrative

Storytelling has been prominent in literature's engagement with the Anthropocene. Ursula Heise's introduction to the *Routledge Companion to the Environmental Humanities* is entitled 'Planet, Species, Justice—and the Stories We Tell about Them'. Serpil Oppermann and Serenella Iovino's collection *Environmental Humanities: Voices from the Anthropocene* includes a section on 'Ecostories'. Houser, too, regards narrative as central to the process by which affective relays in literature can nurture ethical and social dispositions.[97] Because conventional narrative forms are, nevertheless, problematic, some critics have sought alternative, anti-narrative strategies such as narrative silence.[98] Yet, what more typically characterises narrative in the Anthropocene is to subpoena the person-level resolution at which – Astrid Bracke argues in Chapter 4 of this *Companion* – we are 'optimally suited' to see or comprehend things (e.g. the 'small-scale, intimate and immediate experiences' offered by novels) so as to stretch to deeper space and time. As von Mossner puts it, transportation, whether through 'cognitive estrangement or strategic empathizing', can enable us to 'imaginatively experience' other environments or future tipping points. It can bring our present-day 'real world' into dialogue with 'future worlds' that might arise from our impacts, agencies and responsibilities.[99]

For example, while not directly addressing environmental crisis, the potential of incongruity, inherent to allegorical and/or comic forms, for examining *anthropos* has been exploited by English novelist Magnus Mills. *Explorers of the New Century* (2011) and *The Field of the Cloth of Gold* (2016) both examine how human traits of exploration, adventure, migration and settlement can deteriorate into, respectively, hubris and imperialism, or population pressure and a scuffling over resources. *The Maintenance of Headway* (2010) – ostensibly about the unmanageable task of regulating bus timetables! – could be interpreted as a critique of eco-modernism, one that highlights humans' innate inability to manage any phenomena that are not 'self-contained systems'.[100] Displacing his characters into anonymous (albeit vaguely identifiable) places or periods, Mills elicits ontological questions about humans' blind self-interest and the impotence of rational, singular *homo* against both nature and the cumulative movement of *anthropos*.

Michel Houellebecq's *The Possibility of an Island* (2005) depicts the potential result of both the Capitalocene and/or the blind stumbling *anthropos*. The book narrates the interweaving stories of Daniels 1, 24 and 25, the last two cloned into a world, two thousand years ahead, shattered by climate change, tidal waves and nuclear explosions. The 'neohuman' Daniel, who is not unlike us, offers a bridge by which to experience our species haunting the (near) future, to sense, with sadness, a world without us and to encounter the shock that we might survive only in Daniel 25's transhuman form or in the savage 'pre-civilised' condition of the few remaining human inhabitants.[101]

Karen Tei Yamashita's *Through the Arc of the Rainforest* (1990) narrates the commercial exploitation of 'Matacão', a fictional, seemingly magical black substance (formed from industrial waste) discovered in the Amazon rainforest. Yet, the tilted perspective afforded by a non-human narrative focaliser – a fragment of asteroid debris floating six inches above the head of the protagonist, Kazumasa Ishimaru – immediately undermines humans' commercial and technological agency, magnifying the book's chief conceptions: first, that people, environments and (in this case) endangered birds are all entangled by the imperialising, avaricious nature of the Capitalocene; second, that capital itself is entangled equally within the material resources that it supposedly transforms and uncontrollable natural forces, notably when a Covid-like disease sweeps through Brazil and bacteria destroy the Matacão, terminating the corporate spree.

Other novels look back to characters looking forward to suggest ethical lessons. Jean Giono's picture book *The Man Who Planted Trees* (1953) imagines an encounter with a Provence shepherd, Elzéard

Bouffier. Bouffier plants one hundred acorn seeds a day, seeking to revitalise a desolate landscape. The narrator returns, after World War I, to find the land flourishing, the deserted village repopulated, and both water and animals having returned. Chinese novelist Yan Lianke's *The Years, Months, Days* (1997) narrates the sacrifice of Xianye, a seventy-two-year-old man living in a countryside blighted by climate change. Grasping his life's insignificance against environmental history, Xianye, gathering what little water he has, irrigates the soil and literally embeds himself within it. When, in future years, people return to the countryside and a further drought occurs, it is those living on the land fertilised by Xianye's body who survive. Transformation happens in both books because one human visualises their actions within a supposedly 'inconceivably' greater dimension: Lianke scales up Xianye's days to years; Bouffier, in three years, plants a hundred thousand seeds which eventually create a village supporting more than ten thousand inhabitants.

This stress on narrative and stories does risk over-privileging the novel. Yet, other forms also put human and non-human scales into dialogue. To heart-stopping effect, American poet Brenda Hillman, in 'Near Stations', uses negative space – page margins or that between words and lines – to materialise the relation of human time, modernity, to distant, barely conceivable scales of geological time:

> . . . chestnut
> blossoms fall diagonally between
> history and an endish
> time.[102]

Materialising humans' calamitous agency, Solnick, in Chapter 13 of this book, describes slow-ageing characters in Ella Hickson's play *Oil* whose lives stretch beyond a conventional human time frame to embody how oil extends its material ramifications into geological, climatological time. Conversely, in Chapter 17, Marland considers how creative non-fiction conjures (more hopefully) with time. Historian David Gange, gazing up from his kayak, sees cross-sections of rock in the Shetland Island cliffs. His distinctive viewpoint, from the sea, 'brings the passage of thousands and millions of years into view', opening, too, a perspective on the past as 'unfinished business: germs of fruitful routes as yet untravelled'. These routes may yet allow us to struggle free from late capitalism's acceleration towards disaster.

Retaining the individual perspective, even while scaling up or down, remains fundamental to engaging with the Anthropocene. Yet, what these examples also demonstrate is literature's ability to bring the non-human into human space or, conversely, to transport humans into deep time or non-human space. Unnervingly apposite, Dale Pendell's novel *The Great Bay: Chronicles of the Collapse* (2010) narrates a history of humankind after an unidentified global pandemic kills much of the world's population in 2021, a process then compounded by a warming planet and rising water levels. This is not a novel of the 'delimited horizon' that Ghosh laments.[103] While the book is 'set' in California, each chapter begins with a 'Panoptic' documenting the impact of climate change across cities, continents and bioregions. Correspondingly, the novel's twelve chapters progressively zoom out in time: the opening two cover a decade apiece; five and six span a century each; then a millennium (in chapter nine); until the closing chapter, beginning 'ten thousand years after the collapse', encompasses six thousand years in four pages.

Von Mossner argues that Pendell's fragmented narrative, where human protagonists are fleeting, means that we have no investment in what happens.[104] Yet actually, his experiment with narrative scale and eschewal of narrative voice signals further possible directions as literature heads into the Anthropocene. Though partly adopting the epochal and non-human frames of the epic,[105] Pendell's principal technique is to disperse the narrative across genres. The story accumulates from a mishmash of oral history (fictionally archived by a 'Scholar's Guild'), newspaper reports, journals and maps. *The Great Bay* reads, then, as much like a history book as it does a novel, albeit projected forwards. While it is frustrating to invest in characters never seen again (or merely glimpsed, as echoes in their descendants), this hybrid form transfers our empathy from individual characters to humans as a species. This is a critical transition that literature in the Anthropocene must make: conjuring an imagination of *anthropos*. Indeed, working across scale and genre, Pendell even imagines, unusually for an apocalyptic novel, a possibly hopeful future. Without blithely assuming that there won't, one day, be a world without us, he speculates that humans, humanity, might prove to be surprisingly resilient and asserts that if we are to survive, it will be by rediscovering both the land and small-scale, collective, socialist modes of community and coexistence.

Small Acorns: About this *Companion*

This book surveys literary responses to the causes, responsibilities and consequences of the Anthropocene, and where, in some cases, writers have sought to project a more sustainable human condition. Laura

Dassow Walls, in Chapter 1, explores how the 'Anthropocene' compels writers to reimagine the Earth. In the late eighteenth–early nineteenth centuries, planetary awareness emerged from geological research as a new object of fascination across the Western world. While natural scientists from Buffon and Hutton to Humboldt, Lyell and Darwin elaborated Earth's evolutionary development and ecological interdependences, political economists began to suspect humans of having planetary agency while not quite believing that our actions could alter the climate. Regarding the gradually emerging legacy of metaphysical terror sympathetically, Walls argues that our own analogous state of 'not knowing' should not 'end our imagination of possible future worlds but provoke it'.

If the world is being remade by human activity, how can we make truthful statements, depictions or communications about it? In Chapter 2, Sean Cubitt weighs up two procedures for measuring anthropogenic impact – data and anecdote. Each modifies the actuality that it describes, meaning that neither stories, reports, images nor data can ever lead to truth. But they can provide a tool for redirecting those changes. Being human in the Anthropocene actually means being a posthuman assemblage of body, nature and technology. Accept this, and we might 'liberate' all our representational media – whether stories, data or images – towards more utopian ends.

Part I, 'Anthropocene Forms', reappraises the extent to which existing or innovative forms, genres and narratives of literature and culture might help us stay with the trouble or shape better worlds. We include chapters on poetry (Chapter 3), the novel (Chapter 4), popular fiction (Chapter 5), the essay (Chapter 6), theatre and performance (Chapter 7), design (Chapter 8) and digital games (Chapter 9). These explore, in turn, the possibilities that lie in evolving modes such as 'open field' poetry, 'cli-fi', post-colonial crime fiction, green theatre, photography, 'interspecies design' and world-building games.

Exploring contemporary poetry's response to the cognitive, representational and ethical questions posed by the Anthropocene, in Chapter 3, Mandy Bloomfield examines post-war 'open-field' poetics as one alternative to lyric or 'Romantic' nature poetry's engagement with the world through the individual 'I'. Techniques such as collage, spatial composition and an emphasis on the poem as a field of energies and exchanges provoke reconsideration of relations between figure and ground, subject and object, human and non-human. Bloomfield discusses three contemporary writers – Ed Roberson, Evelyn Reilly and Stephen Collis – all seeking (as Collis writes) 'a feeling/for another structure'.

In Chapter 4, Astrid Bracke considers three examples of 'flood fiction' set in the near future: Clare Morrall's *When the Floods Came* (2015), *The Ship* (2015) by Antonia Honeywell, and Natasha Carthew's *All Rivers Run Free* (2018). Bracke deploys cognitive approaches and eco-narratology to dispute the alleged incompatibility of the realist novel with Anthropocene scale and argues that these novels achieve a switching back and forth between the readers' actual world and the text which can transport us to experience the confusion and uncertainty of living in climate crises that our own banal Anthropocene has created.

Turning to genre fiction, in Chapter 5, Saba Pirzadeh explores a South Asian crime fiction that has evolved from accelerated developments in publishing. A cross-genre blend of fictional and non-fictional modes, Osama Siddique's *Snuffing Out the Moon* (2017) and Ghosh's *Gun Island* (2019) incorporate three main elements – historical retelling (relating past to present), partial detection and a quest for environmental justice that traces the Anthropocene's material ramifications (climatic cataclysms, habitat loss, species extermination) to, for example, organised religion and international trade. Investigatory modes of literature, Pirzadeh concludes, might prevent us from becoming 'spectators of our own [and others'] demise'.

In Chapter 6, Byron Caminero-Santangelo likewise draws on Ghosh to propose literary non-fiction as an alternative to the atomising, anthropocentric, fatalistic and apocalyptical fiction of the global North. Postcolonial and creative non-fiction, in particular, might better enable the 'unthinkable': first, by insisting on humans' interrelation to land and other species; second, because a non-hierarchical interplay between literature, history and political writing, as seen in *The Great Derangement*, might facilitate deeper understanding by coupling pragmatic modes with the 'world-making' properties of fictional language and narrative.

Via contrasting examples, in Chapter 7, Sabine Wilke spotlights theatre as a laboratory for exploring (and performing) the Anthropocene. Wilke describes, first, how Georg Kaiser's *Gas* trilogy (1917–20) embodies the potentially catastrophic consequences of flirting with risk: audiences literally feel the gas explosion. In a unique adaptation of another German expressionist play, Heiner Müller's *The Task*, indigenous Australian playwright Mudrooroo demonstrates the value of post-colonial alternatives to the Anthropocene. This aboriginal dance theatre allows its audience to feel human's entanglement in deep history and interspecies networks.

For Stanislav Roudavski, in Chapter 8, design of the artificial – products, infrastructure, information – framed by human timescales and profit motives is directly responsible for the Anthropocene's onset. Noting, though, that animals and plants engineer and build too, he proposes extending 'human-centred design' towards a technologically innovative 'interspecies design' that could preserve or reconstitute habitats. Like a similarly adaptive literature, such practices could help develop new forms of kinship, remodelling environmental ethics to be '*for* and *with* all life'.

Conceding digital games' own implication in the economics and ideology of late capitalism, Alenda Y. Chang reviews in Chapter 9 how varied approaches to 'world-building' games mirror environmental impasses in the contemporary world. While games could prefigure a 'post-wild' future – in which humans artificially maintain ecosystems – Chang argues that in allowing us to explore virtual worlds, which we experience with other players, games also constitute a collective imagining, even realisation, of human futures shaped by multispecies entanglements and obligations.

Part II, 'Anthropocene Themes', addresses the scientific, political, ecological and ontological questions that signifiers or consequences of the Anthropocene raise. It encompasses catastrophe (Chapter 10), animal and human extinction (Chapters 11 and 12), fossil capital and global warming (Chapters 13 and 14), politics and ethics (Chapter 15), interspecies being (Chapter 16) and deep time (Chapter 17). We continue to investigate the pressure exerted on form via discussions of Romanticism (Chapter 10), weird fiction (Chapter 12), petro-fiction, theatre and contemporary poetry (Chapter 13), the global contemporary novel (Chapters 14 and 15), science fiction (Chapter 16) and new nature writing (Chapter 17).

Romanticism emerged alongside industrial innovations that created global carbon capitalism and a sense of catastrophe. Focusing on William Cowper's *The Task* (1783) and Mary Shelley's *Frankenstein* (1818), in Chapter 10, David Higgins and Tess Somervell suggest significant continuities between Romantic writing and discourses of the Anthropocene: specifically, a tension between belief in the power of human imagination to shape environments and humans' inability to manage and control elemental forces, whether nature or technology. The conclusion is hardly reassuring, though, like Walls, they speculate that ontological crisis may compel us to seek alternatives.

Eileen Crist focuses in Chapter 11 on the massive decline of wild animals engendered by human 'civilisation' since antiquity. Divested of animal presence, landscapes and seascapes become disenchanted and humans condemned, writes Erazim Kohák, to 'loneliness in a world reduced to meaninglessness'. Arguing, however, that we are not yet in the Anthropocene, Crist calls for humanity to scale down and pull back in the hope that conceptions of 'multispecies justice', not least from literature, might yet substitute an 'Abundant Earth' for its deadly humanisation.

Turning to humans, in Chapter 12 Hannes Bergthaller suggests that Anthropocene stories pivot on the paradox between *homo* and *anthropos*. Most stories seek to resolve this with humans either wielding their power conscientiously (eco-modernism) or receding into nature (ecological post-humanism). The 'weird fiction' of Jeff VanderMeer's Southern Reach Trilogy – from *Annihilation* to *Acceptance* – holds this paradox in tension. Humans are confronted with an alien entity that embodies the geological force of *anthropos*. Seeking to comprehend their fate, *Acceptance* epitomises literature's task in the Anthropocene: to produce 'faltering stories' that try to (re-)compose the human.

Sam Solnick, in Chapter 13, models the possibilities of this 'faltering' movement in literary form. Fossil fuels epitomise the Anthropocene – they seep into economics ('fossil capital'), politics, climate and bodies. Solnick tracks this through the porous temporal scales, sick polluted bodies and catastrophic disasters embodied, respectively, in Ella Hickson's *Oil* (2016), Jennifer Haigh's 2016 fracking novel *Heat and Light* and Juliana Spahr's 'Dynamic Positioning' (2015). He argues that 'petro-literature' is most interesting when it seeks a formal response – whether in stagecraft, metaphor or metre – to the realisation that oil powers 'the past, present and potential futures of the Anthropocene'.

The four final essays all explore how facing up to social and ecological transformation might help, nonetheless, imagine more sustainable futures. In Chapter 14, Andreas Malm, as we have seen, counters both oil's pervasiveness and the tendency – in genres like cli-fi – to focus on the 'after', the catastrophe, rather than causes or solutions. Where Kanafani crystallises 'the forces and interests' of colonialism and fossil capital, a further tradition of poets (Jabra Ibrahim Jabra, Marwan Darwish) and novelists (Susan Abulhawa, Liyana Badr) remember a fecund Palestinian environment, pre-oil and before the *nakba* ('catastrophe'), the displacement or ethnic cleansing of 70,000 Palestinians in 1948. With the experience of displacement and environmental devastation increasingly becoming globalised, the resistance within Palestinian literature, founded on love for the land, offers a model for literature and the Anthropocene.

Discussing Malaysian literature in English, in Chapter 15, Zainor Izat Zainal traces a bridge between political resistance and an interspecies perspective across three novels: Keris Mas's *Jungle of Hope* (2009),

Zakaria Ali's *The Dam* (2009) and Chuah Guat Eng's *Days of Change* (2010). Reappraising a Malaysia increasingly entangled with capitalist economic development, these novels suggest an alternative environmental ethics based on a realignment of traditional values – subsistence farming, kinship and community – with contemporary modes of grassroots activism, civil society and communication technologies.

The configuration of ethics, politics and posthumanism is further explored by Heather Alberro in Chapter 16 through four ecotopian novels: Aldous Huxley's *Island* (1962), Marge Piercy's *Woman on the Edge of Time* (1976), Kim Stanley Robinson's *Pacific Edge* (1990) and Ursula K. Le Guin's *Always Coming Home* (1985). Unlike science fiction's routine conjunction of technology and transhumanism, ecotopian fiction couples critiques about ecological crisis with 'vibrant world[s] brimming with non-human agency'. It deconstructs human/nature dualism to imply relationality, moving beyond hierarchical or antagonistic 'otherness' to incorporate reverence and respect for species difference.

In Chapter 17, Pippa Marland offers one final argument for how literature might address the scale and complexity of the Anthropocene. She examines five examples of new nature writing about the Scottish islands: from Kathleen Jamie, David Gange, Amy Liptrot, Robert Macfarlane and Adam Nicolson. Complementing ecotopian fiction, this writing makes visible temporal scales from 600 million years ago to millions of years ahead; ocean tides moving to the pull of celestial bodies; and animals whose migrations trace lines across the globe. We can glimpse ourselves as spectres haunting future epochs (in the plastic waste Jamie finds on the Monach islands), but, such writing also invokes alternative narratives by which we might yet become better ancestors for human generations to come.

Pearl Buttons: A Conclusion

The chapters in this *Companion* suggest that, while its limits are being interrogated, literature is being reinvigorated by the Anthropocene and responding in ways that just might assist in steering *anthropos* towards a 'new human condition'.[106] Further appraisal will require more of the concentrated studies of literary traditions, genres and movements evidenced in this book's 'Further Reading' section. I will conclude, however, with a case study underscoring just how literature and culture can mediate the cultural and ontological questions that the Anthropocene poses.

Chile is an epicentre of myriad interlocking systems: the slow violence of entangled forces of imperialism, global trade, capitalism and class; a unique elongated geology assembled from Earth and cosmos; a suppression of indigenous cosmologies which placed human time and space in longer, expansive duration; socio-environmental injustice and the ecological impacts evidenced in Calvillo's visualisation of Santiago; but also an (eco-)cosmopolitan literature and media that exemplify the thematic range and fluid forms demanded by the Anthropocene.[107]

In the nineteenth century, for example, the journalistic sketches of 'Jotabeche' (José Joaquín Vallejo) and the short stories of Baldomero Lillo documented the environmental and social consequences of, respectively, silver mining in the North and coal mining in the South, each of which served a global market. Both writers likewise deployed the hybrid *cuadros de costumbres* genre – sketches of 'customs and manners' characterised by a jumble of history, politics, anecdote, irony and literary technique. This seemingly skittish form was ideally suited, Enrique Pupo-Walker suggests, to 'descriptions of societies besieged by uncertainties'.[108] Later, a generation of twentieth-century writers were imprisoned and/or exiled during Augusto Pinochet's regime (1973–90), a regime underwritten by richer capitalist economies as a bulwark against socialist governments in Latin America. These writers, too, gravitated to multiple genres as a means both of addressing that regime's deadly entanglements and of forming equally complex alternatives that referenced indigenous tradition, subsistence economics, environmental justice or interspecies relationships. Luis Sepúlveda, for instance, produced thrillers, fables, travel writing, children's literature and romance; Isabel Allende's output encompasses magical realism, historical fiction, memoir, romance, YA fiction and even recipe books.

A particularly indicative example is the documentary maker Patricio Guzmán. Known for films about Pinochet and the 'disappeared' supporters of the socialist Popular Unity coalition (1970–3), Guzmán's more recent work has examined the rupturing of the subsistence-based lifestyles of Chile's indigenous people while also signalling 'the impossibility of [humans] extricating themselves from the earth'. *El Botón de Nácar* [*The Pearl Button*] (2015) illustrates the divergent Anthropocene. Guzmán describes Captain Robert FitzRoy's first HMS *Beagle* expedition to Chile in 1830 (Darwin's was second, in 1831). In mapping Chile, FitzRoy opened the country up to gold prospecting, land settlement and large-scale cattle farming. Guzmán summarises the outcome: an economy precariously based, ever since, on a geographically narrow strip of dry land rather than the nation's copious aquatic resources.

Yet, he also contextualises this imperial history in environmental and deep history. Noting that astronomers located in the Atacama Desert in

Northern Chile discovered that water exists throughout space – on planets, in nebula and celestial bodies – Guzmán affirms therefore that water mediates between the cosmos and life on Earth. While the Atlantic Ocean brought imperialism to Chile, the film's opening scene identifies that it was also water, transported to Earth by comets, that formed the Chilean archipelago. Shrinking modernity to Earth's exponentially vaster scale, Guzmán then recounts an alternative indigenous tradition that acknowledged and accepted the scale variance of this relationship. Through extraordinary photographs, interviews with twenty remaining descendants, and poignant re-enactments, the film resurrects subsistence lifestyles founded on water – diving for fish, near-forgotten canoeing skills, long-distance sea journeys.

In *El Botón de Nácar* an oceanographer tells Guzmán that thought, like 'water . . .[,] is always ready to adapt to anything'. If Guzmán's work exemplifies how to juggle environmental and cosmic time with human history and personal experience, equally indicative is how he gets there. An accretion of insight and knowledge forms out of multidisciplinary layers of cinematographic spectacle, literary technique, visual evidence – photographs, film footage – and expert opinion. Indigenous oral history and the testimonies of political exiles and their descendants endow people and place with alternative perspectives. Palaeontologists, archaeologists and anthropologists illuminate longer durations of environmental history and more respectful, sustainable modes of human dwelling; geologists and astronomers locate us in limitless dimensions of Earth and space.

Yet, the film's convergence of scale is ultimately realised in literary mode. For the 'pearl button' is a narrative monad used three times to crystallise both the variegated dimensions of Anthropocene history in which Chile is entangled and ecological possibility. In the first instance, Orundellico, a fourteen-year-old boy from the Yaghan (or canoe) people of Tierra del Fuego, is taken hostage by FitzRoy and removed from Chile to be 'civilised' in England. He is exchanged for one mother-of-pearl button, and renamed 'Jemmy Button', an act signifying the trading away of individual lives, tribal cultures and subsistence economies. The second revisits how iron rails facilitated the drowning of Pinochet's opponents at sea. Accompanied by footage of divers salvaging rails, Guzmán discovers a pearl button encrusted in one, a trace, the only remaining human trace, of military and economic force. Third, though, the film's opening image captures the mediation of life between cosmos and Earth in a single pearl of water encased in a 3,000-year-old block of quartz found in the Atacama.

'In this detail lies everything, condensed, dense.'

Guzmán seizes apparently inconceivable entanglements of cosmos and Earth, land and people, past, present and future in poetic images and his own caesura-laden narration. In Darío Oses's short story 'The Poet, Wine, and Sheep' it is a poet who discerns the threads that tie alienated office workers to globalisation, commodification, the exploitation of natural resources and the elimination of indigenous animals in favour of 'live-stock'. In Sepúlveda's children's book *The Story of a Seagull and the Cat Who Taught Her to Fly*, the baby gull's successful flight is, in the end, facilitated by a poet's intervention: 'Maybe he doesn't know how to fly with bird's wings [says Zorba, the cat], but when I've listened to him it's always made me feel he's flying with his words.'[109] This perhaps is what writers, artists, media practitioners, scholars, too, have to offer. For, alongside our companion historians, astrologists, anthropologists, Earth scientists and geologists, we are all looking, says the poet Raúl Zurita in Guzmán's film, to 'retrieve things' we 'already knew in a poetic sense'; we are all trying 'to bring the universe closer'.

Notes

1. Paul Crutzen and Eugene F. Stoermer, 'The Anthropocene', *IGBP Newsletter* 41 (May 2000), 17–18.
2. quaternary.stratigraphy.org/working-groups/anthropocene/.
3. Christian Schwägerl, 'Neurogeology: The Anthropocene's Inspirational Power', *RCC Perspectives* 3 (2013), 29–37 (p.31).
4. William F. Ruddiman, 'The Anthropogenic Greenhouse Era Began Thousands of Years Ago', *Climatic Change* 61(3) (2003), 261–93.
5. See Simon L. Lewis and Mark A. Maslin, 'Defining the Anthropocene', *Nature* 519 (2015), 171–80; Crutzen and Stoermer, 'The Anthropocene', 17–18.
6. Dipesh Chakrabarty, 'The Human Condition in the Anthropocene', Tanner Lectures on Human Values (2015), tannerlectures.utah.edu.
7. See Andreas Malm, *Fossil Capital: The Rise of Steam-Power and the Roots of Global Warming* (London and New York: Verso, 2016), pp.391–2.
8. Anna Lowenhaupt Tsing, *The Mushroom at the End of the World: On the Possibility of Life in Capitalist Ruins* (Princeton, NJ: Princeton University Press, 2015).
9. See Tom Lancaster and Ellie Brodie, 'What Does Covid-19 Mean for Food, Farming and Nature?', *Insidetrack* (29 April 2020), https://greenallianceblog .org.uk/2020/04/29/what-does-covid-19-mean-for-food-farming-and-nature/. With thanks to Wendy Wheeler for the article and her insights.
10. Anahid Nersessian, 'Two Gardens: An Experiment in Calamity Form', *Modern Language Quarterly* 74(3) (2013), 307–28 (p.318).

11. energyandcleanair.org/air-pollution-deaths-avoided-in-europe-as-coal-oil-plummet.

12. Corinne Le Quére et al., 'Temporary Reduction in Daily Global CO_2 Emissions during the COVID-19 Forced Confinement', *Nature Climate Change* (19 May 2020), www.nature.com/articles/s41558-020-0797-x.

13. Stephen Waring, letter to *The Observer* (7 June 2020).

14. Jeremy Davies, *The Birth of the Anthropocene* (Oakland: University of California Press, 2016), pp.72–5.

15. Alan Weisman, *The World Without Us* (Toronto: HarperCollins, 2010).

16. Jamie Lorimer, *Wildlife in the Anthropocene: Conservation After Nature* (Minneapolis: University of Minnesota Press, 2015), p.4.

17. Kate Rigby, *Dancing with Disaster: Environmental Histories, Narratives, and Ethics for Perilous Times* (Charlottesville and London: University of Virginia Press, 2015), p.18.

18. And see Tobias Boes and Kate Marshall, 'Writing the Anthropocene: An Introduction', *The Minnesota Review* 83 (2014), 60–72 (pp.63–4).

19. Dipesh Chakrabarty, 'The Climate of History: Four Theses', *Critical Inquiry* 35 (2009), 197–222 (p.220).

20. José Joaquín Vallejo, *Sketches of Life in Chile: 1841–1851* [ed. Simon Collier; trans. Frederick H. Fornoff] (Oxford: Oxford University Press, 2002), p.61.

21. Lauren Berlant, 'Genre Flailing', *Capacious: Journal for Emerging Affect Inquiry* 1(2) (2018), 156–62 (p.157).

22. Ibid., p.157.

23. Ibid., p.161.

24. Ibid., p.160.

25. Ibid., p.161.

26. Christophe Bonneuil and Jean-Baptiste Fressoz, *The Shock of the Anthropocene: The Earth, History, and Us* (London and New York: Verso, 2017). Subheading from Warren Ellis, *Freakangels*, vol. 4 [artwork Paul Duffield] (Rantoul, IL: Avatar Press, 2010).

27. Richard Powers, *The Overstory* (London: Vintage, 2018), pp.420, 477–8.

28. Amitav Ghosh, *The Great Derangement: Climate Change and the Unthinkable* (Chicago and London: University of Chicago Press, 2016), pp.7, 9, 66.

29. See, respectively, Jesse Oak Taylor, *The Sky of Our Manufacture: The London Fog in British Fiction from Dickens to Woolf* (Charlottesville: University of Virginia Press, 2016); Byron Caminero-Santangelo, *Different Shades of Green: African Literature, Environmental Justice, and Political Ecology* (Charlottesville: University of Virginia Press, 2014); Adeline Johns-Putra, *Climate Change and the Contemporary Novel* (Cambridge: Cambridge University Press, 2019).

30. Diletta De Cristofaro and Daniel Cordle, 'Introduction: The Literature of the Anthropocene', *C21 Literature: Journal of 21st-Century Writings* 6(1) (2018), 1–6 (p.3).

31. Ghosh, *Great Derangement*, pp.59–60.

32. Timothy Clark, *Ecocriticism on the Edge: The Anthropocene as a Threshold Concept* (London: Bloomsbury, 2015), pp.178, 182.
33. Derek Woods, 'Scale Critique for the Anthropocene', *The Minnesota Review* 83 (2014), 133–42 (pp.134, 139).
34. Woods, 'Scale Critique', p.140.
35. Clark, *Ecocriticism on the Edge*, p.22.
36. Thank you to Dr Nerea Calvillo for permission to reproduce this image.
37. Clark, *Ecocriticism on the Edge*, p.73.
38. Richard Kerridge, 'Foreword' in Serpil Oppermann and Serenella Iovino (eds.), *Environmental Humanities: Voices from the Anthropocene* (London: Rowman & Littlefield International, 2017), pp.12–17 (pp.12–13).
39. David C. Schneider, 'The Rise of the Concept of Scale in Ecology', *BioScience* 51(7) (2001), 545–53.
40. See Jérôme Chave, 'The Problem of Pattern and Scale in Ecology: What Have We Learned in 20 Years?', *Ecology Letters* 16 (2016), 4–16 (p.12); Schneider, p.546.
41. Woods, 'Scale Critique', p.136.
42. See, for example, Timothy F. H. Allen and Thomas W. Hoekstra, *Toward a Unified Ecology* [2nd ed.] (New York: Columbia University Press, 2015).
43. Chave, 'Pattern and Scale', p.13.
44. Ran Nathan, Frank M. Schurr, Orr Spiegel et al., 'Mechanisms of Long-Distance Seed Dispersal', *Trends in Ecology and Evolution* 23(11) (2008), 638–47 (p.638).
45. Chave, 'Pattern and Scale', p.6.
46. Clark, *Ecocriticism on the Edge*, pp.72–3.
47. Timothy Clark, *The Value of Ecocriticism* (Cambridge: Cambridge University Press, 2019), pp.79–81.
48. Thom van Dooren, 'Nature in the Anthropocene? A Reflection on a Photograph', *The Yearbook of Comparative Literature* 58 (2012), pp.228–34.
49. See Walter Benjamin, *The Arcades Project* (Cambridge, MA: Harvard University Press, 1999), p.475.
50. van Dooren, 'Nature in the Anthropocene?', pp.231–2.
51. Clark, *Ecocriticism on the Edge*, p.21.
52. Bruno Latour, 'Imagining Barrier Gestures against the Return to Pre-crisis Production' [trans. Stephen Muecke], *AOC* (29 March 2020), aoc.media/opinion.
53. Bruno Latour interview, Jonathan Watts, *The Observer* (7 June 2020).
54. Chave, 'Pattern and Scale', p.4.
55. Richard E. Miller and Kurt Spellmeyer, *The New Humanities Reader* (Boston: Houghton Mifflin, 2003), p.xix.
56. Robert S. Emmett and David E. Nye, *The Environmental Humanities: A Critical Introduction* (Cambridge, MA: MIT Press, 2017), p.21.
57. Cited in Caspar Henderson, *The Book of Barely Imagined Beings: A 21st Century Bestiary* (London: Granta, 2012), p.192.
58. McKenzie Wark, *Molecular Red: Theory for the Anthropocene* (London and New York: Verso, 2015), p.xx.

59. Ghosh, *Great Derangement*, p.128.

60. Alexa Weik von Mossner, 'Imagining Geological Agency: Storytelling in the Anthropocene' in Robert Emmett and Thomas Lekan (eds.), 'Whose Anthropocene? Revisiting Dipesh Chakrabarty's "Four Theses"', *RCC Perspectives: Transformations in Environment and Society* 2 (2016), pp.83–8 (p.88).

61. Lewis and Maslin, 'Defining the Anthropocene', p.178.

62. Pliny, *Natural History*, vol. IX: Books 33–35 [trans. H. Rackham; Loeb Classical Library] (Cambridge, MA: Harvard University Press, 1952), p.57. My thanks to Ryan Denson for this reference.

63. Rob Nixon, 'The Great Acceleration and the Great Divergence: Vulnerability in the Anthropocene', *MLA Profession* (2014), profession.mla.org.

64. Rob Nixon, *Slow Violence and the Environmentalism of the Poor* (Cambridge, MA: Harvard University Press, 2011).

65. Christine Matzke and Suzanne Mülheisen (eds.), *Postcolonial Postmortems: Crime Fiction from a Transcultural Perspective* (Amsterdam: Rodopi, 2006), p.5.

66. Eva Horn and Hannes Bergthaller, *The Anthropocene* (London: Routledge, 2020), pp.70–4.

67. Alexander von Humboldt, *Views of Nature* (Chicago: University of Chicago Press, 2014 [1849]), p.141. See also p.148n1.

68. For further sources on the divergent Anthropocene, see 'Texts, Authors, Traditions' in 'Further Reading'.

69. Elizabeth DeLoughrey, 'Ordinary Futures: Interspecies Worldings in the Anthropocene' in Elizabeth DeLoughrey, Jill Didur and Anthony Carrigan (eds.), *Global Ecologies and the Environmental Humanities* (New York and London: Routledge, 2015), pp.352–72 (pp.356–7).

70. Ibid., p.358.

71. Eileen Crist, 'On the Poverty of Our Nomenclature', *Environmental Humanities* 3 (2013), 129–47.

72. Heather Anne Swanson, 'The Banality of the Anthropocene', *Fieldsights* (22 February 2017), culanth.org/fieldsights.

73. DeLoughrey, 'Ordinary Futures', pp.357–8.

74. Filippo Bertoni, 'Resources UnLtd: Of Planets, Mining, and Biogeochemical Togetherness' in Serpil Oppermann and Serenella Iovino (eds.), *Environmental Humanities: Voices from the Anthropocene* (London: Rowman & Littlefield International, 2017), pp.215–35 (p.218).

75. Nersessian, 'Two Gardens', p.307.

76. Ibid., p.324.

77. Ibid., pp.311–13.

78. Richard Kerridge, 'Ecocritical Approaches to Literary Form and Genre: Urgency, Depth, Provisionality, Temporality' in Greg Garrard (ed.), *The Oxford Handbook of Ecocriticism* (Oxford: Oxford University Press, 2014), pp.361–76 (pp.368–9).

79. Ibid., pp.369–70, my emphasis.

80. Pippa Marland, '"Heaps of Scrap Metal and Defunct Machinery": Assemblages, Ethics and Affect in W. G. Sebald's Orford Ness', *Ecozon@: European Journal of Literature, Culture and Environment* 5(2) (2014), 123–39 (p.131).

81. Ibid., pp.125, 131–2.

82. Heather Houser, *Ecosickness in Contemporary U.S. Fiction: Environment and Affect* (New York: Columbia University Press, 2014), p.15.

83. Paolo Ruffino, 'Nonhuman Games: Playing in the Post-Anthropocene' in Matt Coward-Gibbs (ed.), *Death, Culture and Leisure: Playing Dead* (Bingley: Emerald Publishing, 2020), pp.11–26. With thanks to Dr Ruffino for sending me his article.

84. Sam Solnick, *Poetry and the Anthropocene: Ecology, Biology and Technology in Contemporary British and Irish Poetry* (London: Routledge, 2016), pp.204–5; Tom Bristow, *The Anthropocene Lyric: An Affective Geography of Poetry, Person, Place* (Basingstoke: Palgrave Macmillan, 2015), p.17.

85. Bristow, ibid., pp.7–8.

86. Ghosh, *Great Derangement*, pp.71–2.

87. Stephanie LeMenager, 'The Humanities after the Anthropocene' in Ursula K. Heise, Jon Christensen and Michelle Niemann (eds.), *Routledge Companion to the Environmental Humanities* (London: Routledge, 2016), pp.473–81 (p.477).

88. Heather Anne Swanson, Nils Bubandt and Anna Tsing, 'Less Than One but More Than Many: Anthropocene as Science Fiction and Scholarship-in-the-Making', *Environment and Society: Advances in Research* 6 (2015), pp.149–66 (p.149).

89. See Adam Trexler, *Anthropocene Fictions: The Novel in a Time of Climate Change* (Charlottesville: University of Virginia Press, 2015), pp.8–9; Johns-Putra, *Climate Change and the Contemporary Novel*.

90. Ghosh, *Great Derangement*, pp.72–3.

91. Deborah Bird Rose, 'Anthropocene Noir', *Arena* 41–2 (2013–14), 206–19 (p.215).

92. David Farrier, 'Animal Detectives and "Anthropocene Noir" in Chloe Hooper's *A Child's Book of True Crime*', *Textual Practice* 32(5) (2018), 875–93 (pp.879–80).

93. Farrier, ibid., pp.879–80; Johns-Putra, *Climate Change and the Contemporary Novel*.

94. LeMenager, 'Humanities after the Anthropocene', p.477.

95. www.extinctionstories.org.

96. www.climatestoriesproject.org.

97. Houser, *Ecosickness*, pp.22.

98. See Adeline Johns-Putra, 'The Rest Is Silence: Postmodern and Postcolonial Possibilities in Climate Change Fiction', *Studies in the Novel* 50(1) (2018), 26–42.

99. von Mossner, 'Imagining Geological Agency', pp.84, 86.

100. Magnus Mills interview, Michael Barron, *Bomb* (21 July 2015), bombmaga-zine.org.

101. See Patricia Malone, 'Less Human, More Ourselves: Michel Houellebecq's Neohumans and the Anthropocene Subject', *C21 Literature: Journal of 21st-Century Writings* 6(1) (2018), 1–24.

102. See Laurel Peacock, 'SAD in the Anthropocene: Brenda Hillman's Ecopoetics of Affect', *Environmental Humanities* 1 (2012), 85–102 (p.95).

103. *Great Derangement*, p.61.

104. 'Imagining Geological Agency', pp.87–8.

105. See Ghosh, *Great Derangement*, pp.61, 64–5.

106. Poul Holm et al., 'Humanities for the Environment—A Manifesto for Research and Action', *Humanities* 4 (2015), 977–92 (p.983).

107. With thanks to my friend Andrea Casals (Pontificia Universidad Católica de Chile), who advised on relevant Chilean authors.

108. Enrique Pupo-Walker, 'The Brief Narrative in Spanish America: 1835–1915' in Roberto González Echevarría and Enrique Pupo-Walker (eds.), *The Cambridge History of Latin American Literature*, vol. 1 (Cambridge: Cambridge University Press, 1996), pp.490–535 (p.490).

109. Luis Sepúlveda, *The Story of a Seagull and the Cat Who Taught Her to Fly* [trans. Margaret Sayers Peden] (Richmond: Alma Books, 2016), p.107.

Earth, Anthropocene, Literary Form

CHAPTER I

Earth

Laura Dassow Walls

Early in January 1834, fresh from his first trip to Europe, Ralph Waldo Emerson offered the first fruits of what he had learned to his Boston audience. Today, he told them, we look at the planet itself 'in quite another light from any in which our fathers regarded it'. Far from being a mere farm, battlefield, market or dwelling-place, the Earth 'is itself a monument on whose surface every age of perhaps numberless centuries has somewhere inscribed its history in gigantic letters', letters so huge and far apart 'that only the most diligent observer ... can read them'. And what do they reveal? That Man is no upstart, 'but prophesied in nature for a thousand thousand ages before he appeared; that from times incalculably remote there has been a progressive preparation for him'. Our planet was made to fit us exactly as a father might build his children a house, 'laying out the grounds, curing the chimneys, and stocking the cellar'. And the fit is precise: so perfectly is human power adjusted to the forces of nature, even to the way our wants lead us to develop those powers still further, that we are entitled to claim 'possession of the globe'. But mere possession is not enough. We must press still farther, altering and amending the globe, 'improv[ing] the face of the planet itself' and thrilling ourselves 'with delight by the choral harmony of the whole'. Thus does Emerson establish his New Organon for modernity: a Promethean path by which patient research 'can make the mind a second Nature, a second Universe', mastering the planet itself.[1]

In August 1856, Emerson's friend Henry David Thoreau inclined towards a different form of epiphany. 'I see that all is not garden and cultivated field and crops', he wrote after an afternoon's walk; 'that there are square rods in Middlesex County as purely primitive and wild as they were a thousand years ago ... little oases of wildness in the desert of our civilization, wild as a square rod on the moon'. Where Emerson was moved to conquest, Thoreau was moved to adoration: 'I believe almost in the personality of such planetary matter, feel something akin to reverence for it, can even worship it as terrene, titanic matter extant in my day.' Why should we reverence only the meteors that fall from another planet? 'Are not the stones in Hodge's wall as good as the aerolite at Mecca? Is not our broad back-door-stone as good as any corner-stone in heaven?'[2] Is not Earth a heavenly body, just as much as the stars above?

Both Emerson and Thoreau are moved by something which had recently emerged as a surprising new object of fascination: the planetary Earth. The natural sciences had been reorienting themselves to this new object for decades, yet even by Emerson's day, this most unsettling of discoveries had still not stabilised. This newest planet, too big to see – and yet, imagined against the vastness of deep space, so absurdly small; this mundane planet underfoot, the ground of our household toils yet composed of incalculable ages receding in unimaginably deep time – did this new object humiliate us in our ancient, Biblical pride? Or, was this God's greatest gift, newly revealed as the yielding substrate for the infinite greatness of Man? Both, and more besides: the literature of the nineteenth century records the eruption of Planet Earth into human consciousness. What they did with this gift gave us in turn our own trauma. In an irony which returns us to Emerson's age, we have named that trauma not after the Earth but after ourselves: the Anthropocene.

That this strange historical loop bonds us tightly with our past is what makes this literature so difficult to read today. In it, we are forced to encounter the history we had buried and ignored as it roars back to life, bearing down upon us with our every measure of rising CO_2, every purchase of plastic-packaged lettuce, every turn of the key in the ignition of our automobiles. As ecocritic Timothy Clark has recently observed, we are now part of the history we study. This deranges all our familiar historicist tricks of exclusion: 'the more degraded and dangerous the once-natural environment becomes, the more the future or possible futures will insist on themselves as part of any context to be considered or critical method to be used.'[3] Despite the chains of causality that bind us with our past, we feel our distance from it; as Anahid Nersessian observes, Romantic literature is '*in* the Anthropocene but not *of* it'.[4] Yet Clark's point remains: we *are* of it, inscribed by its gigantic letters, which we can read even if our ancestors could not – even as they inscribed those letters onto the face of the planet.

Our problem, as literary scholars, is how to stay open to this literature on its own terms while registering the fact that they, as much as we, are gathered into this same massive mutation in the conditions of reality. As Dipesh Chakrabarty announced in 'The Climate of History' (2009), the distinction between human history and natural history has collapsed. Our climate crisis reveals 'the enjambment' of the separate orders 'of recorded and deep histories of the human kind, of species history and the history of the earth systems, revealing the deep connections through which the planet's carbon cycle and life interact with each other'.[5] But the collapse that Chakrabarty locates in recent decades actually began two centuries before. As it intensified, it defined the problem of the nineteenth century. Observers who recognised this emergent crisis responded with great interest and deep anxiety – at least for a time, until this, too, was sealed up and buried, along with so many other unspeakable histories. Given the threat it so evidently posed, planetarity could be honored, even worshipped, in its ancient and terrifying indifference to the humans, it both engenders and reclaims; but couldn't it also be tamed and re-engineered into the mirror of humanity? – into Bacon's crystal ball, the dematerialisation and reassembly of an ancient planet into our globalised modernity of infinite abundance? Yes, and it worked – for a while.

Discovering Earth

Nature didn't always have a history; it became historical during the eighteenth century, as scientific expeditions returned from around the planet bearing immense collections of specimens that exploded once-tidy taxonomies into ramifying messes. Only trained specialists could categorise and describe the planet's immense biodiversity into a comprehensive order of being. As they did so, natural history itself was forced to reorganise from an ordered grid of related phenomena into a temporal network of causal relationships. The breakthrough was led by the Paris naturalist Georges-Louis Leclerc, the Comte de Buffon, who in *Epochs of Nature* (1778) presented the Earth as 'a single integrated system, of living and non-living components—just as we see it today'.[6] Buffon narrativised the static arrangement of minerals, plants and animals, grouped by shared features, into a dynamic tableau of nature's generative power forming and shaping itself through time, starting with the cooling of the molten Earth and culminating with the plenitude of creation – a sweeping tableau that bound mankind together with the planet in a common destiny. As he wrote, surveying that staggering plenitude, 'all that can exist, does'. This meant that nature could be understood only *historically*; 'To understand the present ... one had to know the past.'[7] And for Buffon, that past was disconcertingly deep – seventy-five thousand years, he calculated, laughably short by today's standards. Yet, it was Buffon who placed 'squarely in the public consciousness' the notion of an Earth vastly older than Biblical chronology, and with it, the notion of humanity as 'a global force' whose advent marked the most recent epoch of the planet's historical stages: 'the entire face of the Earth today bears the imprint of human power' – which we could, he reasoned, use for our benefit. For instance, by the judicious use of deforestation and the planting of trees, humans could modify the climate of the Earth itself, adjusting its temperature to our preferred setting – a capacity celebrated by Emerson: 'Climate is ameliorated by cultivation and not only the climate softened, but the air purified, and made healthful .... By the study of nature [man] improves nature, and keeps the world in repair.'[8]

By the 1830s, when Emerson began delivering his popular lectures, geology was the leading edge of natural history. Wildly speculative 'theories of the earth' had given way to the meticulous quest to untangle and define the precise chronology of rock and fossil formations, understood as nothing less than the archives of nature's self-development through untold millions of years.[9] What the rocks revealed was not a single smooth narrative but, rather, long eras of continental uplift, erosion and sedimentary deposition, punctuated by wild episodes of volcanic eruption. For Scottish geologist James Hutton, this pattern mitigated Buffon's troubling conclusion that the cooling Earth would finally lapse into heat-death and the extinction of all life. Instead, Hutton read in the rocks 'a story of stone's energy and constant movement, one in which horizontal layers of sedimentation bend, ripple, melt, interpenetrate'.[10] From this energy, Hutton theorised that Earth could regenerate as well as decay – a 'self-renewing world machine' of erosion, deposition and volcanic uplift creating 'a slow choreography that can never end, or even age, so long as higher powers maintain the current order of nature's laws'. The ringing final line of Hutton's 1788 treatise *Theory of the Earth* has become famous in this literature: 'If the succession of worlds is established in the system of nature, it is in vain to look for anything higher in the origin of the earth. The result, therefore, of our present enquiry is, that we find no vestige of a beginning,—no prospect of an end.'[11] The earth-*machine* was in fact more like an earth-*body*, an organism in which decay could be 'naturally repaired, in the exertion of those productive powers by which it had been formed'. Such a living Earth would cycle on forever: it was Hutton who unleashed upon modernity the challenge of deep time.[12]

Such an Earth also defies history. Time might be deep, but an eternally cycling nature has no narrative to inscribe, no relation to human history – it is beyond human time altogether, unfathomable and infinite. Yet, this was not the direction of mainstream geology, which set about ordering Hutton's physical system of cycling stages into a linear, sequential history, what Stephen Jay Gould calls 'a quirky sequence of intricate, unique, unrepeatable events linked in a unidirectional chain of complex causes (and gobs of randomness)'.[13] This transformation was wrought by Hutton's friend John Playfair, who popularised Hutton's notoriously difficult treatise by casting his ahistorical cycles into a progressive history also in line with Biblical revelation.

Thus when Emerson composed his lecture on the 'Globe', he rifled through his notes on Playfair, perhaps pausing to consider a line that became one of his favourites: 'A method of discovering truths is more valuable than the truths it has discovered.'[14] Emerson's interest in geology led him to Hutton's successor Charles Lyell, whose foundational work was based on a method of inductive reasoning that solidified geology as a true natural philosophy: as Lyell put it in his subtitle, one could explain 'the former changes of the earth's surface, by reference to causes now in operation'. Lyell's *Principles of Geology* (1830–3) was the sort of scientific monument that shifted the public imagination. As Emerson's proverb indicates, it did so not merely by piling on facts but by inculcating a principle of observation. Yet, the effect was paradoxical: even as the evidence of our eyes could make legible the deepest events of Earth's history, the abyss of deep time estranged Earth from human reckoning and experience. The key was time: those twisted strata and horrifying chasms, those 'gigantic letters', told not of some planetary catastrophe or terrible Biblical deluge but merely the slow and steady operation of common causes across an incomprehensible clock – soil eroding from an afternoon's rain, mud settling gently in a streambed, uplift following a distant earthquake. As Emerson put it in his essay 'Nature' (1844): 'All changes pass without violence, by reason of the two cardinal conditions of boundless space and boundless time. Geology has initiated us into the secularity of nature, and taught us to disuse our dame-school measure, and exchange our Mosaic and Ptolemaic schemes for her large style.'[15] Thoreau, reading Lyell in Emerson's library, copied the key idea into his Journal: '[W]e discover the causes of all past change in the present invariable order of the universe.' At the end of his life, on the heels of Darwin's *Origin of Species*, Thoreau reiterated: 'There has not been a sudden re-formation, or, as it were, new creation of the world, but a steady progress according to existing laws.'[16]

All such geological reasoning necessarily ended with the present, a present clearly stamped by human actions on the face of the Earth.

Buffon and Emerson, as noted, both expected that humans would transform their planet for the better; meanwhile, geologists debated what name should be given to denote the obvious impact of recent human activity. In 1854, Welsh geologist Thomas Jenkyn proposed the term '"Anthropozoic," or human life rocks', since the rocks were already recording the influence of humans. In 1873, his term was seconded by the Italian geologist Antonio Stoppani, who regarded humans as already 'a new telluric force that for its strength and universality does not pale in the face of the greatest forces of the globe'.[17] Others, too, proposed variations on the concept, such that the historical puzzle is not how the nineteenth century could have conceived humans as a geological agent but how the twenty-first century could have forgotten this. Taking up this puzzle, Simon Lewis and Mark Maslin trace the parallel rise of a competing term originated by Lyell in 1830: the Holocene, or 'Recent Epoch', naming as one of its distinguishing features the presence of humans. In time, as Lyell's authority became dominant, Western geologists increasingly settled on the term 'Holocene' – yet they shifted its meaning by uncoupling it from Lyell's original association with human impact, thus erasing the concept's troubling associations with human-caused environmental damage. This shift prompted atmospheric chemist Paul Crutzen, in 2000, to name our epoch 'the Anthropocene'. The original, human-centred definition of 'the Holocene' had long since been forgotten and, with it, the nineteenth century's deep engagement with the power of humanity as a force of nature.[18]

The break is registered around the ambivalence of Lyell's method. On the one hand, deep causes for incomprehensible changes in nature could be imagined in familiar terms. Thoreau used Lyell's method to open up the historical meaning of New England's landscapes, seeing in them the agency of common natural causes – wind, rain and floods, erosion and deposition, the dispersion of pollen and seeds, the reciprocity of organism and environment in every moment across scales from intimate to cosmic. On the other hand, the planetary scales of time unfolding across untold millions upon millions of years made nature incomprehensible in human terms. How could any history that unfolded on such scales – whether cyclical or progressive – be imagined or be humanly meaningful? Depending on how one saw it, 'Nature' could be either one's most intimate kin, the neighbouring neighbour for all human life, or an alienating and terrifying force, external, virtually immobile on human timescales, hostile or at best indifferent to the humans who infested it.

Humboldt's Planet

The entire career of Alexander von Humboldt was dedicated to answering this question. This accounts, in large part, for his enormous popularity and prestige: not only did he introduce the planetary Earth to educated readers around the world, his popular writings suggested what it might mean to live on such a planet – to inhabit it not in fear and alienation, nor by seizing control to wrest from nature a wholly artificial world, but in reciprocity and mutual illumination. Christophe Bonneuil and Jean-Baptiste Fressoz remark that, far from dividing humans from nature, 'the period between 1770 and 1830 was marked on the contrary by a very acute awareness of the interactions between nature and society' – ironically, just as Western Europe was precipitating the world into the 'Anthropocene'.[19] This era shaped Humboldt, and he shaped it in turn.

The face of Humboldt's planet was not flat, but deep – he trained himself to see not horizontally across surfaces, but vertically into chains of causality, which he interlaced into growing networks of connections that looped local and present phenomena with planetary, even cosmic, forces. This method allowed Humboldt to work simultaneously across three axes: deep space, deep time and deep mind. His work along the first axis, deep space, is familiar because of his runaway bestseller *Cosmos* (1845–7). Humboldt opened *Cosmos* by taking his readers on an imaginary journey out to 'the depths of space', whence they 'gradually descend through the starry zone . . . to our own terrestrial spheroid, circled by air and ocean'. In this radical new vision, we no longer *ascend* from Earth, escaping and reaching for the stars, but instead we 'descend to our own planet' in order to see it truly, for the first time, as a living planet. Humboldt asks us to envision a world – more, to inhabit a cosmology – that connects 'the realms of infinity' with the swarms of 'minute microscopic animal and vegetable organisms which exist in standing waters and on the weather-beaten surface of our rocks'. As he said towards the end of his life, while our planet may appear 'only like a handful of conglomerated matter in the immeasurable universe', its 'system of co-operating forces . . . shows the dependence of every part of nature upon other parts', seamlessly inter-graded from the most elementary inorganic processes to the organic relations that bring into play forces responsible for 'the production and maintenance of life'.[20] According to cultural theorist Peter Sloterdijk, when scientists in Humboldt's day turned their newly powerful telescopes not to the heavens but, in their imaginations, from the heavens back to Earth, they initiated nothing less than a new phase of modernity: 'the cosmologically sublime' – an aesthetic emergency signalled by Humboldt's *Cosmos*. In Humboldt's day the Earth itself becomes, as Sloterdijk writes, 'the star to which one returns'.[21]

Humboldt set this vision of Earth in deep space along his second axis, deep time, through his work in the emerging geological sciences. His early training as a mining engineer showed him a deep-layered planet thick with fossilised vegetation and riddled with caves and seams, and he applied the cartographic methods of geology to read below the ground, to see where eyes are blind. He taught the world how to see the structure of Earth by comparing rocky outcroppings in local formations, then in regional series, then inferring the underlying structure by relating the strata one could see to analogous series hundreds or thousands of miles away. The result was a dynamic Earth visualised from its molten depths, cooling through the aeons of lithic and organic history, to its present continents and oceans as stitched and separated by chains of volcanoes by which the interior forces of the planet react upon its external crust and vent gases that shape the structure of the atmosphere. And, everywhere, Humboldt traced how the circulations and settlements of human beings, with their domesticated plants and animals, across Earth's continents, oceans and islands, resulted in radical and profound alterations to the Earth's living systems. Rather than separating human history from natural history, Humboldt showed that only through planetary history does humanity become legible.

Third, what binds deep space and deep time together is the mind that can trace their connections through scientific inference and imaginative vision, using language to realise an Earth that we cannot see. Humboldt's 'Nature' does not precede the writing of his oddly disorienting, immersive essays as that which is separate from the 'Human'; instead, nature emanates from them as all that is complexly bound to the creation of the human. For the 'nature' that emanates from Humboldt's writings does so by reimagining the resources of language: when he argues that Earth's strata present traces of the existence and destruction of prior worlds, he shows how the land tells its own story, and how, by learning to read the land's geography, 'earth-writing', we recognise ourselves as part of it. As Humboldt explains in *Cosmos*, in reading the Earth 'we behold the present and the past reciprocally incorporated, as it were, with one another; for the domain of nature is like that of languages, in which etymological research reveals a successive development'. Just as the study of language shows us linguistic relations that animate our present-day speech, the study of Earth shows us geological relations which 'animate the scenery by the associations of the past which they awaken, acting upon the imagination of the enlightened observer like traditional records of an earlier world. Their form is their history.'[22] Thus languages and geological forms not only evidence *analogous* historical processes, they are 'reciprocally incorporated', making human languages an aspect (or in his word, *'Ansichten'*) of planetary geohistory, a living, co-evolving form.

To forge such connections across nature and culture, Humboldt insists on the value of nature writing for rejuvenating languages that modernity has detached from their environmental origins.[23] And as he shows humans to be, in the deepest way, terrestrial beings – profoundly Earth-bound, as Bruno Latour would say – he considers the consequences for ethics and aesthetics as well as science.[24] Humboldt's goal was not to represent a stable reality, either scientifically or poetically, nor to offer a smoothly integrated view of Nature as a whole, but to deploy the act of writing itself to found a science that seamlessly fuses scientific knowledge and literary imagination with ethical concerns, demonstrating how humans and nature compose, together, the evolving and reciprocal relationship that Humboldt called 'Cosmos'. Land, life and language are co-creations. To kill any of them is literally to kill the Cosmos – his own word, reclaimed from the ancient Greek to name the physical, material universe as it is recognised by the mind it engendered, and expressed in the fullness of its order and beauty. Thus, his popular works instantiate Earth, our home, as a planet *both* estranged from us *and* intimately intertwined with everything it means to be human. In doing this, Humboldt announces himself as our first and still primary theorist of planetarity.

On (Not) Sounding the Alarm . . .

In Humboldt's day, problems of environmental reflexivity were shaped by notions of the 'economy of nature', which studied the interface between nature and humanity in order to rationalise human social organisation via natural laws. Humboldt defied traditional views by presuming a planet organised neither like a dead machine, nor like a living body, but as a dynamic and self-organising *world*, an emergent concept that mutated 'economy' into what Ernst Haeckel, in 1866, named 'ecology' – not to nominate a new science but, rather, to rename and reorganise the established tradition of thought in which both Humboldt and Thoreau participated, and which Charles Darwin transformed into the central organising concept of the natural sciences. Nor were political systems excluded – not at first: Darwin's *Origin of Species* (1859) was greeted by early American readers as scientific proof that a global political economy based on slavery was a moral outrage, violating the laws of nature.[25]

Social Darwinism perverted this Humboldtian argument into a racist still-toxic legacy. Yet, that such interlinkages could be quite radical is suggested by Charles Fourier, who, in 1821, concluded from the recent climate disturbance of 1816's 'year without a summer' that the 'health of the globe' was declining owing to the rise of industrial civilisation, which 'overturns everything ... by the struggle of individual interest against collective interest'. Fourier offered to cure this planetary and global sickness by the formation of communal associations, an eco-socialist vision which inspired Utopian communities across France and the United States.[26] Similar warnings lay at the heart of modern liberalism, which sought to balance global markets with the common good. In 1848, fears that industrial capital could not expand infinitely on a bounded planet led John Stuart Mill to propose a 'stationary state', an economy of means towards higher ends.[27] By 1864, George Perkins Marsh was ready to sound the alarm: 'The earth is fast becoming an unfit home for its noblest inhabitant, and another era of equal human crime and human improvidence ... would reduce it to such a condition of impoverished productiveness, of shattered surface, of climatic excess, as to threaten the depravation, barbarism, and perhaps even extinction of the species.'[28] His lesson still terrifies: our war against Nature will render us not master but slave, as she wars against us in return.

Marsh was respected and his book influential – up to a point: while his rational, technocratic solutions to environmental harms were well received, critics scoffed that only 'scientific idiots and crackpots' could believe his ludicrous doomsday warnings.[29] This persistent pattern, of scientists and political theorists sounding ever-more-dire alarms which society mocks or ignores, has, since, become a familiar feature of the Anthropocene. As Bonneuil and Fressoz argue, 'we thus have a history of the marginalization of knowledge and alerts, a story of "modern disinhibition" that should be heeded'. Our ancestors destroyed environments not because they didn't know what they were doing; they knew, and did it anyway. The problem historians face, therefore, is not how to account for the emergence of Anthropocenic discourse, but to understand how it emerged, repeatedly, only to be repeatedly marginalised and subsequently forgotten.[30]

We, of all people, have lost the right to be surprised at ancestors whose practices of denial only dug us in deeper. The shock of planetarity registers in our denial: it upends all our Western cosmologies. The shallow, cyclical time of the Christian Bible becomes the abyssal time of Humboldt's

Cosmos, destabilising the theological plot that has for two millennia organised meaningful human life in the West. The providential promise of infinite territory for capital's infinite expansion and the unregulated externalisation of its excrement has become the finite boundary of a finite planet, destabilising imperial dominance.[31] The wall of separation between human mind and mindless nature becomes the historically emergent mind intuited by Humboldt and theorised by Darwin, a concept so disturbing that the prospect of animal consciousness remains controversial even today. In short, the discovery of Earth destabilised the foundational separation of humans from nature that undergirds the entire Western tradition. The response, however, was not to mitigate but to intensify: ever since the global explorations of the 1400s, modernity has built itself into global dominance by devising ways to restabilise the old binary relationship at any cost. The shock waves define both Romantic and Victorian literature, but the process continues today. Whether humanity, or even a recognisable Earth, can survive its conclusion remains, today, an unsettled question.

One measure of our uncertainty is the anxious search for analogues that might help us understand our current condition. They are not reassuring: four out of five of Earth's previous great extinctions were triggered by rapid rises in CO_2, and the rapidity of our current path outstrips them all by at least an order of magnitude. Thus, scientists, despite their desire to draw predictive power from the deep past, have concluded that we are in a 'no-analogue' state.[32] The difference, of course, lies in the wholesale global swerve, in the mid-nineteenth century, to fossil fuels. Ironically, the Anthropocene future that Thoreau warned against relied on renewables – wind, solar, hydropower. Global warming is but one of the Anthropocene's many faces: Thoreau heated his iconic house with stumps left over from the deforestation he witnessed, as New England's woodlands were clear-cut to build, fill and fuel the locomotives whose screams turned his attention to the future the railroad was bringing. Thoreau named that engine *Atropos*, Fate. As for coal? It came to Thoreau's world as the substitute fuel that would save the forests, just as oil came into Melville's world as the alternative fuel that would save the whales. What the broad Earth was not big enough to supply, a deep Earth, it seemed, would supply in infinite abundance.

The links were drawn by Emerson's own circle. Emerson's Harvard friend Louis Agassiz, back when he had been Humboldt's protégé in Europe, had concluded from studies of the Alpine glaciers of his Swiss homeland that Lyell's grand historical cycles were punctuated by global glaciations that periodically swept the Earth clear of life. But what had caused the Earth to freeze? Another friend, Irish physicist John Tyndall (inspired by his own Alpine mountaineering), traced the cause to atmospheric chemistry. He wrote in 1861: '[A]n almost inappreciable admixture of any of the hydrocarbon vapours would produce great effect on the terrestrial rays and produce corresponding changes of climate.'[33] That is, 'carbonic acid', which we now know as carbon dioxide, trapped heat and warmed the planet. Tyndall's observations confirmed the results of Eunice Foote of Seneca Falls, New York, a scientist and early advocate of women's rights, who, in 1856, had established that carbon dioxide warmed the atmosphere; more, she suggested, would mean a warmer Earth.[34]

Today the link between rising CO_2 and burning fossil fuels that release CO_2 seems obvious, yet, this was not at all obvious to writers and scientists in the nineteenth century. Even glacial theory, as it came to prevail, argued not for human agency over planetary change but for the reverse: ice ages, in their incomprehensibility, only further removed planetary nature from the warm and vital human world. Not until the mid-twentieth century would the links between climate change and human agency be joined into a single picture. Until then, the notion that a trace gas could produce such cataclysmic effect, and that human actions could produce so much of it as to have that effect, was, literally, incredible. What prevailed instead was the wisdom of Charles Lyell: 'We must command nature by obeying her laws . . . and for this reason we can never materially interfere with any of the great changes which either the aqueous or igneous causes are bringing about on the earth.' Or of Ralph Waldo Emerson, who reassured the world that '[Man's] operations taken together are so insignificant, a little chipping, baking, patching, and washing, that in an impression so grand as that of the world on the human mind, they do not vary the result.'[35] Anxieties were resolved, the tracks of the future laid, on this convenient nineteenth-century fiction. Nevertheless, it is we, who have driven the engine to the very edge. Eighty-five per cent of the CO_2 ever released has been released since 1948, when Thoreau's successor Aldo Leopold called for the land ethic; over half has been released since 1988 when the United Nations founded the IPCC.[36] That 'we can never interfere' with the Earth's system has become the rock of faith, or delusion, on which all our lives are built.

Conclusion: Reading the New Earth

Our own close connection to generations before, who both identified the Anthropocene and led us into it, returns us to the question raised by Clark: How might we read the literature of the nineteenth century without closing it down, without building ourselves into its inbuilt future? Nersessian warns against 'dynamic nominalism', a paranoid reading by which we project into the past our knowledge of the ruination of our climate.[37] Against the argument of Bonneuil and Fressoz – *they knew, but did nothing! we know, but it's too late!* – she asks how we might sustain a 'nonanticipatory' relation to the texts we read, by *not* projecting our knowledge onto them, by practising instead a 'nescience, or not knowing'. Nescience acknowledges that in 'calamity form', linear cause-and-effect relations are deranged: we cannot know whether our actions today can make a difference to the future. Does nothing we do matter? Does everything we do matter? Yet, at least we can beware of how 'form exerts the contextual pressure that can turn an event into a signal' – that is, be aware that only in hindsight do some events become signals. Humboldt, offering the geologist's hindsight that the form of a landscape encodes its history, creates a formal logic that makes the incomprehensible (vast accumulations of planetary time) into a regime of history that can be apprehended by Victorian audiences. But how, in a deranged world, where past and future no longer align, can *we* apprehend the *future*? The acute anxiety this generates reminds us that literature gives form to doubt, allowing us to speak from a place of uncertainty. Thus, the anxiety of not-knowing should not end our imagination of possible future worlds but provoke it.[38]

And we might extend that courtesy to the past. Emerson, by aligning his own startling discovery of the Earth to his inheritance of natural theology, resolves his terrified uncertainty at nature's vast 'secular' periods by converting the beneficent designs of God into a mindfully designing Man, who carries God's creative Logos into the material creation to make a 'second nature' through modern technology. He helped his and later generations to rationalise a world that opposed natural limitation, 'fate', with the infinitude of human 'freedom'. While Emerson's logic opened a protective wedge separating human history from the planetary temporality of Earth, Thoreau used Lyell as his primer for reading Earth as a book, turning the landscape's most delicate strata and nuanced features into gradual, ongoing historical processes that were legible as poetry. Both wrote in the optative mood, confident that an accurate reading of a signing Earth would tell us how to live lives adequate to its grand design.

By contrast, Edgar Allan Poe, in his only novel, sends Arthur Gordon Pym off on a Humboldtian voyage to the South Pole, fictionalising the actual polar explorations of his friend J. N. Reynolds, who was inspired by John Symmes's crackpot theory of the Earth as a hollow sphere open at the poles. Poe closed his phantasmagoric voyage with that idea, after mocking Humboldt's vision of racial unity by creating a black polar race of sub-humans, mocking the meaningfulness of non-Western languages with a non-human taunt ('*tekeli-li!*') and, finally, mocking Emerson's notion of Earth writing in 'gigantic letters' by closing with an absurdist play on the gigantic ciphers spelled out by the landforms of Tsalal. Moving, in *Eureka*, from fiction to metaphysics, Poe reveals God's Plot to be the collapse of All into Nothing, a nihilist resolution that, paradoxically, Poe dedicates to Humboldt. Numerous nineteenth-century writers found other ways of engaging with this new planetary sense: one might explore the environmental nihilism of James Fenimore Cooper's late novel *The Crater*, and the answering environmental stewardship of his daughter Susan Fenimore Cooper;[39] one might enquire whether Melville's *Moby-Dick* can be thought of as 'an Anthropocene novel' without violating the pastness of the past, or study, in *Clarel*, the collapse of Humboldt's geological legibility into the abyss of deep time, approaching the limit of human history. As for students of other literatures, Anthropocene historians suggest that the Anthropocene must be understood as an historical process of economic exploitation of Earth coextensive with a longer human lineage that would extend nescience back at least to the early modern era, or, as Marsh suggested, to ancient Greece – or even to the Pleistocene extinctions and the origins of agriculture itself.

My argument here has been that looping back to the nineteenth century is the nearest way to discover the roots of both our insight and our blindness. We join them in wonder, and terror: wonder at the sublime vision of a planetary Earth; terror at the meaning of that vision for humanity, a meaning that even today is still unspooling. This loop has many points of attachment. One is offered by Richard Primack, the botanist whose quest to study the effects of global warming on temperate climates was stymied until he discovered the meticulous daily records of seasonal change kept by Thoreau. Those records, and others kept by Thoreau's followers, yielded the datasets that Primack needed to give reality to the fact of global warming, recruiting, in a Humboldtian way, 'citizen scientists' to register and report changes in local environments. As Primack's team has shown, one-third of the plants that Thoreau knew are locally extinct, and another third are vanishing; warming temperatures alone account for it.[40]

Another loop was drawn in 2000, when the collaborative cluster of sciences known as 'Earth System Science', seeded and inspired by Humboldt's work, emerged into our headlines bearing the name for the geological epoch we have, so obliviously, brought on ourselves: the Anthropocene. A third is drawn by Walt Whitman, who on the brink of the American Civil War seconded Humboldt's faith that human intelligence would naturally follow the currents of the 'Kosmos' towards ever-greater natural and cultural diversity, and that, even if an endlessly warring humanity drove itself to extinction, new life would sprout from the womb of the Earth.[41] Hence Whitman addresses our shared nescience with the prospect of an answer:

> Who, out of the theory of the earth and of his or her body understands by subtle analogies all other theories,
> The theory of a city, a poem, and of the large politics of these States;
> Who believes not only in our globe with its sun and moon, but in other globes with their suns and moons,
> Who, constructing the house of himself or herself, not for a day but for all time, sees races, eras, dates, generations,
> The past, the future, dwelling there, like space, inseparable together.
> ('Kosmos', 1860, 1867)

The questions remain the same: How do we live together in a terrestrial world that binds us all to each other? How do we live in reciprocity with an engendering planet that mocks our dreams of destiny? Scientists are not alone in asking such questions, and literature can play a particular role – of imagining futures in which these as yet unanswered questions might find their form in an inhabitable world.

Notes

1. Ralph Waldo Emerson, 'The Relation of Man to the Globe' in *The Early Lectures of Ralph Waldo Emerson, 1833–1842*, [eds. Stephen Whicher et al.], 3 vols. (Cambridge, MA: Harvard University Press, 1959–72 [1834]), vol. I, pp.28–9, 31–2, 41, 48–9; 'Lord Bacon', ibid. p.327.
2. Henry David Thoreau, *The Journal of Henry D. Thoreau*, [eds. Bradford Torrey and Francis H. Allen], 14 vols. (Boston: Houghton Mifflin, 1906), vol. IX: pp.44–5 (30 August 1856).
3. Timothy Clark, *Ecocriticism on the Edge: The Anthropocene as a Threshold Project* (London: Bloomsbury, 2015), p.66.
4. Anahid Nersessian, 'Two Gardens: An Experiment in Calamity Form', *Modern Language Quarterly* 74(3) (September 2013), 307–28 (p.325).
5. Dipesh Chakrabarty, 'The Climate of History: Four Theses', *Critical Inquiry* 35 (Winter 2009): 197–222; 'Climate and Capital: On Conjoined Histories', *Critical Inquiry* 41 (Autumn 2014), 1–23 (p.15).
6. Simon L. Lewis and Mark A. Maslin, *The Human Planet: How We Created the Anthropocene* (New Haven, CT: Yale University Press, 2018), pp.26–7.

7. Christophe Bonneuil and Jean-Baptiste Fressoz, *The Shock of the Anthropocene* (London: Verso, 2017), pp.27, 177. See also Paul Lawrence Farber, *Finding Order in Nature: The Naturalist Tradition from Linnaeus to E. O. Wilson* (Baltimore: Johns Hopkins University Press, 2000), pp.13–21; Martin J. S. Rudwick, *Bursting the Limits of Time* (Chicago: University of Chicago Press, 2005).

8. Lewis and Maslin, *Human Planet*, p.27; Bonneuil and Fressoz, *Shock of Anthropocene*, p.177; Emerson, 'Relation of Man', p.44.

9. See Laura Dassow Walls, 'Natural History in the Anthropocene' in John Parham and Louise Westling (eds.), *A Global History of the Environment* (Cambridge: Cambridge University Press, 2017), pp.187–200 (p.192).

10. Jeffrey Jerome Cohen, in Jeffrey Jerome Cohen and Linda T. Elkins-Tanton, *Earth* (New York: Bloomsbury, 2017), p.44.

11. Stephen Jay Gould, *Time's Arrow, Time's Cycle: Myth and Metaphor in the Discovery of Geological Time* (Cambridge, MA: Harvard University Press, 1987), p.66; Hutton quoted p.65.

12. Quoted Bonneuil and Fressoz, *Shock of Anthropocene*, p.57; see Cohen and Elkins-Tanton, *Earth*, p.44.

13. Gould, *Time's Arrow*, p.59.

14. See Laura Dassow Walls, *Emerson's Life in Science* (Ithaca, NY: Cornell University Press, 2003), pp.42–3; Playfair quoted p.18.

15. Walls, *Emerson's Life*, pp.156–7; Ralph Waldo Emerson, 'Nature' in *Essays and Lectures* (New York: Library of America, 1983 [1844]), pp.541–55 (p.546).

16. Henry David Thoreau, *Journal I: 1837–1844*, (eds.) Elizabeth Hall Witherell et al. (Princeton, NJ: Princeton University Press, 1981), p.191; Thoreau, *Journal* [1906], XIV: pp.311–13.

17. Quoted and paraphrased from Lewis and Maslin, *Human Planet*, pp.31–4.

18. Ibid., pp.34–9.

19. Bonneuil and Fressoz, *Shock of Anthropocene*, p.76.

20. Alexander von Humboldt, *Cosmos: A Sketch of a Physical Description of the Universe* (Baltimore: Johns Hopkins University Press, 1997 [1845]), vol. I, pp.79–80; *Cosmos: A Sketch of a Physical Description of the Universe* (New York: Harper & Brothers, 1859), vol. V, pp.14–15.

21. Peter Sloterdijk, *In the World Interior of Capital: For a Philosophical Theory of Globalization* (Cambridge: Polity, 2014), pp.24–5, 23.

22. Humboldt, *Cosmos,* vol. I, p.72.

23. In order to immerse us in this sensibility, Humboldt invented a vertiginous, present-tense, immersive nature writing that connects us intimately and viscerally with Earth history. Alexander von Humboldt, *Views of Nature* (Chicago: University of Chicago Press, 2014 [1849]), p.141.

24. Bruno Latour, *An Inquiry into Modes of Existence* (Cambridge, MA: Harvard University Press, 2013), p.247; see also Latour, *Down to Earth: Politics in the New Climatic Regime* (Medford, MA: Polity, 2018).

25. Bonneuil and Fressoz, *Shock of Anthropocene*, pp.182–5; Laura Dassow Walls, *Henry David Thoreau: A Life* (Chicago: University of Chicago Press, 2017), pp.458–9.

26. Fourier quoted in Bonneuil and Fressoz, *Shock of Anthropocene*, p.257.
27. John Stuart Mill, *Principles of Political Economy* (London: J.W. Parker, 1848), vol. 2, pp.310–11.
28. George Perkins Marsh, *Man and Nature, or, Physical Geography as Modified by Human Action* (Cambridge, MA: Harvard University Press, 1965 [1864]), p.43.
29. See David Lowenthal, 'Nature and Morality from George Perkins Marsh to the Millennium', *Journal of Historical Geography* 26(1) (2002), 3–23 (pp.7–8); Lance Newman, *The Literary Heritage of the Environmental Justice Movement: Landscapes of Revolution in Transatlantic Romanticism* (New York: Palgrave McMillan, 2019).
30. Bonneuil and Fressoz, *Shock of Anthropocene*, pp.76, 196–7, 287.
31. Fredrik Albritton Jonsson has detailed the emergence of modernity's 'cornucopian ideology' despite the warnings and cautions of political economists including Adam Smith, Malthus and J. S. Mill. See 'The Origins of Cornucopianism: A Preliminary Genealogy', *Critical Historical Studies* (Spring 2014), 151–68.
32. See Richard E. Zeebe, Andy Ridgwell and James C. Zachos, 'Anthropogenic Carbon Release Rate Unprecedented during the Past 66 Million Years', *Nature Geoscience* 9 (2016), 325–9.
33. John Tyndall, 'On the Absorption and Radiation of Heat by Gases and Vapours', *Philosophical Transactions* (7 February 1861), 1–35 (p.28), royalsocietypublishing.org.
34. Eunice Foote, 'Circumstances Affecting the Heat of the Sun's Rays', *Proceedings of the AAAS*, read on 23 August 1856; cited in Katherine Hayhoe, 'Climate Science: It's a Lot Older than You Think' (2016), blog.ucsusa.org.
35. Charles Lyell, *Principles of Geology*, (ed.) James A. Secord (New York: Penguin, 1997 [1830–3]), pp.312–13; Emerson, *Nature* (1836), *Essays and Lectures*, pp.5–49 (p.8).
36. David Wallace-Wells, *The Uninhabitable Earth: Life after Warming* (New York: Penguin, 2019), pp.4, 235.
37. Nersessian, 'Two Gardens', pp.309, 325.
38. Ibid., pp.311–12, 315, 317.
39. Matthew Wynn Sivils, *American Environmental Fiction, 1782–1847* (Burlington, VT: Ashgate, 2014), pp.154–65; Rochelle Johnson and Daniel Patterson (eds.), *Susan Fenimore Cooper: New Essays on Rural Hours and Other Works* (Athens: University of Georgia, 2001).
40. Richard B. Primack, *Walden Warming: Climate Change Comes to Thoreau's Woods* (Chicago: University of Chicago Press, 2014).
41. Humboldt, *Views of Nature*, p.130.

CHAPTER 2

Data/Anecdote

Sean Cubitt

Delusions of Numeracy

Despite a decline of 1.3 per cent over the previous year, 2018 saw 259.4 million PCs sold worldwide.[1] Over the same period, against declining smartphone and tablet markets, the chip industry increased its revenues more than 13 per cent to $476.7 billion.[2] Optical fibre production increased to 325 million kilometres in 2018, though industry observers say that it was the first year without growth since 2003 owing to falling Chinese demand.[3] Still, the world's total of fixed broadband subscribers passed one billion for the first time in 2018, indicating some growth in domestic connections, now in competition with wireless (which also relies on fibre-optics for background infrastructure).

We are used by now to dealing with these kinds of figure in discussions of the Anthropocene. We know their rhetorical potency and we know how to unpack them. These numbers are significantly incomplete, however. It is all but impossible to get figures for chip production in units shipped, largely because of the structure of supply chains and just-in-time delivery, and because revenue doesn't give direct evidence owing to the cost discrepancy between mass-fabricated chips for general use and high-value specialist chips for security and military uses. Similarly, it is tricky to get up-to-date information on the environmental implications of some activities, although a typical set of figures, in this case for a 6-inch silicon wafer, are that its fabrication requires 3,200 cubic feet of bulk gases, 22 cubic feet of hazardous gases, 2,275 gallons of deionised water, 20 pounds of chemicals and 285 kilowatt hours of electrical power. It is unfortunate, though understandable, that Anthropocene discourse generally focuses more on atmospheric pollution than on terrestrial and pelagic pollution, but even here, we can follow the logic: a lot of energy, a lot of chemicals, many of them extremely dangerous, and a lot of gases and water. Of course, well-regulated plants scrub the water and gas coming out of the process, and an entire industry copes with the waste product. Cleanliness is imperative in digital technologies. Fibre-optics require unbelievably pure glass: purifying it requires temperatures in excess of 2,000 degrees Celsius, and someone has to take care of the impurities that the process removes. Purified water for washing chips after fabrication removes up to 40 per cent of the volume of any ordinary water supply: what happens to the excess? And how much energy does it take to clean it?

Likewise, how much does it take to send signals along those millions of kilometres of cable, and the millions laid over the decades since the internet boom began? What happens to all the old cable that can no longer meet contemporary standards? No one collects it from the bottom of the Pacific. It is clad in plastics, some dating back before the Montreal accords that banned the use of PCBs (polychlorinated biphenyl plastics), and no one knows the chemistry of deep-ocean pressure on old fibre. There are accountings of the environmental costs of satellite launches and of space debris in close earth orbit.[4] We have left exploratory spacecraft, some with nuclear reactors aboard, on the surfaces of other planets. From the deepest oceans to the far reaches of the solar system, our communications media leave footprints even though some of them were only there to take photographs. You can find the carbon footprint of a Google search, and we have bandied about the knowledge that the cloud, the server farms coping with the vast expansion in data production and storage, had already outstripped the airline industry's output of greenhouse gases by 2007, and that corporations install their data farms in the coldest climates to cut their cooling bills but are still pumping heat into the ecosphere. Statistics do not make these actions any more solid than they already are. Beneath the numbers lie other mysteries, other questions, other interpretations. Numbers do not represent, name or indicate truth; they only point at the place where it ought to be, and wave in the direction in which it's travelling.

Nor, correspondingly, do media represent truth: they produce it, not as a discursive formation harnessing power and knowledge to performative statements but by their unavoidable materiality. In order to produce and access the numbers, we use exactly the same machinery we are trying to describe, thereby adding to the total weight of communications as physical installation and as an increasingly significant site of energy consumption. Bear in mind that, as was the case for the postal system since the mid-nineteenth century, about 80 per cent of online traffic is business to business, and another significant tranche is governmental. But now, we are entering the era of the Internet of things (IoT), already in excess of ten billion connected devices, where human-to-human communication is a diminishing part of the traffic. This makes clear why social media corporations are so interested in mining this last preserve of intimate and, from a systemic point of view, random noise generation that human interactions provide: to make a profit. It also helps us to understand that our discussions of data, truth and climate change simultaneously rely on and contribute to global warming, but do so in the margins of a system devoted to an overwhelmingly mechanical internal dialogue, where humans have a diminishing statistical and perhaps semantic role.

Coding the *Anthropos*

Like SETI, the Search for Extra-Terrestrial Intelligence network powered by mass participation and donated computing time that rakes the noisy cosmos for meaningful signals, our communications systems radiate waste heat and electromagnetic waves far beyond our own planet. This creates digital hullabaloo that masks the very signals that SETI seeks and instead provides more and more evidence of that now vanishing species the *anthropos*. The term 'Anthropocene' is challenged on many sides: Capitalocene, Chthulucene, misanthropocene, necrocene and Steigler's French pun the entropocène.[5] Not just a symptom of the Anthropocentric urge, retaining the word 'Anthropocene' perhaps reflects a melancholy wish that our dwindling should leave as its monument not a midden but a heat signature, fading in a corner of the Milky Way. All the same, there is a certain utopianism in keeping the human in play, not as an empirical given (for reasons explored in the section on Compound Truths) but as an unfinished project. Clearly, the environment environs because it is defined as what isn't human, but the act of excluding simultaneously defines what is included, what counts as human. We become human only in relation to a nature that is other-than-human. That unhuman environment now includes the informational equivalent of the factory environment, technologies that chatter among themselves at speeds beyond our comprehension, as well as a world increasingly hostile to the survival of our species. The utopian residue of the Anthropocene would then be not the sustainability of an already defined humanity but a political project: to become human in a different relation to natural and technical environments in rapid evolution.

The Anthropocene thesis is about change, on scales and in time spans that similarly defy human senses. The world has always needed mediation, certainly when approached as the locus of truth as it has been by the scientific concern with knowledge verified by its objects rather than by argument. The self-inscription of tremors on a seismometer's turning drum depends on holding the pen still as the drum moves up and down, while an optical illusion, or more likely a deeply held ideological belief that the moving finger writes, tricks us into believing that it is the pen that moves. The world has agency here; the pen's only task is to stay immobile. The mediation is mysterious to us, and the scrawl it leaves demands a hermeneutic as richly traditional and as formally guided as any scribal culture. Yet, the faith in the world's capacity to record itself, from photography's pencil of nature[6] to real-time meteorological maps, invites a myth of immediacy and transparency that the materiality of lenses and the darkroom, cartographic projection, and translation from arithmetic to geometry belie. The very existence of the Anthropocene depends on its determination through such instruments. The hierarchy of senses that leads us to distrust the proximate senses of taste, touch and scent means that we do not value our own feelings of warmth and cold. The temperature gradients of climate change are imperceptible, too vast and too slow for our eyes. We need time-lapse cinematography, we need cartographic instruments and, increasingly, we demand a combination of these pictorial and symbolic tools in ill-considered hybrids whose veracity we trust more than ourselves. McLuhan's idea of the media as prosthetic senses[7] returns back on itself. For McLuhan, media were prosthetic extensions of human organs, but today, prosthetic media assert themselves against the senses they replace. What is more, the planet-scale instruments we now employ – relays of satellites, automatic buoys in mid-ocean, remote anemometers equipped with cellular communications, all reporting to international computer networks[8] – produce more data than whole cadres of technicians can observe, in granular detail sifted through by devices trained by machine learning to seek patterns that, in their increasing autonomy from direct human design, no longer exclusively conform to the requirements of the science they were built for. The commercial value and consequent restrictions on data sharing, especially for high-resolution local forecasting; the high-end computers and networks needed to access and the high-end skills required to interpret weather data; the mass transformation of weather events into numbers and those numbers into stored databases with their simultaneously idiosyncratic and standardised architectures; all of this produces datasets of stupefying size and fluidity that are scarcely less incomprehensible than the weather itself.

It takes the mediation of what Paul Edwards calls the vast machine of meteorology to produce the new strangeness of weather, the new anxiety about global climate (an entity that has existed only for scant decades) and now the alienation of climate data. This mediating machine prompts two reactions: the truth-claiming of climate science, and our personal and human estrangement from the interactions that constitute the universe we inhabit, as symptomised by an unreadable quantity of data. The communications technologies of the global meteorological network erase human conceptions of distance by synchronising global feeds as well as time through recording and prediction. They confound human distinctions between planetary and microscopic scales of space and time.[9] They displace perception, no longer an exclusively human capability, from the intimacy of *atma*, breath, to atmosphere, a planetary scale where breath, even the combined breathing of the entire species, is a tiny component (although the eructations of cattle do figure). The human, in this perspective, no longer mediates between *atma* and atmosphere but dwells at a mathematical point between the macro-atmosphere and the micro-anatomy of the lungs. In that bounded space-time, a boundary or intersection between dissolution into the cosmos and mastery by measurement, the human persists at a junction between particulate and wave-form, ready to disappear into either; preserved from disappearing into cosmic flux by measurement, and from disappearing into measurement by cosmic flux. This rescaling of the human displaces the species from the core of a semantic universe to a mere message in a communicative one.

Technical mediation implicates the whole ecology. Not only are instruments made of and act in worldly materials; they are nodes of interaction between physical forces, like the seismometer's play between inertia and tremor. Humans, too, are formed in and by mediations of air, water and food. They impact on the environments they create by breathing, eating, excreting and in the built environment via the transport networks and data ecologies they establish. Equally, however, instruments and humans transform mediation into communication by divorcing elements of mediation from one another as senders, channels and receivers, emphasising endpoints and placing under erasure the underlying condition in which both humans and instruments are channels, not termini. The result is that the *anthropos* of the Anthropocene is no longer the Renaissance humanists' Man that saw itself as the centre of the universe. The subject of Science, the subject that knows to count the two trillion galaxies in the universe and also, simultaneously, to calculate the mathematics of the Higgs boson, is collective and distributed, and increasingly reliant not only on prosthetic senses but also on prosthetic memory and prosthetic understanding. The actually existing cyborg is not an enhanced human but a corporate network of computers with implanted human functionaries. The actual humans who function as biochips in the massive cyborg operation of Science defer to Science as the site of knowing. They are in the vanguard of historical transformation, humans at last recognising that they are not messages but channels. Rather than an organic conjuncture mutating the flows passing through it, the new human is a digital processor of inputs. The human as code not only alters its inputs but, like code, is formally performative: like any software, its processing necessarily makes a difference in the world. This is one reason why so many 'environmentalities',[10] especially natural resource management and biodiversity conservation, are not only neo-liberal in content[11] but systems-theoretic in form. For they are anchored in a belief that a world explicable in terms of code is fundamentally composed of code.

Our estrangement from the climate thus also raises the question of truth: if the climate is truly the mathematically describable system that atmos-pheric science says it is, then its truth does not include our senses, and, given the scale and speed of the physical actuality as well as the digital description, humans are excluded from that truth. On the other hand, humans can contemplate its meaning in a way that the pure, 'objective' gathering and storage of weather data cannot. Meaning and truth have drifted apart in the Anthropocene, truth becoming increasingly machinic while meaning is increasingly an effect of communication in the nodes of networks, we call human beings. This marginalisation, surely a key reason why climate change denial is possible, provokes a reaction of resentment to the bullying assertion that what any of us thinks no longer counts. Counting, the numerical, has overwhelmed all other symbol systems, especially those such as religion whose task has always been to produce meanings and to conform meaning to truth. The divorce of meaning from truth, which produces the professional modesty of scientists, instead produces for denialists an embattled defence of human privilege founded on human exception, its apparent capacity for freedom underpinning the modern worldview at least since Kant.

Visualisations

It is clear that the human has changed. The utopian Anthropocene project of becoming human otherwise, is then by no means doomed. The division of human from nature means that there is no determinate human nature. The divorce of meaning from truth is a corollary of Gödel's theorem, which states that no consistent set of axioms can prove all the truths of a formal system such as mathematics and logic, and that no system can demonstrate its own consistency. In everyday terms, a system can be coherent or complete but not both. Because climate science treats the planet as a formal system, the truth it proposes can only be either complete or consistent. Scientists tend to dispute the idea that their data are mediated, as if that detracted from their truth; but for humanists, mediation contributes to, even brings about meaning, and incompleteness and inconsistency are intrinsic qualities of mediation. The ecocritical category of the human is torn, in this historical moment, between formal truth and mediated meaning.

Scientists emphasise the consistency of facts with observable reality; humanists stress that facts are statements about what is the case, not the case itself. Etymologically, data are a class of facts that ostensibly give themselves. The status of the gift was once underwritten by the generosity of the gods or God, and subsequently by Mother Nature whose gendered fecundity colonialism transformed into the infinitely exploitable *terra nullius*, thus transforming Nature's generosity – the given – into the prerogative of wealth to seize whatever it wants – the fact. Evolving, language has recognised the ambiguity of the given when we spoke first of 'taking' photographs and now of 'capturing' data, in an incongruous paradox of seizure and gift. To take a photograph was a relatively innocuous activity. To capture information is less immaterial: ordering needs energy and material infrastructure, and processing and transmission have implications for observer, observed and the channels that link them. Current databases store not only data – statements about reality – but relations between data – statements about statements. Contextual relations become metadata, treated in exactly the same way as primary data. This relational architecture deprives data of any context, any environment, beyond the database itself. There is no outside of data. Like the Derridean 'il n'y a pas de hors-texte',[12] a database is a self-enclosed world whose formal systems make it impossible for it to refer to any referent beyond itself. And yet, the autonomy it claims is impossible since, as a physical entity, the database exists inside the ecology which it attempts to substitute for and exclude. Denying the conditions for their own existence, data substitute for the world rather than interpreting or representing it.

This is rarely more apparent than in financial trading software, engine of the economy and therefore of the present and future exploitation of nature, where the concept of real-time communication reaches its practical boundary (trading companies pay premium rates for office space in the immediate vicinity of major stock exchanges to shave milliseconds off the response times of their high-frequency trading computers). Finance software combines displays from premium financial news suppliers – public delivery of stock prices is far too slow – with automated and rapidly evolving buy–sell algorithms[13] which account for 80 per cent of the total number of trades on contemporary markets. Watching video screen-grabs of the 36-minute flash crash of 6 May 2010, which wiped a trillion dollars off US stocks – and then restored them – is a lesson in illegibility. The screen displays are intended to translate into visible form a more or less exclusively algorithmic activity: computer-mediated trading whose principle is that extreme speed is itself a source of profit. Software responding to incoming news of volatility places bets that prices will carry on descending or bounce back, creating feedback loops veering between wilder and wilder extremes. If, on the one hand, they reveal the profound irrationality hidden by the concept of the market's invisible hand (rather like the authoritative pen of the seismometer that proves to have no agency at all), on the other, the fine print – the alphanumeric codenames of corporations whose shares are yo-yoing up and down – tells us that these absurd diagrams have intensely real effects on the environment. Abstract prices on screen denoting the price of an equally abstract idea, next year's copper, for example, change the investment and planning of mining companies, their equipment purchasing and the order books of equipment manufacturers, and reverberate through the environmental consequences of each falling domino.

At this period in its history, it is as silly to describe money as 'fundamentally' a medium of exchange as it is to describe language as fundamentally a substitute for beating each other round the head with sticks. Figures bouncing across screens bear the same relation to the real economy as meteorological databases do to the clouds passing by the window: a relation of exclusion, so that even though the real economy includes the data-storms of stock exchanges, *they* do not include *it*. This contradiction is part of what drives economic crises that in the end do have a performative relation to the ecology they otherwise studiously ignore. This collision of worlds is enacted, in medialogical terms, in the collocation of screens and their displays. The physical presence of the glass rectangle and its plastic frame disappears into the far greater apparent reality and urgency of the activities they are the vehicles of. Likewise, the backend technical processes of data capture, processing, storage and transmission, together with their energy budgets and physical infrastructures, vanish. Despite stock exchanges being among the heaviest users of computer memory, and despite the significance of records to the training and operation of autonomous finance software, despite even the external consequences of futures trading on local economies months or years later, these systems present themselves as present, as operating exclusively in a 'now' that goes on and on and whose dimensions are measured in milliseconds, faster than even unconscious human reflexes. Climate change denial is written into this systemic eternal now.

The lively diagrams that flitter across these screens are neither narrative nor illusion. They belong to a new mode of image making. Geometry, cartography, even theology made use of schematic ways of showing relationships for two thousand years before the rise of modern data visualisation, which can be dated to William Playfair's *Statistical Breviary* of 1801, when pie charts, bar charts and the horizontal time axis came into use. Playfair inaugurated the first new visual order since perspective. Like perspective, it provides a visual grammar capable of containing an effectively infinite number of visual statements, and like perspective it constructs a viewing position from which its grammar makes sense: perspective conformed to the Man of Western humanism. In data visualisation, that subject, individual and generic at the same time, the singular species-being, the reader-in-the-text, is eradicated in favour of a form that reconciles the subject with its object while asserting the absolute objectivity of its presentation. What this subsumption of the subject under the object hides, but then asserts again, is the master subjectivity for which the survey of the world-as-data performs its truth. The influential information designer Gyorgy Kepes phrased it thus: 'The essential vision of reality presents us not with fugitive appearances but with felt patterns of order.'[14] At that point, it was the fugitive that was the enemy. Kepes sought the endurance of pattern, but today's instruments, from the meteorological network to Facebook, are devoted precisely to the ephemeral. This is the first of three ways in which twenty-first-century data visualisation differs from its predecessors. The master subject of the new, real-time visualisation technologies is entranced by the exception as much as by the repetitive. Without the bandwidth and storage limitations of its print forebears, contemporary data visualisation can include the extreme, the limit case, the aberrant statistic, without recourse to the normative adjustments that characterised an older visualisation practice. Still, some characteristics have remained, most of all the depiction of time in a spatial form. Like Duchamp's concept of post-retinal art – for instance, contemporary neo-conceptual art that celebrates the idea over the visible – data visualisation celebrates the triumph of the concept over the senses. Even where it embraces the abnormal, it does so by including it within a taxonomy that benefits from its extension into new domains without sacrificing the principle that everything can be assimilated into its system.

A second novelty of twenty-first-century data visualisation is its new relational topology. In relational databases, there is no fixed hierarchy to the taxonomies structuring the data. Every search and interaction reconfigures the data into new orderings. At the same time, each search generates new data (the user's IP address, search history, location and so on) which leaves its trace in the evolving relations between items and sets of data. It is these relations, rather than the data themselves, which are of greatest value. If I do a picture search today for, let's say, 'climate change diagram', I will get different results from yours, and other results tomorrow, both because of my intervening search activity and because other searchers will have generated other relations between similar search terms and results, adding their behaviours (clicking on this or that result) to the total set of relations clustered around the search terms. Under these conditions, the 'knowledge' represented by a screenful of images is constantly evolving, perpetually and even infinitely malleable, so long as we recognise that what is on offer is a bounded infinity, an infinite that can never exceed the borders of its character as an infinity of data. Since every point in a network is its centre, the view from any point, the viewpoint of any data subject, gives on to an apparent infinity. It is only when we step out of the network that we can see that it exists entirely behind the screen which, in our fascination, we took for an immaterial, im-mediate (unmediated) transparency.

The third moment of this transformation arrives in the hybridisation of the two great symbolic forms of modernity's visual culture. For the Anthropocene, as cultural formation and discursive artefact, depends on a double mediation in both perspective and data visualisation. Long since built into the elaborate lenses on which analogue and digital cameras alike depend, perspective is deeply embedded in photographic and cinematographic culture (experiments with lenseless imaging notwithstanding). And photography is crucial to the semantic dimension of Anthropocene culture. Data visualisation culls large-scale dynamics from massive collections of data. The photographic media seize on unique instances of the confluence of forces, specific and unrepeatable encounters of physical, social and technical agents, tailored to the human sensorium. The attempt to bend photography to normative social science, for example, in the images of street children and criminals analysed by John Tagg,[15] cannot restrain the viewer from seeing in them the evidence of lives lived and of the capacity for those lives to have been lived otherwise. At the same time, as Tagg argues in a later work,[16] a photograph is only one instance in a larger apparatus of institutions and discourses. Sarah Kember spies something similar in a liminal technology, facial recognition, which supplements photographic imaging with biometric data that, even supported through artificial intelligence and so potentially free of institutional and discursive prejudice, still operates a sexist and racist taxonomy.[17] Retention of human societies' worst aspects into quasi-autonomous data technologies is one of the more depressing aspects of the emerging formation. The hybridisation of perspectival and diagrammatic symbolic orders extends from biometrics to the intricate imbrication of iconic images, such as the polar bear on an ice floe, and photographic tools such as time-lapse with cartographic and geographic information systems (GIS), data visualisations and animations. Animation, as a time-based medium, informs the assembly of photo-image and data visualisation into montage forms, often overlaid with a mix of environmental sound and generated soundtracks, and interspersed with text and voice-over from older media – language, music, writing. Collapsing millennia of media practice into a single compound form would appear syncretic were it not shaped under the overarching architectonics of data.

Compound Truths

Nonetheless, in this compound of montage and palimpsest, multiple internal contradictions arise, of the kind that plague the well-meant documentary of Al Gore's PowerPoint presentation *An Inconvenient Truth* (2006). Like all of us, Gore speaks in language, but not under conditions, of his own choosing. His skilful performance of the classical humanist lecture form binds together but cannot entirely dispel the frictions between two regimes of truth, the anecdote and the dataset. Anecdotes typically narrate unique, often but not necessarily symptomatic or emblematic events. In Eastern European usage, this includes fictions, a feature that emphasises that it is not just brevity that characterises them; rather, they are acts of telling. An anecdote includes not only the situation narrated, but the circumstances of the narration: teller, tale and audience. It actively participates in the mutation of the told in the telling, and, like language, the anecdote thrives on its evolution through multiple retellings, each of which is likely to alter it, knowingly or unknowingly. As anecdotes, pictures provide snapshots of a situation: a conjuncture of histories in a uniquely concrete moment pregnant, like the photographs of criminals mentioned by Tagg, with the possibility of becoming otherwise.

This subjunctive mode of the image as anecdote speaks of and from a different order of truth to the insistence on the actual in data forms. Accumulated data in conjunction with powerful algorithms and machine learning become capable of performative statements directed towards conforming the future to the will of the present. Anecdotes, on the contrary, recognise in the actual the accumulation of acts that form it, but, in so doing recognise the non-identity of the present: not only its capacity to become other than it is but its failure to exist in any fully completed form. The profound instability of anecdotal evidence, rather than its uniqueness, is what makes it so despised in natural and social sciences. In the unstable domain of political rhetoric, anecdotes are, surprisingly, simultaneously despised in the highly ideological arena of 'evidence-based policy', and deployed as popular wisdom wherever a politician finds that an appeal to common sense can trump data. Like many statistical arguments, the pseudo-anecdotes of table-thumping campaigners can always be identified by their monocausality. In the eyes of expert culture, anecdotes are constantly trumped by statistics.

Gore's humanism should not be dismissed too easily as anthropocentric, if only because to do so avoids the more challenging task of understanding how his narration, oscillating between data and anecdote, rests ultimately on a third truth-procedure: logic. The construction of an argument on the basis of well-formed axioms lies at the root of Western truth. Given the empty set as axiom, it is possible to derive all the counting numbers and the basic arithmetic functions (Here is an empty set: how many sets are there? One. So now we have the empty set as the contents of a new set which is the set of all sets whose contents are zero, so we have two sets. That makes a new, third set with two members, and so on ad infinitum). If it is true that all men are mortal, a host of further statements present themselves, and fundamental tools like the law of the excluded middle (which holds that a proposition is either true or untrue: men are either mortal or not) allow listeners to discriminate between true and false arguments. Gore's lecture mixes logic, anecdote and data. He moves among them to produce a rhetorical rather than purely logical effect. However, there is in his script a deep respect for the rules of argument. The effect is to produce an audience position which should blend various older forms into a single subject capable of political action. Yet the impersonal subject of logic, the individual subject of perspective and the collective subject of data do not blend in any simple convolution. Their product is instead best caught in the category of the data subject, deleted from the European Union's General Data Protection Regulation (GDPR) in 2018, but a potent concept still. The data subject is not a person but the cloud of data points assembled around a network user. This data subject should be understood as a first indication that the once mighty social form of the individual is beginning to pass, through its representations online, into its own environment, dissolving the boundary between human and datasphere. The data subject already fulfils, then, its necessarily performative economic and biopolitical tasks in social and workplace media.

The mass image databases of Instagram, or Google Earth and Google Maps, and their governmental and military analogues, are not simply collections but, in relational topologies, construct a single mass image of the world, connecting photographic and metadata – GPS locations, user IDs, previous shots with similar filenames – with, increasingly, data produced by reading within the image, like face recognition and algorithms that read represented signs and logos. The resultant mass image is not intended for human reading: the visual elements appear to the favoured computer algorithms as alphanumeric files of colour values and interaction records. The presentation of search results and the personalised menus typical in social media treat the data subject in exactly the same way as the data object: conditioned and defined by its relations with other data. This is why it is now possible to argue that the human-environment barrier is dissolving. This data environment has assimilated the entire machinic sensorium – instruments that count and picture,[18] often in spectra invisible to humans – into a closed world which nonetheless depends on the physical, 'natural' environment which it seeks both to exclude and to enclose.

The contradiction runs through the failure of visual forms to produce a subject other than one entirely subsumed into the database, where it only ever finds itself in the estranged form of a commodity. We discover that we are data – givens – with no consciousness of ever having consented to give. This allies us with the unconscious donations of nature, or indeed the unwilling gift of common land to rapacious landlords and colonists that forms the long history of savage appropriation and accumulation[19] that undergirds the Anthropocene catastrophe. The very act of giving has been reft from us humans. Like Baudrillard's silent majorities,[20] and in the spirit of the anecdote which holds back as much as it reveals, we are learning to withhold something of ourselves from dissolution. This may, however, be a more radically conservative stance than populist resentment and denialism, clinging to the self after post-structural demands for its splitting have come to pass, and to meaning long after linguistics' and philosophy's turn to language began to unpick its foundations. Truth, meanwhile, has become as alien to us as the nature it derives from, relies on and denies.

Photographic images do, however, retain their subjunctive quality, even after uploading into mass image databases. The excluded environment is not self-identical but historical, redefining its borders and internal flows in response to shifting forms of the *anthropos*. Photographs, too, lack self-identity. In light of the non-identity of environments and of photography, we should not mourn but embrace their condition as it extends to the non-identical heart of contemporary subjectivity. The Anthropocene is not a matter of scientific fact. The encounter with the Anthropocene is not an encounter of the human with truth but one where humans, data technologies and natural processes are ostensibly divided but ontologically connected, and historically wholly permeable to one another. The new humanity will evolve only out of recognising that its media, in all their autonomy, now form a third party in the encounter, and are ripe for liberation.

Notes

1. 'Gartner Says Worldwide PC Shipments Declined 4.3 Percent in 4Q18 and 1.3 Percent for the Year' (10 January 2019), www.gartner.com/en/newsroom/press-releases/2019-01-10-gartner-says-worldwide-pc-shipments-declined-4-3-perc.
2. 'Gartner Says Worldwide Semiconductor Revenue Grew 13.4 Percent in 2018; Increase Driven by Memory Market' (7 January 2019), www.gartner.com/en/newsroom/press-releases/2019-01-07-gartner-says-worldwide-semiconductor-revenue-grew-13-#:~:text=January%207%2C%202019-,Gartner%20Says%20Worldwide%20Semiconductor%20Revenue%20Grew%2013.4%20Percent%20in%202018,preliminary%20results%20by%20Gartner%2C%20Inc.
3. Michael Finch and Richard Mack, 'Optical Fibre and Cable Industry Review' (2019), CRU, www.crugroup.com/knowledge-and-insights/spotlights/2019.
4. See 'Final Environmental Impact Statement for the Cassini Mission' (Washington: National Aeronautics and Space Administration, 1995), saturn.jpl.nasa.gov; *The Space Debris Mitigation Guidelines of the Committee on the Peaceful Uses of Outer Space* (Vienna: United Nations, 2010), orbitaldebris.jsc.nasa.gov.
5. Jason W. Moore, *Capitalism in the Web of Life: Ecology and the Accumulation of Capital* (London: Verso, 2015); Donna Haraway, 'Tentacular Thinking: Anthropocene, Capitalocene, Chthulucene', *e-flux* 75 (September 2016), www.e-flux.com/journal/75/67125/tentacular-thinking-anthropocene-capitalocene-chthulucene/; Joshua Clover and Juliana Spahr, *#Misanthropocene: 24 Theses*. First presented at Curds and Whey Oakland, 13 June 2014 (Oakland: Commune Editions, 2014); Bernard Stiegler, 'Sortir de l'anthropocène', *Multitudes* 60(3) (2015), 137–46; Ghassan Hage, *Is Racism an Environmental Threat?* (Cambridge: Polity, 2017).

6. Henry Fox-Talbot, *The Pencil of Nature* (London: Longman, Brown, Green and Longmans, 1844).

7. Marshall McLuhan, *Understanding Media: The Extensions of Man* (London: Sphere, 1964).

8. Paul N. Edwards, *A Vast Machine: Computer Models, Climate Data, and the Politics of Global Warming* (Cambridge, MA: MIT Press, 2010).

9. Janine Randerson, *Weather as Medium: Toward a Meteorological Art* (Cambridge, MA: MIT Press, 2018).

10. Arun Agrawal, 'Environmentalities', *Current Anthropology* 6(2) (April 2005), 161–90.

11. Robert Fletcher, 'Neoliberal Environmentality: Towards a Poststructuralist Political Ecology of the Conservation Debate', *Conservation and Society* 8(3) (2010), 171–81.

12. Jacques Derrida, *Of Grammatology* [trans. Gayatri Chakravorty Spivak] (Baltimore: Johns Hopkins University Press, 1976), p.158.

13. Ian Stewart, 'The Mathematical Equation that Caused the Banks to Crash', *The Observer* (12 February 2012).

14. Gyorgy Kepes (ed.), *The New Landscape in Art and Science* (Chicago: Paul Theobald and Co., 1956), p.24.

15. John Tagg, *The Burden of Representation: Essays on Photographies and Histories* (London: Macmillan, 1988).

16. John Tagg, *The Disciplinary Frame: Photographic Truths and the Capture of Meaning* (Minneapolis: University of Minnesota Press, 2009).

17. Sarah Kember, 'Face Recognition and the Emergence of Smart Photography', *Journal of Visual Culture* 13(2) (2014), 182–99.

18. Peter Galison, *Image and Logic: A Material Culture of Microphysics* (Chicago: University of Chicago Press, 1997).

19. Rosa Luxemburg. *The Accumulation of Capital* [trans. Agnes Schwarzschild] (London: Routledge & Kegan Paul, 1951).

20. Jean Baudrillard, *In the Shadow of the Silent Majorities, or, The End of the Social and Other Essays* [trans. Paul Foss, John Johnston and Paul Patton] (New York: Semiotext(e), 1983).

PART I

Anthropocene Forms

CHAPTER 3

Poetry

Mandy Bloomfield

How is contemporary poetry responding to a current state of rapid and ongoing environmental change? What aesthetic and philosophical legacies are poets drawing on to address current transformations of our material world and their cultural meanings? How are practitioners and theorists of poetics contributing to discussions of the Anthropocene and its ramifications? This chapter will explore such questions by focusing on recent writing that uses the resources of experimental poetics to engage with some of the cognitive, ethical and representational challenges of the Anthropocene. Rather than extending the traditions of nature poetry, this work draws on an alternative, and more recent, legacy: that of post-war open-field poetics as developed by writers such as William Carlos Williams, Robert Creeley and, most especially, Charles Olson. Through techniques such as the decentring of the lyric persona, collage and spatial composition, as well as an emphasis on the poem as a field of energies and exchanges, open-field poetics provokes a rethinking of relations between figure and ground, subject and object, human and non-human entities. This chapter will investigate how contemporary writers have reworked these poetic strategies to refigure human relations with the rest of material reality in the context of ecological crisis.

Beyond Nature Poetry

Poetry's prominent role within environmental criticism is well established. Ever since its formative years in the 1990s, ecocriticism has valued poetry's long-running traditions of pastoral and nature writing for their negotiation of changing environmental imaginaries. Early ecocritical discourse on poetry focused predominantly on British and American Romantics such as William Wordsworth, John Clare and (as discussed in Chapter 1) Ralph Waldo Emerson and Henry David Thoreau, as well as modern poets who extended this tradition, such as A. R. Ammons, Wendell Berry,

W. S. Merwin and Gary Snyder.[1] Jonathan Bate's *The Song of the Earth* argued for the capacity of such poetry to reveal and critique modern humanity's alienation from nature in industrialised society, but also to restore an ethos of 'dwelling upon the earth'.[2] Such criticism valued the Romantic tradition and its legacies in more recent nature writing for its potential to inculcate an ethos of care towards nature in times of ecological threat.

However, as Lynn Keller points out in her seminal work on poetry in the Anthropocene, 'nature poetry alone . . . is an insufficient poetic response to the radical instabilities of the environmental mess in which we find ourselves'.[3] In its celebration of the natural world as a reinvigorating space of escape from the alienation of human civilisation, the pastoral mode relies on embedded dualisms between the urban and the rural, the human and the natural. The Romantic privileging of experiences of the sublime in awe-provoking spectacles such as towering mountains or stormy seas, meanwhile, depicts natural forces as beyond human influence. But one implication of the Anthropocene is that 'nature' can no longer be imagined as an autonomous organic system impervious to human activity, nor as a space of escape from the contaminations of human civilisation. Climate change and pollution affect even the remote mountains and wild seas that were such potent sources of the Romantic sublime. By the late 1980s, growing awareness of global environmental change led Bill McKibben and others to declare 'the end of nature', in a dramatic gesture that asserted not the end of planetary life itself but the demise of an understanding of 'nature as eternal and separate'.[4] It was the end of nature as we knew it. One could no longer imagine wandering lonely as a cloud, because clouds now jostle in our imaginations with an awareness of atmospheric concentrations of carbon dioxide and other airborne pollution. Such changed states of 'nature' are out of joint with the aesthetic and representational resources of traditional forms of nature poetry. The material phenomena and conceptual challenges of the Anthropocene, as Tobias Boes and Kate Marshall argue, require, therefore, 'novel modes of articulation'.[5]

The publication in 2001 of the first issue of the journal *ecopoetics*, edited by Jonathan Skinner, highlighted the potential for contemporary poetry to pursue such 'novel modes of articulation'. The inaugural issue's opening statement lambasted '"[e]nvironmentalist" culture' for a blinkered vision that ignored avant-garde traditions of poetry and that demonstrated, 'for a movement whose scientific mantra is "biodiversity," an astonishing lack of diversity in approaches to culture, to the written and spoken word'. At the same time, Skinner also criticised late twentieth-century avant-gardes for largely failing to turn their 'linguistically sophisticated approaches' to the task of exploring environmental issues. And yet, he insisted, '[e]xamples of sustained investigations of nature . . . can be found throughout "postmodern" poetry – from Lorine Niedecker, through Charles Olson or Larry Eigner, to contemporary poets'. *Ecopoetics* formed a gathering place for both creative and critical work, encompassing a range of poetic experiments and environmental concerns in 'recognition that human impact on the earth and its other species, is without a doubt the historical watershed of our generation'.[6]

The contemporary writing examined in this chapter combines poetic experimentation with an attention to ecological dilemmas. This is poetry, that, rather than figuring nature as a space of renewal, engages with anthropogenically compromised environments. Rather than positing nature as separate from human culture, this work emphasises entanglement and contingency. And instead of engaging with the material world through individual lyric personae, as in much nature poetry, it explores alternative forms of agency and collectivity pertinent to an era of ecological crisis.

Open-Field Poetics

An important point of reference for experimental strands of ecologically oriented poetry is 'open-field' poetics, as developed by American post-war writers such as William Carlos Williams, Robert Creeley, Robert Duncan and Charles Olson. Open-field poetics emerged from a context in which World War II, and most particularly, the detonation of the atomic bomb in 1945, had highlighted the devastating capabilities of anthropogenic forces, catalysing new kinds of thinking about the socially and ecologically destructive potentials of modern 'progress'. At the same time, recent scientific innovations, particularly, within branches of theoretical physics that had been crucial to the bomb's development, suggested new understandings of the material world and humanity's place within it.

From the discourses of physics, poets such as Williams and Olson appropriated the concept of the 'field' to advocate modes of composition that would construct the poem as a dynamic nexus of energies and exchanges, rather than an expression of a univocal lyric persona. In 1948, William Carlos Williams proposed the notion of 'The Poem as a Field of Action', explicitly invoking 'Einstein's theory of relativity, affecting our very conception of the heavens about us of which poets write so much' to suggest new methods of composition.[7] Einstein's theories revealed that, rather than constituting a stable background reality, time and space stretch and contract relative to the observer. For Williams, poets needed to avoid the hubristic fallacy of 'think[ing] we stand outside the universe' and to 'come into contact with reality' by responding to new understandings of the material world in their compositional techniques and poetic structures.[8]

The new modes of scientific knowledge proposed by early twentieth-century physics did not only challenge conventional understandings of how the physical world works and how it can be known. Because of its role in making the atomic bomb, such science also demonstrated, Olson reflected, 'how suddenly and strikingly [humanity] could extend himself'.[9] Anna Tsing writes that 'grasping the atom was the culmination of human dreams of controlling nature. It was also the beginning of those dreams' undoing. The bomb at Hiroshima changed things. Suddenly, we became aware that humans could destroy the livability of the planet – whether intentionally or otherwise.'[10] As Margaret Ronda argues, American poets of the post-war moment onwards inherited 'emerging paradigms of crisis' that involved an increasing sense of environmental calamity, 'generat[ing] not only ecological and economic arguments but also aesthetic sensibilities that shape the poetry of this period'.[11] In contrast to the transcendent 'spirit' of Romantic celebrations of nature, and the cerebral intellectualism of much early twentieth-century Modernism, the post-war poetics of writers such as Williams, Olson, Creeley and others acknowledged an intimate relationship between aesthetic practices and a material world increasingly shaped – and threatened – by human activity.

Although not specifically concerned with environmental issues, the theories and practices of early open-field poetics have profound ecological implications which resonate with our own moment, thereby forming an important legacy for contemporary ecopoetics. Many contemporary poets interested in ecological questions have taken up and reworked the compositional and philosophical resources of the open field. This chapter will now outline aspects of Olson's poetic theories and practices that are particularly pertinent for ecopoetics. It will then discuss three contemporary North American writers – Evelyn Reilly, Ed Roberson and Stephen Collis – who extend this legacy in different ways to engage with the specific conceptual, material and ethical dilemmas of the Anthropocene.

Charles Olson and the Open Field

Williams had proposed the notion of the poem as a 'field of action' in 1948. But, it was Olson who extended this idea in his 1950 manifesto 'Projective

Verse'. This essay would become a defining statement of American avant-garde poetry, and highly influential for subsequent generations on both sides of the Atlantic. Unlike Williams, Olson does not explicitly refer to the new physics as a context to which poetry must respond. Instead, he assimilates the imagery of energies, particles and fields into his rhetoric. He asserts that the new 'projective' poem 'must, at all points, be a high energy-construct and ... an energy-discharge'. To generate such energy, 'ONE PERCEPTION MUST IMMEDIATELY AND DIRECTLY LEAD TO A FURTHER PERCEPTION'. Syllables are understood as 'particle[s]' arranged within 'the large area of the whole poem ... the FIELD'.[12] Echoing the idea of matter transformed into energy, as encapsulated in Einstein's $E=mc^2$, such formulations present the work of prosody as an emphatically physical assemblage involved in dynamic processes of exchange between poetic matter and energy.

For Olson, the open-field poem was not just a new mode of composition but a 'stance *toward* reality outside a poem as well as a new stance towards the reality of a poem itself'.[13] This aspect of his poetics, which he called 'objectism', has important ecological implications. Olson defined 'objectism' as

> the getting rid of the lyrical interference of the individual as ego, of the 'subject' and his soul, that peculiar presumption by which western man has interposed himself between what he is as a creature of nature ... and those other creations of nature which we may, with no derogation, call objects. For a man is himself an object, ... the more likely to recognize himself as such the greater his advantages, particularly at that moment that he achieves an humilitas sufficient to make him of use.[14]

While the interrogation of the lyric 'I' is a familiar tenet of avant-garde poetics, Olson's stance is distinctive; his rejection of the 'individual as ego' is also a denunciation of the Western (masculinised) inheritance of human exceptionalism and superiority over the non-human world. Consequently, his poetics aspires to articulate the human in a non-hierarchical ontological relation among others, as an object among other objects, a form of being and making defined through a relation with other entities. Human being and creative activity are imagined not as distinct from but as co-emergent with 'nature'.

Numerous contemporary writers working in Britain and America have identified Olson's objectism as a productive model for ecopoetics. British poet and critic Harriet Tarlo writes:

> [W]e need to get beyond not just the confessional obsession with identity, but also the obsession with the fracturing of identity which has characterized

recent theoretical thought. As we move into the twenty-first century, Olson's words gain in eco-ethical significance, as we try to reduce human egotism, anthropocentrism and subjectivism.[15]

Evelyn Reilly draws on objectism in 'a search for language congruent with a world that is not filled with objects or subjects, that is not "the context," nor "the setting" for subjects or objects but that is a permanent state of flux between subject-objects and object-subjects'.[16] For Skinner, Olson's poetics yield the insight that 'the more we attend to the objecthood of the artefact we are shaping . . . as constituted in a field of relations, the more we let ourselves be used, as objects in our own right, by the field in which the object participates'.[17] Each of these statements sees in Olson's objectism a politics of attention and an ontological ethics, where what is habitually considered the 'background' or surrounding 'environment' for human subjectivity is acknowledged as relationally, dynamically and *actively* entangled with human being and creativity. Objectism offers modes for understanding the human and the other-than-human, the poem and the material world, as inseparably enmeshed and co-producing.

Olson's own compositional methods often embody these ontological and ethical principles by opening up the poetic page as a typographic and semantic space for the performance of dynamic relations between entities. These methods are evident in his long serial work *The Maximus Poems*, begun in the same year as the publication of 'Projective Verse'. The following, aptly ecological, example comes from the first poem of the *Maximus* sequence, which presents the poet's hometown of Gloucester, Massachusetts as an assemblage of heterogeneous but entangled entities and histories, human and non-human. In this poem and throughout this long series, Olson laments the appropriative and alienating forces of capitalist modernity inscribed upon the town. But he also aspires to imagine an alternative form of collectivity (or, in Olson's terms, 'polis'), a striving which the opening poem figures through the activity of a gull nest building:

> one loves only form,
> and form only comes
> into existence when
> the thing is born
>
>   born of yourself, born
>   of hay and cotton struts,
>   of street-pickings, wharves, weeds
>   you carry in, my bird

of a bone of a fish
of a straw, or will
of a color, of a bell
of yourself, torn[18]

The poem performs its thought process and its investigation of a particular geography by moving in space, down and across the page. In so doing, its attention moves outwards – from the ambiguous 'one' of the first line, to the second-person address in the second stanza, to a collective of entities in the final stanza. It also moves from propositional logic, to dialogue with an other, to a catalogue form that suggests relations among multiple entities. Thematically and formally, the poem conducts an enquiry 'into existence' understood as collective coexistence. This sensibility is embodied in the poem's spatial layout, and also in rhythmic and arrhythmic patterns of repetition and sound resonance, between 'form', 'born' and 'torn', for example. The field of the poem upon the page embodies the processual and relational dimensions of Olson's ontology as articulated in his notion of objectism.

Evelyn Reilly's Relational Poetics

New York-based poet Evelyn Reilly explicitly invokes Olson's open-field poetics as an important model for ecopoetics in the late twentieth and early twenty-first centuries. Reilly declares wariness of 'the mesmerizing spell of the transcendent' and 'compensatory notions of nature as retreat' associated with traditional nature writing, turning instead to precursors such as Olson, Susan Howe, George Oppen and others, whose techniques suggest ways of 'dismantling' dualisms of 'self/other, nature/culture, indigenous/alien and central/peripheral' as well as subject/object as part of a necessary decentring of human power and agency.[19] Although the Anthropocene concept would seem to position the 'anthros' as a central agent of a new era, it also entails recognition that human activity has triggered multifarious processes beyond its control. As Boes and Marshall put it, 'human beings in the new epoch can no longer simply be defined (as they have been in most ... strains of humanistic discourse during the late Holocene) as acting upon the natural world. Instead, they must also be described as being acted upon by that same world on an ontological, rather than merely existential, level'.[20] The poetic corollary to this destabilisation of human agency is a move away from an individualistic lyric 'I' and 'the abandonment of the idea of center for a position in an infinitely extensive net of relations' which can 'enact connections rather than ... mark distinctions'.[21] Reilly cites Olson's 'Objectism and the poetics of vector relationships' as an important model for this ecopoetics and identifies Olson's own practice of 'opening the page both topo- and typo-graphically as a surface for juxtapositions' as an embodiment of this ethos.[22]

Reilly's book-length serial poem *Styrofoam* draws on these resources of open-field poetics to explore the 'extensive net of relations' involved in plastic production, consumption and waste, and its implications for human agency as it escapes human control, permeating numerous habitats, human and non-human animal bodies, forms of language and cultural imaginaries. Plastic pollution is one potential geological marker of the Anthropocene, and recent years have seen increased media attention and public awareness of this issue. Many 'disposable' plastic objects will not degrade in our lifetimes; some will take up to five hundred years to decompose, leaching toxic chemicals into their surroundings in the process. Most common plastics never truly biodegrade but merely break down into smaller particles, or microplastics, which then become widely dispersed in the surrounding environment.

One of the poems in *Styrofoam*, 'A Key to the Families of Thermoplastics', maps out the vast array, or 'CORNUCOPIA',[23] of polymers in common usage. One of Reilly's techniques is to list the abbreviated names of thermoplastics, their qualities and uses phrased in banal industry and marketing language, juxtaposed with a wide range of unexpected verbal and visual materials which cast these seemingly ordinary substances in a different light:

> PET, with exceptional clarity, but "notch sensitive"
>
> carbonated drink bottles MATERIAL FLOOD
> throw-away condiment tubs MATERIAL STORM[24]

This common polymer's acronym, description and uses render it homely and unassuming, but Reilly's capitalised interjections work against these connotations to recast PET as a new force of nature, and a particularly destructive one, on a par with calamities such as floods and storms.

As well as representing plastic substances in a strange new light, the poem foregrounds their disturbingly intimate relations with human bodies, emphasising their entanglement with our physical and emotional lives:

POM, translucent, with good processing qualities
DEVELOPS A "MEMORY" AND GRADUALLY
CONFORMS TO THE USERS GRIP[25]
. . .
so PB, which can withstand mild chemical attack

boil-in-the-bag films WARM MEMORY (HI MOM)[26]

The poems of *Styrofoam* present plastics as 'actants'. For Bruno Latour, an actant is 'any entity that modifies another entity'.[27] Plastics are not just a product of modern capitalist humanity; they are also mobile and tenacious entities which 'modify' us and our material world through a series of relational interactions. In the lines above, polymers actively develop a 'memory', are capable of defence and are also entangled with fond familial memories. Although these actions might seem benign and even enriching to human lives, such close physical and emotional relations with plastics give pause for thought in the light of scientific research on the endocrine disrupting capacities of many of the chemical additives in polymers, which can leach into our bodies through contact and ingestion where they may modify hormonal activity. Common plastics additives such as BPA and phthalates have been associated with fertility problems, obesity, diabetes, cancers and other health issues, although much is still unknown. Earlier sections of Reilly's book invoke such risks, associating plastic substances with 'environmental sources of hormonal activity'.[28] Through such chemical interactions permeating bodily boundaries, plastics have the capacity to act upon and even reshape human organisms from the inside.

Reilly's series also highlights the unintended consequences of plastic production and waste for other species:

the ankle bracelets of the birds
(a pvc resin cut from extruded sheets)[29]
. . .
(for all averred, we had killed the bird)   [enter albatross stand-in of choice[30]

Replacing Coleridge's 'I' for 'we' in her rewriting of these famous lines indicates how, as Keller has pointed out, '"we" who are transforming habitats around the globe are collectively responsible for vastly more deaths' than the guilt-wracked Ancient Mariner of the earlier poem.[31] Furthermore, these lines intimate how little volition 'we' have over the everyday substances we use, since, unlike the Ancient Mariner, we have not even consciously '*killed the bird[s]*' of Reilly's poem. Furthermore, because of their longevity – referred to in *Styrofoam* as 'deathlessness', 'immortality' and 'THE UNDYING (ZOMBIE CONRUCOPIA)'[32] – the 'lives' and actions of plastics will outlast our own, as individuals and possibly even as a species.

Reilly's poem indicates that, while the concept of the Anthropocene positions 'the human' as the dominant material force on the planet, nonetheless, as Derek Woods has pointed out, 'paradoxically, the present is a moment of human disempowerment'. Woods continues: 'The subject of the Anthropocene is not an individual or species-based "intelligence"' but, rather, 'modern terraforming assemblages', by which he means assemblages of humans, non-humans and technologies collectively capable of material planetary transformation.[33]

Scale Effects in the Poetry of Ed Roberson

Reilly's emphasis on the inconceivable longevity of plastics in *Styrofoam* highlights how, as many commentators have observed, the concept of the Anthropocene requires cognitive engagement with scales incommensurate with the human.[34] For Woods, 'terraforming assemblages' function at multiple and discontinuous scales, which 'can no longer be understood or controlled by analogy with the human perceptual mesocosm'.[35] Likewise, Timothy Clark argues that 'the Anthropocene enacts the demand to think of human life at much broader scales of space and time'. However, because these are '[p]erhaps too big to see or even to think straight ... the Anthropocene challenges us to think counter-intuitive relations of scale, effect, perception, knowledge, representation and calculability'.[36]

In his 2010 collection *To See the Earth Before the End of the World*, American poet Ed Roberson ponders such scalar challenges, with a particular emphasis on the limitations and capacities of human perception. The collection's title poem explores the disjunction between the scales of human experience and those of anthropogenic environmental change:

> the world's death piece by piece each longer than we.
>
> Some endings of the world overlap our lived
> time, skidding for generations
> to the crash scene of species extinction
> the five minutes it takes for the plane to fall,
> the mile ago it takes to stop the train,
> the small bay   to coast the liner into the ground ...[37]

Although appearing to offer effective analogies for large-scale catastrophe, on closer consideration, the human-scale disasters here indicate radical incommensurability between events spanning 'five minutes' or a 'mile' or 'a small bay' and the scales of phenomena such as species extinction and climate change (addressed later in the poem through the metonym of melting glaciers). Unlike the straightforward, linear collisions of these lines, processes of species extinction and climate change involve complex networks of factors, interactions, agencies and feedback loops. Because of this, Anthropocene scale effects defy analogy with human scales of perception. There is no perceptible 'crash scene' of species extinction. And the problem is exacerbated if this is our own 'small human extinction' which, unlike the disasters of Roberson's lines, we cannot observe or measure from an external position.[38]

Although the poem signals the failures of human perception, it also explores the possibilities for poetic form itself to yoke together incommensurate scales, to negotiate, even if disjunctively, the 'very subtlety of time between // large and small', and, in so doing, to reach for new modes of attention and ways of seeing.[39] When asked about environmental catastrophe in an interview, Roberson says, 'I'd really like people to take *a big look*. And I don't want *a big look* to imply helpless, voyeuristic tourism, to sound like backing off, definitely not sounding like backing off from the human responsibility for things.'[40] Provoking a process of looking in this account, then, means redefining what it means to look at or perceive the material world we inhabit.

As an African American poet for whom 'nature' is a central concern, Roberson is highly attuned to how perceptions of the material world are culturally and historically specific. Common motifs of nature poetry such as trees and ocean waves, for example, have different connotations in relation to African American historical experience than they do in white traditions of nature poetry (since trees were often sites of lynching and oceans are historically entangled with the Middle Passage). If perceptions of landscape and geography are always, then, refracted through specific historical and cultural lenses, Roberson's poetry asks whether it might be possible to shift the perceptual frames through which we currently perceive our material world.

Roberson explores such possibilities by working through the distinction between 'earth' and 'world' as repeatedly highlighted and revisited in his collection. He understands 'earth' as the material planet, whereas 'world' is what humans have constructed out of it, including the limited lenses through which it is seen. The poem 'We Look at the World to See the

Earth' highlights how instances of looking at the earth, such as in whole-earth images taken from space in the late 1960s and 1970s, not only catalysed environmentalist awareness but also demonstrated modern humanity's ability to perform profound scalar adjustments of perspective. Looking 'at the silver, pedestal-ed globe to see the grounds,/ we see what we've done with it, what it has/ to do with'.[41] However, merely scrutinising the earth to 'see what we've done with it' risks reasserting an anthropocentric perspective in which the image of the earth is only a reflection of 'humanity's conception of itself';[42] as Roberson's poem puts it, 'we see our face bent to a surface'.[43]

One of Roberson's strategies for shaking up habitual ways of seeing in his poetry connects to Olson's compositional principle that 'ONE PERCEPTION MUST IMMEDIATELY AND DIRECTLY LEAD TO A FURTHER PERCEPTION'.[44] In contrast to the abrupt collage-like juxtapositions at work in Reilly's *Styrofoam*, in Roberson's work, perceptual movement occurs through his 'syntactically double-jointed lines',[45] as in the following:

> but what of the world is seen in looking at the earth
> any more than the world's measure of minute to a rock
> looking, but seeing gets
> a return   begets return   gets returned:
> the rivers come back, the salmon[46]

In a convoluted poetic acrobatics, syntax and lineation dart, sidestep, circle back, repeat and rework key phrases, as if from a different direction. Here, the 'LINE' is 'the threshing floor for the dance'.[47] Formally, as well as thematically, Roberson's poem enacts a dynamic process of pursuing new modes of cognition. Part of this endeavour involves recognising how other things of the earth, 'a rock', 'the rivers' and 'salmon', are not just objects of the human gaze but capable of active 'return' and 'looking' back. Twists and folds of syntax are crucial to the attempt to present these ideas while also avoiding an anthropomorphism that would simply project a human gaze through non-human entities. This technique frustrates straightforward explanations and models complex entanglements of agency, interaction and forms of non-human perception that cannot be subsumed to human modes of experience but nevertheless warrant acknowledgement.

Roberson's decentring of anthropocentric perspectives here also parallels Olson's 'objectist' attempt to depict human consciousness in non-hierarchical relation with other entities of the material world. Roberson's poem is primarily concerned with the potential and the limitations of a human 'we' to recognise our contingent existence as embedded within a material earth, an earth which exceeds our capacity to both perceive and control it. But if the poem is to achieve 'an humilitas sufficient to make [it] of use',[48] then the act of looking must acknowledge the existence of other perspectives, including non-human ones.

Stephen Collis's Poetics of Collectivity

Canadian poet and activist Stephen Collis takes the Olsonian 'objectist' stance a step further to articulate new forms of collectivity and allegiance. Collis prefers to frame our contemporary moment of ecological crisis as 'the era of Geophysical capitalism' rather than the Anthropocene, because the latter implicates all humans, as if equally, in anthropogenic damage. This move chimes with the thinking of Jason Moore and Andreas Malm, who propose the term Capitalocene to indicate 'the geology not of man-kind, but of capital accumulation'.[49] Collis reasons that under capitalism, '*life itself*—all planetary biological material—is now subject to, and the substance of, the extraction of wealth', and this engenders a new kind of political class:

> a biotariat: that portion of existence that is *enclosed* as a "resource" by and for those who direct and benefit from the accumulation of wealth. So: workers and commoners; most animals and plants, including trees and forest and grassland ecosystems; water; land, as it provisions and enables biological life; minerals that lie beneath the surface of the land; common "wastes" and "sinks" too ... —the atmosphere and the oceans. It's that large. **The enclosed and exploited life of this planet.**[50]

Formed through shared assimilation within capitalist structures of exploit-ation, a 'biotariat' might also be the basis for new kinds of collective agency. There is resonance here with Olson's understanding of the human as 'a creature of nature' among 'other creations of nature which we may, with no derogation, call objects'.[51] For this, too, aspires to reject structures of thinking that separate humanity from 'nature' and in so doing opens up possibilities for revaluing and strengthening connections between these 'creations of nature'.

In Collis's work (as in many of Olson's articulations of poetics) it is above all through the creaturely body that these affinities – and their political potentials – are tangible. A poem entitled 'Come the

Revolution' from Collis's collection *To the Barricades* (2013) enacts this sensibility:

> wrap the sensuous body
> of human tongue in animal revolution
> self-governance in bios in animal
> wrap sound all lifted to be level
> to small habitations and
> habits to be level
> animal and sound and sensuous bodies
> small hearths of animals own
> all of us all animals
> come the revolution we will
> come to be animal to be sound[52]

These lines articulate a relational field of 'sensuous bodies' and 'habitations'. Radical enjambment and a syntax of interconnection that flows between phrases and propositions embody the relations of entanglement that constitute Collis's 'biotariat'. Unlike in Roberson's poems, which use 'we' to mean (narrow) human perspective, in Collis's poem, the 'we' is sometimes human, but at other times, as in the lines above, it also encompasses the (non-human) 'animal'. Manipulating 'the sensuous body of language'[53] provides opportunities to forge connections through 'sound' and creaturely sensuous embodiment. The enactment of 'return' (or, literally, 'revolution') to recurring words and phrases, reworked differently each time, foregrounds the sensuous materiality of language, as well as the process of unmaking and remaking. In so doing, the poem feels its way towards a poetic articulation of interconnected 'self-governance in bios'. Or, as the poem later puts it: 'Here is a feeling/ for another structure.'[54]

Conclusion

All three contemporary poets examined in this chapter seek 'a feeling/ for another structure' in the languages, modes of perception and forms of knowledge which articulate human relations with non-human materiality. In so doing, they extend the open-field poetics developed by post-war writers such as Olson, which was also responsive to its own moment's seismic shifts in understandings of material reality and humanity's place within it. The concept of the Anthropocene is, like its cultural implications, still very much under debate. But the entry of this term into our collective vocabulary registers genuine, shared recognition of the profound implications of anthropogenic ecological degradation in its many forms. It also works as an acknowledgement that this era demands new kinds of language, thinking and perception. Ecopoetic interventions into the vocabularies through which we articulate ecological relations have the potential to model more ethical forms of knowledge, perception and natural-cultural entanglement. The poets whose work I have examined in this chapter do not aspire to simply raise awareness of ecological crises, nor to connect readers to an idealised 'nature'. Instead, through poetic language they seek to forge new grammars of ontological relation, thinking and feeling.

Notes

1. Jonathan Bate, *The Song of the Earth* (London: Picador, 2000); Lawrence Buell, *The Environmental Imagination: Thoreau, Nature Writing, and the Formation of American Culture* (Cambridge, MA: Belknap Press of Harvard University Press, 1995); Leonard M. Scigaj, *Sustainable Poetry: Four American Ecopoets* (Lexington: University Press of Kentucky, 1999).
2. Bate, *Song of the Earth*, p.205.
3. Lynn Keller, *Recomposing Ecopoetics: North American Poetry of the Self-Conscious Anthropocene* (Charlottesville and London: University of Virginia Press, 2017), p.19.
4. Bill McKibben, *The End of Nature* (London: Bloomsbury, 2003), p.7.
5. Tobias Boes and Kate Marshall, 'Writing the Anthropocene: An Introduction', *Minnesota Review* (2014), 60–72 (p.66).
6. Jonathan Skinner, 'Editor's Statement', *Ecopoetics* (2001), 5–8 (pp.6–7).
7. William Carlos Williams, 'The Poem as a Field of Action' in *Selected Essays* (New York: New Directions, 1969 [1948]), pp.280–91 (p.283).
8. Ibid.
9. Charles Olson, *Collected Prose*, (eds.) Donald Allen and Benjamin Friedlander (Berkeley: University of California Press, 1997), p.121.
10. Anna Lowenhaupt Tsing, *The Mushroom at the End of the World* (Princeton, NJ and Oxford: Princeton University Press, 2015), p.3.
11. Margaret Ronda, *Remainders: American Poetry at Nature's End* (Stanford, CA: Stanford University Press, 2018), p.4.
12. Olson, *Collected Prose*, pp.240, 241, 243.
13. Ibid., p.246, my emphasis.
14. Ibid., p.247.
15. Harriet Tarlo, 'Open Field: Reading Field as Place and Poetics' in Ian Davidson and Zoë Skoulding (eds.), *Placing Poetry* (Amsterdam and New York: Rodopi, 2013), pp.113–45 (p.141).
16. Evelyn Reilly, 'Eco-noise and the Flux of Lux' in Brenda Iijima (ed.), *)((Eco(Lang)(Uage(Reader))* (New York: Portable Press at Yo-Yo Labs & Nightboat Books, 2010), pp.255–74 (pp.256–7).

17. Skinner, 'Thoughts on Things: Poetics of the Third Landscape' in *)((Eco(Lang)(Uage(Reader))*, pp.9–51 (pp.11–12).
18. Olson, *The Maximus Poems*, (ed.) George F. Butterick (Berkeley and London: University of California Press, 1983), p.7.
19. Reilly, 'Eco-noise and the Flux of Lux', p.257.
20. Boes and Marshall, 'Writing the Anthropocene', p.61.
21. Reilly, 'Eco-noise and the Flux of Lux', pp.257, 258.
22. Ibid., pp.258, 261.
23. Evelyn Reilly, *Styrofoam* (New York: Roof Books, 2009), p.54.
24. Ibid., p.51.
25. Ibid., p.51.
26. Ibid., p.53.
27. Bruno Latour, *Politics of Nature: How to Bring the Sciences into Democracy* (Cambridge, MA: Harvard University Press, 2004), p.237.
28. Reilly, *Styrofoam*, p.9.
29. Ibid., p.20.
30. Ibid., p.11.
31. Keller, *Recomposing Ecopoetics*, p.79.
32. Reilly, *Styrofoam*, pp.9, 20, 56.
33. Derek Woods, 'Scale Critique for the Anthropocene', *Minnesota Review* 83 (2014), 133–42 (pp.140, 138).
34. Dipesh Chakrabarty, 'The Climate of History: Four Theses', *Critical Inquiry* 35 (2009), 197–222; Timothy Clark, *Ecocriticism on the Edge: The Anthropocene as a Threshold Concept* (London: Bloomsbury Academic, 2015); Woods, ibid.
35. Woods, ibid., p.139.
36. Clark, *Ecocriticism on the Edge*, p.13.
37. Ed Roberson, *To See the Earth before the End of the World* (Middletown: Connecticut Wesleyan University Press, 2010), p.3.
38. Ibid.
39. Ibid.
40. Lynn Keller, and Steel Wagstaff, 'An Interview with Ed Roberson', *Contemporary Literature* 52 (2011), 397–429 (p.419).
41. Roberson, *To See the Earth*, p.22.
42. Clark, *Ecocriticism on the Edge*, p.31.
43. Roberson, *To See the Earth*, p.22.
44. Olson, *Collected Prose*, p.240. Unlike Reilly, Roberson does not explicitly invoke Olson's open field as an influential reference point, even remarking in an interview that he 'wasn't that impressed' when he encountered Olson's work. However, like other experimental poets of his generation, he did inherit the aesthetic legacies to which Olson contributed, and he does identify with other figures who contributed to mid-century open field poetics, such as Robert Duncan, Creeley and Williams. See Kathleen Crown, '"Down Break Drum": An Interview with Ed Roberson (Part 1)', *Callaloo* 33(3) (2010), 651–82 (p.673).

45. Nathaniel Mackey, quoted in Roberson, *To See the Earth*, endmatter.
46. Roberson, ibid., p.22.
47. Olson, *Collected Prose*, p.243.
48. Ibid., p.247.
49. Andreas Malm, *Fossil Capital: The Rise of Steam-Power and the Roots of Global Warming* (London: Verso, 2016), p.391.
50. Stephen Collis, 'Notes towards a Manifesto of the Biotariat' in *Beating the Bounds: Notes on Commons, Poetry, and Climate Justice* (2014), beatingthe bounds.com, emphasis in original.
51. Olson, *Collected Prose*, p.247.
52. Stephen Collis, *To the Barricades* (Vancouver: Talonbooks, 2013), p.105.
53. Ibid., p.103.
54. Ibid., p.106.

CHAPTER 4

The Novel

Astrid Bracke

The novel, it seems, is in its final throes – at least, that is what some recent scholarship suggests. Faced with global anthropogenic climate change, the novel may no longer be able to adequately capture human experience. Critics who argue along these lines tend to identify several ways in which they believe the novel to fall short of the Anthropocene's representational challenges. For instance, they suggest that the vast temporal and spatial scales of climate crisis cannot be captured in conventional narrative forms such as novels. The Anthropocene, as Timothy Clark puts it, 'enacts the demand to think of human life at much broader scales of space and time' than those typically depicted in a novel.[1] An argument has developed in the environmental humanities that the Anthropocene requires new narratives: new ways of imagining and depicting the world that move 'environmentally oriented thought into the future', rather than 'shackle environmentalism to outdated templates' by relying on older imaginations of nature such as that of the pristine wilderness.[2] Non-conventional narrative forms such as Google Earth, Modernist collage or samples of ice-cores might grasp those scales in much more effective ways than the novel does.[3] A related shortcoming of the novel identified by critics is the parallel between its development and the epoch of the Anthropocene. Suggesting that the novel has emerged out of the same circumstances that caused widespread climate crisis, some scholars argue that the conventional, realist novel has run its course, and is unable to imagine the new circumstances that humanity faces in the twenty-first century.[4] As the Indian novelist Amitav Ghosh suggests, it is the genre's development 'in precisely that period when the accumulation of carbon in the atmosphere was rewriting the destiny of history' that requires authors and critics to look beyond the realist novel in order to imagine life in a time of environmental crisis.[5] Another point of critique often voiced is that the novel's typical subject-matter is one or a group of humans. This anthropocentrism, Clark and others hold, needs to be challenged by an awareness of the way in which 'still-dominant conventions of plotting, characterisation and setting in the novel [are] pervaded by anthropocentric delusion'.[6] A decentring and defavouring of the human perspective may better befit the Anthropocene, the epoch brought into being by anthropogenic climate change.

Against these critiques, a body of work is emerging that explicitly holds faith with the capacities of the novel in the Anthropocene. These scholars emphasise the possibilities that the novel as form holds for imagining what it feels like to live in a time of climate crisis. In the first book-length study of fiction in the Anthropocene, Adam Trexler holds that '[t]he imaginative capacities of the novel have made it a vital site for the articulation of the Anthropocene'.[7] Jesse Oak Taylor expresses a similar argument when he compares the workings of the novel to computer simulation. He envisions the novel as 'a space of simulation, in which hypothetically possible outcomes can be tested (and contained) under safe conditions'.[8] The pessimism voiced by critics such as Clark, then, is countered by scholarship exploring the potential of the novel in helping readers feel through life in the Anthropocene. The tension between the vastness – spatially, temporally and conceptually – of climate crisis and the constraints of novelistic form does not lead these scholars to dismiss the novel but rather has them focus on the Anthropocene as 'an opportunity for the novel to do what it has always done—innovate'.[9] The rising popularity of climate fiction, one central example of Anthropocene writing, in the past decades underwrites these scholars' claims. Though lacking a precise definition, climate fiction is, in Axel Goodbody and Adeline Johns-Putra's words, 'best thought of as a distinctive body of cultural work which engages with anthropogenic climate change, exploring the phenomenon not just in terms of setting, but with regard to psychological and social issues, combining fictional plots with meteorological facts, speculation on the future and reflection on the human-nature relationship, with an open border to the wider archive of related work on whose models it sometimes draws for the depiction of climate crisis'.[10] The speculation on the future that Goodbody and Johns-Putra identify as part of the genre results in most climate fictions being set in the future rather than the present, showing the genre's affinities with science fiction and speculative fiction. Novels such as Margaret Atwood's *MaddAddam* trilogy (2002–13) and Jeff Vandermeer's *Southern Reach* trilogy (2014) show a distant future world in which climate change has further wrecked the planet as we know it today, leading to extensive population reduction, war and disease. While these kinds of climate fiction tend to receive most attention in the scholarship on the topic, works that take place closer to the present of their first readers may be just as interesting in studying the novel in the Anthropocene. Climate fictions like Barbara Kingsolver's *Flight Behaviour* (2012) and Nathaniel Rich's *Odds Against Tomorrow* (2013) may enable readers to better understand and imagine the effects of climate crisis in their own time. As Stephanie LeMenager suggests, fictions that depict the 'everyday Anthropocene' show 'what it means to live through climate shift, moment by moment, in individual, fragile bodies. It is at best a project of reinventing the everyday as a means of paying attention and preparing, collectively, a project of staying home and, in a sense distant from settler-colonialist mentalities, making home of a broken world.'[11] Such climate fictions – closer to realist fiction than to science or speculative fiction – may more adequately capture what it means to live in the Anthropocene.

Flood Fictions

I'll explore in this chapter how a number of narratological strategies challenge scholarship that foregrounds the novel's shortcomings, and instead demonstrate the potential the novel holds at a time of crisis. I will develop this line of thought by focusing in particular on a subset of climate fictions that I term flood fictions: twenty-first-century literary narratives set in the present or near future that portray floods as an effect and image of climate crisis. Floods are one of the most visible consequences of climate change, and are expected to increase in many areas around the world in the lifetimes of contemporary readers. Even recent floods are increasingly connected to anthropogenic climate change.[12] Flood fictions consist of a range of narratives that show a familiar world submerged by extensive flooding. As such, they constitute a broad cultural response to climate crisis in which literal and figurative floods are used to imagine the Anthropocene. Flood fictions include novels such as Maggie Gee's *The Flood* (2004), Amitav Ghosh's *The Hungry Tide* (2004), Sarah Hall's *The Carhullan Army* (2007), Clare Morrall's *When the Floods Came* (2015), Megan Hunter's *The End We Start From* (2017), as well as short stories like Ross Raisin's 'Submersion' (2013) and Hall's 'Sudden Traveller' (2018). These narratives tie in with a visual response to climate crisis offered by graphic novels and films, for instance, Richard McGuire's 2014 graphic novel *Here*, as well as well-known dystopian and post-apocalyptic films such as *Waterworld* (1995), *The Day After Tomorrow* (2004) and *Flood* (2007). Flood narratives, moreover, include stories in which floods are depicted figuratively as a watershed moment of irreversible change and crisis: from Atwood's *MaddAddam* trilogy, Emily St. John Mandel's *Station to Eleven* (2014) and Ali Shaw's *The Trees* (2016), to figurative flooding in the 2017 film *Downsizing* and Leonardo DiCaprio's 2016 documentary *Before the Flood*. While some of these narratives may fall under the umbrella of climate fiction in their direct treatment of climate crisis, most of these works depict worlds in which climate crisis is rarely made explicit. It is precisely the way in which climate crisis is no longer exceptional but part of everyday life that makes them such interesting test cases through which to imagine life in the Anthropocene.

In what follows, I'll use flood fictions as a case study for contemporary novels that address some areas of critique voiced by Clark and others: the vast temporal and spatial scale of the Anthropocene, in contrast to the perceived limited scale of the novel; and the central role that human characterisation plays in the novel. The novels' utilisation of time, space and character is vital to giving readers access to a world in crisis. In combining my focus on climate crisis flood fiction with an attention to the narratological elements of time, space and character, this chapter develops work done in the field of econarratology. Econarratology combines the attention to the environment familiar to ecocriticism with a close attention to the effects of narratological elements, as such maintaining 'an interest in studying the relationship between literature and the physical environment . . . with sensitivity to the literary structures and devices that we use to communicate representations of the physical environment to each other via narratives'.[13] An econarratological approach foregrounds the effects that narratological choices have on the depiction of climate crisis, and the extent to which readers gain access to it and are able to connect narrative worlds to their own realities.

Time

Flood fictions stretch backwards in time to ancient flood myths lodged in many cultures' collective memory, and forwards by prefiguring the face of climate crisis in the near future. In scenarios for the future, flooding features high on the list of climate crisis effects. In Britain, changing environmental and climatological circumstances will make floods twenty times more likely by 2080, affecting at least twice as many people as are currently at risk from flooding.[14] As such, a timescale of crisis is created, taking in not only a history of flood myths but especially the causes of future flooding, and present blame. The effectiveness of flood fictions in depicting the temporal scale of environmental crisis lies particularly in a kind of doubling of time that happens in these works, in which pasts and futures are connected. As Stef Craps and Rick Crownshaw note, '[t]he ways in which climate is mediated are often more visible in hindsight', as happens in novels 'that project future climate-changed worlds from which retrospection on and cultural remembrance of the changing climate and its causes is staged'.[15] This turn towards the future anterior, or the dramatisation of that which will have been, has become a stock feature of many climate fictions, flood fictions included. Thinking about the effects of climate change requires us to imagine a time in which our future has become the past. This move is not merely a matter of imagining the future; it is also essential to giving readers access to a world distant to them. At the same time, in flood fictions and many other dystopian fictions, the past as much as the future is important. The characters' past, often depicted as a kind of rupture or watershed moment, is our present.

My focus is particularly on Morrall's *When the Floods Came, The Ship* (2015) by Antonia Honeywell and the 2018 novel *All Rivers Run Free* by Natasha Carthew. In *When the Floods Came*, a young woman called Roza lives a secluded life with her family in a Britain ravaged by disease and flooding. A similar collapse of British society, as we know it today, is portrayed in *The Ship*. The father of Lalage, the novel's teenage protagonist, buys a ship, fills it with supplies and people, and takes to the sea while the world burns and floods. Much like in this novel, the main character in *All Rivers Run Free*, a young woman named Ia, tries to survive in a Britain that has crumbled into civil war and flooding. She undertakes a risky journey back home to southern England in an attempt to escape her violent partner in Cornwall. All three of these novels are set, therefore, in their first readers' near future: although none of the novels make the date specific, temporal cues in the works suggest them to be set in the middle of the twenty-first century. Economic, political and climate crises have led to global or at least national British collapses. What is left is a world of conflict, warfare and extensive flooding. Explicitly or implicitly, many characters in these novels reflect on the past: either by referencing it as a moment when things went wrong, or by detailing the things that have changed in their world but that are familiar in ours. In *The Ship*, for instance, Lalage reaches out to the novel's first readers by addressing their culpability. She is angry 'at the stupidity of the generations before mine that had brought us to this place'.[16] Comments such as these do more than merely tell the reader about the textual world. They provide a submersion or way in which the reader can enter the storyworld through what Marie-Laure Ryan calls the principle of minimal departure. Readers always use their own time and environment as the starting point for understanding a narrative and its world: 'we construe the central world of a textual universe . . . as conforming as far as possible to our representation of AW [the actual or real world]. We will project upon these worlds everything we know about reality, and we will make only the adjustments dictated by the text.'[17] Determining the temporal and spatial setting of a story can happen quickly or slowly: when aliens or medieval knights are mentioned on the first page of a novel, a reader is quickly transported into different times and places. In the flood fictions I explore here, transportation from the readers' world to the textual world happens by almost literally taking the reader out of her own familiar environment and showing the demise of this familiar world. For instance, the world of the novels' initial readers is a time that Lalage in *The Ship* can barely remember: a time of restaurants, when Regent's Park was a park, rather than a holding pen for unwanted people, a time when there were still some private cars and electricity was widely and reliably available. Similarly, the protagonist in *All Rivers Run Free* provides a cue that the novel is set in a time different from that of the novel's first readers when she mentions 'those days when petrol was still a thing you could buy'.[18] Through the principle of minimal departure and emphasising time in other ways, flood fictions point to the future, illustrating the effect of current events on future people. As such, they establish a timeline of change that requires the reader to move back and forth between her own present, the characters' past, the reader's future and the characters' present, thereby getting a sense of the temporal scale of the Anthropocene and our own place in it.

Space

Of course, the challenge of imagining climate crisis and the Anthropocene does not just lie in imagining its vast temporal scale, its encompassing of past, present and future. Imagining the Anthropocene also means coming to terms with its vast spatial scale; of events that have their cause in one place, but effect in another; of global inequality and interconnectedness. Perhaps counter-intuitively, one of the ways in which flood fictions tackle this challenge of scale is by depicting very constricted spaces. Much of *The Ship* takes place on a ship, and Lalage has never known much of the world outside of her parents' apartment and its immediate surroundings. Similarly, the family in *When the Floods Came* keep largely to their flat, save for some illicit expeditions the children undertake to the centre of what used to be Birmingham. The one time the family do venture out and spend a few days on the road, they are nearly murdered. *All Rivers Run Free* is the only one of the three novels not set predominantly in a single place: while in the first half of the novel the main character Ia is confined to the trailer in which she lives with her partner, the second half of the novel relates her journey along the river Tamar, in south-west England. Yet even on the road, the spaces available to her are constricted: most areas are dangerous, especially for a woman travelling alone, and many areas have become inaccessible because of the floods: 'As far as the eye could see was water. That was just about all that was left of the streets and corners: water punctuated with a tree a post a steeple.'[19] The constricted spaces of flood fictions demonstrate how novels may function as what Oak Taylor calls spaces of simulation: the relatively limited space of literary narrative, as well as the small spaces depicted in the flood fictions function as spaces of elucidation and experimentation, in which the large-scale issues of climate change are played out. While narratology has been relatively late to in-depth explorations of space, recent scholars such as Marco Caracciolo, David Herman and Erin James have foregrounded the role that space plays in the reader's experience of a narrative.[20] They emphasise how spatial cues are central to the shift that the reader makes from her own world to that of a novel's characters. The connection between the world outside of the text and the world inside of a text also works the other way around, transport-ing experiences from the textual world into the actual world. Much as Oak Taylor implies, making sense of the spatial world within a text affects our understanding of the larger world.[21] As James points out, the construction of the storyworld is an 'inherently comparative process', in which readers become aware of the differences between the world in which they live, and the world that they are reading about.[22] This comparison or negotiation is not only what gives the reader access to the textual world but also the reason why the novel can function so powerfully as a site to try out experiences of and responses to environmental crisis.

Yet, constricted spaces are not merely a narrative device used in flood novels. Despite the emphasis often put in the environmental humanities on the vastness of global climate change, our world is also getting smaller, almost literally, owing to environmental crisis. In a 2018 article, environ-mentalist Bill McKibben argues that the earth, for humans at least, has begun to shrink: 'Until now', he notes, 'human beings have been spreading from our beginnings in Africa, out across the globe ... But a period of contraction is setting in as we lose parts of the habitable earth.'[23] We are especially losing parts of the habitable earth owing to flooding, as flood fictions demonstrate so well. The narrow settings of these novels, moreover, make instances of what Rob Nixon has termed slow violence visible. Slow violence, as Nixon defines it, is 'a violence that occurs gradually and out of sight, a violence of delayed destruction that is dispersed across time and space, an attritional violence that is typically not viewed as violence at all'.[24] A dark story of such slow, attritional, almost invisible violence underlies both *When the Floods Came* and *The Ship*. In the former novel, Birmingham is one of the British cities that is surrounded by barriers, built by the government during the outbreak of Hoffman's disease. Described by Roza as 'a giant protective ring around the city',[25] this wall is a little like the Berlin Wall: built not to keep people out but, rather, to keep people in. The people left inside the city were ill, contaminated with the disease. Those who weren't ill yet would soon catch it, unable to leave the city. The city, then, became a massive graveyard which no one was able to escape. As someone living outside of the city, and being immune to Hoffman's disease, Roza is one of the fortunate ones. Lalage, in *The Ship*, lives a similarly privileged life, in relative safety. The differences between the haves and the have-nots in a time of crisis become especially glaring once Lalage boards the ship that her father has acquired. His plan is to fill it with a select group of people from all over the world – hand-picked by him. Once he has enough food for all of these people to last a long time, the ship leaves. The sacks of rice that Michael stores on the ship, Lalage realises, 'altered the world's balance ... the ship was not so much an escape from hunger as the cause of it', causing hunger for those in need now, while providing sustenance for the lucky few in the future.[26] Lalage's realisation is a thinly veiled reference to developing and underdeveloped nations bearing the brunt of the growth of the developed world, whether through the outsourcing of pollution or the use of land to feed cattle. The constricted spaces in these flood fictions, then, carry different meanings for different people. On the one hand, they serve as safe, though boring, spaces for the lucky few, such as Roza and Lalage. On the other hand, they are graveyards, spaces that the already disadvantaged are unable to escape from, symbols of the violence that characterises the Anthropocene.

Characterisation

In critiques of the novel as genre, some scholars have suggested that characterisation ought to be less central to Anthropocene narrative. Oak Taylor, for instance, argues that adapting the novel to the Anthropocene 'will demand alternative models for what we think about, value, and emphasize when we read novels, de-privileging character and plot and paying renewed attention to setting, atmosphere, and description'.[27] Likewise, Johns-Putra explores narrative silence as a means of recuperating 'a nuanced view of human agency that enables humans to engage more fully with the unprecedented crisis now engulfing human and nonhuman organisms and environments'.[28] While much can be said for being critical of modes of reading and storytelling – for example, in emphasising character as a means to privilege an anthropocentric point of view – the importance of characterisation in gaining access to the storyworld requires equal attention. Few textual elements are as efficient in transporting a reader from her own world to the textual world than characters. Flood fictions are generally characterised by a small cast of characters, frequently family groups. This kind of construction 'privileges people's local ties over the wide social networks of which they are part'.[29] In early realist novels, such as Jane Austen's *Pride and Prejudice*, such small character groups create a sense of intimacy. Even though the wider world is present – glimpsed, for instance, in Austen's novels through the appearance of soldiers and letters from distant family – the characters have the luxury to retreat, and be concerned largely and exclusively with their own concerns. Yet, in flood fictions, as in many novels set in the Anthropocene, the emphasis on the small group is not a matter of choice or luxury, but an inevitability. Climate crisis and socio-political collapse have led to the severing of connections and much of the population has died in conflict, natural disaster or because of disease. This happens in *When the Floods Came* because of a fictional illness – Hoffman's disease – which has also spread across the world. Pandemics, hunger, war and floods have similarly decimated the human race in *The Ship*, and Ia in *All Rivers Run Free* hears reports of civil unrest, social collapse and internal warfare on the radio. Rather than intimacy, then, character construction in these novels causes a feeling of claustrophobia: the claustrophobia of living through a global climate crisis that has shrunk rather than expanded the world. This sense of claustrophobia is heightened by the danger posed by anyone outside of the small (family) group. Instead of causing a pleasant sense of excitement, as the arrival of a stranger might have done in early realist novels, meeting a stranger in flood fiction can be a matter of life or death – usually the latter. In Morrall's book, the sudden appearance of Aashay, a mysterious teenager, motivates Roza and her family to look beyond their own circle and travel to a fair where they meet other survivors. On the way back, however, it soon becomes apparent that Aashay is not a friend, but is out to kill and rob them, just as he kills Roza's fiancé Hector. The danger that strangers pose is likewise present in *All Rivers Run Free*. As a woman, Ia is vulnerable even in her own small community. She is dependent almost completely on her violent partner, and tries to stay away from the groups of people nearby. Once she decides to leave the Cornish coast and make her way up the river Tamar, she becomes even more vulnerable. Within days, she falls into the hands of one of the many gangs roaming the country and is briefly imprisoned until she manages to escape, only to be followed by them for much of the rest of the book.

Given the small casts of characters in flood fictions, the loss of the family unit is a particularly powerful trope in these works. Unlike most other families in Britain, Roza's family is still intact – at least it seems that way. As the novel progresses, however, it becomes clear that Roza's younger sister Lucia is not the family's first of that name. The 'first Lucia' was lost in a flood, and soon after another girl was found wandering outside the flat in which Roza lives. The family took her in, called her Lucia and never spoke of the event again. *The Ship* depicts another seemingly idyllic family setting, of father, mother and daughter. It crumbles, however, when Lalage's mother is murdered shortly before the family boards the ship. Lalage later learns that this murder was planned, a way for her father to get rid of his wife's criticism of the ship. Ia is the only member of her family left in *All Rivers Run Free*. Her parents committed suicide as the country crumbled and her twin sister was left behind when Ia herself travelled west. This trope of the loss of the family unit achieves several things in flood fictions, and in apocalyptic fiction in general. It ties in, for instance, with the importance of the child in (post-)apocalyptic works, in which the survival of the child becomes synonymous with the survival of the human species and the belief that there is a future for humankind.[30] Moreover, the destruction of the family unit adds a sense of emotional resonance to the narrative, inspiring the reader to feel along with the surviving characters, as well as experience direct emotions in response to the narrative. Creating an emotional response is an effective way to provide the reader access to the storyworld, tying her to the textual world and enabling her to really feel what it is like to experience climate crisis first-hand.

Characterisation is, then, a powerful tool of providing access to a narrative of climate change. It may also be used on a meta-fictional level to create confusion in the reader, and thereby deliberately make access difficult. While this may, at first sight, prevent the reader from feeling alongside the characters and the story, creating an alienating experience through characterisation also reflects the nature of the Anthropocene. The sense of claustrophobia that the reader gets from the character construction – paired with the constricted spaces I explored earlier – is heightened by the intense and exclusive focalisation of flood fictions. The novels tend to be focalised solely through one person, who is often also the narrator, eliminating any possibility for the reader to get a wider perspective, or to find out what is actually happening. In *All Rivers Run Free*, focalisation through Ia is used to maximise the confusion that she herself experiences when trying to navigate the Anthropocene world. Her feelings about her environment are probably normal given the state of Britain in *All Rivers Run Free*. Yet, as becomes clear as the novel progresses, Ia is not even sure about events in her own life. For instance, she finds a child in the water, but this is no regular child. In fact, the girl – who Ia calls Geeva – may not be real at all. More confusion ensues as Ia travels up the river Tamar, back to her childhood home. During this journey, Ia is motivated primarily by making her way back to her sister Evie, who for much of the novel she suggests is still alive. However, once Ia reaches the cave in which she last saw Evie, she reveals to the reader what actually happened to her sister: she died while Ia went to get help. While at first it seems that Ia herself is surprised to find Evie's suicide note in the cave, it is soon revealed that she knew all along that Evie was dead. She remembers carrying her sister's dead body into the waves and letting her go. On the level of the narrative, this revelation can be read as a consequence of the trauma Ia experienced as a girl, and later with her partner. On a more meta-fictional level, however, the fact that the reader cannot fully trust Ia, and that Ia cannot even fully trust her own perceptions and memories, points to the profoundly alienating experience of life in the Anthropocene. While Ia's confusion and possible unreliability may prevent the reader from connecting with her on an emotional level, the experience of not getting access fully to the storyworld echoes the larger experience of what it means to live through climate crisis.

Conclusion

There are several reasons to remain sceptical about the novel as a genre. Yet at the same time, for a growing group of authors and readers, the novel can still provide answers to the great question of our time, namely how to live in the Anthropocene. The novel may face challenges in depicting the Anthropocene, but it also provides possibilities for representing it. Indeed, literary narratives such as the novels that I have discussed are optimally suited to coming to terms with environmental crisis. They enable a different, potentially deeper, sense of engagement than some of the suggested alternatives like Google Earth and ice-cores. For while these alternatives might more effectively depict large temporal and spatial scales, they much less allow readers and viewers to empathise, almost co-experience crisis with the characters of novels. What's more, literary narratives fit human sense-making capacities well. Human minds, Herman holds, are best at grasping 'person-level experiences' and humans' mental capacities, 'are optimally suited for navigating situations and events that are encountered at a particular spatiotemporal scale or degree of resolution'.[31] Narratives themselves, Herman suggests, are 'instruments for sense making that are optimally calibrated for molar minds',[32] which seems to hold especially true for the small-scale, intimate and immediate experiences offered by literary narratives such as novels. The potential of literary narrative lies, therefore, in the depiction of the everyday through the narrative categories of time, space and character, giving the reader access to a world of increased climate crisis. Temporal and spatial cues enable transportation from her own world to that of the characters, while reflecting on the role of the present generation on future change as well as global issues of inequality and privilege. Character is perhaps the novel's most powerful tool of transportation, allowing the reader to empathise and experience with fictional people who are adjusting to an Anthropocene world. The novel, indeed, is neither dead nor in crisis, but is a vibrant and important form in which to come to terms with life in the Anthropocene.

Notes

1. Timothy Clark, *Ecocriticism on the Edge: The Anthropocene as a Threshold Concept* (London: Bloomsbury, 2015), p.13.
2. Ursula K. Heise and Allison Carruth, 'Introduction to Focus: Environmental Humanities', *American Book Review* 32(2) (2010), 3.
3. See Ursula K. Heise, *Sense of Place and Sense of Planet* (New York: Oxford University Press, 2008); for ice cores as a way of depicting the scale of climate crisis see Alessandro Antonello and Mark Carey, 'Ice Cores and the Temporalities of the Global Environment', *Environmental Humanities* 9(2) (2018), 181–203.
4. See for instance Jesse Oak Taylor, 'The Novel After Nature, Nature After the Novel: Richard Jefferies's Anthropocene Romance', *Studies in the Novel* (50(1) (2018), 108–33 (p.110).
5. Amitav Ghosh, *The Great Derangement* (Chicago and London: University of Chicago Press, 2016), p.6.
6. Clark, *Ecocriticism on the Edge*, p.191. Adeline Johns-Putra engages with the anthropocentric bias of the novel in a set of novels that counter this anthropocentrism through narrative silence, see 'The Rest Is Silence: Postmodern and Postcolonial Possibilities in Climate Change Literature', *Studies in the Novel* 50 (1) (2018), 26–42.

7. Adam Trexler, *Anthropocene Fictions: The Novel in a Time of Climate Change* (Charlottesville: University of Virginia Press, 2015), p.23.

8. Taylor, 'The Novel After Nature', p.115.

9. Axel Goodbody and Adeline Johns-Putra, *Cli-Fi: A Companion* (Oxford: Peter Lang, 2019), p.12.

10. Ibid., p.2.

11. Stephanie LeMenager, 'Climate Change and the Struggle of Genre' in Tobias Menely and Jesse Oak Taylor (eds.), *Anthropocene Reading: Literary History in Geologic Times* (Pennsylvania: Pennsylvania State University Press, 2017), pp.220–38.

12. Lorenzo Alfieri et al., 'Multi-model Projections of River Flood Risk in Europe under Global Warming', *Climate* 6(16) (2018), 1–19; Nathalie Schaller et al., 'Human Influence on Climate in the 2014 Southern England Winter Floods and Their Impacts', *Nature Climate Change* 6 (2016), 627–34.

13. Erin James, *The Storyworld Accord* (Lincoln: University of Nebraska Press, 2015), p.23.

14. Paul H. Whitfield, 'Floods in Future Climates: A Review', *Journal of Flood Risk Management* 5 (2012), 336–65 (p.337).

15. Stef Craps and Rick Crownshaw, 'Introduction: The Rising Tide of Climate Change Fiction', *Studies in the Novel* 50(1) (2018), 1–8 (p.5).

16. Antonia Honeywell, *The Ship* (London: Weidenfeld & Nicolson, 2015), p.36.

17. Marie-Laure Ryan, *Possible Worlds, Artificial Intelligence and Narrative Theory* (Bloomington: Indiana University Press, 1995), p.51.

18. Natasha Carthew, *All Rivers Run Free* (London: riverrrun, 2018), p.24.

19. Ibid., p.211.

20. See David Herman, *Story Logic: Problems and Possibilities of Narrative* (Lincoln: University of Nebraska Press, 2002); David Herman, *Storytelling and the Sciences of Mind* (Cambridge, MA: MIT Press, 2013); James, *Storyworld Accord*; Marco Caracciolo, 'The Reader's Virtual Body: Narrative Space and Its Reconstruction', *Storyworlds* 3 (2011), 117–38.

21. Herman, *Storytelling and the Sciences of Mind*, p.283.

22. James, *Storyworld Accord*, p.22.

23. Bill McKibben, 'Life on a Shrinking Planet', *The New Yorker* (26 November 2018), p.49.

24. Rob Nixon, *Slow Violence and the Environmentalism of the Poor* (Cambridge, MA: Harvard University Press, 2011), p.2.

25. Clare Morrall, *When the Floods Came* (London: Sceptre, 2015), p.4.

26. Honeywell, *The Ship*, p.111.

27. Taylor, 'The Novel After Nature', p.127.

28. Johns-Putra, 'The Rest Is Silence', p.26.

29. Marta Figlerowicz, 'Novels and Characters' in Eric Bulson (ed.), *The Cambridge Companion to the Novel* (Cambridge: Cambridge University Press, 2018), p.125.

30. I explore this at greater length in 'Worldmaking Environmental Crisis: Climate Fiction, Econarratology and Genre' in Erin James and Eric Morel (eds.), *Environment and Narrative* (Columbus: Ohio State University Press, forthcoming).
31. Herman, *Story Logic*, p.81.
32. Herman, *Story Logic*, p.83.

CHAPTER 5

Popular Fiction

Saba Pirzadeh

Accelerated developments in the publishing industry and the digital revolution of recent years have brought about a marked shift in the conception, proliferation and reception of South Asian Anglophone literature. The readership and the consumption of such fiction have also changed since the original 'double audience' at home and abroad expanded to include a new readership in the local market.[1] Fiction is slowly moving away from established templates and branching into other sub-genres to question the historical-political formations of post-colonies. The trope of social interrogation is also being used to examine the implications of ecological degradation since 'environmental consciousness and nature awareness has permeated popular and commercial fiction'.[2] Notable examples include Mahasweta Devi, Kiran Desai, Ruchir Joshi, Indra Sinha, Nadeem Aslam, Mohsin Hamid and Uzma Aslam Khan, who incorporate the environment as a formal and stylistic presence in their novels to underscore issues of uneven development, ecological imperialism and environmental degradation.[3]

Linking ecological degradation to the current Anthropocene epoch, recent South Asian texts such as Pakistani writer Osama Siddique's *Snuffing Out the Moon* (2017) and Indian writer Amitav Ghosh's *Gun Island* (2019) stand out owing to their careful consideration of the local and regional implications of destabilising anthropocentric climate change on human and animal lives. Examining the climatic focus, this chapter establishes these texts as ecological crime fiction that investigates the unfolding and intensification of the climate breakdown. Despite the absence of conventional crime fiction elements such as the hard-boiled detective, police procedure, and the resolution and restoration of social order, both novels adhere to the conceptual premises of the genre in investigating climate decline and underscoring the criminality of an anthropocentric instrumentalisation of nature.

Snuffing Out the Moon consists of six separate storylines ranging from 2084 BCE to 2084 CE, based largely on the Punjab and Sindh provinces of Pakistan – and using a diverse set of characters to explore themes of religion, morality, savagery and justice. *Gun Island* blends mythology and adventure to trace the bookseller Deen's efforts to decode a local legend about a merchant fated to travel the world as he sought a safe haven from the goddess of snakes, Manasa Devi. Deen embarks on a global journey spanning from the Sundarban mangroves to the Los Angeles forest fires to a flooded Venice. Despite the differing timelines and locales, both novels interweave history and reality to explore the human and ecological harm generated by anthropogenic climatological mutations. While it is true that climate change is not a new phenomenon, contemporary climate change differs from past shifts in two crucial respects: it is man-made, and it is happening more rapidly than at any time in the last fifty million years.[4] This highlights the importance of decoding the complexities of anthropocentric climate change.

In this regard, the term Anthropocene describes both the primacy of human agency in shaping the planet's chemistry and the engendering of complex transformative processes over which humanity's geophysical agency has little control.[5] The concept of the Anthropocene also entails experiencing dynamic (and mostly damaging) change by humans on animals, plants, soils, oceans and atmosphere in an extremely dynamic biosphere.[6] A key challenge is relaying the massive scale and reach of the Anthropocene. Storytelling – fiction and non-fiction – can help us to imaginatively experience the impact of the geophysical force that is the human.[7] Ghosh's and Siddique's works relay the risks of the Anthropocene by fusing fictional and non-fictional modes of narration to explore 'the relationship between climate change and humanity in psychological and social terms, exploring how climate change occurs not just as a meteorological or ecological crisis "out there" but as something filtered through our inner and outer lives'.[8] In this regard, this chapter establishes how Siddique and Ghosh use crime fiction elements of historical retelling, partial detection and perpetual quests for social justice – to generate a critical investigation of the causality and culpability of anthropocentric climate breakdown. This analysis aligns with Anthropocene Noir scholarship – for example, notable work by David Farrier (which looks at ecological transgression and detection in Chloe Hooper's *A Child's Book of True Crime*) – but extends it into a South Asian perspective by emphasising the counter-discursive potentiality of historical myth in dismantling

anthropocentric logic and highlighting the importance of pursuing interspecies justice for planetary survival.

Historical Retelling

Historical retelling foregrounds the narrative relationship at the heart of
most crime fiction, namely the relationship between the past and the
present.[9] Specifically, Ghosh's and Siddique's novels work as 'trans-
historical crime fiction' since they are characterised by transitions from
the present to the past.[10] These novels attain this through the narrative
device of framing one story within another story.[11] Siddique's novel narra-
tivises life in Mohenjodaro about nature and human civilisation while
Ghosh's novel scaffolds an Indian legend within a transnational narrative
journey about climate crisis and refugees.

Snuffing Out the Moon delves into the lives of the denizens of the
Mohenjodaro civilisation (2084 BCE) – one of the most advanced
human civilisations which 'knew the arts of writing, town planning,
metallurgy, monumental architecture, and mass production and had considerable engineering skills'.[12] The novel fuses historical and fictional
modes of narration by imagining the demise of this advanced river-based
civilisation owing to the natural catastrophe of floods. The text introduces
us to the fictional character of Prkaa, a wise young man portrayed as
a prescient character, who carefully observes and interprets nature in his
everyday encounters with the land. Despite experiencing a series of intense
rainstorms, most denizens seem to be unconcerned about the changing
climate patterns and their implications for the community. Prkaa seems to
perceive the danger of ignoring nature's warnings: 'The rains last longer
and the river tides are more unpredictable than before. We need to protect
the jungle and rebuild those embankments and city walls. Have you seen
how the city's riverside area is crumbling and how much water got in
during the last floods?'[13] This impassioned questioning emphasises the
power of climate in shaping the agricultural and residential dimensions
of human society and highlights climate as a part of the embodied experience of living amidst nature.

Moreover, a major factor behind the success of Mohenjodaro is attrib-
uted to the attention given to a climatic phenomenon in anticipating and
protecting the settlement – a practice which slowly starts to disappear with
the onset of anthropomorphised religion. Siddique indicates the cultural
shift that takes place with the arrival of priests who steadily accrue authority and resort to rituals such as 'special water puja [for] placating the

weather gods and abating the floods' (p.139). This decision induces severe anxiety and worry in Prkaa who scorns the proposed solution: 'How will such idle splashing around ward off the threat of flooding? Don't we have enough water already pouring from the skies and overflowing from the river that we now have to see that ugly lecher wading before the public, offensively semi-naked; muttering incantations?' (p.139). The inefficacy of the ritual is suggested by Prkaa's condemnation of it as 'idle splashing' that will do nothing to curtail the potent 'threat of flooding', suggesting how pantheism is quickly supplanted by anthropomorphic religion. Moreover, the spectacle of religious ritual gradually diminishes the communal willingness to maintain a balance between human and natural environments as indicated by the master architect Mahweel's observations about the stark ruination of wells, drains and passages constructed by earlier generations to store excess water from the deluges (p.161). The architect wistfully remembers the past when people 'deliberated over how much to take from the jungle' (p.161), thereby praising the previous approach of respectfully using and conserving natural resources. This fictional representation is supported by historical studies which confirm that the people of Mohenjodaro worshipped an Indus goddess who was the universal symbol of life and inexhaustible fertility and had a subsistence economy based on agriculture, hunting and fishing.[14]

Thus, Siddique's work interprets history in an expansive manner to help readers recognise the embodied experience of living amidst nature. As the narrative progresses, though, the text indicates the oncoming demise of the civilisation owing to people's disengagement from nature: 'Mahweel . . . looked at Prkaa with an expression of the deepest sadness: 'The rains aren't letting up and neither are the floods . . . only a fool would deny that we are entering a very wet epoch . . . And yet we have been sitting around and doing nothing about it' (p.162). This dialogue relays how estrangement from nature terminates human–nature kinship such that humans lose the ability to adapt to nature and give way to their violent demise, as indicated by the narrative depiction of Mohenjodaro's destruction by floods – a conclusion also reached by some archaeologists.[15] Thus, Siddique's narrative re-presents history ecocritically to convey the potent dangers of estrangement from nature – one temporally extended by Ghosh to the Anthropocene.

This concept is framed mythically in Ghosh's novel, which begins with the introduction of a local Indian legend that propels Deen's journey across the world. It is a 'legend of a merchant called Chand Sadagar – who is said to have fled overseas in order to escape the persecution of Manasa Devi, the goddess who rules over snakes and all other poisonous creatures'.[16] This casual reference piques Deen's interest in travelling back to the Sundarbans (an expansive mangrove delta area of 3,860 miles which extends from north-eastern India to southern Bangladesh) to explore the origins of the myth. Upon his arrival, Deen reads local literature and discovers that: 'The legend was probably born amidst the original, autochthonous people of the region and was perhaps sired by real historical figures and events ... to this day, scattered across Assam, West Bengal and Bangladesh, there are archaeological sites that are linked, in popular memory, to the Merchant and his family' (p.7). This fictional element also has a factual component as attested by historical accounts of the legend's popularity whereby the deity is worshipped in Bengal and its neighbouring regions for her ability to cure chronic diseases and to bestow fertility.[17] Historians have also found that the Manasa Devi myth has been preserved through rich folk-literature (from the thirteenth century AD) such as narrative poetry which, to this day, has been carried down generations and publicly performed in different parts of Bengal.[18]

Upon arrival in the Sundarbans, Deen discovers the myth to be part of the everyday vernacular and belief systems such that local people have built multiple shrines to pay homage to the Devi. This religious devoutness is seen as a necessary prerequisite to ward off harm and misfortune, such that any defiance of the Devi is seen as an invitation to her wrath, as reflected in the outcomes of the Merchant's refusal to become the Devi's devotee. As a result, the merchant was 'plagued by snakes and pursued by droughts, famines, storms and other calamities, he had fled overseas to escape the goddess's wrath' (p.17). Local people such as Horen believe that 'the Gun Merchant's misfortunes were due to his own arrogance, and his conviction that he was rich enough, and clever enough, to avoid paying deference to the forces represented by the goddess of snakes' (p.60). This fear is in line with religious beliefs about Manasa Devi's power: 'She destroys ruthlessly and wantonly, the innocent with the guilty, to demonstrate her might. She is full of wrath and violence. But she has a strange and equally wanton compassion. She has the power to bring her victims back to life, and this she often does once she has conquered them.'[19] Intrigued by the quasi-factual basis of the legend, Deen embarks on a transcontinental journey to uncover the gun merchant's story. It is through this journey that Deen witnesses the violent assault of anthropocentric climate change (such as extreme weather fluctuations, floods, mass animal deaths, insect invasions) on human and animal populations, which also becomes a metaphorical signification of the deadly effects of the human drive to tame and control nature. This is similar to Manasa Devi's legend that warned about the cursed existence of humans who refuse to yield to nature. Thus, Ghosh deftly uses myth as parable and as a warning against the abuse of nature within the Anthropocene.

Siddique and Ghosh use history and folklore, then, to highlight human–nature interdependence such that their texts become 'noir folk narrative[s] in which social diatribes are replaced by archetypal folkloric motifs'.[20] In this context, the historical retelling of the Mohenjo-Daro civilisation and the Manasa Devi legend are used to convey grave warnings against the human instrumentalisation of nature 'by giving the natural world itself agency and identity and complexity [to] provide an antidote to the anthropocentrism that might be said to motivate, perpetuate, and aggravate the ecological crises of our time'.[21]

Partial Detection

The motif of historical retelling becomes a narrative device for the detection of the global dimensions of climate change by the primary characters Afaqi (the historian) in Siddique's work and Deen in Ghosh's work. Both Afaqi and Deen are cast in the role of detectives who, in contrast to the traditional detective role of investigating murdered bodies, are charged with the role of examining bodies of historical and experiential knowledge concerning climate cataclysms. These post-colonial detective novels demonstrate that ecological crime is not an isolated phenomenon but is part of a larger field of social disorder and inequality in which the detective is unable to fight the wrongs of the social system.[22]

Snuffing Out the Moon extends the water metaphor counter-chronologically from 2084 BCE (Mohenjodaro civilisation) to 2084 CE (South Asian Corridor) whereby water surplus is inverted into scarcity. In 2084 CE there exists a new global order whereby the nation-state system has been dismantled and replaced by the rule of conglomerates that retain power through their control of natural resources – specifically water. Siddique focuses on the geopolitics of this futuristic world order in the South Asian region wherein populations have been divided largely into two groups – the Conglomerates themselves (the dominant group) and the Regressives (the peripheral group). The text describes how the rise of new age technology enabled the rapid dissemination of opposing meta-historical narratives (about the return to an idyllic past) with the result that the ideological clash gave way to war and political breakdown, thereby creating space for the militarised new world order of the Conglomerates.

The regime maintains its biopolitical power through control of information such that there is a strict censorship of oral or written discourse about the past. This forces the population to remain uncritical subjects entrenched in the present. While this order ensured that the opposing faction of the Regressives was banished from the mainland to remove them from cultural memory, a small discordant minority nevertheless endeavours to understand the Regressives' worldview. In this context, the academic Alexander Afaqi assumes the role of detective as he reclaims historical archives that trace new world order origins. The text informs us that his descent from a pioneering stalwart historian (p.238) to one 'who lost his path' began when he started to cast doubts on the 'undeniable progress of the human civilizational project' of the Conglomerates (p.239). His resultant book, *A Very Concise History of the Post Later Days Period*, was interpreted to be subversive since it critiqued the Conglomerates' origins. It was pulled 'out of circulation and the public domain' (p.239).

However, the novel exposes us to textual snippets that serve as illuminating evidence into the Conglomerates' rise to power in the wake of climatic disaster. Afaqi's text documents the rise of the order: 'after the conflicts, meltdowns and disintegration of the Area formerly known as South Asia (AFKA-SA), the anarchic situation was exacerbated by intense climate changes' (p.254). These climate changes included 'failing rains, acute deforestation and worsening ecological imbalance which caused a scramble for freshwater resources and led to mass displacements and full-scale conflicts' (p.254). This retrospective narration denotes how the acceleration of the anthropocentric economic order exacerbated existing climatic imbalances to the tipping point of ecological calamities which destabilised the world order. Afaqi's treatise further declares that the environmental catastrophes ushered in a new order of re-colonisation whereby Western powers moved into the global South since 'the primary object of attraction for conquests had changed. No longer was it advantageous trade, cash crops, raw materials, cheap labor, oil and gas, precious minerals or even territorial domination ... but fresh water resources and the surrounding tracts of arable land' (p.255).

In this war, the Conglomerates emerged victorious through the ruthless deployment of new age weapons and techniques of mass rationalisation (p.255). This treatise records a new phase of war as resource wars with global powers such as the Conglomerate, deploying technologies to usurp untapped natural resources, thus showing how a capitalist logic (that undergirds the Anthropocene) works by monetising crisis to its growth. The treatise also exposes the regime's brutality by documenting its reintegration process: 'The imperative was to [decrease the] pressure on scarce resources and retain only [people] that were highly skilled in certain technologies and sciences and were therefore necessary to operate local water facilities and reservoirs' (p.255). The remaining population becomes disciplined into instrumentalised bodies used to maintain the operations of water reservoirs, demarcating their slavish existence in a biopolitical regime.

Upon discovery of the indicting treatise, Afaqi is seized by the Conglomerates and subjected to an inquisition, after which the text suggests that he might have been killed or subjected to memory erasure. He is never heard from again. On one level, Afaqi's disappearance suggests a partial detection, but on a metaphorical level, Afaqi's detection positions instrumentalised technology as a constitutive element of the Anthropocene and condemns the ways that this technology violates the environment.[23] This fictional detection mirrors, therefore, our current suicidal relation to nature whereby climatologists predict that global warming will accelerate the shrinkage of drinkable water resources, as well as intensifying droughts in arid and semi-arid regions in the world.[24] In narrativising this climatological phenomenon, Siddique seems to criticise the current nation-state's lack of reaction to climate change not to 'dispassionately abandon human life to the reality of its coming extinction but to deploy narrative to affirm the continuing value of human life'.[25]

Likewise, Ghosh's novel uses the travel trope to give Deen an acute insight into the ground-level realities of living amidst the socio-economic destabilisation of climate change – specifically floods. The novel demonstrates that 'fictionalizing climate change is not about falsifying it, or making it imaginary, but rather about using narrative to heighten its reality'.[26] Through encounters with multiple characters of various socio-economic standing (scholars, scientists, Bengali people), Deen detects the nuances and implications of climate change across the ages.

With the help of his friend Cinta (an Italian academic), Deen surmises that the gun merchant's travels were precipitated by 'droughts and floods brought on by the climatic disturbances of the Little Ice Age [whereby] he loses everything including his family and decides to go overseas to recoup his fortune' (p.155). While this highlights the temporal longevity of geological climate change, the current climate disturbances are presented as a consequence of anthropogenic ecological failure spread across the globe – from the Sundarbans to Los Angeles to Venice. It is through interactions with the locals that Deen learns about the everyday devastation caused by climatic upheaval such as the growing deprivation of subsistence-based survival for the Sundarban fishermen: 'When people tried to dig wells, an arsenic-laced brew gushed out of the soil; when they tried to shore up embankments the tides rose higher and pulled them down again. Even fishermen could barely get by; where once their boats would come back loaded with catch, now they counted themselves lucky if they netted a handful of fry' (p.53). These poignant lines allow us to see the ways in which the most marginalised people are assaulted and threatened by a sentient nature that has been repeatedly used and abused by anthropogenic activities (such as the state-led development of the landscape).

Moving from the Sundarbans to other continents, Deen continues to detect, note and reflect on the unfolding of climate cataclysms across different geographies and countries. He witnesses Los Angeles's forests being ravaged by wildfires (p.128), learns that floods occur regularly in Venice (p.180), and is nearly killed by a massive tornado there (p.272). The temporal juxtaposition and the bodily detection of these climatic disasters enable Deen to detect and convey how the uncanny events of anthropogenic derangement have become an ordinary occurrence. Deen finds out the various forms that 'strange weather' takes: 'Soon we learnt that the strange weather was not just a local phenomenon: all of Italy had been affected in different ways. Some northern cities had been deluged with rain and hail; many parts of the country had been struck by gale-force winds; in the mountains of the Sud Tirol entire forests had been flattened ... damaging houses and blocking roads' (p.276). By presenting an array of weather disturbances – rain, hail, gale – through Deen's keen observational powers, Ghosh conveys to us the factual complexity of anthropogenic climate change. This distinguishes his novel from other climate fictions that 'concentrate the disaster into a single tsunami [despite the fact that] climate change's real effects are more distributed: desertification, contamination of freshwater, fiercer tornadoes, extinctions, destroyed mangrove barriers, crop failures, and so on'.[27]

Moreover, in his role as detective, Deen also forays into peripheral space and encounters the shadowy figures of illegal immigrants detained in camps in the Italian borderlands. The necessity of such migration is reinforced by the character of Tipu, who smuggles people for money. When Deen critiques Tipu for his work, he retorts: '[W]hat I'm doing is offering an essential service. In these parts, there's a whole bunch of dirt-poor, illiterate people scratching out a living by fishing or farming or going into the jungle to collect bamboo ... but now the fish is catch down, the land's turning salty, and you can't go into the jungle without bribing the forest guards. On top of that every other year you get hit by a storm that blows everything to pieces. So what are people supposed to do?' (p.65). Tipu's retort yields keen insight into the bodily experience of living amidst and with anthropogenic climate imbalance that has ruptured indigenous, earth-based livelihoods and generated such extreme socio-economic vulnerability in the lives of marginalised groups that they are forced to illegally migrate (to the West) hence exposing themselves to further unknown dangers.

Furthermore, this example shows how climate refugees are a growing concern, thus highlighting how anthropogenic climate change threatens to upend nation-state borders and global securitisation. And though Deen's detection doesn't conclude on an all-explanatory note, it is effective in conveying the chaotic ground-level realities of a contemporary risk society characterised by 'unintended consequences of modernity' such as climate change risks.[28] Indeed, such risks, indeterminately distanced over space and time, stretching social and natural relations of cause, effect and responsibility, have become inescapable for both developing and developed countries.[29]

Thus, in their roles as post-colonial detectives, both Afaqi and Deen offer a partial detection of bodily and experiential knowledge of the socio-economic implications of the Anthropocene to underscore how 'power and authority can be investigated through the magnifying glass of other knowledges, against the local or global mainstream, past and present, or against potential projections of a dominant group and a (neo-)imperial West'.[30] This partial detection serves an ecocritical purpose by ensuring that readers do not have the freedom to imagine that the environmental conflicts have been solved by the novels' end; those conflicts remain a problem in the world beyond the fictional works.[31]

Narrating Social and Interspecies Justice

Adding to the affective dimensions of post-colonial detection is the narrativisation of the precarious plight of the victims of climate catastrophes, indicating social justice to be an important characteristic of post-colonial crime fiction.[32] In Siddique's novel the quest entails the re-inscription of new subject positions for the previously oppressed.[33] In *Snuffing Out the Moon* the textual encounter between a Conglomerate pilot, Farooqi, and the Regressives opens up communication between two supposedly antagonistic factions. The text informs us how the Conglomerates have devised structural barriers to protect themselves and their water settlements from the Regressives (p.76). Air rider Farooqi has been given the order to flush out the Regressives who left their jungle hideouts to seize the opportunity to channel water from the main river system (p.78). A closer reading of this seemingly factual description of the settlement allows us to see the acute power imbalance between the two groups, the Conglomerates using structural fortification to enclose and usurp water, thereby forcing the subordinate group (the Regressives) to adopt guerrilla tactics to gain access to this fundamental life resource. The Conglomerates' worldview continues to be dismantled through the sustained textual encounter that occurs as a result of Farooqi's plane crash into Regressive territory. By choosing to forgo the opportunity to kill some members of the Regressive group, Farooqi gains slow acceptance into the group, who provide him with shelter.

In the days that follow, Farooqi converses with the group members and discovers the truth about their marginalised status. Farooqi is told how, with the advent of water wars, 'children, women, and men had gone forth in caravans, small and large, clinging together for fear of persecution, in dire need of water and security. After the stabilization of the extant global power balance among the Conglomerates, their places of exile became semi-permanent abodes' (p.233). These lines reveal how poor and vulnerable groups were purposely expelled by the Conglomerates and left to fend for themselves in harsh, unsafe conditions, thereby unveiling the inherent violence of the new empire. Furthermore, Farooqi is informed of the inhuman Conglomerate governance policies whereby the rulers did not see any incentives to subjugate and rule the indigenous populations; so instead the imperative became to destroy or cast them out with the result that they eventually perished in the drought-struck wilderness and wastelands (pp.255–7). This insight into the Conglomerates' hidden past exposes the criminal aspects of the ostensibly advanced civilisation and indicts them for the large-scale expulsion and murder of people in pursuit of an accumulation of ecological capital. Upon discovery of the regime's sordid past, Farooqi decides to forgo his affiliation with the Conglomerates and to live with the Regressives. And though the text's conclusion indicates that the Conglomerates remain in power, Farooqi's narrative arc becomes an important counter to the 'misframing of indigenous peoples and underlines the necessity to integrate the perspectives of marginalized, transnational groups'.[34] Facilitating human connectivity across different groups, not least through narrative, could inspire collective action for socio-environmental justice.

In *Gun Island* the quest for justice entails environmental witnessing which makes readers see and understand the trauma inflicted on non-human species[35] – specifically aquatic creatures and insects. The text does a highly effective job of mapping the various anthropogenic factors that are contributing to the psychological and corporeal trauma inflicted upon animals. One such factor is the global warming that is rendering animal habitats unliveable and forcing them to seek new places. This is narrated, for instance, in the sudden appearance of the yellow-bellied sea snakes in southern California (pp.147–8), the migration of the brown recluse spider to other parts of Italy (p.234) and the Venetian shipworm invasion wherein the insects are literally eating the city's foundations (p.251). By documenting these unexpected changes in the movements and behaviours of insects, Ghosh establishes the planetary impact of anthropocentric climate change on human and natural spaces.

Ghosh also charts the affective and psychological dimensions of habitat modification by global warming through the example of the Sundarban dolphins. Rising sea levels have made their familiar waterways too saline, forcing the dolphins to seek new paths by venturing further upriver, into populated, heavily fished areas where they can be snared by fishermen's nets and get hit by motorboats (p.102). By explaining the change in the dolphins' movement, the text dismantles the idea of animal behaviour as inexplicable and instead attributes it to the ecological havoc created by anthropocentric climate change that can threaten the existence of an entire animal species. The text invites readers to consider the dolphins' cognition, in the face of such alarming ecological changes, through the perspective of Piya, a marine scientist who senses that this habitat alteration will hit Rani (the matriarch dolphin) hardest. She 'must have felt that everything she knew, everything she was familiar with – the water, the currents, the earth itself – was rising up against her ... We're in a new world now. No one knows where they belong anymore, neither human nor animals' (p.106). This close attention to Rani's interiority allows readers to feel her acute psychological pain at the unrecognisable transformation of her natural environment, and in turn makes Rani a metonym for all life (human and animal) displaced and dispossessed because of anthropocentric climate disruptions.

In addition to the psychological trauma, the text also depicts the corporeal trauma inflicted upon animals whereby the rapid poisoning of natural spaces owing to anthropocentric activities – such as industrial pollution and effluent discharge – is creating oceanic dead zones over tens of thousands of square miles of ocean – some as large as middle-sized countries (p.104). These zones 'have been growing at a phenomenal pace, mostly because of residues from chemical fertilizers' (p.106). Ghosh's fictional account visually captures the scale and scope of the real-life environmental catastrophe of dead zones, which are one of the most detrimental anthropogenic threats to marine ecosystems worldwide. They have been doubling in every decade since the mid-1900s and have significant consequences for the biodiversity and functioning of marine ecosystems.[36]

Furthermore, the text informs us that these dead zones are 'vast stretches of water that have a very low oxygen content [such that] only a few, highly specialized organisms can survive in those conditions – everything else dies' (p.106). As a consequence, there has been a corresponding increase in the phenomenon of fish kill with thousands of dead fish found floating on the surface or washed up ashore (p.106). This directs our attention to the violent assault on sea species (amongst others) and highlights the corporeal trauma inflicted on animals. Thus, the generic concern with social justice that we find in post-colonial crime fiction is extended by Ghosh to encompass an insistence on interspecies justice in the face of the Anthropocene. Through a careful mapping of the habitat rupture, behaviour modification and corporeal violence inflicted on animals as a result of anthropocentric activities, Ghosh encourages readers to feel the trauma of persecuted animals in order to advocate justice and responsibility for the well-being of these animals and other life-forms.

An ecocritical examination of Siddique's and Ghosh's two novels establishes the writers' use of crime fiction elements of historical retelling, partial detection and perpetual quests for social (and interspecies) justice – to investigate the causes of and culpability for anthropocentric climate breakdown. These authors expand the conventional notions of climate as statistical data. They instead denote its importance as a material phenomenon wherein 'climate is omnipresent in the history of cultures ... as a condition *and* product of life, as responsible for *and* a threat to human existence',[37] thereby highlighting, in turn, the destabilising impact of anthropocentric processes on the earth's ecosystems. Ghosh and Siddique, furthermore, underscore the criminality of an instrumentalisation in which we, humans, are actors 'in the mass deaths of other creatures and in the misery of numerous and diverse forms of life including humans'.[38] In doing so, the works chosen highlight how 'Anthropocene fiction must account for crimes that are at the same time incalculable and urgently in need of recognition'[39] and how we might turn to literature to help us avoid becoming 'spectators of our own demise'.[40]

Notes

1. Alex Tickell, *South-Asian Fiction in English: Contemporary Transformations* (Basingstoke: Palgrave Macmillan, 2016), p.6.
2. Patrick Murphy, *Ecocritical Explorations in Literary and Cultural Studies* (Lanham, MD: Lexington, 2009), p.143.
3. Pablo Mukherjee, *Postcolonial Environments: Nature, Culture and the Contemporary Novel in English* (Basingstoke: Palgrave Macmillan, 2010), p.11.
4. Catriona McKinnon, *Climate Change and Future Justice: Precaution, Compensation and Triage* (New York: Routledge, 2011). p.1.
5. Richard Crownshaw, 'Speculative Memory, the Planetary and Genre Fiction', *Textual Practice* 31(5) (2017), 887–910 (p.888).
6. Deborah Bird Rose, 'Anthropocene Noir', People and the Planet: Transforming the Future Conference, Global Cities Research Institute, RMIT University (2–4 July 2013), global-cities.info, p.2.
7. Alexa Weik von Mossner, 'Imagining Geological Agency: Storytelling in the Anthropocene' in Robert Emmett and Thomas Lekan (eds.), 'Whose Anthropocene? Revisiting Dipesh Chakrabarty's "Four Theses"', *RCC Perspectives: Transformations in Environment and Society* 2 (2016), 83–8 (p.84).
8. Adam Trexler and Adeline Johns-Putra, 'Climate Change in Literature and Literary Criticism', *WIREs Climate Change* 2(2) (2011), 185–200 (p.196).
9. See John Scaggs, *Crime Fiction* (London: Routledge, 2005), p.32.
10. Ibid., p.125.
11. Ibid., p.131.
12. Gregory L. Possehl, 'The Mohenjo-Daro Floods: A Reply', *American Anthropologist* 69(1) (1967), 32–40 (p.32).
13. Osama Siddique, *Snuffing Out the Moon* (India: Penguin Books, 2017), p.10.
14. Herbert P. Sullivan, 'A Re-examination of the Religion of the Indus Civilization', *History of Religions* 4(1) (1964), 115–25.
15. See Robert Raikes, 'The End of the Ancient Cities of the Indus', *American Anthropologist* 66(2) (1964): 284–99; Robert Raikes and George Dales, 'The Mohenjodaro Floods—A Rejoinder', *American Anthropologist* 70(5) (1968), 957–61.
16. Amitav Ghosh, *Gun Island* (New York: John Murray Publishers, 2019), p.6.
17. Pranabananda Jash, 'The Cult of Manasa in Bengal', *Proceedings of the Indian History Congress* 47 (1986), 169–77 (p.170).
18. Asutosh Bhattacharyya, 'The Serpent as a Folk-Deity in Bengal', *Asian Folklore Studies* 24(1) (1965), 1–10 (p.10).
19. Edward C. Dimock, 'The Goddess of Snakes in Medieval Bengali Literature', *History of Religions* 1(2) (1962), 307–21 (p.317).
20. Andrea Goulet and Susanna Lee, 'Editors' Preface: Crime Fictions', *Yale French Studies* 108 (2005), 1–7 (p.3).
21. Patsy Callaghan, 'Myth as a Site of Ecocritical Inquiry: Disrupting Anthropocentrism', *ISLE: Interdisciplinary Studies in Literature and Environment* 22(1) (2015), 80–97 (p.80).

22. Emily Davis, 'Investigating Truth, History, and Human Rights in Michael Ondaatje's Anil's Ghost' in Neal Person and Marc Singer (eds.), *Detective Fiction in a Postcolonial and Transnational World* (Abingdon: Routledge, 2009), pp.15–31 (p.17).

23. Senayon Olaoluwa, 'Dislocating Anthropocene: The City and Oil in Helon Habila's *Oil on Water*', *ISLE: Interdisciplinary Studies in Literature and Environment* 27(2) (2019), 243–67 (p.244).

24. Claire Perrin, 'An Ecocritical Study of Cli-Fi Novels' in Andre Dodeman and Nancy Pedri (eds.), *Negotiating Waters: Seas, Oceans and Passageways in the Colonial and Postcolonial Anglophone World* (Delaware: Vernon, 2019), pp.165–81 (p.166).

25. Pieter Vermeulen, 'Future Readers: Narrating the Human in the Anthropocene', *Textual Practice* 31(5) (2017), 867–85 (p.879).

26. See Adam Trexler, *Anthropocene Fictions: The Novel in a Time of Climate Change* (Virginia: University of Virginia Press, 2015), p.75.

27. Ibid., p.170.

28. Ulrich Beck, *Risk Society: Toward a New Modernity* (London: Sage, 1992).

29. Harriet Bulkeley, 'Governing Climate Change: The Politics of Risk Society?', *Transactions of the Institute of British Geographers* 26(4) (2001), 430–47 (p.432).

30. Christine Matzke and Suzanne Mülheisen (eds.), *Postcolonial Postmortems: Crime Fiction from a Transcultural Perspective* (Amsterdam: Rodopi, 2006), p.5.

31. Patrick Murphy, *Ecocritical Explorations in Literary and Cultural Studies* (Lanham, MD: Lexington, 2009), pp.119–20.

32. Sam Naidu, 'Teaching Postcolonial Crime Fiction' in Charlotte Beyer (ed.), *Teaching Crime Fiction.* (Basingstoke: Palgrave Macmillan, 2018), pp.83–98 (p.84).

33. Ibid., p.85.

34. Anna Roosvall and Matthew Tegelberg, 'Media and the Geographies of Climate Justice: Indigenous Peoples, Nature and the Geopolitics of Climate Change', *Triple: Communication, Capitalism and Critique* 13(1) (2015), 39–54 (p.39).

35. Sarah Grieve, 'Environmental Justice Witnessing in Muriel Rukeyser's *The Book of the Dead*', *ISLE: Interdisciplinary Studies in Literature and Environment* 26(4) (2019), 968–85 (p.969).

36. Andrew Altieri and Keryn Gedan, 'Climate Change and Dead Zones', *Global Change Biology* 21 (2015), 1395–1406 (p.1395).

37. Mike Hulme, *Weathered: Cultures of Climate* (London: Sage, 2017).

38. Bird Rose, 'Anthropocene Noir', p.4.

39. David Farrier, 'Animal Detectives and "Anthropocene noir" in Chloe Hooper's A Child's Book of True Crime', *Textual Practice* 23 (2017), 1–19 (p.15).

40. Bird Rose, 'Anthropocene Noir', p.4.

CHAPTER 6

The Essay

Byron Caminero-Santangelo

In Amitav Ghosh's *The Great Derangement*, the author sets out to explore how 'the grid of literary forms and conventions that came to shape the narrative imagination' since the eighteenth century has been entangled with collective delusion regarding climate change and its threat.[1] His primary generic focus is the contemporary novel which, he claims, is a productive site for identifying the characteristics of culturally embedded 'modes of concealment' since it is particularly resistant to thinking 'the unthinkable' (p.11). Supporting this argument, he notes that climate change figures only obliquely, if at all, in 'what is now considered serious fiction' (p.9); 'we need only glance through the pages of a few highly regarded literary journals and book reviews' to see that 'when the subject of climate change occurs in these publications, it is almost always in relation to nonfiction' (p.7).

Yet, Ghosh does not explore what the elements of creative non-fiction might be that would make it amenable to addressing climate change, even though it is the form that he himself uses. If he is right 'that when novelists do choose to write about climate change it is almost always outside of fiction' (p.8), then, given also the relative paucity of critical work on non-fiction's relationship with climate change, examining its potential benefits and limitations for shaping a 'narrative imagination' that might disrupt our derangement is an important step in furthering Ghosh's project.

The 'derangement' to which Ghosh refers is not really explicit denial of anthropogenic climate change, which he discusses only briefly. Instead, his focus is people's more general inability to reckon with 'the realities of their plight' (p.11) and to develop a sense of urgency and primacy. Central to our delusion are concepts based on discontinuity and exclusion that render the actual threats of climate change unreal and that suppress holistic, relational modes of apprehending reality. Ghosh's use of creative non-fiction demonstrates how it can help dislodge this delusional conceptual framework. However, *The Great Derangement* also reflects how the genre tends towards a form of representational closure that is, given Ghosh's own analysis, especially problematic for thinking about our present and imagining the future in the age of the Anthropocene.

Colonial Modernity, Culture and Concealment

In many ways, Ghosh's analysis echoes other analysts' conclusions about the relationships among climate change, culture and modernity. We need, he asserts, to recognise the 'forces of unthinkable magnitude that create unbearably intimate connections across vast gaps in time and space' (p.63). Such recognition entails a sense both of proximate, improbable catastrophic change and of our intimate relationships with non-human presences. However, Western modernity has bestowed a sense of mastery, of relatively static everyday existence and of very gradual change which renders the uncanny and the catastrophic unrealistic. We blindly embrace an illusion of nature as orderly, manageable and free from non-human constraints. This illusion suppresses the *wildness* of proximate 'nonhuman interlocutors' and mutual mediation (p.30).

In terms of human relations, climate change requires a sense of collective threat and action but, instead, we are enthralled by fantasies of sequestered autonomy. A focus on individual conscience leaves us paralysed since 'the scale of climate change is such that individual choices will make little difference unless ... collective decisions are taken and acted upon' (p.133). In addition, the stark divide between denialism and climate activism partly results from what he calls 'the politics of self-definition', climate change becoming another issue entangled with 'extreme political polarization' (pp.136–7). As politics gets reduced to the performance of personal expression, we end up with a 'deadlocked public sphere' (p.131).

At the same time, colonial forms of national political consciousness short-circuit efforts to grapple with climate change. While colonialism shaped a conception of national security in the metropole based on maintaining dominance, differentials of power between nations have been closely related to carbon emissions and a carbon economy set up by colonial violence, in order, writes Ghosh, 'to ensure that poor nations remained always at a disadvantage' (p.110). As a result, security apparatuses and political elites in the global North undermine efforts to tackle emissions and climate injustice, and the imagining of national interest and identity is a major obstacle to mitigation. Furthermore, notions of nationally delimited security prevent a recognition that the real threat is already to be found everywhere and 'cannot be held at bay by reinforcing man-made boundaries' (p.144). Meanwhile, in the former colonies the prevailing response to climate change remains tied to national imaginaries shaped by colonialism and hardened over time through the historical configuration of the carbon economy. Nations in the global South rightfully focus on climate injustice; however, they also remain enthralled by colonial concepts of national development and interest based on industrialism and consumption and, ultimately, carbon emissions. This enchantment disables a reckoning with transnational threats and responsibilities that extend beyond borders and stem from carbon-fuelled growth everywhere.

As his decolonial analysis suggests, Ghosh sees the disruption of modernity's temporality as crucial for overcoming our derangement. This temporality projects 'the modern' as a state of exceptional enlightenment that brings security from the threats faced by those who lived or are living in an unenlightened past. The modern worldview renders obsolete other modes of apprehension by designating them as primitive, traditional and backward. Yet, if 'one of modernity's most effective weapons' is 'its insistence that it has rendered other forms of knowledge obsolete' (p.20), this, nevertheless, threatens hope for the future, for *a* future; such hope, according to Ghosh, necessitates drawing on marginalised, non-Western and unmodern ways of understanding reality. In arguments echoing Jean and John Comaroff's assertion that understanding the present and the future requires theory from the global South, Ghosh claims that we must listen precisely to those whose knowledge is discounted as ignorance, but who actually understand better the forces and conditions with which we contend.[2]

In terms of which literary genres might offer an alternative temporality, he primarily turns to narrative forms predating the modern novel and, in particular, to epic traditions. Drawing on examples such as *The Odyssey*, the *Ramayana* and the sixteenth-century Chinese folk epic *The Journey to the West*, Ghosh notes how the epic ranges 'over eons and epochs', brings 'multiple universes into conjunction' (p.59), delights 'in the unheard-of and the unlikely' (p.61) and draws on non-humans to provide much of the narrative momentum: 'In the Indian epics—and this is a tradition that remains vibrantly alive to this day—there is a completely matter-of-fact acceptance of the agency of nonhuman beings of many kinds' (p.64). Such a narrative sensibility has been banished by modern ideals of 'serious' fiction, resulting in a contemporary novel form which, aligned 'with the avant-garde', focuses on moving forward by erasing 'every archaic reminder of Man's kinship with the nonhuman' (p.70). It results, ultimately, in a literary imagination poorly suited to 'the earth of the Anthropocene' (p.62).

Ghosh also highlights, specifically, what he sees as science fiction's limitations, even though the genre includes many of the attributes he endorses. He argues that science fiction too easily places the 'unheard-of and improbable' events of the Anthropocene in 'an imagined "world" apart from ours' or 'in another "time" or another "dimension"'. We need, he claims, a narrative form that can place such events and 'the transformations that are now under way' in 'a time that is recognizable as our own' (pp.72–3). In this sense, he perceives particular promise in realist post-colonial fiction that is both focused on events in the past or present and informed by a narrative sensibility that contrasts sharply with the atomis-ing, anthropocentric orientation of the contemporary novel in the West. If 'in many parts of the world' there are novelists who continue to write 'very effectively' about 'men in the aggregate' and about the presence of 'the nonhuman', such writing is part of a 'sly' decolonial reversal whereby writers who would be considered backwards by the standards of the modern novel have been 'actually ahead of their peers elsewhere' (p.80).

Truth and Heresy in Non-fiction

Nonetheless, although Ghosh himself is best known as a post-colonial novelist, he does not use the novel as a means to think about 'the unthinkable' and our derangement. Instead, he turns to the essay (the three parts of *The Great Derangement* represent separate but connected essays), a choice supporting his claim that novelists more generally turn to non-fiction when addressing climate change. What is it about the essay that might make it amenable to Ghosh's purpose?

The beginnings of an answer can be found in Rob Nixon's analysis of politically engaged creative non-fiction by environmental writer-activists in the global South. Such writers strive to make 'unseen or imperceptible violence … accessible and tangible by humanizing drawn-out threats inaccessible to the immediate senses'.[3] Creative non-fiction's focus on rendering 'reality' and its association with 'truth' and 'veracity' is well suited to its purposes.[4] The use of personal narrative foregrounds the act of witnessing, helps establish the trustworthiness and truthfulness of the author, and enables that humanising work to which Nixon refers. At the same time, the genre enables connections among the personal and the political, individual experience and collective or professional knowledge; thus, memoirists are able to draw 'on intimate energies while offering the reader a social depth of field'.[5] In other words, though drawing on first-person narrative, creative non-fiction does not necessarily focus on individual perspective and concerns. The writer-activists' witnessing has a collective quality that links individual perception with often violently suppressed 'socioenvironmental memory' and modes of apprehension.[6] More generally, creative non-fiction fits well with their goals in challenging accepted truths. Tending to disrupt 'the official story' and 'the authority of the sanctioned story tellers', the genre entails a challenge to assumptions about objectivity and disinterestedness embedded in specialised writing and 'systematized . . . approaches to knowledge'.[7] Indeed, Adorno associates the creative essay with 'heresy' in its 'antimethodological' orientation.[8] Such heretical deviation from disciplinary norms gives the form a discursive flexibility and adaptability. The benefits of the genre for writer-activists such as Ken Saro-Wiwa, Arundhati Roy and Wangari Maathai are made clear in Nixon's explication of how they employ the essay simultaneously to appeal to different audiences and to generate a sense of urgency and responsibility.

The value of non-fiction's qualities for addressing our derangement and thinking 'the unthinkable' becomes even clearer when one considers Ghosh's account of what this work entails. He seeks a form that will defamiliarise the everyday, make visible what we normally cannot apprehend and denaturalise what is rendered natural by modernity's modes of concealment. It must have the potential to inculcate a way of perceiving reality to which we are cognitively and perceptually resistant. At the same time, this form must be able to convince an audience that what is being described is 'real', precisely because part of our derangement is in the ease with which we can distance ourselves from the dangers of climate change and relegate them to stories of some far-off future (even if we acknowledge them in the abstract). Such a goal entails creating a sense of a reliable witness, one whom we can trust to tell the truth. Yet, the form must avoid valorising or reifying individual perception and, more generally, any single vantage point for apprehending reality. It must be up to the task of examining the complex, multiscalar intersections of culture, history, politics and climate change by connecting a wide range of expert and cosmopolitan forms of knowledge and narrative. At the same time, it must be able to foreground marginalised or discounted perspectives and knowledge and disrupt projections of an 'enlightened' subject with a monopoly on truth.

Ghosh's use of personal story is especially telling in terms of matching form with purpose. At the beginning of the first section, 'Stories', he tells us that his 'ancestors were ecological refugees long before the term was invented' as a result of the Padma river 'one day in the mid-1850s ... suddenly changing course, drowning the village; only a few of the inhabitants had managed to escape to higher ground' (p.4). Ghosh first heard this story as a child when he journeyed down the Padma with his family. Looking into the 'swirling waters', he imagined the 'catastrophe' and had a recognition, one that has remained important 'to this day', of the 'circumstances that have shaped my life ... the elemental force that untethered my ancestors from their homeland and launched them on the series of journeys that preceded, and made possible, my own travels' (p.4). He began to be aware both of the relationality of his identity in respect to ancestral history and of what his 'forebearers' came to recognise: 'the urgent proximity of nonhuman presences', of the incredible power of 'the energy that surrounds us ... an all-encompassing presence that may have its own purposes about which we know nothing' (p.5). In turn, his story of his family history and childhood represents a reversal by which what is supposedly backwards, childish and fantastic – including ancestral knowledge and a recognition of non-human agency – exposes the limitations of modernity's narrative of enlightenment and development.

When he was in the Sundarbans writing his novel *The Hungry Tide*, Ghosh became more fully aware and wrote in his notes of how the 'land' is 'alive' and 'is [itself] a protagonist' (p.6). Still later, he came to recognise that the struggle he'd had to put such 'perceptions' into his novel was the result not just of the particular challenges of writing it, as he'd thought 'back then', but also of the 'literary forms and conventions' that came to shape modernity's 'narrative imagination' (pp.6–7). This recognition is central to the first section of *The Great Derangement*, and it informs the arguments throughout the text about the origins of our derangement.

Yet, Ghosh does not valorise the epistemological positioning of the older self, reflected, for example, in that self's cosmopolitan understanding of 'the accelerating impacts of global warming'. Instead, he emphasises that understanding is always relational; it is not transcendence but re-engagement:

> [A] moment of recognition occurs when a prior awareness flashes before us, effecting an instant change in our understanding of that which is beheld. Yet this flash cannot appear spontaneously; it cannot disclose itself except in the presence of its lost other. The knowledge that results from recognition, then, is not of the same kind as the discovery of something new: it arises rather from a renewed reckoning with a potentiality that lies within oneself. (pp.4–5)

Ghosh's claim disrupts the notion of an enlightened self, since any understanding that supposedly represents a leap from ignorance to knowledge is actually a productive engagement with a prior recognition and self that one does not simply move beyond. In addition, there is no recognition that represents an endpoint; knowledge, instead, is in the non-teleological relationality between past and present, the lost and the found. Finally, if Ghosh's 'self' has been shaped by family, community and the non-human, then any apparently new understanding also renews connection with the recognitions of those 'lost others' whom modernity suggests that he has surpassed. In pursuit of such heretical truth telling and relationality, Ghosh uses non-fiction's discursive hybridity to connect different types and times of recognition without reinscribing hegemonic hierarchies.

This point is made evident by Ghosh's use of another seminal story, his sublime experience of a tornado 'on the afternoon of March 17, 1978 . . . in north Delhi' (p.11). Rushing to escape a sudden, extreme turn in the weather, he observes a 'gray, tube-like extrusion forming on the underside of a dark cloud' and hears a 'rumbling sound' that soon rises 'to a frenzied pitch'. Eventually, astonished, he sees 'an extraordinary panoply of objects flying past' and has the sense that 'gravity itself' has 'been transformed into a wheel spinning upon the fingertip of some unknown power'. Afterwards, he is 'confronted by a scene of devastation such as I had never before beheld' (pp.12–13). This uncanny experience confounds him and, initially, the journalists who try to understand it; even they struggled to find the 'right word' – 'tornado' – for the phenomenon, the first 'to hit Delhi . . . in recorded meteorological history' (p.14). Nevertheless, his embodied experience rendered an important recognition of the still not entirely explicable relationship between himself and the tornado; what happened 'was strangely like a species of visual contact, of beholding and being beheld. And in that instant of contact something was planted deep in my mind, something irreducibly mysterious' (pp.14–15).

In the present, Ghosh has been able to give a wider meaning to the experience because he has moved outward in time and space and to a higher level of abstraction. Connecting it with more recent events, such as Hurricane Sandy, and with his knowledge of climate change, he uses it as a means to represent the relationship between our uncanny intertwining with the non-human and our present predicament (p.24). In other words, as with the previous story, he reads the experience through cosmopolitan and expert knowledge that can render a significance he could not have perceived before. While drawing on individual perception, he does not privilege this in the way that, he argues, is so problematic in the modern novel and in contemporary politics.

At the same time, Ghosh neither represents his current self as enlightened in comparison with his earlier self nor valorises the perspective bestowed by modernity. In fact, he suggests that the supposed maturity of his older, more modern self has resulted in a kind of ignorance. His further education and his development from young 'part time journalist' to internationally known novelist did not necessarily represent a movement towards a better sense of 'reality'. The older self struggles to include in his own fiction exactly the kind of improbable experience represented by the tornado. His recognition of why reveals a disciplining that is blinding: he realises that if he were to 'come across [the experience] in a novel written by someone else', his 'response would be one of incredulity'; he would think it a 'contrivance of last resort' because of the misguided assumptions about reality in which 'the modern novel' traffics (p.16). This recognition requires linking the perspectives of the older and younger selves, without privileging one over the other. Recovery from our derangement necessitates making non-hierarchal connections between past and present, the human and the non-human, and widely different scales and kinds of knowledge.

The connection between Ghosh's rhetorical purpose and literary form is also reflected in the way he draws on and intermingles an enormous range of literature, scholarly sources, genres and disciplinary methods throughout *The Great Derangement*. The layout of the three parts in the table of contents – 'Stories', 'History', 'Politics' – in a triangle suggests that we must understand the movement from one part and category to another not as a progression towards a higher level of understanding and priority but in non-linear, relational terms. Just as importantly, the delimitation of the categories is erased as they are brought into proximate relationships within each of the sections. For example, the literary focus of the first essay is broken up by forays into a history of colonial urban planning while in the final section, 'Politics', he does a close (and explicitly) literary analysis of two different kinds of text (Pope Francis's encyclical letter *Laudato Si'* and the Paris Agreement on climate change) in order to bring out their contrasting political significance. Ghosh likewise brings together a vast array of literary authors and genres from different places and times – from the folk epic of the Sundarbans to Barbara Kingsolver's *Flight Behavior*, from Homer to Abdel Rahman Munif's *Cities of Salt*. His challenge to the boundaries typically imposed by literary studies and to assumptions about form is but another example of the epistemological and narrative work that, he argues, is crucial in addressing the age of climate change and to the potential of politically engaged, creative non-fiction to enable this.

Non-fiction and Concealment

However, *The Great Derangement* also points towards some possible pitfalls in this use of non-fiction. These are entailed by the form's pedagogical aspect: the focus on enlightening an audience, on rendering 'versions of reality with sufficient power to compel ... belief' and on exposing the fraudulence of dominant narratives.[9] In the case of politically oriented non-fiction, such work often entails representing the 'truth' about a problem, its causes and possible courses of action. Yet, when it comes to climate change, this focus leads to at least four potential, connected limitations. First, the effort to represent the 'reality' of the problem clashes with climate change's many contradictions, its scope and scale, and its status as an 'unprecedented' threat. Second, the focus on 'truth' all too easily returns us to polarising, possibly useless debates about who is a 'realist' and who is a 'dupe'. Third, the drive to make an audience believe in a particular version of reality is in tension with Ghosh's relational mode of enquiry and his rejection of 'enlightenment'. Finally, the effort 'to be real' all too easily leads to a fatalistic closure of the future. In the final section of *The Great Derangement* there is an increasing sense of unavoidable collapse. This narrative trajectory is understandable; when it comes to enlightening an audience to the realities of climate change, based on what we know in the present, it is difficult to avoid telling a story of catastrophic checkmate. And, such closure is problematic. It potentially shuts down imagination, strengthens a sense of authoritative representation, encourages inaction and, in the process, ironically brings into question the very purpose of truth-telling.

The challenge of avoiding apocalyptic closure is apparent in Ghosh's conclusion. Despite the pessimistic narrative trajectory of the entire final section, with its particular focus on the uselessness or extreme limitations of current courses of action, he ends on an optimistic note. Following a reading of Pope Francis's encyclical letter as disrupting the forms of consciousness underpinning the great derangement, he claims that 'the increasing involvement of religious groups and leaders' in the struggle against climate change offers a basis for hope in collective action (p.159). He considers religious orientations as potentially resistant to the institutions and guiding principles of modernity: 'nation states'; 'economistic ways of thinking'; and the foreclosure of 'imagining nonlinear change'.

Perhaps most significantly, he argues that 'if already-existing communities and mass organizations will have to be in the forefront of the struggle', those organisations 'with religious affiliations possess the ability to mobilize people in far greater numbers than any others' (p.160). Such potential leads to a final hope; he 'would like to believe that out of the [struggle for action] will be born a generation that will be able to look upon the world' in ways that move beyond the derangement of the present and enable less suicidal ways of living and being (p.162).

This hopeful conclusion seems a stretch, given the rest of the book, and, in fact, might have the opposite effect. Anecdotally, my students in a course on environmental ethics were having none of it; given Ghosh's narrative of the problem, they found the solution and basis for hope disingenuous. Critics and interviewers have had a similar response (see, for example, Fa-ti Fan[10]), while Ghosh himself has acknowledged that 'the last section of *The Great Derangement* is "forced"': 'the only excuse I can offer is that I felt it necessary to look, as does nearly everyone who writes about climate change, for some rays of hope; very few of us can claim to possess the clarity of vision that allowed Martin Heidegger to say . . . "only a God can save us"'.[11]

The conclusion reveals a contradiction that stems from the intersection of climate change and the genre of politically engaged creative non-fiction. On the one hand, the effort to 'enlighten' an audience about the problem risks creating a fatalistic apocalyptic narrative. On the other, the drive to offer a 'realistic' basis for action – for what the audience can do once they 'see' – all too easily serves to further emphasise the gap between the unprecedented challenge of climate change and our current means of addressing it. The pedagogical aspects and expectations of political non-fiction can foreground a mismatch that strengthens the sense that there is nothing to be done and that the future is foreclosed. In turn, a sense of inevitability attenuates consideration of other possibilities and doubt about an authoritative apocalyptic narrative. In other words, Ghosh's choice of genre has some significant limitations in relation to the approach to cognition and perception that he claims we need to foster and with an acknowledgement of the resistance that climate change poses to 'enlightenment'.

Non-fiction and the Apostles of Apocalypse

Yet, Ghosh does *attempt* to resist both foreclosure of the future and, more generally, authoritative representational closure. For example, even in his conclusion, he acknowledges the possibility of not yet accessible forms of knowing and being that *might* emerge through collective action. The problems to be found at the intersection of non-fiction and climate change are, in this regard, actually more striking in the literary non-fiction of a growing number of authors who *explicitly assert*, some might even say embrace, the equation between fatalistic apocalyptic narrative and enlightenment. Like Ghosh, these authors aim to challenge the delusions they regard as embedded in existing solutions and modes of political action. However, unlike Ghosh, they are authoritative in their rejection of any hope and in their representation of mitigatory action as the clichéd moving of deckchairs on a sinking ship. They insist that acceptance of the inevitable is the only logical and ethical response; all we can do is bravely face the music. The novelist Jonathan Franzen does not 'have any hope that we can stop the change from coming. My only hope is that we can accept the reality in time to prepare for it humanely, and my only faith is that facing it honestly ... is better than denying it.'[12] Such 'climate nihilism', to use David Wallace-Wells's apt term,[13] may *seem* honest, consistent and logical given all that we know, yet it also reflects, more fully than *The Great Derangement*, the problems to be found at the intersection of climate change and non-fiction's focus on reality and truth. There is an increased projection of epistemological transcendence (they *know* what is coming) and of a singular enlightened perspective of the kind that Ghosh argues has both shaped and now prevents a grappling with climate change.

In turn, the sense of representational authority risks reinforcing the narratives of identity and delimitation that Ghosh associates with the coloniality of our derangement – despite these realists' denunciation of modernity's delusional perspectives. For example, they project a forceful separation between those who are enlightened and those who remain in darkness. This is particularly overt in poet Jan Zwicky's 'A Ship from Delos'. She asserts that we must face the fact that 'catastrophic global collapse is on the horizon' with equanimity and dignity. However, she says, we ought not to ask that those 'whose cultures have been systematically savaged by colonial empires' should 'reach for enlightenment' since 'they are simply trying to stay alive'; instead, it is up to 'those of us who do have enough to eat and the time and freedom to think' to 'see clearly what their situation is'.[14] This position is striking in its colonial paternalism and its repetition of precisely the notions of knowledge and enlightenment which Ghosh aims to challenge.

The reiteration of colonial discourse, despite the appearance of iconoclasm, is even more ubiquitous and subtle in the courses of action that the climate nihilists endorse. A prominent recommendation is withdrawal from forms of mitigatory action or collective political transformation. And what do we do when we withdraw? The answers tend to focus on individual redemption, the embrace of wildness/wilderness, and conservation. The poet Robert Bringhurst, for example, encourages us to spend 'a day in the wild – alone with reality' and to embrace ecocentric identification.[15] Meanwhile, Franzen focuses on 'the meaning' that 'the individual can still find' through biodiversity 'conservation work' in 'specific threatened habitats', informed by a 'novelistic' sensibility that foregrounds a delimited sense of place (unwittingly supporting Ghosh's arguments about the modern novel).[16] Novelist Paul Kingsnorth explicitly advocates in his essay 'Dark Ecology' that we 'withdraw', 'root' ourselves in 'places' and 'physical work in clean air', and build 'refuges' (in order to preserve what is of value).[17] In other words, the authoritative projection of an inescapable apocalyptic future enables a return to projects enshrined in forms of environmentalism and nature writing that have been brought into question by post-colonial ecocriticism and environmental justice advocacy. There is a retreat from the messiness of global processes and responsibilities and from people who are already displaced or do not have the luxury of withdrawal. Moreover, the equation between enlightenment and the voices of relatively privileged middle-class white authors from the global North shuts out the perspectives of those who might know the world 'otherwise' (a term used by the decolonial theorist Arturo Escobar).[18]

In the essay 'Elegy for a Country's Seasons', Zadie Smith offers one such alternative perspective in critiquing these apostles of apocalypse. She pointedly notes how a focus on who has a monopoly on truth and a concomitant intellectual detachment are the products of privilege. In the global North, weather events (e.g. superstorms and polar vortexes) are the basis of 'a game' between right and left about who is a realist. Meanwhile, for those in places like 'Jamaica or the many other perilous spots', the cascade of ever-worsening weather events 'do not fall . . . in the category of ontological argument'. With 'apocalypse . . . always usefully cast into the future', the fatalists have the luxury of focusing on an eschatological apocalyptic narrative and on the nostalgia of elegy, as well as of escape from uncertainty and responsibility to act:

> Sometimes the global, repetitive nature of [the] elegy is so exhaustively sad – and so divorced from any attempts at meaningful action – that you can't fail to detect in the elegists a fatalist liberal consciousness that has, when you get right down to it, as much of a perverse desire for the apocalypse as the evangelists we supposedly scorn.[19]

Resisting such narrative closure includes bringing close what seems distant and bringing the future into the present while claiming not to know that future or what the 'right' course of action might be. Smith ends by imagining what she will tell her granddaughter, for whom withdrawal and nostalgia may not be possible; in the process, she recognises not what will come but the danger that we will help fulfil a prophecy of doom by believing in our knowledge of the future. We need to use our sense of 'the intimate loss of the things we loved' not as traction for closure but as spur for action and for an open-ended temporal question; we need 'to turn from the elegiac *what have we done?* to the practical *what can we do?*'[20]

Smith's essay is not free from the dangers entailed by truth-telling. For example, the categorical rejection of apocalyptic narrative suppresses the possible need for it. Moving from the 'intimate loss of things we love' to the question '*what can we do*' may very well require the imagining of all that could be lost and 'the visions of apocalypse conjured by climate scientists'.[21] Furthermore, her concluding question cannot necessarily forestall the sense of dread and helplessness I so often see in my environmental studies students. Yet, unlike the nihilists, and like Ghosh, Smith does strive to keep the future open, instil doubt about what we can know, and imagine 'other' voices and narratives.

Conclusion

Although Ghosh does not discuss literature in his conclusion, he does at an earlier point allude to the possibility that fiction can play a beneficial role in the age of climate change because 'it makes possible the imagining of possibilities'; it enables us 'to approach the world in a subjunctive mode, to conceive of it *as if* it were other than it is'. Moreover, 'to imagine other forms of human existence is exactly the challenge that is posed by the climate crisis: for if there is any one thing that global warming has made perfectly clear it is that to think about the world only as it is amounts to a formula for collective suicide' (p.128). Yet, he argues, at the very moment when we need an imaginative movement, fiction remains entrapped within problematic modes of apprehension. He asserts that there is only a very slender library of novels that meet the required standards. And, given his analysis of deeply problematic and embedded modes of representation, one is left wondering how even those texts might still traffic in them. Something similar might be said of creative non-fiction. Even if there are many texts that address climate change in a non-oblique and sustained way, the library that might meet Ghosh's standards is narrow.

Furthermore, the question of whether or not potentially exemplary texts transcend the limitations of genre remains. In this sense, what we may most need is not the right library or genre but the relational ways of reading that Ghosh enacts regardless of the genre. For example, we might read fiction that has little to do with climate change or the Anthropocene in the light of non-fiction about climate change with its 'aura of the real' and its 'information carrying capacity'.[22] And, we may need to read non-fiction – including *The Great Derangement* – in the light of fiction's world-making potential and its attention to the construction of reality through language and narrative.

Notes

1. Amitav Ghosh, *The Great Derangement: Climate Change and the Unthinkable* (Chicago and London: University of Chicago Press, 2016), p.7. Subsequent references are cited parenthetically in the main text.
2. Jean Comaroff and John L. Comaroff, 'Theory from the South: Or, How Euro-America Is Evolving toward Africa', *Anthropological Forum: A Journal of Social Anthropology and Comparative Sociology* 22(2) (2012), 113–31.
3. Rob Nixon, *Slow Violence and the Environmentalism of the Poor* (Cambridge, MA: Harvard University Press, 2011), p.15.
4. Mark Doty, 'Bride in Beige' in David Lazar (ed.), *Truth in Nonfiction* (Iowa City: University of Iowa Press, 2008), p.13; John D'Agata, 'Mer-Mer: An Essay about How I Wish We Wrote Our Nonfictions', in Lazar, *Truth in Nonfiction*, pp.71–2.
5. Nixon, *Slow Violence*, p.26.
6. Ibid., p.24.
7. See Lynn Z. Bloom, 'Living to Tell the Tale: The Complicated Ethics of Creative Nonfiction', *College English* 65(3) (2003), 276–89 (pp.278, 286); Carl H. Klaus, 'Essayists on the Essay' in Chris Anderson (ed.), *Literary Nonfiction: Theory Criticism, Pedagogy* (Carbondale: Southern Illinois University Press, 1989), pp.155–75 (p.163).
8. Klaus, ibid., p.163.
9. Bloom, 'Living to Tell the Tale', p.278.
10. Fa-ti Fan, 'Imagining Ourselves Out of Modernity and Climate Crisis' in Julia Adeney Thomas et al., 'JAS Roundtable on Amitav Ghosh, "The Great Derangement: Climate Change and the Unthinkable"', *Journal of Asian Studies* 75(4) (2016), 929–55.
11. Amitav Ghosh, 'Author's Response' in Thomas et al., 'JAS Roundtable', 929–55.
12. Jonathan Franzen, *The End of the End of the Earth: Essays* (New York: Farrar, Straus and Giroux, 2018), p.22.

13. David Wallace-Wells, *The Uninhabitable Earth: Life After Warming* (New York: Tim Duggan Books, 2019), p.214.

14. Robert Bringhurst and Jan Zwicky, *Learning to Die: Wisdom in the Age of Climate Crisis* (Saskatchewan: University of Regina Press, 2018), p.52.

15. Ibid., pp.31, 38.

16. Franzen, *The End of the End of the Earth*, pp.21, 55, 64.

17. Paul Kingsnorth, 'Dark Ecology', *Orion* (2012), 13–14.

18. Arturo Escobar, 'Worlds and Knowledges Otherwise: The Latin American Modernity/Coloniality Research Program', *Cultural Studies* 21(2–3) (2007), 179–210.

19. Zadie Smith, *Feel Free: Essays* (New York: Penguin, 2018), p.17.

20. Ibid., p.19.

21. Ibid., p.15.

22. Nixon, *Slow Violence*, p.25.

CHAPTER 7

Theatre and Performance

Sabine Wilke

The recent turn to a renewed reflection on the role of catastrophe in literature and culture has received special attention from scholars in the environmental humanities. In particular, the connection between catastrophe and violence came into focus more prominently in an effort to understand how catastrophes have been framed rhetorically and culturally. By bringing the concept of the Anthropocene to this discussion, the connection between catastrophe, risk and culture can be explored as an effect of the increasing human influence on nature and the environment and the resulting more nuanced interconnectivity of nature–culture beyond already existing approaches to posthumanism and actor–network frames.[1] As documented in this *Companion*, scientists have recently identified the Anthropocene as the geologic epoch in which we now live and in which humankind has become a force that is capable of altering Earth systems.[2] The theatre, I argue in this chapter, is an effective venue for staging Anthropocene interweavings among humankind, natural environments and their complex interrelationships in a variety of modes that can be experienced by different audiences at different times and intensity levels.[3] Staged performances involve the spectator intellectually but also physically and emotionally. I show how the theatre functions as a laboratory for exploring the Anthropocene by way of proposing (in the first section) a reading of a German Expressionist play, the second part of Georg Kaiser's (1917–20) *Gas* trilogy from 1918, that focuses on the connection among catastrophe, violence and the negotiation of environmental risks in a culture of heightened risk assessment. In the second section, I consider how these consequences and risk assessments might be perceived from a culturally decentred position by focusing on a unique conversation that took place in the 1990s between the German tradition of political theatre that developed from Expressionism – Heiner Müller's most canonical political play *The Task* – and its redaction by Australian playwright Mudrooroo. In conclusion, I examine the results of this unique blending of

German political theatre with indigenous traditions and suggest the continued need for a post-colonial critique of the concept of the Anthropocene.[4]

In a recent essay, I explored Anthropocene theatre from a theoretical angle with examples from a few select contemporary performance pieces.[5] The concept of Anthropocene performance that I developed there captures new modalities of contemporary theatre that lay to rest the remnants of humanism that are so characteristic for the institution itself. Instead, Anthropocene performances embrace a new materialist practice that builds on a vision of global interconnectedness, a vision of human culture that embraces perspectives from deep history, an exploration of how bodies are entangled in their environments, and a broad sense of agency and crisis combined with an acute sense of volatility and risk. These performances begin where Erika Fischer-Lichte's project of re-enchanting the world with the help of a new aesthetics of the performative leaves off: they do not 'govern over nature – neither their own nor that surrounding them – but instead [the aesthetics of the performative] encourages them to enter into a new relationship with themselves and the world'.[6] While providing models for enjoying greater complexity in a new age,[7] Anthropocene performances no longer hide behind the energy systems that facilitate this complexity. While unleashing the transformative power of performance, they call attention to the collusion of aesthetic regimes based on fossil cultures with environmental depredation and other results of radically interconnected nature–culture and states of in-between.[8] A more refined understanding of the interwovenness of modern aesthetic practices and energy regimes is what is at stake when the challenge of the Anthropocene brings together projects of critical theory, ecology and performative practice. Georg Kaiser's *Gas* trilogy – comprising *The Coral*, *Gas I* and *Gas II* – and especially its second part serves as an example for rethinking theatre as a laboratory of the Anthropocene. It brings into focus Expressionist drama as an early articulation of a heightened connection among catastrophe, violence and risk assessment.

German Expressionism

In a thought-provoking opinion piece from 5 January 2014, Brad Evans blogged about 'The Promise of Violence in the Age of Catastrophe'.[9] He brings up the idea of resilience as a new dominant trope for thinking about the environment from an Anthropocene perspective, and how a vision of future catastrophes has to build on the ruins of the present –

referencing a framework from Walter Benjamin for thinking about catastrophe.[10] I am interested in the cultural aspects of how this concept of risk management helps us understand the connection between catastrophe and violence. Georg Kaiser's *Gas I* features a crisis, a catastrophic explosion in a gas factory, on centre stage. The play briefly investigates the events that led to the explosion, then turns to the theatrical happening of the catastrophe itself, and from there mostly focuses on the reconstruction of the factory and society in its aftermath. Through this theatrical lens and its performative aspects, the audience – because it is drawn into the play on an intellectual, physical and emotional level – is provided with experiences that empower it to analyse the connection between catastrophe and risk management strategies in an age of radical inflections of human culture and natural/environmental processes.

As a natural element used for energy but, at the same time, a manufactured element produced by workers in a factory, Kaiser's matter, gas, transcends the difference between natural and social catastrophes.[11] With this conflation of two modes of framing catastrophe, Kaiser's play effectively engages the deep entanglements that characterise life in the Anthropocene. To investigate the complexities of gas as matter, a variety of theatrical scenarios are created on stage, offering audience members a platform for experiencing the interconnections between catastrophe and violence intellectually, physically and emotionally. Theatre transforms these scenarios into artfully shaped images and tropes. As such, theatre 'serves as a cultural archive which mediates between humans and ecology and facilitates strategies of renaturalization through the retranslation of nature's language and through reflection on human embeddedness in nature'.[12]

Watching a performance of Kaiser's play amounts to what Kate Rigby recently called, as a more modern way of framing eco-catastrophes, not endgames but 'dancing with disaster'.[13] Rigby shows how literary works invite ethical reflections and complex human responses to the age's calamities by framing the stories we tell about them. Theatrical scenarios of disasters heighten the audience's ability to experience culture as a material-discursive process. Performances of catastrophes emerge 'as something that arises from the complex and sometimes chaotic interaction of a diversity of human and nonhuman factors and actants, rather than as something that is neither divinely orchestrated, purely natural, or exclusively societal in its etiology'.[14] As a blueprint for an Anthropocene performance, Kaiser's catastrophe draws close attention to these complex interactions by having some of the characters dance with disaster in their renewed appreciation of dependencies and entanglements in Anthropocene futures.[15]

The trilogy is rarely performed on stage in its entirety. However, it was recently shown at the Deutsches Theater, Göttingen in a stage version that emphasised the environmental risk of gas as the sole source of energy for any given society. In that version, gas stands in for pure energy, that is, an addictive drug pervasive in all industrialised societies that depend on it for growth. *Gas I* asks its readers and its audience to choose between enlightenment and catastrophe. It was received by this contemporary audience mainly in terms of articulating a critique of alienation, mass society and increasing social impoverishment.[16] A more modern ecocritical perspective on the problem of industrial automation and the systematic production of violence in political conflicts and warfare might also enable us to see beyond the limits of the aesthetic models developed in German Expressionism for staging catastrophes and challenging established positions of environmental risks.

Gas I stages catastrophe with an explosion at the end of Act One. The remaining four acts are then dedicated to the discussion of this event and how to move forward among the surviving characters and remaining stakeholders. Read as Anthropocene performance, the play provides critical commentary on these positions from the perspective of a vision for a new materialist practice, a sense of global interconnectedness and a minimal ethics for the appreciation of deeper entanglements that is required in order to reveal its ecocritical dimension.[17] As an Anthropocene performance, the Expressionist technique of collage – with its specific focus on character and speech – in the end complicates the individual positions presented on stage and signals towards the development of a broader sense of agency and crisis. As an artistic technique that assembles different forms and materials, collages have the unique advantage of juxtaposing individual dramatic characters and thematic events without having to bring them to a resolution, tragic or otherwise. Crises can thus be perceived as the product of difference more clearly and transparently.

One of the key moments in which this theatrical technique can be observed is a scene in Act Three in which a number of characters referred to as Gentlemen in Black are trying to convince The Billionaire's Son of the fact that he should fire the Engineer who invented the formula for producing gas. These Gentlemen in Black intend to continue using the same old formula thereby ending the strike of the workers who are demanding the Engineer's resignation:

FIFTH GENTLEMAN IN BLACK: A new Engineer – and the same old formula!
THIRD GENTLEMAN IN BLACK: And thereby the strike comes to an end.
FIRST GENTLEMAN IN BLACK: We are assembled here to present our demands – the
    dismissal of the Engineer!
BILLIONAIRE'S SON (STARING): – Have you forgotten – are you still deaf – is the
    thunder and the crushing no longer rolling on your ears – are you no longer
    shaken upon your seats? – are you paralyzed?
SECOND GENTLEMAN IN BLACK: The catastrophe is a dark page –
FOURTH GENTLEMAN IN BLACK: We book it to profit and loss –
FIFTH GENTLEMAN IN BLACK: And turn over a new leaf![18]

This 'dark page' has to be turned over, yet the turning leads either to the
proto-ecological vision that the Billionaire's Son articulated in an earlier
scene – a life and society before gas – or to the necessary repetition of
catastrophe and violence. As Anthropocene performance, Kaiser's theatre
confronts its audience with an impasse that the characters on stage are
unable to overcome since the problem lies in the energy regime that fuels
the performance itself.

In this context, we might consider the theatrical stage from the perspective of cultural ecology. Hubert Zapf's *Literature as Cultural Ecology:
Sustainable Texts* outlines a new approach of reading literary texts as spaces
in which the question of how we want to live in a future society is
considered from a variety of perspectives.[19] Dramatic texts and theatrical
performances that stage risk scenarios encourage us to step back from the
positions taken by some of the stage characters and develop models of
interconnected being-with that embrace more complex Anthropocene
futures. Even the green utopia offered by the Billionaire's Son as an
alternative to reconstructing the factory that exploded can be understood
as continuing to hold on to an anthropocentric worldview based on
humanism. The theatre as laboratory of the Anthropocene, however,
encourages us to go beyond humanism and intellectually, physically and
emotionally explore greater complexities. An ecocritical reading of the play
urges us to look beyond character and figure constellations, foreground
questions of energy and ultimately experience the stage as a system of
cultural ecology.

Given that *Gas I* focuses on debates about energy and the catastrophic
consequences of a failed modern technology, it is perhaps not surprising
that the play still references the classical tradition of European drama. The
list of figures, however, breaks away from that tradition and affirms the
contemporary tendency of rethinking character from a perspective of
typification and as defined, therefore, by a lack of depth, psychology and

motivation. Act One, for example, presents the dramatic enactment of the catastrophe from the perspective of the event itself. The explosion is first referenced by several characters, then described again in the metatextual stage descriptions, and eventually performed on stage eliciting intellectual as well as physical responses from the audience. This first act takes place in a vast square room, the Billionaire's Son's office, where the 'rear wall is composed entirely of glass in large squares' through which one can see 'in a murky violet light, the steep close-thronged shapes of great chimney-stacks from which flame and smoke pour in horizontal lines'.[20] This serves as the backdrop for a discussion between the Clerk and the Gentleman in White about the economic conditions behind the production of this new, revolutionary energy that fuels millions of machines and is produced by workers around the clock.

When the Gentleman in White poses a question about the risks of this new energy, the Clerk is unable to give an answer. However, the performance puts him in a position in which he has to observe the explosion through a glass window. With this device, the Clerk is confronted with the consequences of his cluelessness – and is showcased dancing with disaster. The audience is, in turn, put into a position from which they can watch the unravelling of the catastrophe in the background and, at the same time, observe the Clerk's 'dance' on stage: 'A terrible sibilance tears asunder the silence without. A grunding thunder bursts—the smokestacks crack and fall. A silence, empty and smokeless, ensues. The great glass windows rattle into the room in a cascade of fragments.'[21] In the theatre, the physical explosion of the gas factory cannot only be seen on stage, it can be heard and physically experienced by the audience as thunder bursts; it can even be felt as a consequence of the pressure that shatters the glass, thus eliciting tangible physical responses in the audience. Finally, the explosion becomes part of the report of the Engineer and of one of the Workmen in ways that graphically echo this physical response:

WORKMAN: Report from Shed Eight – Central – white cat burst – red eyes torn open – yellow mouth gaping – humps up crackling back – grows round – snaps away girders – lifts up roof – bursts – sparks! (*Sitting down in the middle of floor and striking about him*): Chase away the cat – Shoo! Shoo! – smash her jaws – shoo! Shoo! – bury her eyes – they flame – hammer down her back – hammer it down – thousands of fists! – It's swelling, swelling – growing fat – fatter – Gas out of every crack – every tube! (*Once more half erecting himself*): Report from Central – the white cat has – exploded! (*He collapses and lies prone.*)[22]

This excessive repetition of the description and staging of the explosion at the end of Act One creates a theatrical scenario that is quite literally engaging the two main tropes of energy cultures identified by ecocritic Fredrick Buell – exuberance and catastrophe.[23] An exuberant aesthetics shapes the audience's perception of catastrophe as performed on stage and their reaction. The scene ends with the melodramatic death of the Workman who collapses in front of the Billionaire's Son who, in uttering the last words of the act ('O mankind!'), evokes humanism as a framework for a society beyond gas.[24]

I suggest that we can read this scene in light of Ulrich Beck's insights about modern risk societies which, according to Beck, are on their way to a different, more global modernity.[25] A reflexive form of modernity is characterised, however, by the systematic production of inherent risks that are themselves potentially reflexive. They can aid and/or endanger the process of modernisation. The risks of a reflexive modernity envisioned by Beck encompass the collapse of all central institutions, environmental catastrophes of various kinds, and increasingly drastic social and environmental injustices that lack any conceptual framework capable of regulating and containing these risks. The conditions of nature, the environment and modern society at the beginning of the twentieth century were the foundation for these inherent contradictions in the process of modernisation.[26] The dramatic action that unfolds post-apocalyptically over the remaining four acts of the play shows how this process of self-reflexive modernisation needs to be realised by the audience in a reception of the play that builds on the intellectual, physical and emotional reactions elicited by the performance.

Act Two takes place in the same room seventeen days after the explosion. The Billionaire's Son – according to Sol Gittleman a 'Zarathustrian character'[27] – is working on an aesthetic concept for his utopian vision for a global and sustainable society and culture, post-gas. He wants to use the tragic occurrence of the explosion as an incentive for radical change: the White Horror, as the explosion is referred to by the characters, can 'fling us forward a thousand years'.[28] To take such a radical step forward, the Billionaire's Son advocates that society revert to a condition before gas and adopt an economic model that is independent from it – a reversal towards utopia that voluntarily abandons the technical progress of modern society. Yet, the workmen demand that the engineer be fired and the factory rebuilt to produce gas with the same formula that led to the explosion. Creating an impasse, the play provides the Billionaire's Son with a platform to articulate his ideas. When he shows the Engineer his drawings, however, the Engineer is unable to make sense of them:

BILLIONAIRE'S SON: These green lines? (*The Engineer stares at the plans.*) Can you guess? Have you no suspicions? You sly duck! You feeder on figures! Are you puzzled by the multi-coloured riddle? You are blind – colour-blind from the eternal monotony of your doings – up to this very day. Now a new day is born to greet you, and smiles upon you like springtime. Open your eyes and let them sweep over this domain. The vary-coloured earth is all about you (*Pointing to the plans.*) The green lines – streets bordered by trees. The red, the yellow, the blue circles – open space full of flowering plants, sprouting from smooth lawns. The squares – houses, human dwellings with a small holding of land – shelters. Mighty streets go forth here – penetrating, conquering under domains, great roads trodden by pilgrims, our pilgrims, who shall preach simplicity – to us – to all!

(*His gestures are grandiose.*)[29]

The Billionaire's Son praises the colours of nature to which humans have become immune. He invokes the spring-like new beginning of a new era, the greening of old industrial sites, simple homes surrounded by small yards and mighty arterials that lead outside of the city into untouched wilderness. His model rests on the principle of reawakening the deteriorated senses in humans that were 'lost' during the process of industrial modernisation. Nonetheless, in his model, nature continues to be subdued and functionalised for the aims of humans. It is a vision that turns the clock back to a time before intensive energy consumption; but where the imagined future remains haunted by the past. In this laboratory of the Anthropocene, a model that rests on advocating reduced consumption habits is, however, presented in terms of an aesthetic project that lacks a corresponding viable ethics or framework for a global vision of interconnectedness.

The model of a return to pastoral conditions propagated by the Billionaire's Son becomes centre stage in Act Three in which different stakeholders and representatives from a variety of social strata appear on stage. The workmen are on strike because the Engineer has not been fired yet; the representatives from the business community demand more gas; a consensus is emerging among these different groups that the factory should be rebuilt and the same formula used to produce gas in the hope that – with improved technology to be developed sometime in the future – the distance between explosions can be widened. Confronted, though, with the Billionaire's Son dismissing this project of reconstruction,[30] the representatives of the various stakeholders regurgitate the classic arguments against change: the costs would be ruinous, energy production would need to be reduced, technological progress would be endangered and the socio-economic model it rests on would collapse.[31] Even slowing down energy production is dismissed. The eco-utopian humanism proposed by the Billionaire's Son is dismissed. Instead, the Gentlemen in Black give him a deadline for the resignation of the Engineer. At the end of this scene, the Billionaire's Son is sitting at his drawing table, lonely and defeated; meanwhile, the Officer – his son-in-law who lost all his money to gambling and who now turns to him for financial help – shoots himself with his revolver when the Billionaire's Son refuses to bail him out. This turn in the plot refocuses the action on stage away from abstract socio-political debate and towards the familial, thereby eliciting powerful emotional responses from the audience. As a result, the concept of a return to pre-industrial society is never developed on stage. The performance leaves this model behind, yet, because of this, elicits further reflection. For the project of a vision for global interconnectedness and deeper entanglements will need to be realised, it is implied, by the audience, in later steps of building complex Anthropocene futures. The Billionaire's Son is, himself, unable to convince the rest of society about the benefits of rethinking the social and cultural modes of existence beyond gas since his model lacks an ethics for the future.

Act Four introduces new voices on stage as counterweights to the opinions of the Gentlemen in Black that dominated the third act. The women, however, speak not as representatives of their sex but as sisters, wives and mothers, thereby emphasising again the familial over the socio-political and socio-cultural. The workmen respond correspond-ingly in their roles as sons, husbands and brothers and all these voices eventually come together in demanding the dismissal of the Engineer. At the end of the scene, the voice of the Billionaire's Son speaks to the assembly and encourages them to demand more rather than less: 'Was there a single man in all the works who was whole and sound? What havoc could the Explosion wreak upon you? – You who were shattered before the walls fell – you who were bleeding from many wounds before the crash came ….'[32] He addresses the workers as human beings and offers them again his pastoral concept of small domains and green alleyways:

> Pastures broad and green shall be your domains. The settlement shall cover the ashes and the wreckage which now cover land. You are dismissed from bondage and from profit-making. You are settlers – with only simple needs and with the highest rewards –you are men – Men![33]

Interestingly the Billionaire's Son establishes a connection between the economy and a culture of energy dependence. However, a reduction in desires, needs and consumption habits that is tied to a rise in symbolic capital for humanity will remain tied to an anthropocentric value system unless accompanied by a viable ethics for the future. The Engineer, on the other hand, is able to convince the masses to end their strike and embrace the reconstruction of the factory by calling them heroes, the winners of the world, and the masters of nature and technology: 'How can you become peasants again – after you have been workmen! – Do we not expect you to climb still higher? The peasant in you has been overcome – and now the Workman must be overcome – and Man must be the goal!'[34] Act Four ends with the Billionaire's Son alone on stage reflecting on his vision for humanity – a vision that evidently needs to be protected from human beings themselves. His failure to sell this vision to the workmen is tied to the lack of a common narrative for a sense of purpose in a complex Anthropocene future. As a memorial, it represents a ruin in the landscape of humanism that needs to be overcome.

That vision is not even part of the action and discussion in Act Five, however. To get to this point, we are witness to a scene in which the Billionaire's Son, who is still resisting the idea of firing the Engineer, has a conversation with a government official in which the idea of risk management is crucial. We learn that the government only accepts so-called facts, not alternatives to facts (i.e. interpretations). Future options and possible future catastrophes cannot be considered as facts. With the help of a power of attorney, the Billionaire's Son is then removed from running his own factory, and the government takes over the reconstruction project. Subsequently, the play's actual pastoral ending is a seemingly idyllic family scene that features the dispossessed Billionaire's Son and his widowed daughter and which links the project of ecological humanism not with social change and a new human condition but with notions of bourgeois subjectivity, family and rebirth. In other words, while Expressionist theatre can provide an early articulation of how theatre can function as a laboratory of the Anthropocene, if read from an ecocritical perspective, it is unable to perform the reflexive turn that Beck's world risk society calls for, leaving us instead with models of modern tragedy still inspired by bourgeois family norms. For a truly radical critique of theatre and performance in the Anthropocene, it is necessary to introduce a response to this model from a decentred perspective.

Decentring Political Theatre

In 1991, the Sydney German Studies scholar Gerhard Fischer embarked on an interesting project: he asked Western Australian playright Mudrooroo to write a play about Aboriginal protest of the proclamation of the Australian Republic on 26 January 2001 and to frame that protest as an indigenous response to Heiner Müller's play *The Task* (or *The Commission* as it was newly translated by Fischer).[35] The East German playwright Müller followed in Georg Kaiser's and Bertolt Brecht's footsteps in shaping post-war German political theatre. *The Task* (1979) features three French Revolutionaries who receive a task or commission from the revolutionary government to incite a rebellion among slaves in slave-holder societies in the Caribbean and who ultimately founded a 'Negro Republic'; yet, by the time they receive their task/commission the French Revolution is over.[36] In other words, Müller stages the problematic aspects of political theatre in post-revolutionary times where it is unclear who gives, receives and executes orders. In this play, Müller also experiments with race and its representation on the European stage. One of his revolutionaries is a descendent of slaves and the characters debate the complex issue of black masks and white actors among themselves but from a Western European perspective. Müller's play is, then, an early articulation of a postmodern Western theatre aesthetic as well as an excellent example of post-dramatic theatre in a post-revolutionary political context.[37]

What happens when this post-revolutionary scenario is rewritten from a transcultural and post-colonial perspective? Fischer explains:

> Mudrooroo constructs a frame play around *Der Auftrag:* on the eve of the proclamation of the Republic, planned for 2001, a group of Aboriginal lay performers – they are young, middle-class Black professionals – are rehearsing Müller's play, to be publicly performed as part of a protest demonstration against the declaration of a republic that does not address the aspirations of the Aboriginal people of Australia. In the end, the Aboriginal performers take a vote, and decide – with a majority of one – not to continue with *Der Auftrag.* Ironically, the whole of Müller's text has by then been shown within the fictional rehearsal that constitutes the plot of the frame-play.[38]

To devise a play that confronts the Western European perspective of Müller's script, Mudrooroo adds a second frame in which the historical material and the political nature of the project are contained within a realistic play-by-play narrative that finds interesting intersections with political protest over Aboriginal rights. By adding a future dimension, that is, setting the play ten years from now, Mudrooroo shows how the past projects into the future and how the future projects back into the present.[39] In this case, Aboriginal performers represent invisible spirits in the form of giant white moths (*djangara*) thus making visible deep entanglements between human history and deeper histories. The *djangara* performers envelop slaves, the audience and musicians, as well as characters within the play, into a dance sequence. They dance around the stage playing discordant music, providing commentary and supporting the action on stage. Aboriginalising Müller becomes a theatrical project in which voices are given to those who have been denied one. Specifically, 'the *djangara* are on stage at all time, observing and commenting on the action. In this, and the physicality of the performance, they establish a link between twentieth-century Aboriginal culture, more specifically contemporary dance theatre, and the age-old traditions of the dream time.'[40] By bringing the European tradition of political theatre into conversation with contemporary Aboriginal dance theatre, the performance presents a dramatic re-enactment of complex histories that signal new departures to help address complicated futures. In other words, Mudrooroo extends Müller's historical frames (1794, 1808 and 1979) by adding a mythological frame and a perspective on linking characters that goes even further back into deep history to document and bring to life the continuity of a cultural tradition that dates back tens of thousands of years. Through the performance of this mythological frame, performers and audience alike are able to experience this tradition intellectually, physically and emotionally and to envision a sense of interconnectedness based on a much broader sense of agency and crisis.

Aside from the dance performance of the *djangara*, a vision of theatrical ritual emerges in which Aboriginal performers appropriate for themselves the roles of Müller's revolutionaries: 'There are clapsticks and didgeroos, three of the performers take up position in the middle of the circle, two male and one female; they begin to put on the clothes of white people while the others watch and assist. Slowly the three are dressed entirely in white, with shoes and gloves to match, finally white masks are put on to complete the metamorphisis.'[41] This reversal of the European theatrical tradition of blackface is part of a vision for theatre as laboratory of the Anthropocene that mixes different historical levels, places and performance styles in order to experiment with a model of staging complex futures that, articulated through a highly physical mode of performance, embrace deeper entanglements of humans, their immediate histories and non-human environments.

I suggest that we read this performance through the lens of transcultural adaptation and/or post-colonial theory in an attempt to highlight indigenous agency, showcase the loss of dominance of the Western framework over indigenous material, and add complexity to the portrayal of the shape of political struggle in a post-colonial context: 'Whereas in Müller's text the Black characters, with the exception of Sasportas, are extras, nameless and voiceless slaves, ... the six Aboriginal characters in Mudrooroo's frame play are complex contradictory persons with minds of their own and effortless eloquence.'[42] While this addition of diversity and complexity constitutes an important perspective for rethinking the shape of political drama, let me suggest by way of conclusion that an Anthropocene perspective adds further nuance to a transcultural and/or post-colonial framework for interpreting theatre and performance. For what Mudrooroo's adaptation and reframing of Müller's revolutionary play illustrates is a keen sense of deep entanglement among different life forms, time frames, spirits and realities beyond rather firm and nostalgic notions of the local, the native or the indigenous body and culture. These entanglements are examples of Anthropocene interweavings that highlight the common responsibility of human culture to embrace deep history and geology as an additional perspective for analysing the meaning and functioning of individual cultures and societies, indigenous or otherwise.[43]

This conversation between German Expressionism, the European political tradition, and Aboriginal protest cultures and dance traditions creates an awareness of a state of being in-between and liminality that does not rely on naively recreating the pastoral sense of local identity envisaged by the Billionaire's Son in Kaiser's play. This awareness participates in the production of an Anthropocene framework for the creation of participatory forms of ethics, politics and culture that interweave European theatrical/ historical discourse and dramatic structures with Aboriginal frames without sidestepping the display and critique of power relations. At the same time, such frames address the communal responsibility of humanity for the future of the Earth. Theatre emerges then as an important platform and medium for the discussion and display of these dynamics.

Notes

1. See Jeremy Davies, *The Birth of The Anthropocene* (Oakland: University of California Press, 2016), p.6.
2. See Paul J. Crutzen and Eugene F. Stoermer, 'The Anthropocene', *IGBP Newsletter* 41 (2000): 17–18; Jan Zalasiewicz, Mark Williams, Will Steffen and Paul J. Crutzen, 'The New World of the Anthropocene', *Environmental Science & Technology* 44 (2010), 2228–31.

3. This chapter was written during my fellowship period at the Centre for Interweaving Performance Cultures at the FU Berlin. I thank the directors, Erika Fischer-Lichte and Gabriele Brandstetter, for granting me this extraordinary experience.

4. See Sabine Wilke, 'Anthropocene Poetics: Aesthetics and Ethics in a New Geological Age' in Helmuth Trischler (ed.), *Envisioning the Future of the Age of Humans, Rachel Carson Center Perspectives* 3 (2013), 67–74; Sabine Wilke and Ninad Bondre, 'Beyond the Anthropocene's Common Humanity', *Geocritique* (14 May 2014), geocritique.org.

5. Sabine Wilke, 'Critical Theory and Ecology: The Shape of Performance in the Anthropocene', *Telos* 183 (2018), 25–46.

6. Erika Fischer-Lichte, *The Transformative Power of Performance: A New Aesthetics* [trans. Jain Saskia Iris] (New York and London: Routledge, 2008), pp.206ff.

7. See Jens Kersten, 'The Enjoyment of Complexity: A New Political Anthropology for the Anthropocene?' in Trischler (ed.), *Envisioning the Future*, pp.39–55.

8. See Erika Fischer-Lichte, 'Interweaving Cultures in Performance: Different States of Being In-Between', *New Theatre Quarterly* 25 (2010), 391–401.

9. Brad Evans, 'The Promise of Violence in the Age of Catastrophe' (5 January 2014), www.truth-out.org.

10. See Walter Benjamin, 'On the Concept of History' in *Selected Writings* (eds.) Howard Ellands and Michael W. Jennings (Cambridge: Belknap, 1972), vol. 4, pp.389–400.

11. Early articulations of some of the ideas in this section of the chapter were first presented in an essay on '"Die Katastrophe ist ein schwarzes Blatt": Katastrophenmanagement und Umweltethik in Georg Kaisers Schauspiel *Gas*', *Monatshefte* 107(4) (2015), 590–604.

12. Gabriele Dürbeck, 'Writing Catastrophes: Interdisciplinary Perspectives on the Semantics of Natural and Anthropogenic Disasters', *Ecozon@* 3 (2012), 1–9 (p.3).

13. Kate Rigby, *Dancing with Disaster: Environmental Histories, Narratives, and Ethics in Perilous Times* (Charlottesville: University of Virginia Press, 2015), p.15.

14. Ibid., p.50.

15. Ibid., p.177.

16. See Peter K. Tyson, *The Reception of Georg Kaiser (1915–45): Text and Analysis* (Frankfurt: Lang, 1984), vol. 1, pp.15ff.

17. See Joanna Zylinska, *Minimal Ethics for the Anthropocene* (Ann Arbor, MI: Open Humanities Press, 2014).

18. Georg Kaiser, *Gas I: A Play in Five Acts* [trans. Herman Scheffauer] (New York: Ungar, 1963), pp.53–4.

19. See Hubert Zapf, *Literature as Cultural Ecology: Sustainable Texts* (Rochester: Bloomsbury Academic, 2016), pp.15ff.

20. Kaiser, *Gas I*, p.9.

21. Ibid., p.20.
22. Ibid., p.21.
23. See Fredrick Buell, 'A Short History of Oil Cultures: The Marriage of Catastrophe and Exuberance', *Journal of American Studies* 42(2) (2012), 273–93.
24. Kaiser, *Gas I*, p.21.
25. See Ulrich Beck, *World at Risk* (London: Polity, 2009), pp.15ff.
26. Ibid., pp.154ff.
27. Sol Gittleman, 'Fritz Lang's *Metropolis* and Georg Kaiser's *Gas I*: Film, Literature, and the Crisis of Technology', *Die Unterrichtspraxis* 12 (1979), 29.
28. Kaiser, *Gas I*, p.23.
29. Ibid., p.36.
30. 'Never again shall smokestacks belch here! Never again shall machines pound and hammer. Never again shall the cry oft he doomed be mingled with the – unavoidable – Explosion!' Ibid., pp.55–6.
31. Ibid., pp.56–7.
32. Ibid., p.75.
33. Ibid., pp.77–8.
34. Ibid., pp.81–2.
35. See Gerhard Fischer, 'Performing Multicultural and Post-Colonial Identities: Heiner Müller "Aboriginized" by Mudrooroo (With a Postscript on Mudrooroo's Dilemmas)' in Wolfgang Kloos (ed.), *Across the Lines: Intertextuality and Transcultural Communication in the New Literature in English* (Amsterdam: Rodopi, 1998), p.215. See also Gerhard Fischer, '"Twoccing" *Der Auftrag* to Black Australia: Heiner Müller "Aboriginized" by Mudrooroo' in Gerhard Fischer (ed.), *Heiner Müller: ConTEXTS and HISTORY: A Collection of Essays from the Sydney German Studies Symposium 1994* (Tübingen: Stauffenburg, 1995), pp.141–64; Gerhard Fischer (ed. with Paul Behrendt and Brian Syron) *The Mudrooroo/Müller Project: A Theatrical Casebook* (Kensington, Australia: New South Wales University Press, 1993).
36. See Heiner Müller, 'The Task' in Carl Weber (ed. and trans.), *Hamletmachine and Other Texts for the Stage* (New York: Performing Arts Journal Publications, 1984), pp.81–101. See also Arlene A. Teraoka, *The Silence of Entropy or Universal Discourse: The Postmodernist Poetics of Heiner Müller* (Bern: Peter Lang, 1985), pp.73ff.
37. See Hans-Thies Lehmann, *Postdramatic Theatre*, (ed.) Karen Jürs-Munby (London and New York: Routledge, 2006).
38. Fischer, 'Performing Multicultural and Post-Colonial Identities', p.217.
39. See Fischer, *The Mudrooroo/Müller Project*, p.17.
40. Ibid., p.217.
41. Ibid., p.12.
42. Ibid., p.218.
43. See Dipesh Chakrabarty, 'The Climate of History: Four Theses', *Critical Inquiry* 35(2) (2009), 197–222 (p.198).

CHAPTER 8

Interspecies Design

Stanislav Roudavski

Design is a distinct form of practice with a typical focus on human aspirations for products, buildings, infrastructure, urban spaces, services and land use. As such, design affects all planetary environments, societies and the capabilities of individual humans. This chapter begins by establishing design as both a force responsible for the current situation and a primary concern of the future. Next, the chapter uses cities as a characteristic example of significantly modified habitats that are simultaneously biological and cultural. The cultures within such habitats combine the behaviours and traditions of many lifeforms. Consequently, the chapter argues that design approaches to the management of future habitats – conceptualised as 'interspecies design' – must engage with non-human as well as human cultures. This has implications for theoretical and practical engagements with the Anthropocene, pointing to the significance of design and the need for a transformation of design practices.

Design in the Future

By now, the concept of the Anthropocene is familiar in many disciplines. Conceptualisations of a pervasive human impact emerged at least in the early nineteenth century and developed in the work of Carl Ritter (1810s), George Perkins Marsh (1860s), Jacques Élisée Reclus (1870s), Vladimir Vernadsky (noosphere, 1920s) and Nikolai Vereshchagin (technocene, 1970s), among others. However, the proposal to formalise the Anthropocene as a geological epoch at the turn of the twenty-first century resulted in much more attention. The desire to highlight the detrimental impact of human activities and motivate remedial action underpinned this proposal. As one of the authors wrote in 2002: '[M]ankind will remain a major environmental force for many millennia. A daunting task lies ahead for scientists and engineers to guide society towards environmentally sustainable management.'[1] This chapter

147

understands the term Anthropocene as a label for the situation where human activities substantially affect the Earth system. Two characteristics of the Anthropocene are especially relevant. Firstly, the Anthropocene is important as the prevailing condition of the future: future cultures (human and non-human) will have to live within its effects. Secondly, many of the Anthropocene's effects are undesirable. A reasonable response is to change current human practices.[2]

The focus on the future and the responsibility for managing change are – also – the key characteristics of design. This point requires elaboration because public opinion associates design with styles and forms of objects. Business practices cultivate this focus as a marketing instrument. For them, human users are factors that determine the look and comfort of 'pleasurable products'.[3] The end goal of such design is financial gain.

Theories of design advance beyond such popular definitions. A common goal is to encompass all possible design practices, as is evident in an early and popular definition by Herbert A. Simon: 'Everyone designs who devises courses of action aimed at changing existing situations into preferred ones.'[4] Simon believed that all professions design. He included engineering, architecture, business, law and medicine as examples. His list stopped there. For him, scientists were not designers: 'Design . . . is the principal mark that distinguishes the professions from the sciences.'[5]

This focus on paid occupations makes Simon's influential definition inadequate because it makes presumptions that do not match the observable effects of the Anthropocene. For example, Simon's definition assumes that a preferred future state can exist. This is not always the case. Situations where a preferred state is attainable are increasingly rare. As a rule, destroyed ecosystems, like extinct species, cannot return to life. Ecosystem dynamics and biological evolution are irreversible. Novel ecologies such as those that exist in urban parks might be more attractive than treeless cityscapes or monoculture farming. However, such environments almost never constitute preferred states. They are compromises that are substantially less desirable than pristine ecosystems. People might prefer such ecosystems, but no design can make them attainable.

Furthermore, Simon's definition presumes the existence of professionals who can distinguish existing situations from preferred states. However, this is always difficult and often impossible. Modification of ecosystems leads to complex, often surprising results. In most cases, the only way to understand the consequences is to obtain new evidence through experimentation. The job of producing such evidence rests with the scientists and other experts that he excludes.

Crucially, Simon's definition of design presumes the possibility of an agreement between designers and those they design for. However, such agreements are rare. Biologically and culturally, forms of life can and do have incompatible interests. In most cases, relationships between interests, life histories, abiotic events and other factors prevent stakeholders from agreeing on a preferred future state. In a large city, these stakeholders might include coffee-loving bankers, elderly homeless, rats and birds. For example, peregrine falcons struggled in 1930s New York. During the 1940s, their wintering population in the city increased because the war effort removed pigeon fanciers, falconers and other interfering humans. In this period, female falcons seemed at home in the city and developed territorial attractions to certain skyscrapers. However, with the 'golden age' of the 1950s, peregrine numbers dropped and by 1961 the entire population was extirpated.[6] Tom Cade and others bred and reintroduced falcons in the 1970s and 1980s. In this post-DDT era, New York provided artificial shelters and bright lights that illuminated prey. The new generation of falcons took to the city and their return continues to attract media attention and public support.[7] The measure of this success at the time of writing is sixteen couples.[8] By contrast, up to 230,000 birds per year die in New York through collisions with buildings. In the United States as a whole, the annual figure can be as high as one billion.[9] Such deadly interactions between the drive for human occupation density and the migratory routes of avian life indicate that it is too early to celebrate urban interspecies harmony. These examples show that designerly agreements between birds and humans are not impossible, but neither are they easy. In many cases, human and non-human stakeholders struggle to cohabit. Even where co-presence is obvious, communication about possible futures or necessary actions will remain challenging. As a result, all relevant (human and non-human) stakeholders are unlikely to be present when professionals assess states or devise plans.

The term 'preferred future state' suggests a goal within a configuration of some situation, a state of affairs. A city without overcrowding, or sprawl, or slums would be an example. Design Studies inherits the notion of states from Future Studies. Neither field defines this notion clearly. In practice, states are local, limited and pragmatic. A developer's brief for a high-rise building might ask for the maximum possible area of office space within a predefined footprint and fixed budget. This confines designing to a search for configurations that can satisfy given conditions.

The focus on 'states' in the 'preferred future state' conception is also problematic. States are subjective. Designers or clients can attempt to specify future states to represent problems and ideas. However, resulting specifications are invariably partial and discontinuous. Design theories that build on Simon's definition operate with cultural constructs that remain coherent only within narrow boundaries. Such boundaries confine design projects in time, space and complexity. Professional designers begin by excluding most of the world and proceed to define states and devise courses of actions within these artificial confines. Professional projects often inherit such exclusions from powerful stakeholders in the form of briefs, laws, regulations, disciplinary training and budgets. Because Simon's definition depends on exclusions, it cannot be compatible with the demands of the Anthropocene and its global, continuous, inescapable impacts.

Other design theorists have sought to expand the notion of design to include 'everyday design'. Harold Nelson and Erik Stolterman propose that '[d]esign is a natural and ancient human ability – the first tradition among many traditions of human inquiry and action. Everyone is designing most of the time – whether they are conscious of it, or not.'[10] Klaus Krippendorff calls this approach to design 'the realization of everyday life'.[11] Design theory that follows these trends seeks to apply 'design approaches' to a broader spectrum of activities, including management and governance. However, much of this focuses on professional services and capitalist business practices. As a result of recent expansion, more paid consultants claim that they use 'design thinking'. Textbooks advocate 'design-focused problem solving' for organisational management,[12] and practitioners within the lucrative field of business leadership argue that design thinking is the best tool for creating empathetic and responsive organisational cultures.[13] Reframing such practices as types of 'designing' validates the limitations of existing approaches, not least their anthropo-centrism, disregard for non-proximal implications and compliance with the injustices of the political status quo.

An enduring focus on narrowly understood benefits is an example. The contribution of Krippendorff's approach is to see design as a meaning-making activity: design as a discursive practice that discusses designed artefacts within its discourse communities. These communities develop traditions and institutions. The discourse therefore occurs within perme-able but distinguishable boundaries. It seeks to justify and promote its methods and achievements. Krippendorff's goal is to expand the positive impact of design. His approach to such expansion is through 'human-centred design'. The objective of human-centred design is to derive solutions from and for stakeholders' lives. He prefers this approach to 'technology-centred design' where experts impose solutions on 'users'.

According to Krippendorff, the desired result of human-centred design is an artificial world filled with designed artefacts that play various social roles. The transparently anthropocentric aim of this insular world is to make sense to humans, be useful and give them 'a feeling of home'.[14] Unfortunately, environmental history demonstrates that humans can value or love highly damaging, even suicidal practices. Easter Islanders dedicated a large proportion of their resources to the construction of giant statues. It is likely that they had a most powerful 'feeling of home' among them. However, the commitment to this much-admired example of human-centred design did nothing to prevent the severe exploitation of the island's ecosystem, a dramatic thirty-fold reduction in the number of human inhabitants and the disappearance of the statue-making societies in the ensuing starvation.[15] The debate on the complete composition of causes – from ecocide to genocide – is still ongoing.[16] However, the human contribution to a rapid near-total deforestation and the resulting cascade of societal and environmental degradations seem undeniable.

So far, this chapter has outlined the significance of design and introduced existing understandings of design as well as their limitations. The next section advances this narrative of design as a cause of destruction.

Design as the Problem

Many understandings of design seek to explain existing practices and give them logic and credence. This approach is limiting because the combined outcome of all past design in all its diversity is the current condition of acute environmental crisis. Innovative design is responsible for introducing all major contributors to the crisis including technologies for hunting and fishing, agriculture, urban settlements, transportation or fossil-fuelled devices. Power to re-engineer the world comes at a cost. Professional designers or any humans that engage in design should be wary of promoting inherited approaches. The anthropocentric bias of most current practices prevents the consideration of all possible futures and limits opportunities for reassessing human-induced impacts.

Human designing has a long history of interference with planetary systems. Many commentators link the Anthropocene with effects of industrialisation initiated by the patenting of Watt's steam engine in 1764 and magnified by the 'great acceleration' after World War II. However, impacts of intentional human activities resulted in significant environmental degradations long before that. Examples include the global destruction of megafauna by various Homo species,[17] desertification and pivotal societal transformations in the fertile crescent under the influence of agricultural innovations from about ten thousand years ago[18] and some six thousand years of European deforestation.[19] With industrialisation, the consequences are more serious, though not entirely novel. Consequently, it is important to rethink the pervasive influence of design on the future of life in the Anthropocene. Conditions of the future will offer novel, difficult (but interesting) challenges that will necessitate the refashioning of design.

For example: design, along with many other creative practices – from literature to engineering – prizes ingenuity, innovation and impact. However, creativity is a force of destruction as well as making. In a world where resources such as materials or energy are finite, making something new requires a destruction of the old. On Earth, life had enough time to spread into every place that can work as a habitat. Scientists find organisms deep in the Earth's crust, in the stratosphere, in hot springs and at the bottom of ocean trenches. When newly evolved *Homo sapiens* began to colonise the planet, other creatures already occupied most available spaces to their maximal carrying capacity. The introduction of a new species, especially one as successful as humans, can occur only at the cost of diminishing the opportunities of others. Today, this is approaching catastrophic proportions. Consequently, an urgent need for design is to develop approaches that prioritise balance over efficiency and a small footprint over large impact.

Another difficult challenge is the need to plan for substantially different futures. Many ongoing trends have crossed or will soon cross qualitative thresholds that can lead to substantially altered habitats. Examples include technological advances, biodiversity loss, global warming and urbanisation. For example, insect populations are in sharp decline, globally. Estimates claim that more than 40 per cent are threatened with extinction.[20] Designed land use that transfers habitats to intensive agriculture or urban uses is the main driver. Industrial deployment of poisons is another cause. Beyond agricultural industries, most families have and apply poisons at home. The retail trade in designed insecticides and the related designed narratives of hygiene, safety and efficiency are worth billions of dollars each year. The result is a decline in ecosystem productivity and health. Among other consequences, loss of insects leads to a precipitous increase in bird deaths and equally large decreases in pollination, shifting whole regions towards ecosystem collapse.

Life, human and non-human, seeks to adapt in response to numerous pressures. The result is novel environments and novel relationships among their inhabitants. Societal values, education and business practices –

including procurement, development and implementation of designs – struggle to match this novelty.

Appropriate responses to novelty are especially difficult because of multiple uncertainties. Ignorance is one factor. Human impact outpaces the accrual of human knowledge in many domains. For example, most biological species remain unknown and undescribed. Current estimates say that there are 8.7 million species on Earth with more than 86 per cent still undiscovered.[21] About fifteen thousand to twenty thousand new species are described each year. It will take hundreds of years to find the rest. At the same time, some 50 per cent of species will be unviable by mid-century.[22] Humans are still largely ignorant about their environment and in many cases lose the opportunity to learn more. The intrinsic unpredictability of complex systems is another factor that limits planning and modelling. These challenges become even more difficult in the presence of differing cognitive abilities and the resulting perceptions of relevant stakeholders. Any efforts towards more holistic design will have to develop methods that can alleviate such constraints on shared knowledge.

Cultural Habitats

Cities provide a characteristic example. Urbanisation is accelerating globally, and this trend will persist into the foreseeable future. Even if human societies arrest the spread of cities, existing artificial environments will remain. Urban effects include waste, pollution, destruction of old ecosystems and depletion of resources well beyond the confines of cities. These effects inhibit the population of many organisms through heightened mortality, ill health and poor quality of life. At the same time, cities and adjacent areas act as significant habitats for many organisms.[23] Some individuals and species prefer cities. Others, such as urban pigeons, mice and most domesticated animals, can no longer survive without cohabiting with humans. Many more non-human organisms could live in cities but are excluded by prevailing human cultures, design and management practices.[24] Often, design choices exclude unintentionally.[25] Examples include the sealing of road surfaces, removal of old trees, introduction of non-native vegetation and light pollution. Careful management of urban ecosystems can be necessary, for example, for safety or disease control. However, the form and regulation of cities emerged to enable an expansive growth of human civilisations. Resulting environments neglect habitat requirements and negatively affect all lifeforms, including humans themselves.

The proposal of this chapter is that the participation of all lifeforms in design is a prerequisite to the viability of future habitats. Three propositions underpin this hypothesis: firstly, that habitats are necessarily cultural; secondly, that cultures involve human and non-human lifeforms, even if unknowingly and; thirdly, that design can learn from and support such interspecies cultures.

Developing approaches in urban ecology seek to study cities as ecosystems.[26] However, this field predominantly focuses on the observation and understanding of existing cities. Parallel, and more recent, areas such as political urban ecology seek to understand the management of urban environments in the context of societal interactions.[27] Here, green design methods seek to minimise urbanisation's damage.[28] Yet, these approaches continue to prioritise the needs of humans, interpreting them as distinct from the needs of the other lifeforms and considering them over relatively short timescales. For example, most 'green building standards' attempt to minimise energy consumption but do not seek to provide habitat opportunities for non-human life. Most 'nature-based solutions' seek to purify water and air, reduce heat island effects and provide recreational opportunities for humans. Such approaches use other lifeforms as tools, dispensing with them as human needs change. The scope of a typical urban masterplan is thirty years. A typical lifespan of a commercial building is about fifty years. By contrast, most trees become valuable as habitats after 150 years and can live much longer. Their communities, with all the associated wildlife, can be many magnitudes older.

A body of work on animals, plants and other non-humans considered in relation to human cultures has grown in a variety of disciplines including geography, philosophy, political science, law and environmental history.[29] However, these recent advances are yet to penetrate the field of design or inform other, related professional practices and public opinion. In 1990, distinguished ecologist Daniel B. Botkin wrote that 'our beliefs about nature have fallen well behind our knowledge'.[30] These beliefs are important because they guide design. Unfortunately, since the 1990s, the gap has only widened despite recent efforts to address the needs of non-human stakeholders such as animals.[31] For example, a recent systematic review of 200 studies on urban biodiversity revealed 'critical knowledge gaps about the people-biodiversity interface in cities'[32] while a group of prominent researchers argued that future urban-design research ought to encompass non-human inhabitants.[33] Reciprocally, researchers in biological conservation argue that the discipline needs to develop an integration with urban planning.[34] The literature, therefore, indicates substantial gaps in the knowledge about the interaction of human culture, including design, with biology and ecology.

Cultural barriers often prevent beneficial actions. For example, as diurnal animals, humans prefer brightly lit environments. They associate darkness with danger and crime. Yet, outdoor lighting is hugely harmful to many forms of life, including humans.[35] Information on harmful effects is not penetrating design disciplines. With further research, design could support the required cultural shift in the homes, business spaces and public areas of cities. This shift must involve multiple cultural interactions, including education, communication, regulation and technologies. Parts of this shift can occur only if non-human lifeforms adjust their cultures. For example, the introduction of artificially constructed nest sites in urban areas invite birds that do not typically dwell in cities to recognise new opportunities for habitation.[36] To accept this invitation, birds need to learn to recognise and accept artificial nesting sites, be tolerant of noise and the presence of humans and their devices, modify their hunting strategies, adjust their diets and modify how they socialise. The next section sketches a conception of design that can benefit from integrating more-than-human cultures.

Interspecies Design

The extent of environmental degradation poses risks to numerous forms of life, including many or most humans, especially those less privileged.[37] A century ago, only 15 per cent of Earth's surface was used to grow crops and raise livestock. Today, more than 77 per cent of land (excluding Antarctica) and 87 per cent of the ocean have been modified by the direct effects of human activities.[38] Humans have destroyed a tenth of Earth's wilderness in twenty-five years.[39] New forms of interspecies responsibility should, therefore, guide all future practices.[40] Yet, human societies struggle to modify their behaviours, as illustrated by failures in setting and meeting environmental-protection goals. The inability to imagine an attractive future that diverges from business-as-usual is an important constraint.[41] Current policies acknowledge culture and design as major organisational forces in the cities. However, the notion of culture used in these policies emphasises human production and consumption.[42] This understanding sees humans and other forms of life as fundamentally different: only humans have cultures and their needs trump those of others.

However, many (maybe even all) lifeforms have cultures. Consequently, it is possible to promote shared cultures that can better reflect ecosystem interactions among forms of life. The abstract nature of environmental ethics is one of the barriers preventing consideration of morality within environmental politics.[43] Yet, cultures that encompass human and non-human lives can foster critically important support for environmentally responsible behaviours and policies. As Paul Downton has written:

> Because cities are the drivers of environmental degradation the challenge is to turn them into agents of ecological restoration, supporting massive human populations and simultaneously repairing the damage to the world that humans have already done. The survival of our species' civilisation depends on how we make our cities work.[44]

The absence of a framework theorising interspecies cultures in the context of design makes a meaningful choice between alternative approaches towards environmental management difficult, or impossible. This impasse results in coexistence of dramatically incompatible attitudes, ranging from the extreme modifications of geoengineering[45] to the arrant protectionism of 'affluent environmentalism'.[46]

The emerging understanding of cities as living ecosystems is an important advancement. Nonetheless, leading literature in urban ecology inherits the anthropocentric bias of previous scholarship. It sees the urban environment as 'a dynamic interaction between the natural environment and human culture'.[47] In such interpretations, human culture gets a privileged position. The anthropocentric bias situates other forms of life as separate from humans, undifferentiated as individuals, inferior and mechanical: co-mixed as the 'environment'. For example, undetected, undescribed and many 'lower' species – insects, worms or fish – remain unprotected by laws. New construction can remove or kill them if the viability of known non-human inhabitants is not affected. In similar situations, humans would receive compensation or even acquire protective status as refugees. Illustrating relevant recent thinking, proposals for animal property rights constitute one attempt to address this gap.[48]

Positioning that sees humans as valuable individuals but other life-forms as environmental forces devoid of individuality or culture is often unintentional. Yet, this is detrimental to the environmental-protection goals of urban ecology. Theory and practice need, therefore, to advance beyond such separations. The study, management and design of urban ecologies need to see them as cultural as well as physical, chemical or biological phenomena. Necessary to developing practices that can address the future challenges of such environments is the study of interspecies cultures.

Humanist traditions define culture as something unique to humans. Ellwood insists that 'there is a qualitative difference between the social behavior of men and the social behavior of animals'.[49] Yet, recent scientific work disproves this.[50] It argues that many forms of life have rich cultures that are definable in terms of outcomes such as survival and well-being. For Allen et al., culture is 'shared behavior propagated by social learning'.[51] Laland and Janik understand 'culture (or tradition) as all group-typical behaviour patterns, shared by members of animal communities, that are to some degree reliant on socially learned and transmitted information'.[52] This chapter follows a similar definition proposed by Ramsey: '[C]ulture is information transmitted between individuals or groups, where this information flows through and brings about the reproduction of, and a lasting change in, the behavioral trait.'[53] This definition typifies a large and rapidly growing body of work in multiple disciplines.

Human and non-human cultures are always shared. They evolve in constant interaction within ecosystems and implicate multiple forms of life. Thus, cultures are always interspecies. Such cultures constitute a crucial mechanism of evolution and will have a pervasive impact on the health and well-being of humans and all other lifeforms.[54] This understanding of culture also has important implications for established bodies of knowledge in ethics, aesthetics, governance and other areas important for design.

The notion of interspecies cultures will require practical trials of a new ethics that builds upon existing work. This work includes forms of 'land ethic' that expand the socio-environmental community to include soils, waters, plants and animals.[55] Such an ethic has precedents but will necessitate innovation in rapidly changing environments.[56] Such innovation will have to deal with novel ecologies and social relationships. Andrew Dobson suggests that socio-environmental ethics should constitute a way of being rather than a code of conduct.[57] Future work must trial novel but plausible patterns of lived multispecies interactions.[58]

Consequently, interspecies design can be understood as a subset of interspecies culture, one that rejects speciesism. It is a form of design that seeks to involve and benefit both human and non-human lifeforms; to design *for* and *with* all life. Interspecies design can have human or non-human clients, consider human and non-human stakeholders and seek participatory contributions from human and non-human parties. It is committed to further research and conceptual innovation in areas of more-than-human co-habitation, interspecies culture, aesthetics and communication. To illustrate, modifications of existing seawalls into welcoming habitats for marine life respond to the needs and preferences of both human and non-human inhabitants.[59] Recent installations in Sydney illustrate how biodiversity-sensitive designs can improve the habitat capabilities of protected architectural heritage while enhancing humans' aesthetic appreciation of the shoreline. In Melbourne, digitally fabricated owls' nests combine ecologists' understandings of habitat needs with advances in design technologies.[60]

The definition of culture that frames this chapter emphasises, then, the transmission of information content. The practical implementation of interspecies design is likely to depend, therefore, on technologies of data gathering, representation, analysis, modelling, communication and generation. Capabilities provided by computation are a qualitative leap that could restructure socio-environmental relationships. The resulting changes can be detrimental as well as beneficial. The continuing impact of increasingly automated technology seems unavoidable, however, and this chapter proposes its judicious integration into constructive approaches that can support design with scientific evidence and measurable performance criteria. The bulk of the work in this area focuses on physical functions such as structural stability or energy efficiency. In extension, computation can have substantial positive effects on cultural interactions. Such effects are clear in the case of human cultures. It is likely that the impact of digital technologies on interspecies cultures will be as important.

Conclusion

An unfolding era of environmental collapse calls for new forms of interspecies responsibility, including new types of science, new scientific data and reconfigured relationships between science and politics.[61] Within this interdisciplinary endeavour, design plays a particularly significant role. Broadly understood, design encompasses all planning. Past designs affected all planetary environments, societies and the capabilities of individual humans. The conditions of the Anthropocene make it clear that human-centred design will continue to result in increasingly diminished living worlds. Thus, human impact in the Anthropocene makes the role of design in the future even more important. This chapter proposes an interspecies design that will engage with all life and encourage a productive rethinking of concepts such as culture, traditions, intelligence, sentience and language. Design relies on agile try-and-adjust methods supported by technical creativity. Reoriented to include more-than-human stakeholders, such methods can usefully extend the purviews of sciences and humanities. For example, design can serve as a testing ground that can combine scientific evidence on the ethology of a species with radical proposals for its legal status and evocative narratives of possible neighbourly friendship with humans. Expressed as inspirational demonstrators, reproducible recipes, guidelines, regulations or curricula as well as functional practical projects, the resulting scenarios can help to mobilise research and imagination in the exploration of preferable – and plausible – futures.

Notes

1. Paul J. Crutzen, 'Geology of Mankind', *Nature* 415(6867) (2002), 23.
2. Libby Robin, Sverker Sörlin and Paul Warde (eds.), *The Future of Nature: Documents of Global Change* (New Haven, CT: Yale University Press, 2013).
3. Patrick W. Jordan, *Designing Pleasurable Products: An Introduction to the New Human Factors* (London: Taylor & Francis, 2000).
4. Herbert A. Simon, *The Sciences of the Artificial* [3rd ed.] (Cambridge, MA: MIT Press, 1996 [1969]), p.111.
5. Ibid.
6. Richard A. Herbert and Kathleen Green Skelton Herbert, 'Behavior of Peregrine Falcons in the New York City Region', *The Auk* 82(1) (1965), 62–94.
7. Joel E. Pagel et al., 'Peregrine Falcons: The Neighbors Upstairs' in Clint W. Boal and Cheryl R. Dykstra (eds.), *Urban Raptors: Ecology and Conservation of Birds of Prey in Cities* (Washington: Island Press, 2018), pp.180–95.
8. New York City Department of Environmental Protection, 'Peregrine Falcons in New York City' (2019), www1.nyc.gov.
9. Scott R. Loss et al., 'Bird-Building Collisions in the United States: Estimates of Annual Mortality and Species Vulnerability', *The Condor* 116(1) (2014), 8–23.
10. Harold G. Nelson and Erik Stolterman, *The Design Way: Intentional Change in an Unpredictable World* [2nd ed.] (Cambridge, MA: MIT Press, 2012 [2002]), p.1.
11. Klaus Krippendorff, *The Semantic Turn: A New Foundation for Design* (Boca Raton: CRC, 2006), p.32.
12. Joan Ernst van Aken, Hans Berends and Hans van der Bij, *Problem-Solving in Organizations: A Methodological Handbook for Business Students* (Cambridge: Cambridge University Press, 2007).
13. Jon Kolko, 'Design Thinking Comes of Age', *Harvard Business Review* (1 September 2015).
14. Krippendorff, *The Semantic Turn*, p.39.
15. Jared M. Diamond, *Collapse: How Societies Choose to Fail or Survive* (London: Allen Lane, 2005).
16. Valentí Rull, 'Natural and Anthropogenic Drivers of Cultural Change on Easter Island: Review and New Insights', *Quaternary Science Reviews* 150 (15 October 2016), 31–41.

17. Nicole L. Boivin et al., 'Ecological Consequences of Human Niche Construction: Examining Long-Term Anthropogenic Shaping of Global Species Distributions', *Proceedings of the National Academy of Sciences* 113(23) (2016), 6388–96.

18. Simone Riehl et al., 'Mid-to-Late Holocene Agricultural System Transformations in the Northern Fertile Crescent: A Review of the Archaeobotanical, Geoarchaeological, and Philological Evidence' in Liviu Giosan et al. (eds.), *Climates, Landscapes, and Civilizations* (Washington: American Geophysical Union, 2013), pp.115–36.

19. Yuval N. Harari, *Sapiens: A Brief History of Humankind* (Toronto: Signal, 2014); Diamond, *Collapse*.

20. Francisco Sánchez-Bayo and Kris A. G. Wyckhuys, 'Worldwide Decline of the Entomofauna: A Review of Its Drivers', *Biological Conservation* 232 (2019), 8–27.

21. Camilo Mora et al., 'How Many Species Are There on Earth and in the Ocean?', *PLOS Biology* 9(8) (2011).

22. Chris D. Thomas et al., 'Extinction Risk from Climate Change', *Nature* 427 (6970) (2004), 145–8.

23. Jenni Garden et al., 'Review of the Ecology of Australian Urban Fauna: A Focus on Spatially Explicit Processes', *Austral Ecology* 31(2) (2006), 126–48.

24. Alexandra Botzat, Leonie K. Fischer and Ingo Kowarik, 'Unexploited Opportunities in Understanding Liveable and Biodiverse Cities: A Review on Urban Biodiversity Perception and Valuation', *Global Environmental Change* 39 (2016), 220–33.

25. Thomas Elmqvist et al. (eds.), *Urbanization, Biodiversity and Ecosystem Services: Challenges and Opportunities* (Dordrecht: Springer, 2013).

26. See, for example, Ian Douglas and David Goode (eds.), *The Routledge Handbook of Urban Ecology* (London: Routledge, 2011).

27. Nik Heynen, Maria Kaika and Erik Swyngedouw (eds.), *In the Nature of Cities: Urban Political Ecology and the Politics of Urban Metabolism* (London: Routledge, 2006).

28. See, for example, Timothy Beatley, *Green Urbanism: Learning from European Cities* (Washington: Island Press, 2000).

29. See, respectively, Chris Philo and Chris Wilbert, *Animal Spaces, Beastly Places: New Geographies of Human-Animal Relations* (London: Routledge, 2000); Matthew Hall, *Plants as Persons: A Philosophical Botany* (Albany: State University of New York Press, 2011); Robert Garner and Shiobhan O'Sullivan (eds.), *The Political Turn in Animal Ethics* (Lanham, MD: Rowman & Littlefield, 2016); Christopher D. Stone, *Should Trees Have Standing? Law, Morality, and the Environment* [3rd ed.] (New York: Oxford University Press, 2010 [1974]); Sue Donaldson and Will Kymlicka, *Zoopolis: A Political Theory of Animal Rights* (New York: Oxford University Press, 2011); Clay McShane and Joel A. Tarr, *The Horse in the City: Living Machines in the Nineteenth Century* (Baltimore: Johns Hopkins University Press, 2007).

30. Daniel B. Botkin, *Discordant Harmonies: A New Ecology for the Twenty-First Century* (New York: Oxford University Press, 1990).
31. Jennifer R. Wolch, 'Zoöpolis', *Capitalism Nature Socialism* 7(2) (1996), 21–47; Jennifer R. Wolch, 'Green Urban Worlds', *Annals of the Association of American Geographers* 97(2) (2007), 373–84.
32. Botzat, Fischer and Kowarik, 'Unexploited Opportunities', p.220.
33. Kirsten M. Parris et al., 'The Seven Lamps of Planning for Biodiversity in the City', *Cities* 83 (2018), 44–53.
34. Briony A. Norton, Karl L. Evans and Philip H. Warren, 'Urban Biodiversity and Landscape Ecology: Patterns, Processes and Planning', *Current Landscape Ecology Reports* 1(4) (2016), 178–92.
35. Davide M. Dominoni, Jeremy C. Borniger and Randy J. Nelson, 'Light at Night, Clocks and Health: From Humans to Wild Organisms', *Biology Letters* 12(2) (2016), 1–4.
36. Ed McNabb and Jim Greenwood, 'A Powerful Owl Disperses into Town and Uses an Artificial Nest-Box', *Australian Field Ornithology* 28(2) (2011), 65–75.
37. J. Baird Callicott, *Thinking Like a Planet: The Land Ethic and the Earth Ethic* (New York: Oxford University Press, 2013).
38. James E. M. Watson et al., 'Protect the Last of the Wild', *Nature* 563(7729) (November 2018), 27.
39. James E. M. Watson et al., 'Catastrophic Declines in Wilderness Areas Undermine Global Environment Targets', *Current Biology* 26(21) (2016), 2929–34.
40. Jamie Lorimer, *Wildlife in the Anthropocene: Conservation after Nature* (Minneapolis: University of Minnesota Press, 2015).
41. Stephen M. Gardiner, *A Perfect Moral Storm: The Ethical Tragedy of Climate Change* (New York: Oxford University Press, 2011).
42. Tüzin Baycan and Luigi Fusco Girard, 'Case Study Window: Culture in International Sustainability Practices and Perspectives: The Experience of "Slow City Movement – Cittaslow"' in Greg Young and Deborah Stevenson (eds.), *The Ashgate Research Companion to Planning and Culture* (Farnham: Ashgate, 2013), pp.273–92.
43. Donald A. Brown, 'The Importance of Creating an Applied Environmental Ethics: Lessons Learned from Climate Change' in Ben A. Minteer (ed.), *Nature in Common? Environmental Ethics and the Contested Foundations of Environmental Policy* (Philadelphia: Temple University Press, 2009), pp.215–27.
44. Paul Downton, *Ecopolis: Architecture and Cities for a Changing Climate* (Collingwood, Australia: CSIRO, 2009), p.21.
45. Clive Hamilton, *Earthmasters: The Dawn of the Age of Climate Engineering* (New Haven, CT: Yale University Press, 2013); Jack Stilgoe, *Experiment Earth: Responsible Innovation in Geoengineering* (London: Routledge, 2015).
46. Peter Dauvergne, *Environmentalism of the Rich* (Cambridge, MA: MIT Press, 2016); Hannah Holleman, *Dust Bowls of Empire: Imperialism, Environmental Politics, and the Injustice of Green Capitalism* (New Haven, CT: Yale University Press, 2018).

47. Ian Douglas and Philip James, *Urban Ecology: An Introduction* (London: Routledge, 2015), p.9.

48. Karen Bradshaw, 'Animal Property Rights', *University of Colorado Law Review* 89(3) (2018), 809–62.

49. Charles A. Ellwood, 'Culture and Human Society', *Social Forces* 23(1) (1944), 6–15.

50. Charles T. Snowdon, 'Introduction to Animal Culture: Is Culture Uniquely Human?' in Jose M. Causadias (ed.), *The Handbook of Culture and Biology* (Hoboken, NJ: John Wiley & Sons, 2018), pp.81–104.

51. Jenny Allen et al., 'Network-Based Diffusion Analysis Reveals Cultural Transmission of Lobtail Feeding in Humpback Whales', *Science* 340(6131) (2013), 485–8.

52. Kevin N. Laland and Vincent M. Janik, 'The Animal Cultures Debate', *Trends in Ecology & Evolution* 21(10) (2006), 542–7.

53. Grant Ramsey, 'Culture in Humans and Other Animals', *Biology & Philosophy* 28(3) (2013), 457–79 (p.464).

54. Eva Jablonka, Marion J. Lamb and Anna Zeligowski, *Evolution in Four Dimensions: Genetic, Epigenetic, Behavioral, and Symbolic Variation in the History of Life* (Cambridge, MA: MIT Press, 2014).

55. Aldo Leopold, *A Sand County Almanac and Sketches Here and There* (New York: Oxford University Press, 1949).

56. See Philippe Descola, *Beyond Nature and Culture* (Chicago: University of Chicago Press, 2013); Tim Ingold, *The Perception of the Environment: Essays on Livelihood, Dwelling and Skill* (London: Routledge, 2000).

57. Andrew Dobson, *Green Political Thought* [4th ed.] (London: Routledge, 2007 [1990]).

58. Alasdair Cochrane, *Sentientist Politics: A Theory of Global Inter-species Justice* (Oxford: Oxford University Press, 2018); Donaldson and Kymlicka, *Zoopolis*; Nicole Rogers and Michelle M. Maloney (eds.), *Law as if Earth Really Mattered: The Wild Law Judgement Project* (Abingdon: Routledge, 2017).

59. Elisabeth M. A. Strain et al., 'Eco-engineering Urban Infrastructure for Marine and Coastal Biodiversity: Which Interventions Have the Greatest Ecological Benefit?', *Journal of Applied Ecology* 55(1) (2018), 426–41.

60. Roudavski, Stanislav, and Dan Parker. "Modelling Workflows for More-than-Human Design: Prosthetic Habitats for the Powerful Owl (Ninox Strenua)." In Impact - Design with All Senses: Proceedings of the Design Modelling Symposium, Berlin 2019, edited by Gengnagel, Christoph, Baverel, Olivier, Burry, Jane, Thomsen, Mette Ramsgaard, and Weinzierl, Stefan, 554–64. Cham: Springer, 2020. https://doi.org/10/dbkp.

61. Lorimer, *Wildlife in the Anthropocene*.

CHAPTER 9

Digital Games

Alenda Y. Chang

It would be simply too much work to give everything meaning. This is why so many virtual worlds have windows that don't break, chairs you can't sit on, grass you can't pull up, trees you can't chop down . . .
(Richard A. Bartle, *Designing Virtual Worlds*)[1]

We've forever altered the Earth, and so now we cannot abandon it to a random fate. It is our duty to manage it. Luckily, it can be a pleasant, even joyful task if we embrace it in the right spirit.
(Emma Marris, *Rambunctious Garden*)[2]

Why devote so much energy to imagining other worlds, when we do such a poor job of maintaining the one we now occupy? Perhaps what the discourse of the Anthropocene reveals to us, above all, is that world-building is an innate human tendency, whether or not it is sustainable or manifests on geological, biological or computational timescales. In what follows, I tender a schematic history of world-building across art forms, in order to underscore the distinct design opportunities and challenges presented by life and creative labour in the early twenty-first century. As reality and fancy increasingly converge in billionaires' proposals for space colonisation, planetary-level geoengineering and voluntary state and industrial targets for emissions reduction, thinking our collective environmental quandaries through the multiplicity of worlds articulated within contemporary media, particularly digital games, may come to seem less far-fetched than altogether fitting.

There are, inevitably, further ironies inherent to any discussion of building digital worlds in the Anthropocene – from our desire to use the Anthropocene as a means of decentring the human, even as the term itself reinscribes the centrality of human experience, to digital media's outsize complicity with destructive regimes of resource extraction, energy use and disposal. Yet, as I have argued before, digital games offer a potent avenue for designing and partaking in environmental scenarios.[3] In many ways informed by Donna Haraway's and Bruno Latour's long-standing critiques of nature/culture divides in modern thought,[4] this chapter aims to trouble a similar split between the wild and the domesticated through the hybridity of interactive or 'playable' media.[5] I contend that games are fitted to imagining the 'rambunctious gardens' of a 'post-wild' future, marked by multispecies entanglements and obligations. Despite, in fact because of, their compromised provenance, contemporary games excel at Anthropocenic world-building, as evident in recent formal and generic experiments in non-human gameplay and so-called 'permanent death' and 'legacy' mechanics.[6] As a review of the varied approaches to ludic world design also suggests, differences in opinion as to who or what constitutes a viable game world – broadly speaking, designers, players, software or spaces – bear on environmental impasses in the 'real' world, namely who or what gets to determine what lives remain viable here on Earth. I conclude that the essence of world-building does not lie primarily in singular, authorial intent or vision but in a collective imagining and realisation, where designed worlds may serve as both inspirations and cautionary tales for our ecologically compromised times.

A History of World-Building

The idea of world-building is arguably as old as imagination itself, although the term arises much more recently in contexts as disparate as game design and theory, science fiction and the Hollywood pitch. To begin, some sense of world creation has been central to literary hermeneutics from its earliest stages. It is for instance encapsulated in M. H. Abrams' well-known interpretive model from *The Mirror and the Lamp*, in which a literary work must be approached from a variety of angles, that not only of the work itself but also of the artist or creator, the audience for the work and, most crucially in this context, the world or universe from which the work is drawn. World-building is also frequently invoked in the growing scholarship on speculative fiction, fantasy and science fiction. Science fiction especially has long been guided by the hazy mantra of a 'sense of wonder',[7] but all of these genres have often been lauded or criticised for putting more emphasis on world development than story structure.[8]

Correspondingly, world-building has become de rigueur in the cut-throat world of current cinematic enterprise, not only for aspiring writers, but also for would-be directors, showrunners and producers. As the new dogma goes, where once you used to proffer a snappy storyline – the plot pitch – now you do your best to conjure up an entire world. It is no longer enough to describe the hero's journey; now, you must also evoke the universe to which that journey belongs, be it a superhero multiverse, the alternate magical worlds of *Harry Potter* or *A Wrinkle in Time*, or J. R. R. Tolkien's high-fantasy realms. Cynics grumble that world-building is largely an economic pretext, allowing industry-aligned actors to extract more money from audiences because the *full* story is available only to those who purchase every last bit of content. Certainly, the common denigration of the seemingly endless, formulaic entries in the Marvel or DC Comics universes accords with such a complaint. Yet others see world-building as a productive complement to previous stresses on story and character, one that leverages the multi-platform affordances of the modern media matrix.[9] As Henry Jenkins has repeatedly clarified in his theories of convergence culture and transmedia storytelling,[10] world-building need not represent a zero-sum game in which accenting the imaginative housing of a story detracts from the story's realisation.

Most recently, similar trade-offs between narrative and world design have been posited in the arena of digital games, although the latter is more readily seen as constitutive of player experience. Game scholarship has popularised terms like virtual world and virtual reality, and to a lesser extent immersive virtual environments or multi-user virtual environments (MUVEs), for example, with the first wave of writing on massively multi-player online games (MMOGs) like *EverQuest* (Sony Online Entertainment, 1999) and *World of Warcraft* (Blizzard Entertainment, 2004). In the very first issue of *the Journal of Virtual Worlds Research* published in 2008, Mark Bell points to early definitions from self-professed economist of virtual worlds and currencies Edward Castronova,[11] but also multi-user dungeon (MUD/MOO) designer Richard Bartle and game designer Raph Koster. Bell himself defines a virtual world as comprising '[a] synchronous, persistent network of people, represented as avatars, facilitated by networked computers',[12] a definition that applies equally well to a game like *EVE Online* (CCP Games) or a simulated world like *Second Life* (Linden Lab), both released in 2003. The *Journal of Gaming & Virtual Worlds*, a kindred publication, meanwhile first began publication in 2009.

All of this is to say that, depending on which of the aforementioned perspectives prevails, world-building as a concept or set of practices may slide awkwardly between the poles of interpretation and visualisation, or storytelling and interaction, even as each requires a degree of inventiveness. Importantly, world design as I wish to invoke it here is not solely a matter of aesthetics but an inherently *environmental* set of questions – again, who or what constitutes a world in which we want to live? Or play (recognising that these are not always the same thing)? How is world-*building* also a project of 'becoming worldly' with other species or of *autre-mondialisation*, a phrase that Haraway borrows from Paul Preciado and a network of European activists who hope to advance a peaceful and equitable 'other-globalization' outside dominant military and neo-liberal frameworks.[13] The worlding capacities of our creative media therefore matter a great deal.

In *The Great Derangement*, Amitav Ghosh laments what he sees as the shameful failure of the realist novel to come to terms with the improbabilities of climate change.[14] Although Ghosh allows that this omission may, in part, stem from the novel's period of origin, that it came to maturity at the very time when carbon was first being delivered into the atmosphere at an unprecedented rate, he finds little to excuse a more recent reticence. Corresponding to the nineteenth-century origins of the realist novel, digital games have developed in tandem with some of the worst excesses of late capitalist economies as well as growing concern over human environmental impact. Even as the devices that support gaming partake of unsustainable and often toxic manufacturing and disposal practices,[15] while games that encourage players to marshal, rationalise and dominate nature are perennially popular,[16] games regularly reverse highbrow novelistic convention by indulging in the counterfactual and the cataclysmic, where players not only bear witness but are also encouraged to tinker with, jury-rig, exploit, expend and otherwise intervene in game environments. Ghosh notes that poetry and the stereotypically 'lowbrow' genres of science fiction and fantasy have more commonly taken up the charge of climate crisis in print, but my own contention is that contemporary digital and analogue games are formally and generically suited to Anthropocene storytelling. For games can dramatise the impact of humans on *a* world, if not *the* world; they may deal with a disastrous series of choices that culminates in world death or takes place 'after the end', to quote James Berger;[17] even more radically they might rethink the status quo.

In this chapter, I want to look closely at several divergent strands of world-building discourse in games – roughly characterised as software-centred or human-centred – which inadvertently illuminate parallel tensions in real-world approaches to environmental crisis. These strands inevitably intertwine, but tellingly locate agency in different places. For some, world design and governance are foremost a matter of code or legislation via software, while for others, the production of game space is marked primarily by the creative authorship of either designers or players.

Ultimately, both ecocentric (or systemic) and anthropocentric perspectives must be taken into account, as figured in serious games like *Eco* (Strange Loop Games, 2018) and serious proposals for future planetary flourishing, like journalist Emma Marris's realist vision of a well-managed Earth as 'rambunctious garden'.

Elements of World-Building in Digital Games

Software

In the lingo of game development, a typical world-building workflow might unfold as follows: after brainstorming and mock-ups, whether of the paper-and-pencil or digital variety, designers would a) select a platform, programming language or game engine like Unity or Unreal, which essentially acts as a blank slate with embedded physics, b) laboriously populate discrete scenes with self-made or purchased assets (game objects like 3D models, sprites, textures, sound files and so on) and c) compile, debug and run the resulting code. Artists and designers often espouse rapid prototyping cycles in which versions of the game or parts of it are partially fleshed out and evaluated in order to quickly sustain or scuttle development efforts, perhaps sending employees back to the drawing board before too much time has been wasted on something that won't work.[18] Game creators must not only navigate their own schedules and conflicts[19] but also choreograph the everlasting dance between a computer's affordances and limitations (in terms of processing power, graphics and energy demand) and the desired world as laid out in code, texture wraps, objects, routines and so on. Elsewhere, I have tried to draw attention to just one small facet of this sprawling ecosystem of game studios, each with its own organisational units, independent designers, publishers, middlemen, contractors and service providers, by looking more closely at developers' use of pre-existing asset libraries and 'middleware' software packages like SpeedTree, which enable time- or cash-strapped developers to download, purchase or license art, objects or other 'things' for use in their budding games.[20] SpeedTree, as the name suggests, is in the business of selling digital vegetation to any and all customers wanting off-the-shelf trees, bushes and so forth. This is literally world-building, leaf by leaf, sometimes even one blade of a grass at a time!

Far from being only mundane technical decisions or simply a question of aesthetic preference (for instance, whether or not one prefers realistic trees or more stylised ones, or both as in the game *Firewatch* [Campo

Santo, 2016]), these building blocks of game worlds (and, increasingly, cinematic, televised and architecturally visualised worlds) represent distinct investments and choices by creators, in part a reflection of their own constraints and beliefs (cost, labour-saving, attention to detail), and in part what players are perceived to prioritise (game performance, immersion). So far, these largely inward-facing aspects of game design, often business-to-business (B2B), have received little attention even as digitally realised worlds have steadily infiltrated the mass media and some of the most visible imaginative media worlds of our time, from Pandora to Westeros. Tarleton Gillespie has thoughtfully articulated a similar need for scrutiny in relation to algorithms and platforms outside the domain of virtual worlds and games and more squarely in the ranks of social media and online applications.[21] Echoing Gillespie, as well as Audre Lorde's famous dictum that one may not dismantle the master's house with the master's tools,[22] sociologists William Youmans and Jillian York have analysed inflated claims of social media's role in the Arab Spring and expressed concern that no true activist potential can be realised until activists develop their own software tools and platforms, rather than using commercially available ones like Twitter, Facebook and YouTube.[23] Digital world-building faces much the same constraints, if not in so overtly political a fashion.

Analysing Game Space

Like design software, spatial analysis of games has historically taken a backseat to the more clearly cultural and performative elements of game design and experience. A few notable exceptions include Espen Aarseth's early use of the myth of Theseus and the minotaur's maze to characterise video games as 'ergodic' texts, meaning that they require significant effort to traverse.[24] To this, I would add the work of Mark J. P. Wolf on the spatial construction of video game worlds, including their use of the 'z-axis' and on-screen/off-screen space.[25] While Wolf draws heavily on mythology, literature and cinema in his work, Clara Fernández-Vara, José Pablo Zagal and Michael Mateas have taken a slightly different tack, eschewing comparisons to prior media and instead emphasising the unique spatial properties of games.[26] Treating the screen as the fundamental unit of game space, Fernández-Vara et al. create a spatial taxonomy that can be used to classify games according to whether or not they are one-dimensional, two-dimensional or three-dimensional (the 'cardinality' of the game world and gameplay allowing vision and movement along one, two or three axes), and whether or not they are discrete or continuous in their use of the screen as spatial unit (single-screen games, stitched-screen games like *King's Quest* or games that show no obvious zone lines). For them, the present trend is towards seamless experiences of game space, where the cardinality of game world and play align in three dimensions. However, both Wolf and Fernández-Vara et al. stress that space is not just an objective feature of a game world but experienced and in some sense created by the movement through that space. All also leave open the possibility that game designers can or will develop spaces or spatial relations that do not exist in reality. This interest in navigation and imagination propels us back towards another strand of world-building discourse more closely aligned with the human.

Social World-Building and the Game Designer as Auteur

Predating the extensive scholarship on MMOGs,[27] but buoyed by the postmillennial work on social networks and media, a social rather than spatial approach to ludic world-building has become more prevalent. Initial analyses centred on the behaviour of player populations, as first MUDs and MOOs and later immersive graphical worlds were considered for their aggregation of co-present player-characters. Many experts studied membership in common player groups inspired by medieval guilds (though social rather than trade-based), while others charted fundamental difficulties around virtual-world governance, as journalist Julian Dibbell memorably chronicled in 'A Rape in Cyberspace', the story of the textual violation of avatars and unspoken community norms in LambdaMOO.[28] Legal philosophers like Lawrence Lessig and the late technology evangelist John Perry Barlow have all mused on the potential for 'cyberspace' to be either a wild west of unenforceable behaviours or a bastion of freedom from the bureaucracies and control schemes of the fleshly world. Although there is no imperative that in creating a world one must create an *ideal* world, the utopian impulse has long coloured world design, with conspicuously mixed success. As Wolf recounts, early utopias were typically political, social and philosophical commentaries written by men (think Plato's Kallipolis in *The Republic*, or Thomas More's *Utopia*), and were only later expanded to female-authored feminist utopias and proto-science-fictional worlds like those of Margaret Cavendish. This historical gender lag highlights the relativism of utopic fantasies, that what counts as utopian for one person or group may not qualify as such for another. After all, Plato famously banned poets and other misleading creatives from his ideal city even as he enshrined philosophers as kings, while the celebrated *demos* of ancient Greek society excluded slaves, women and men who did not own property.

In many ways, Plato's dictums bring us to the standard paradigm of game design, one in which a human world-builder exercises authorial vision and intent. The Web and print libraries are awash with books and articles offering mentorship to aspiring game designers. Some are more philosophical, like Bernard Suits's famed treatise *The Grasshopper*, and others more practical, often drawn from the author's experience. They include Raph Koster's *A Theory of Fun for Game Design*, Jesse Schell's *The Art of Game Design: A Book of Lenses* and Richard A. Bartle's *Designing Virtual Worlds*. Setting aside eternal questions like what constitutes a game, what makes play fun and so on, a book like Bartle's matter-of-factly presents the nuts and bolts of 'successful' world-building. For Bartle, virtual world design is inarguably driven by players; spatial design is a mere technical precursor to meaningful inhabitation by players, so worlds must be shaped according to their needs and purposes. In contrast to the 'scientific' view of the real world, virtual worlds demand what Bartle calls a more 'religious' view, where design is knowingly guided by deities, in this case game designers. As his epigraph to this chapter implies, Bartle prefers a no-nonsense attitude towards world design, describing by turns the business aspects of building a virtual world (sales, marketing), the technical aspects (software development/IT), and his specialty, the structuring of gameplay.

Evidently, the spatial and social strains of world-building (what I am also calling the system-centred and the human-centred lines of approach) end up mingling despite my efforts here to tease them apart. Both software and game designers exercise world-defining powers; space and sociality operate in tandem to imbue virtual worlds with meaning, despite Bartle's advice to the contrary. That utopia – so frequently imagined in terms of idealised human relations – etymologically indicates both a 'good place' and a 'no place' seems particularly pertinent to the entertaining and invented worlds of game-building and emblematic of their distributed co-constitution.

Granted, given these roots and the generally progressive bent of utopian fiction, such worlds might appear diametrically opposed to the sobering realities of the Anthropocene. As the now ample Anthropocenic literature reminds us, all of us are ensconced on this planet for the foreseeable future. Far from dwelling nowhere, we are bound to the here and now and, as such, to the repercussions of our own actions and those of our ancestors. To date, therefore, Anthropocene storytelling is largely synonymous with the dystopian. Witness the rise of so-called 'cli-fi' or climate fiction, including works such as Jeff VanderMeer's *Southern Reach* trilogy, in which (as discussed in Hannes Bergthaller's Chapter 12 in this book) the known world is steadily engulfed by an 'area X' inimical to humans, or Paolo Bacigalupi's *The Windup Girl*, set in a future, sub-sea-level Thailand in which fossil fuel has become an obscenity replaced by muscular exertion. Yet to invoke the long history of utopias in relation to digital world-building is to quickly realise that games partake of both utopian and dystopian impulses. Not only can they model both the 'good' (eu-) and the 'bad' (dys-), but they are simultaneously some place (where the player plays, both in-game and out) and no place (ou-). Further, as Eric Hayot and Edward Wesp have written in relation to *Everquest*'s land of Norrath, game geographies partake of both imagined and real places. Hayot and Wesp draw on Marc Augé's well-travelled concept of non-spaces, like airports, waiting rooms and grocery stores, which are often seen as negatively valenced by-products of supermodernity. However, Hayot and Wesp suggest that Norrath may be seen as providing players real pleasure in non-space, not unlike the no-place of utopian worlds. These worlds apart reflect not only lived geographies but also current mores: 'insofar as what *EverQuest* aims to produce defines itself and is understandable as a world – it communicates a great deal about what its designers and players believe a world to be'.[29]

Instructive in this regard are Rob MacDougall and Lisa Faden's reflections on using gameplay and game design in the history classroom, in part to promote a disciplinarily aberrant kind of counterfactual thinking.[30] For MacDougall and Faden, the point is less to get a student to wonder whether Napoleon may have ruled the world in an alternate universe, than to use games to heighten students' sensitivities to contingency, causality and context. MacDougall and Faden celebrate critical game play, but even more so critical game design, for an ability to drive home questions of structure and agency vital to historical enquiry. Yet clearly, structure and agency do not belong solely to human historical record, for what is climate change, or the Anthropocene, if not human history writ large upon the atmosphere, the planet and its denizens? As Anna Tsing carefully explains, in her exploration of global matsutake supply chains, '[m]aking worlds is not limited to humans'.[31] If we were to similarly interrogate the benefits of playing games with environmental content as compared to designing our own interactive environmental scenarios, we would likely find that the task of rendering the world playable quickly becomes staggeringly complex – what parts of the natural world should we include in our game? Who or what are considered players, and how do they interact with each other and the game world (which is also to say, what parts of the game world are actionable)? What value do we place on each aspect of the game world, from terrain to species to weather systems? Already, these design-oriented questions mimic long-standing debates in economics, environmental psychology and history, landscape architecture and so on, for instance around the much-contested term 'natural capital' or the idea that environmental services may be valued by means of a cost–benefit analysis. Ultimately, both trying and failing to build our own worlds and trying others on for size may lead to a productive irreverence for existing arrangements.

Games Have Never Been Wild

In other words, the same questions that expert game designers pose to aspiring amateurs easily substitute for more general questions about our collective, planetary future: What do you want your world to look like? How will it sound and feel? What will you be able to do in that world and what will remain off limits? While world-building may seem little different from other customary but deeply acquisitive game activities, like civilization-building, the construction of massive armies or the amassing of fortune, I would argue that the difference is qualitative – it is not just that world-building demands a wider view but that it is rather closer to the venerable feminist and activist traditions of intersectional coalition-building, a way of joining together without erasing any particular group's distinctive investments or concerns. World-building as I hope to see it taken up in relation to games can be less about painstaking craftsmanship or immersive texture than about imagining and making visible equitable human–non-human relations.

As unpopular as this sentiment may be, there may be distinct advantages to silicon-based forms of life. For one way to view the patent artificiality of games, and to recuperate a medium better known for its exploitation of natural elements than its subtler negotiations, is to embrace games' impure status. The game industry is undeniably complicit in unsustainable economies of resource extraction and use, yet a growing number of games expressly allegorises these very shortcomings. From *Phone Story* (Molleindustria, 2011), a game about the compromised provenance of smartphones designed to be played *on* smartphones, to *Submerged* (Uppercut Games, 2015), a game that takes place in a drowned future in which only one human city remains visible above sea level, games occasionally share the scepticism expressed by countless environmental historians towards collective fantasies around wilderness, or sometimes the wild, and the Romanticisation of unmanaged or putatively pristine natural space untouched by people.

Conveniently in fact, games are rather more like Marris's 'rambunctious gardens', her moniker for scenes from a post-wild future in which humans have come to terms with new ideals of conservation and active management. Unlike the calls for 're-wilding',[32] perhaps most dramatically expressed in biologist E. O. Wilson's desire to set aside a *Half-Earth* solely for non-human animals and plants (spatial and not social world-building, if ever there were an example), Marris's vision of the unruly but still tended garden has more in common with scientists Erle Ellis and Navin Ramankutty's notion of anthromes, which takes the classic taxonomy of the world's major ecological regions (biomes) and reinserts into them people and their planet-shaping ways. To 'save' nature in a post-wild world, as the subtitle to Marris's book proclaims, we must learn to accept things such as assisted migration (for instance, moving species to assist them in climate change adaptation), 'invasive' or 'exotic' species, and designer ecosystems. Although not all games have ecosystems, all game ecosystems are, of course, designer ones. To toy with game environments is automatically to relinquish any dream of communion with unadulterated nature, whether games adhere to realist conventions (like Ghosh's novels, except less as story than graphical visualisation) or range more widely in ways akin to poetry's intimacy with climatic events or other modes of speculative literature or media.

I am influenced in this regard by attempts to articulate multispecies justice, either through multispecies ethnography (particularly Thom van Dooren's work on corvids and other bird species) or multidisciplinary engagements with environmental representation (Ursula Heise's work on discourses of extinction). Van Dooren's *Flight Ways* underscores that extinction is not a clean-edged or cauterised wound so much as a messy tear, and that species losing life and land to human settlement invite equal parts despair and hope as they make ad hoc arrangements with the help of still other humans. Heise engages directly with environmental justice discourse even as she ranges across laws, taxonomic categories, fiction, art, television commercials, toys and even comedy. Reminiscent of similar musings in *Sense of Place, Sense of Planet*, in *Imagining Extinction* she 'helps us see what kinds of stories and genres might be more successful at generating this concern [care about the well-being of non-human species] than others'.[33] Faced with unfathomable losses, there is no single affect to which we might retreat. There are, however, moments of grief, empathy, righteous anger, laughter and playful disrespect, which Anthropocenic digital worlds strive to evoke.

Games today offer manifold outlets for world-making and worldly play, whether escapist (building and balancing), corrective (solving) or heedless (destroying and breaking). While there is no single genre, format or mode of gameplay that trumps all others when put to ethical purposes, Colin Milburn has offered a taxonomy of 'green' games in which the most powerful are games of environmental responsibility,[34] evoking the 'becoming-with' and 'response-ability' of Haraway's companion-species thinking. For some, environmental responsibility might emerge from interaction with a richly realised virtual world, one so large and detailed that no player could single-handedly see all of it. For others, a tightly delimited game might best emphasise the dangers of closed systems or careless inaction on known issues, from Bethesda Softworks' advice to 'recycle everything' in the sci-fi horror game *Prey* (Arkane Studios, 2017), which takes place aboard an alien-infested space station, to *Fate of the World* (Red Redemption, 2011), one of many educational simulation games designed to put players in the bureaucratic hot seat as climate change engulfs various regions of the planet. Methodical turn-based gameplay (as opposed to real-time strategy), prevalent in simulation games like *Civilization* (MicroProse, 1991), invites a managerial approach, while open-world, persistent-state games more readily mimic the indifference and momentum of real-world events. As Mark Bell reminds us: 'A virtual world cannot be paused.'[35] If you log off, the virtual world trundles on and will be changed by other players. Even something as deliberately minimal as Anna Anthropy's text game *Queers in Love at the End of the World* (2013) evokes radical response-ability. Although the end of Anthropy's game world may have been sparked by anything from nuclear war to alien invasion, the game's tautly hyperlinked choices – offered under the duress of a ten-second countdown – embolden us to try, and try again, even if we are destined to fail.

Framed in terms of social versus spatial approaches to world-building, digital worlds tinged by Anthropocene doubts plainly demand careful exploration of underlying systems as well as spirited engagement with others, both human and non-human, sharing those worlds. As Bartle opines, a virtual world is not just its physical geography but also its economy, social structure, even combat system. For Bartle, virtual world economies and ecologies work in largely the same way, seen abstractly, gesturing to their shared etymology in the Greek term for household, *oikos*.[36] Acknowledging that players will inevitably carry part of their real-world attitudes, beliefs or 'culture' into the virtual world, Bartle nevertheless remarks that 'virtual worlds let you rethink what you've been taught at every level'.[37] Virtual worlds can be different by design, and therein lies their abiding appeal.

Notes

1. Richard A. Bartle, *Designing Virtual Worlds* (Berkeley, CA: New Riders, 2004), p.263.
2. Emma Marris, *Rambunctious Garden: Saving Nature in a Post-Wild World* (New York: Bloomsbury, 2011).
3. Alenda Y. Chang, 'Games as Environmental Texts', *Qui Parle* 19 (2011), 57–84.
4. Donna Haraway, *Simians, Cyborgs, and Women: The Reinvention of Nature* (New York: Routledge, 1990); Bruno Latour, *We Have Never Been Modern* [trans. Catherine Porter] (Cambridge, MA: Harvard University Press, 1993).
5. Soraya Murray, *On Video Games: The Visual Politics of Race, Gender and Space* (London: I. B. Tauris, 2017).
6. Alenda Chang, Jesús Costantino and Braxton Soderman, 'Introduction: The Multiple Lives of Permadeath', *Journal of Gaming and Virtual Worlds* 9 (2017), 103–21.
7. Leigh Ronald Grossman, *Sense of Wonder: A Century of Science Fiction* (Cabin John, MD: Wildside Press, 2011).
8. Cixin Liu, 'Beyond Narcissism: What Science Fiction Can Offer Literature' [trans. Holger Nahm and Gabriel Ascher], *Science Fiction Studies* 40 (2013), 22–32.
9. See Michael Curtin, 'Matrix Media' in Graeme Turner and Jinna Tay (eds.), *Television Studies after TV: Understanding Television in the Post-Broadcast Era* (New York: Routledge, 2009), pp.9–19. The World Building Institute (Wbi), founded in October 2008 at the University of Southern California, fulfils both charges. Directed by Alex McDowell, the Wbi's list of financial and creative partners is dizzying – testament to how many parties are eager to make media (and money) under the auspices of world-building. At the same time, the Wbi bills itself as a 'non-profit Organized Research Unit dedicated to the dissemination, education, and appreciation of the future of narrative media through World Building'. Its network of world-builders 'transcends borders and boundaries in film, animation, fashion, gaming, theatre, television, music, architecture, science, interactive media and more'. See worldbuilding.institute/about.
10. Henry Jenkins, *Convergence Culture: Where Old and New Media Collide* (New York: NYU Press, 2006); and Henry Jenkins, 'Transmedia Storytelling', *MIT Technology Review* (2003), www.technologyreview.com /Biotech.

11. Mark W. Bell, 'Toward a Definition of "Virtual Worlds"', *Journal of Virtual Worlds Research* 1 (2008); Edward Castronova, *Synthetic Worlds: The Business and Culture of Online Games* (Chicago: University of Chicago Press, 2006).

12. Bell, 'Toward a Definition of "Virtual Worlds"', p.2.

13. Donna J. Haraway, *When Species Meet* (Minneapolis: University of Minnesota Press, 2008), p.3.

14. Amitav Ghosh, *The Great Derangement: Climate Change and the Unthinkable* (Chicago: University of Chicago Press, 2016).

15. See Richard Maxwell and Toby Miller, *Greening the Media* (Oxford: Oxford University Press, 2012); and Nicole Starosielski and Janet Walker (eds.), *Sustainable Media: Critical Approaches to Media and Environment* (New York: Routledge, 2016).

16. Take the criterion of 'destructibility' now common in game reviews, for example George Reith, '10 Games with Great Destructible Environments' (2011), GamingBolt.com; Lorenzo Veloria, '12 Games that Do Destructible Environments Right', *GamesRadar+* (2014), www.gamesradar.com.

17. James Berger, *After the End: Representations of Post-Apocalypse* (Minneapolis: University of Minnesota Press, 1999).

18. Tracy Fullerton, *Game Design Workshop: A Playcentric Approach to Creating Innovative Games* [3rd ed.] (Boca Raton: CRC Press, 2014).

19. Casey O'Donnell, *Developer's Dilemma: The Secret World of Videogame Creators* (Cambridge, MA: MIT Press, 2014).

20. Alenda Y. Chang, 'Between Plants and Polygons: SpeedTrees and an Even Speedier History of Digital Morphogenesis', *Electronic Book Review* (2019), https://electronicbookreview.com/essay/between-plants-and-polygons-speedtrees-and-an-even-speedier-history-of-digital-morphogenesis/.

21. Tarleton Gillespie, 'The Relevance of Algorithms' in Tarleton Gillespie, Pablo J. Boczkowski and Kirsten A. Foot (eds.), *Media Technologies: Essays on Communication, Materiality, and Society* (Cambridge, MA: MIT Press, 2014), pp.167–93.

22. Audre Lorde, 'The Master's Tools Will Never Dismantle the Master's House' in *Sister Outsider: Essays and Speeches* (Berkeley, CA: Crossing Press, 2007), pp.110–13.

23. William Lafi Youmans and Jillian C. York, 'Social Media and the Activist Toolkit: User Agreements, Corporate Interests, and the Information Infrastructure of Modern Social Movements', *Journal of Communication* 62 (2012), 315–29.

24. Espen J. Aarseth, *Cybertext: Perspectives on Ergodic Literature* (Baltimore: Johns Hopkins University Press, 1997). Other notable exceptions include Henry Jenkins, 'Game Design as Narrative Architecture' in Katie Salen and Eric Zimmerman (eds.), *The Game Design Reader* (Cambridge, MA: MIT Press, 2006); and Michael Nitsche, *Video Game Spaces: Image, Play, and Structure in 3D Game Worlds* (Cambridge, MA: MIT Press, 2008).

25. See Mark J. P. Wolf, 'Z-axis Development in the Video Game' in Bernard Perron and Mark J. P. Wolf (eds.), *The Video Game Theory Reader 2* (New York: Routledge, 2009), pp.151–68; Mark J. P. Wolf, 'Theorizing Navigable Space in Video Games' in Stephan Günzel, Michael Liebe and Dieter Mersch (eds.), *DIGAREC Keynote-Lectures 2009/10* (Potsdam: Potsdam University Press, 2011), pp.18–49; and Mark J. P. Wolf, 'World (of a Video Game)' in Mark J. P. Wolf (ed.), *Encyclopedia of Video Games: The Culture, Technology, and Art of Gaming* (Santa Barbara: Greenwood, 2012), vol. 1, pp.692–3.

26. Clara Fernández-Vara, José Pablo Zagal and Michael Mateas, 'Evolution of Spatial Configurations in Videogames', Proceedings of Digital Games Research Association (DiGRA) 2005 Conference: Changing Views – Worlds in Play, digra.org.

27. For example, see Nicholas Yee, 'Ariadne – Understanding MMORPG Addiction' (October 2002), www.nickyee.com; Constance A. Steinkuehler and Dmitri Williams, 'Where Everybody Knows Your (Screen) Name: Online Games as "Third Places"', *Journal of Computer-Mediated Communication* 11 (2006), 885–909; Castronova, *Synthetic Worlds*; and Bonnie A. Nardi, *My Life as a Night Elf Priest: An Anthropological Account of World of WarCraft* (Ann Arbor: University of Michigan Press, 2010).

28. Julian Dibbell, *My Tiny Life: Crime and Passion in a Virtual World* (New York: Henry Holt and Company, 1998).

29. Eric Hayot and Edward Wesp, 'Towards a Critical Aesthetic of Virtual-World Geographies', *Game Studies* 9 (2009), gamestudies.org.

30. Rob MacDougall and Lisa Faden, 'Simulation Literacy: The Case for Wargames in the History Classroom' in Pat Harrigan and Matthew G. Kirschenbaum (eds.), *Zones of Control: Perspectives on Wargaming* (Cambridge, MA: MIT Press, 2016).

31. Anna Lowenhaupt Tsing, *The Mushroom at the End of the World: On the Possibility of Life in Capitalist Ruins* (Princeton, NJ: Princeton University Press, 2015).

32. Rewilding is a favourite trend of magazines like *Condé Nast Traveller* and *Orion*, which have featured items including a column from the editor-in-chief on the merits of African 'rewilding' safaris, and interviews with George Monbiot and Jeff VanderMeer on topics like 'rewilding your lawn'.

33. Ursula K. Heise, *Imagining Extinction: The Cultural Meanings of Endangered Species* (Chicago: University of Chicago Press, 2016), p.13.

34. Colin Milburn, 'Green Gaming: Video Games and Environmental Risk' in Sylvia Mayer and Alexa Weik von Mossner (eds.), *The Anticipation of Catastrophe: Environmental Risk in North American Literature and Culture* (Heidelberg: Universitätsverlag Winter, 2014), pp.201–19.

35. Bell, 'Toward a Definition of "Virtual Worlds"', p.3.

36. Bartle, *Designing Virtual Worlds*, p.267.

37. Ibid., p.251.

PART II

Anthropocene Themes

CHAPTER 10

Catastrophe

David Higgins and Tess Somervell

When Paul Crutzen and Eugene F. Stoermer outlined their newly coined term 'Anthropocene' two decades ago, they proposed a start date for the new geological epoch of 'the latter part of the 18th century', in part because it 'coincides with James Watt's invention of the steam engine in 1784'.[1] Since then, other start dates have been suggested, but if we accept that the Anthropocene is intertwined with the rise of what Andreas Malm calls 'fossil capital', then 1784 seems as plausible as any.[2] This chapter argues that Romantic literature is Anthropocene literature in its concern with human–non-human entanglements and with what it means to be alive at a catastrophic turning-point in planetary history.[3] As well as being characterised by increasing numbers of environmental catastrophes, such as extreme weather events and species extinctions, the Anthropocene is itself a catastrophe in the etymological sense, from the Greek *katastrophē* meaning an 'overturning' or 'sudden turn'. Its beginning, whenever that might have been, is a turn from the Holocene to a new geological epoch. This shift is also an epistemological catastrophe, a turning-point in individual and cultural self-consciousness: the catastrophe of perceiving the catastrophe. Kate Rigby suggests that 'true catastrophes' are 'opportunities for deeper understanding and, potentially, new directions'.[4] However, Timothy Clark has argued that a catastrophe like the Anthropocene may preclude deeper understanding owing to the 'derangement of given norms' that it produces.[5] Through readings of William Cowper's *The Task* (1785) and Mary Shelley's *Frankenstein* (1818), we not only show how Romantic texts responded to specific environmental conditions but also how they evinced a catastrophically destabilising shift in humanity's relationship with the more-than-human world.

The period first suggested as the start of the Anthropocene was also the period in which a geologic timescale was first formulated, owing to developments in practical stratigraphy and the development of the concept of deep time. This was an epistemological catastrophe (i.e. a 'sudden turn') on a scale to match recent theorisations of the Anthropocene. Although catastrophist models of earth history – which understood past geological changes to be the results of dramatic, violent events such as floods, volcanic eruptions and earthquakes – had largely been superseded by the middle of the nineteenth century, they remained powerful in the Romantic period and were often used as literary tropes for reflecting on political revolution.[6] A number of texts central to the Romantic canon depict the present as an overturning in which both the natural and the social orders undergo dramatic change, and existing paradigms for understanding the planet and our relation to it are no longer sufficient. While it challenged older paradigms, Romantic literature also challenged modernity's tendency to separate nature and culture into discrete ontological realms. According to Bruno Latour, this separation allows for a proliferation of hybrids that is simultaneously denied.[7] We argue that Cowper and Shelley, in different ways, address the complex natural-cultural entanglements that characterise the Anthropocene.

William Cowper wrote his six-book poem *The Task* (1785) in the wake of the 1783 eruption of the Lakagígar volcanic fissure in Iceland, which had deadly and far-reaching effects on the atmosphere. His employment of Christian tropes – apocalyptic imagery and weather events as divine punishment – demonstrates clear continuities with ostensibly secular discourse around climate change in the twenty-first century. He also makes use of the georgic literary model and its conventions for depicting changeable weather. Nonetheless, he emphasises the limitations of these Holocene paradigms for explaining the crisis or offering a solution to it. Mary Shelley's novel *Frankenstein* (1818) was conceived and written during the climate crisis largely caused by the massive eruption of the Indonesian volcano Mount Tambora in 1815. If that novel is about human vulnerability to elemental forces, it is also concerned with our capacity to manipulate the elements and to create new and unpredictable natural-cultural hybrids. It may therefore be seen as an apt parable for the Anthropocene. However, like *The Task*, it does not offer easy solutions to complex problems. Both texts are sceptical of the capacity of existing modes of thought and behaviour to explain, let alone control, human–non-human entanglements; they are also sceptical as to whether divine or technological miracles can solve the contemporary catastrophe.

The Task and the Unprecedented Anthropocene

As well as the first proposed start date for the Anthropocene, 1784 was the year that William Cowper completed *The Task*. It is an Anthropocene poem insofar as the objects of its critique are a catalogue of subjects that have been frequently identified as the epoch's defining features, including capitalism and consumerism, imperialism, the exploitation of animals, pollution, fossil fuels and climate change. It is an Anthropocene poem, furthermore, in that it conceives of its historical moment as a turning-point in planetary climate history. *The Task* depicts a catastrophic time in which a past characterised by a (mostly) hospitable and predictable natural environment is giving (or has already given) way to a present characterised by a hostile climate and natural disasters. Tobias Menely identifies *The Task* as a 'sustained reflection on the obscurity of the present'. Developing his argument that 'Cowper came to regard the [contemporary] atmospheric turmoil as a symptom of modern time' and its radical difference from the past,[8] we explore the extent to which Cowper's articulation of this catastrophic turning-point leaves space for a 'cure' for such symptoms of modernity, or for the underlying disease.[9] If the present belongs to a new age, what, if any, use do historical precedents and paradigms – including those that constitute his own poem – have in helping us to understand and respond? Cowper attempts to contextualise the catastrophic present in a longer timeline of natural, religious and literary history, but questions whether the cultural strategies of the past are and will be viable still. He is sceptical as to whether any existing paradigm of humanity's relationship with nature can explain or solve the present crisis. Between a past that offers no answers and an unknown future, the present catastrophic moment is one in which meaningful action stagnates.

The year 1783–4 was one of strange weather across the world. From February 1783 months of earthquake activity in southern Italy killed between thirty thousand and fifty thousand people. There were several volcanic eruptions, the most dramatic and deadly being that of the Lakagígar volcanic fissure in Iceland. The 'Laki' eruption lasted from 8 June 1783 till 7 February 1784, and released into the atmosphere around 120 million tonnes of sulphur dioxide that caused an aerosol veil to cover Europe in a thick, dry fog from June to winter 1783.[10] In Europe the summer of 1783 was extremely hot and stormy, and the winter extremely cold.[11] Around a fifth of Iceland's population, and tens of thousands more across Europe, were killed as a result of poisoning or famine caused by the eruption. News of it did not reach the continent of Europe until September 1783, and it was not immediately known to be the cause of the strange weather.[12] Thus, *The Task* responds to climate change that Cowper does not know is neither permanent nor anthropogenic.

In Book II of *The Task* Cowper reflects on the weird weather and general sense of catastrophe:

> Sure there is need of social intercourse,
> Benevolence and peace and mutual aid
> Between the nations, in a world that seems
> To toll the death-bell to its own decease,
> And by the voice of all its elements
> To preach the gen'ral doom. When were the winds
> Let slip with such a warrant to destroy,
> When did the waves so haughtily o'erleap
> Their ancient barriers, deluging the dry?
> Fires from beneath, and meteors from above
> Portentous, unexampled, unexplained,
> Have kindled beacons in the skies, and th' old
> And crazy earth has had her shaking fits
> More frequent, and foregone her usual rest.
>
> (II.48–61)

Cowper's questions are an attempt to understand the changes in the climate by contextualising them within a longer narrative. He looks back through the history of the 'old' earth but finds no answers because the present is 'unexampled'. He alludes to the Deluge as a possible precedent, but later states, in his description of the earthquakes in Sicily, that 'Never such a sudden flood, / Upridged so high, and sent on such a charge, / Possess'd an inland scene'. (II.115–17) Cowper seems to be articulating 'the prospect of unprecedented change', which Zoltán Boldizsár Simon has argued is a defining experience of the Anthropocene.[13] He uses familiar tropes from Christian apocalyptic discourse, such as the phrase 'gen'ral doom' (a quotation from *Romeo and Juliet*, III.2.68; itself an allusion to Revelation 8–9). But they exist in a strange disjunction with the stated unfamiliarity of the present. In this way the passage relies on, even as it disclaims, continuities.

Whereas Simon argues that unprecedented change produces a 'demand for immediate and preventive action', for Cowper the lack of precedent paralyses.[14] He uses the weather to make the political argument that now is no time for disputes between humans, but he does not claim a causal relation between natural and political disorders. Peace is not said to offer any kind of solution to the sickening of nature, only temporary comfort in the shared nature of the suffering: 'brethren in calamity should love' (II.74). The 'close of all' still seems to approach, regardless of human action (II.65).

In the lines that follow, Cowper looks forward to a future that extends beyond this catastrophic moment, but is unable or unwilling to describe it in any detail:

> But grant her [the earth's] end
> More distant, and that prophecy demands
> A longer respite, unaccomplished yet;
> Still they are frowning signals, and bespeak
> Displeasure in His breast who smites the earth
> Or heals it, makes it languish or rejoice.
> (II.65–70)

Here Cowper finds an explanation for this catastrophic climate change. He invokes the 'punishment paradigm': the ancient theory that God controls the weather so as to reward or punish human behaviour.[15] While this 'way of making sense of calamities ... began to wane in earnest with the rise of a mechanistic and atomistic view of matter during the seventeenth and eighteenth centuries ... Christian versions of the punishment paradigm persist[ed] well into the nineteenth century'.[16] Narratives of divine intervention are now more often associated with denials of anthropogenic climate change, but we can, nevertheless, recognise the punishment paradigm as an older model for understanding humans as a climatic force. It allowed Cowper to reassert the correlation between human action and climate.[17]

Accordingly, *The Task* utilises several existing models for understanding the interrelationship between nature and human culture, from Christian narratives of apocalypse and punishment to secular scientific explanations to other generic models such as georgic. But in the poem, these old models repeatedly fall short of offering practical guidance for the 'unexampled' present and unknown future. Cowper's appeals to God's intervention quickly work to mystify as well as assert that correlation, and to diminish rather than increase the sense of human control over climate. As Menely suggests, 'what is illuminated by providential meteorology is the opacity of natural signs'.[18] 'Such evil sin hath wrought', Cowper states with confidence, implying that the earthquakes in Sicily are, at least in part, a 'judgment' of unjust imprisonment there (II.131–3); but shortly afterwards the sin is defined loosely as 'an atheist life' (II.180), and elsewhere even more broadly as 'guilt' or wickedness (II.155). In Cowper's version of the punishment paradigm, which refuses to pinpoint one specific cause of the judgement, the global scale and multifaceted nature of the sin makes it unmanageable. All '[s]tand chargeable with guilt', and 'the less' guilty may be punished 'to warn / The more malignant' (II.155–8).

Like political peace, faith is offered as a source of comfort rather than a solution to the present crisis. Cowper argues that perceiving God's hand in nature brings comfort and happiness, but although it 'resolves' 'good and ill' into God's will, it does not eliminate those ills themselves:

> Happy the man who sees a God employed
> In all the good and ill that chequer life!
> Resolving all events, with their effects
> And manifold results, into the will
> And arbitration wise of the Supreme.
>
> (II.161–5)

This passage is Cowper's version of the 'Happy Man' set piece, a popular trope of georgic poetry based on examples by Virgil and Horace. As with the punishment paradigm, an idea or trope that we initially expect to demonstrate human control over nature is turned around to demonstrate lack of control. Whereas Virgil's Happy Man is 'he who can fathom the causes of things', including earthquakes and floods, Cowper's Happy Man knows the ultimate, divine cause rather than the natural one.[19] The georgic model, with its emphasis on the promise and satisfaction of empirical knowledge, is no longer sufficient, and its trope about the pleasures and powers of natural science is twisted to make the point that knowledge of the cause is not knowledge of the solution. Cowper mocks 'the spruce philosopher' who tells 'of causes how they work ... their sure effects' (II.189–92):

> He has found
> The source of the disease that nature feels,
> And bids the world take heart and banish fear.
> Thou fool! will thy discov'ry of the cause
> Suspend th' effect, or heal it?   (II.193–7)

Cowper does not offer a clear political, moral or spiritual solution to the catastrophe, but he is confident that science does not offer a solution either. Cowper is not straightforwardly anti-science, but like Shelley, as we discuss in the second half of this chapter, he is sceptical about its curative capacity and suspicious that it fosters an arrogant and complacent notion of human power over nature.[20]

In Book III, Cowper continues to subvert his generic model of georgic. Describing the frivolous but difficult task of growing cucumbers in his garden, he concludes:

> It were long,
> Too long to tell th' expedients and the shifts
> Which he, that fights a season so severe
> Devises, while he guards his tender trust,
> And oft, at last, in vain. The learn'd and wise
> Sarcastic would exclaim, and judge the song
> Cold as its theme, and like its theme, the fruit
> Of too much labor, worthless when produced.
>
> (III.558–65)

Georgic has always incorporated an acknowledgement of nature's hostility and the risks associated with human dependence on climate. But it is essentially a Holocene genre: its instructions are premised on a mostly stable and moderate climate, which is changeable but at least predictable, and even its extremes have been seen before. Cowper's discussion of the likely failure of the cucumber-grower is within the conventions of georgic – albeit with a particularly heightened emphasis on the lack of solutions: 'Heat and cold, and wind and steam . . . oft work / Dire disappointment that admits no cure' (III.554–7). The real rejection of the georgic model comes when Cowper adds to the failure of the grower the failure of the poem to provide worthwhile instruction. The final lines invite comparison between the cultivation of the cucumber and the construction of the poem, depicting both as products of labour and as commodities: 'the poem-as-luxury-item', as Kevis Goodman puts it, '—*The Task* as giant cucumber'.[21] Book III closes with a reflection on the inefficiencies and inequalities of modern agriculture, casting a damning light back upon the waste of labour that went into Cowper's gardening: growing cucumbers for the town while '[t]he country starves' (III.757). This waste of labour is also the waste of labour of writing *The Task*: writing poetry while Sicily burns.

In *The Task*, no existing paradigm for humans' relationship with the natural world offers an explanation for the present or guidance to effect a desirable future. The result is a poem that advocates stasis rather than action, and itself occupies a kind of nervous stasis, constantly unclear in its 'task' and unwilling to commit to one theme or genre. This state resembles Clark's description of the effects of recognising the Anthropocene: 'a kind of inertia or potential paralysis'.[22] At the end of the poem, Cowper returns to the georgic Happy Man who had been advised in Book II to look for spiritual consolation rather than natural causes. Now he is '[n]ot slothful . . . though seeming unemployed, / And censured oft as useless' (VI.928–9). Cowper then suggests that he might have a use, in the ability to bring about better weather through prayer: 'Perhaps she [the world] owes /

Her sunshine and her rain, her blooming spring / And plenteous harvest, to the pray'r he makes' (VI.945–7). Menely argues that this demonstrates that 'As the poem ends, Cowper is more confident about his capacity to influence the seasons ... than he is about his capacity to recognize the prevailing weather. The weatherman has become a weather maker.'[23] But the doubt in that 'Perhaps' rises as the poem continues to its close:

> In vain the poet sings, and the world hears,
> If he regard not, though divine the theme.
> 'Tis not in artful measures, in the chime
> And idle tinkling of a minstrel's lyre
> To charm his ear, whose eye is on the heart ...
>
> (VI.1018–22)

The 'idle tinkling' of poetry offers no solutions, but the outcomes of the poet's life and the current political, social and ecological catastrophes are still said to be dependent on God who is driven, ultimately it seems, by the human 'heart'. What kind of behaviour will be rewarded with good weather, however, the poem has already failed to reveal; it has asserted only that a change in human behaviour, at a global scale, is necessary to mitigate, if it cannot halt, the current climate catastrophe.

Frankenstein and the 'Good Anthropocene'

Around thirty years after Cowper wrote *The Task* in the strange atmosphere created by the Laki eruption, Mary Shelley began work on *Frankenstein* during the 'Year Without a Summer' of 1816. Like Cowper, she did not know the origin of the unusual weather conditions, but they had a significant impact on her writing. Modern versions of the *Frankenstein* story tend to follow a traditional understanding of the novel as a warning against the dangers of anthropocentricism. In this reading, *Frankenstein* criticises scientific attempts to manipulate non-human nature without paying due attention to the risks involved, and suggests that there are boundaries that our technologies should not cross. Bruno Latour has argued for a very different interpretation of the novel. Victor Frankenstein's crime 'was not that he invented a creature through some combination of hubris and high technology, but rather that he abandoned the creature to itself'. The lesson, therefore, is that rather than trying to limit our effects on the environment, we should take responsibility for those effects; we should continue 'innovating, inventing, creating, and intervening', and show 'the same type of patience and commitment to our creations as God the Creator, Himself.[24] This may be a reasonable intellectual position, and it is consistent with Latour's argument in *We Have Never Been Modern* that modernity represses its reliance on hybrids by understanding nature and culture as separate. However, it is a reductive reading of the novel. *Frankenstein* endorses neither an anti-technological agenda nor humanity's supposed elevation to the role of 'God species'. Rather, it challenges utopian ideas about scientific progress while also suggesting that returning to a more 'primitive' state is itself a fantasy. It therefore speaks to some of the tensions that trouble Anthropocene thinking.

Latour's interpretation was published under the title 'Love Your Monsters' in the online journal of the Breakthrough Institute, a think tank based in California. The Institute describes itself as 'a global research center that identifies and promotes technological solutions to environmental and human development challenges'.[25] Its mission statement suggests 'that human prosperity and an ecologically vibrant planet are not only possible, but also inseparable', and describes its 'unique approach' as 'rooted in a positive, optimistic paradigm called ecomodernism'.[26] The signatories of 'An Ecomodernist Manifesto' are all closely associated with Breakthrough. Latour is not among them; indeed, he has been critical of eco-modernism.[27] However, his article on *Frankenstein* supports the manifesto's aspiration that a 'good Anthropocene demands that humans use their growing social, economic, and technological powers to make life better for people, stabilize the climate, and protect the natural world'. Ecomodernism, in effect, wants us to double down on the Anthropocene by embracing our power as a species to shape the world. It sees technologies such as 'urbanization, agricultural intensification, nuclear power, aquaculture, and desalination' as interventions that will reduce environmental degradation and improve human life.[28] It therefore offers a narrative of hope rather than the narrative of loss associated with other forms of environmentalism, which tend to see global capitalism, at least in its current form, as part of the problem. Thus Ian Angus suggests that the Breakthrough Institute 'consistently couples a professed concern for the environment with rejection of actual pro-environmental policies, on the grounds that new technology, growth and capitalism are the only solution to all environmental concerns'.[29] According to Angus, rather than understanding the Anthropocene as a severe crisis in the Earth system caused by industrial capitalism, Breakthrough members present it simply as a continuation of the human manipulation of the environment over many millennia and therefore not really a crisis at all.

Victor Frankenstein can be understood as a prototypical eco-modernist. He is thrilled by the prospect of harnessing the power of electricity, first brought home to him by viewing what he describes as the 'catastrophe' of an oak tree destroyed by lightning.[30] He is optimistic about the potential of technology to improve the world and ascribes to it a kind of magical power. He is partly inspired by a 'panegyric' on modern scientists delivered by one of his university tutors: '[They] have indeed performed miracles. They penetrate into the recesses of nature, and shew how she works in her hiding places ... They have acquired new and almost unlimited powers' (p.29). As Anne K. Mellor has influentially argued, this language draws on scientific discourse in the early nineteenth century; its characterisation of 'nature' as a woman to be penetrated suggests an aggressively masculine desire to impose human will on to the world.[31] Victor's ambition is to defeat death itself, not only by creating a 'new species' from apparently 'lifeless matter' but also by learning how to 'renew life where death had apparently devoted the body to corruption' (p.33). His reasons for pursuing this project are presented as a curious mixture of the rational – a desire to benefit future generations – and an emotional obsession: 'I pursued my undertaking with unremitting ardour ... a resistless, and almost frantic impulse, urged me forward' (p.33). Explorer Robert Walton, within whose letters the story of Frankenstein and his creation is framed, similarly combines rational and emotional aspirations. He emphasises 'the inestimable benefit which I shall confer on all mankind to the last generation' (p.8), but he is also a poetic fantasist. Both men are seemingly blind to the catastrophic consequences of their endeavours: as reflected in Victor trying to return to his normal life once the Creature has been animated (also a 'catastrophe' (p.35), according to Victor) and in Walton refusing to turn back even though half his crew have died. Given that, by pursuing their dreams of a better world, both characters end up destroying the people around them, it seems reasonable to suggest that Mary Shelley is wary of the Enlightenment utopianism apparent in the writings of her father William Godwin and husband Percy Bysshe Shelley, which shows a deep faith in the perfectibility of humanity even while it rejects the traditional apparatus of religion. Eco-modernism can be understood as the latest iteration of this utopianism, with even apparently secular groups such as the Breakthrough Institute having a quasi-religious belief in the eventual triumph of 'Progress'.

The Creature's narrative lies at the centre of the novel and presents a kind of counterpoint to Walton's and Victor's schemes. Rather than imposing his will on to the world, he seeks only the sympathy of others and, when this proves impossible, to find somewhere free of human influence:

> I will go to the vast wilds of South America. My food is not that of man; I do not destroy the lamb and the kid, to glut my appetite; acorns and berries afford me sufficient nourishment. My companion will be of the same nature as myself, and will be content with the same fare. We shall make our bed on dried leaves; the sun will shine on us as on man, and will ripen our food. The picture I present to you is peaceful and human. (pp.102–3)

This is exactly the sort of primitivism that eco-modernists lambast. It presents an ideal of 'wild' untouched nature that offers a refuge from the problems of modernity and, in the Creature's case, the cruel treatment that he receives from humanity. It also offers an ecocentric view of mutual coexistence with non-human creatures based on a vegan diet. The Creature implies that his vision is more authentically 'human' than the modern world; resembling the 'state of nature' celebrated by Jean-Jacques Rousseau, whose works had a major influence on *Frankenstein*.[32] However, by the time that he presents this vision to Victor, the Creature has already discovered fire. He therefore has access to a source of energy that – unlike the sun's rays – he can manipulate and control, and he has experienced the benefits of this technology.

After being rejected by his creator, the Creature, in a state of confusion and pain, spends several days wandering around a forest. Eventually he finds a 'fire which had been left by some wandering beggars':

> [I] was overcome with delight at the warmth I experienced from it. In my joy I thrust my hand into the live embers, but quickly drew it out again with a cry of pain. How strange, I thought, that the same cause should produce such opposite effects! I examined the materials of the fire, and to my joy found it to be composed of wood. I quickly collected some branches; but they were wet, and would not burn. I was pained at this, and sat still watching the operation of the fire. The wet wood which I had placed near the heat dried, and itself became inflamed. I reflected on this; and, by touching the various branches, I discovered the cause, and busied myself in collecting a great quantity of wood, that I might dry it, and have a plentiful supply of fire ... I found some of the offals that the travellers had left had been roasted, and tasted much more savoury than the berries I gathered from the trees. (pp.71–2)

It is hard to imagine a more innocent account of scientific experimentation. Unlike Walton and Victor, the Creature is not trying to change the world with technology; he is simply trying to make his own life a little more bearable. Through trial and error, he learns to master fire and traverses the boundary between energy regimes (solar and biomass, respectively). However, as with the energy transitions experienced by Homo sapiens – which potentially includes Victor's discovery of the principle of life – the technology that makes life more comfortable also brings with it the potential for catastrophic change. When he is rejected by the family whom he has spent several months observing, he burns down their cottage. And it is fitting that his chosen method of suicide is through fire, as he tells Walton: 'I shall ascend my funeral pile triumphantly, and exult in the agony of the torturing flames' (p.161). It seems unlikely, therefore, that the Creature would really be able to resist the temptations of fire in his South American paradise. And would the 'lamb and the kid' be safe from him and his companion, now that he has learnt of the 'savory' taste of cooked meat?

The novel never makes it to the 'wilds of South America'. It offers instead a kind of parody of that utopian vision of the state of nature when Victor travels to 'one of the remotest of the Orkneys'. In this 'desolate and appalling landscape', he is able to find the solitude that he requires in order to make the Creature a companion (p.117). As he comes close to completing his task, he reflects on the risks involved and particularly the idea that a new species might be propagated that would threaten the existence of humanity. When he sees the Creature observing his labours, he is overcome with 'a sensation of madness' and, 'trembling with passion', tears apart the body of the Creature's companion (p.119). This language suggests, as with the initial creation, that Victor's apparently rational reasons for acting as he does are in the service of motives that are much more obsessive and pathological. The novel's problem is certainly not with science per se – Mary Shelley was very much a child of the Enlightenment – but may well be with a science that lacks reasonableness. In the introduction to the 1831 version of the novel, she associates Victor's experiment with an attempt 'to mock the stupendous mechanism of the Creator of the world', suggesting that technology should not seek to cross divinely set boundaries (p.168). However, this claim does not reflect the unruly energies and intellectual excitement of the 1818 version of the novel, from which God is notably absent. Even after the suffering that their actions have led to, Walton and Victor refuse to take the obvious moral lesson from their experiences. Shelley's novel is certainly alert to the unintended consequences of technology and the dangers of utopian thinking. But Victor's and Walton's unwillingness to let go of their hopes suggests, like the Creature's discovery of fire, that Shelley sees catastrophic change as an unavoidable part of human culture.

That is not to say that such change can only take us in one direction. Thinking about the Anthropocene genealogically has the value of showing its history as contingent rather than inevitable. Fire becomes a destructive force in the Creature's hands because of his sense of alienation, not because of the nature of fire; the current hegemony of carbon capitalism is primarily owing to political, economic and cultural factors rather than technological 'progress' or the nature of fossil fuels. Latour's argument that we should embrace catastrophic technologies is a powerful one, but it may also distract from the socio-political overturnings required at a time of climate catastrophe.[33] *Frankenstein* offers a more nuanced approach than he suggests. In its complex portrayal of the Creature as a marginalised other, it asks us to be wary of invocations of humanity as a unified agent, given the inequalities that drive, and are driven by, catastrophic change. Yet the novel also shows how difficult it can be to control our technologies, even if we wish to do so. For when one reads the myriad of statistics and reports reflecting our Anthropocene catastrophe, it is hard to share the eco-modernists' optimism about our capacity to make well-managed interventions to the Earth's systems. We live on a volatile planet and the idea that we can shape it to our whims is a fantasy.[34]

Cowper likewise understands climate change in relation to political, economic and cultural factors and he calls for individual and social transformation. But in *The Task*, as in *Frankenstein*, any optimism in perceiving the contingency of the Anthropocene is undercut by the scale and complexity of the problem, and by our limited capacity to comprehend it. Both *The Task* and *Frankenstein* therefore articulate the catastrophic nature of the Anthropocene as a turning-point, one where existing paradigms for understanding the entanglements between humans and non-human nature are frustratingly ineffective, and solutions elusive. While it draws heavily on Christian apocalyptic tropes, *The Task*'s sense of paralysis is ultimately more akin to secular catastrophism. Similarly, *Frankenstein* mounts a catastrophic *reductio ad absurdum* of the quasi-religious technological utopianism most recently adopted by the eco-modernists. In doing so these two texts articulate our current position: still at a turning-point, part of the same continuous catastrophe that has extended, so far, over at least two centuries. We seem unable to progress, with any meaningful action stymied by the magnitude, variety and unruliness of the hyperobject of global environmental change. The texts remind us that paradigms that attempt to explain our catastrophic present and future, and those which offer solutions to it, whether technology or poetry, may in fact be part of the problem. Gloomy as it may sound, that recognition is perhaps a necessary precondition for finding a better way of doing things.

Notes

1. Paul Crutzen and Eugene F. Stoermer, 'The Anthropocene', *IGBP Newsletter* 41 (May 2000), p.17.
2. Andreas Malm, *Fossil Capital: The Rise of Steam Power and the Roots of Global Warming* (London and New York: Verso, 2016).
3. For a discussion of further ways in which Romantic literature can usefully be read as Anthropocene literature, see Thomas H. Ford, 'Punctuating History Circa 1800: The Air of Jane Eyre' in Tobias Menely and Jesse Oak Taylor (eds.), *Anthropocene Reading: Literary History in Geologic Times* (University Park: Pennsylvania State University Press, 2017), pp.78–95.
4. Kate Rigby, *Dancing with Disaster: Environmental Histories, Narratives, and Ethics for Perilous Times* (Charlottesville and London: University of Virginia Press, 2015), p.18.
5. Timothy Clark, *Ecocriticism on the Edge: The Anthropocene as a Threshold Concept* (London: Bloomsbury, 2015), p.195.
6. See Martin J. S. Rudwick, *Bursting the Limits of Time: The Reconstruction of Geohistory in the Age of Revolution* (Chicago: Chicago University Press, 2005); and Mary Ashburn Miller, *A Natural History of Revolution: Violence and Nature in the French Revolutionary Imagination, 1789–1794* (Ithaca, NY and London: Cornell University Press, 2011).
7. Bruno Latour, *We Have Never Been Modern* [trans. Catherine Porter] (Cambridge, MA: Harvard University Press, 1993).
8. Tobias Menely, '"The Present Obfuscation": Cowper's Task and the Time of Climate Change', *PMLA* 127(3) (2012), 477–92 (p.480).
9. William Cowper, *The Poems of William Cowper*, ed. John D. Baird and Charles Ryskamp (Oxford: Clarendon Press, 1995, reprinted 2002), vol. 2, *The Task*, III, 557. Subsequent references to *The Task* are to this edition, cited parenthetically by book and line number.
10. Thorvaldur Thordarson and Stephen Self, 'Atmospheric and Environmental Effects of the 1783–1784 Laki Eruption: A Review and Reassessment', *Journal of Geophysical Research Atmospheres* 108(D1) (2003), AAC 7, 1–29.
11. G. R. Demarée and A. E. J. Ogilvie, 'Bons Baisers D'Islande: Climatic, Environmental, and Human Dimensions Impacts of the Lakagígar Eruption (1783–1784) in Iceland' in P. D. Jones, A. E. J. Ogilvie, T. D. Davies and K. R. Briffa (eds.), *History and Climate: Memories of the Future?* (New York: Kluwer Academic, 2001), pp.219–46 (n.228).
12. Ibid., p.220.
13. Zoltán Boldizsár Simon, 'Why the Anthropocene Has No History: Facing the Unprecedented', *The Anthropocene Review* 4(3) (2017), 239–45 (p.243).
14. Ibid.

15. Rigby, *Dancing with Disaster*, p.3.

16. Ibid.

17. See Mike Hulme, *Weathered: Cultures of Climate* (London: Sage, 2017) for a history of different cultures' conceptions of human behaviour as a climatic force.

18. Menely, '"The Present Obfuscation"', p.488.

19. Virgil, *The Georgics: A Poem of the Land* [trans. Kimberly Johnson] (London: Penguin, 2009, reissued 2010), p.69.

20. For an in-depth introduction to Cowper's ambivalent views on science, see Harry P. Kroitor, 'Cowper, Deism, and the Divinization of Nature', *Journal of the History of Ideas* 21(4) (1960), 511–26.

21. Kevis Goodman, *Georgic Modernity and British Romanticism: Poetry and the Mediation of History* (Cambridge: Cambridge University Press, 2004), p.104.

22. Clark, *Ecocriticism on the Edge*, p.15.

23. Menely, '"The Present Obfuscation"', p.488.

24. Bruno Latour, 'Love Your Monsters', *Breakthrough Journal* 2 (2011), thebreakthrough.org.

25. Ibid.

26. thebreakthrough.org/about/mission.

27. See bruno-latour.fr/sites/default/files/downloads/00-BREAKTHROUGH-06-15_0.pdf.

28. See John Asafu-Adjaye et al., 'An Ecomodernist Manifesto' (2015), ecomodernistmanifesto.squarespace.com.

29. Ian Angus, 'Hijacking the Anthropocene' (19 May 2015), climateandcapitalism.com.

30. Mary Shelley, *Frankenstein: The 1818 Text*, ed. John Paul Hunter (New York: Norton, 2012), p.24. Subsequent references to *Frankenstein* are to this edition, cited parenthetically.

31. Anne K. Mellor, 'Possessing Nature: The Female in Frankenstein' in Hunter (ed.), *Frankenstein: The 1818 Text*, pp.355–68.

32. For a useful early ecocritical discussion of *Frankenstein* and Rousseau, see Jonathan Bate, *The Song of the Earth* (London: Picador, 2000), chapter 2.

33. Andreas Malm, *The Progress of This Storm: Nature and Society in a Warming World* (London: Verso, 2018), pp.153–6.

34. Nigel Clark, *Inhuman Nature: Sociable Life on a Dynamic Planet* (London: Sage, 2011).

CHAPTER 11

Animals

Eileen Crist

Defaunation: *a neologism coined in the early twenty-first century to refer to (1) the massive decline of wild animal populations and species; (2) empty forest, empty landscape, empty reef and empty ocean syndrome; (3) the de-animation of the world; (4) wild vertebrate biomass trumped by the biomass of livestock and humans.*

The Human–Animal Rupture

The humanisation of the world began unfolding when agricultural humans separated themselves from wild nature, and started to tame landscapes, subjugate and domesticate animals and plants, treat wild animals as enemies of flocks and fields, engineer freshwater ecologies, and open their psyches to the meme of 'the human' as world conqueror, ruler and owner. Permanent settlements, surplus food production, engineering projects, population growth, defence of territories and the drive to expand territories – all these developments were entangled with the further emergence of empire, social stratification and militarism. With the advent of Western civilisation in particular, a human–non-human hierarchical worldview took shape. 'A cultural formation', as environmental philosopher Val Plumwood wrote, 'going back thousands of years that sees the human as part of a radically separate order of reason, mind, or consciousness, set apart from the lower order that comprises the body, the animal and the pre-human'.[1] Thus was the forging of a new human identity initiated with the birth of civilisation. Defaunation was incepted.

Over time, the new human elaborated a view of the animal that ruptured from the totemic, shamanic and relational past. Animals were disempowered politically and psychically. Politically, for no longer being related to as co-citizens of place – as beings with whom to enter into conversation, partnership or negotiation. Psychically, for no longer being deemed as embodying a spiritual force that humans might learn from, avail of, defer to, harmonise or contend with. This rupture between human and animal was like shutting a door, an interspecies portal where human beings and animals would meet within quotidian and liminal spaces of physical encounter, ritual, dialogue, quest, alliance, dreaming and thanksgiving.

The new human of militarised, hierarchical mass societies embarked on defining, shaping and consolidating a newfound identity *in contrast to* the animal. This contrast was paramount to the elevation of the human into distinguished status. The animal, after all, most often has a face, and a face undeniably signifies physical and mental continuity: kinship. Looking into the face of an animal – rhino, bear, dog, tiger, manatee, swallow, frog, lobster – resembles looking into a mirror that shape-shifts the human face. In order to elevate the human above the animal, the mirror had to be broken; this required protracted work, including the elaboration of human-supremacist ideas in philosophy, political thought, science, theology and spirituality.[2] Dominant systems of thought that arose after the advent of civilisation – with its interconnected systems of territorialism, large-scale agriculture, livestock keeping, caste/class/gender stratification and militarism – gave pride of place to *the* (distinguished) *human*. In civilisations both Western and Eastern (but most especially Western), the image of the 'dumb brute' came into prominence, even as that image was perennially precarious and ever contested by minority voices from antiquity forward. In our time of global ecological deterioration brought on by the 'distinguished' human, the representation of the 'dumb brute' – the animal as lacking by comparison to the human – is finally crumbling. A new human consciousness is labouring to birth itself and struggling to restore the broken mirror.

A Long History of Defaunation

Killing wild animals goes back. Wherever 'civilised' humans went, wild animals receded and wildlife shrank. Neither ferocity towards nor fear of the human presence is an automatic reaction of wild animals; rather, civilised behaviour turned such responses into default settings. Stories of 'first encounters' often conveyed curious and fearless animals, like Charles Darwin's descriptions of Falkland Island wolves and naturalist Georg Wilhelm Steller's experiences with Steller sea cows.[3] Both species were slaughtered out of existence by people who took advantage of their gentle, inquisitive spirits. Wild animals have learned to fear civilised humans to the extent that there exist 'genes for fear', which have surely been favoured by natural selection.

Relations between humans and animals have not always been warped by violence, exploitation and terror. Nor is it likely that humanity will remain on that path indefinitely. Indigenous people cohabited with wild animals in more egalitarian, neighbourly relations that fostered links of common understanding. To draw on an example, the anthropologist Barbara Smuts describes how the Ju/wa hunter-gatherers in the Kalahari Desert of southern Africa 'had a truce with the local lions such that neither harmed the other'. One day:

> Four Ju/wa hunters were tracking a wildebeest that one of them had hit with a poison arrow. When they caught up with the dying wildebeest, a pride of about thirty lions surrounded it. The men, who were unarmed and of small stature, moved slowly toward the lions and announced that the meat belonged to the people. Several lions retreated. Others held their ground for a little while, but as the men descended on the wildebeest, still speaking quietly but firmly, the rest of the lions faded into the bush. The Ju/wa, apparently unworried, killed the wildebeest and processed the carcass.[4]

'Years later', Smuts continues, 'the situation was very different. The Ju/wa were gone, forced to move into settlements, and the new people in the area did not understand lions. An ancient interspecies tradition was broken, replaced by mutual fear and mistrust.'[5]

Animals were hounded and slain, or else fled before civilised incursions. Asian elephants, for example, inhabited most of Asia, but were extirpated from 85 per cent of their historic range.[6] Tigers spanned from the Caspian Sea through China and from Siberia to India and Oceania; they were also annihilated from the greatest portion of their former habitats. In Europe, from antiquity onward, lions, wolves, bears and other carnivores were killed or pushed to marginal lands, while the auroch, Europe's native herbivore, was driven to extinction by the early seventeenth century. This trend of extinguishing big carnivores and big herbivores, which began millennia ago, has accelerated in our time. Big animals are globally imperilled. They need expanses of habitat to live, eat and move, but civilised humans have not respected their livelihoods, have not recognised that wild animals morally count, and have not deigned to share the world equitably with Earth's non-human citizens.[7]

It is, however, important to recognise the long history of this civilised posturing and its continuities with the modern moment. Otherwise, the ecological crisis, including defaunation, appears fully explainable by the consumption and demographic J-curve trends of the post-1950s 'Great

Acceleration'.[8] Understanding a long history matters for discerning and divulging the deep causes of defaunation.

The new human that emerged with empire-building was, and is, the one with absolute power over the non-human realm, including the power of life and death over animals. The Roman Empire, for example, which spanned centuries and sizable geographic regions, installed a dominant motif for human relations to wild animals, who the Romans variously configured as property, commodities, foods, trophies, nuisances or entertainment. Regarding the last, millions of wild animals were trapped, traded and subsequently slaughtered in 'games' held across the empire over the span of centuries.[9] The new human was trained in many ways, including through these gruesome spectacles that, in the West, the Romans institutionalised and bequeathed as forms of amusement.

That training of the human was a training into and about power, an affirmation of supremacy, a turning of heart to stone and a prolonged teaching about the expendability of animals – as well as of certain humans, since the constructed human-nature hierarchy included, in its very design, stratification of the human realm, too.[10] The training into violence-as-entertainment involved the induction of indifference before the suffering of the other, an inurement that became imbricated into history in sundry conventional relations of the elevated human with the denigrated animal. Yet this unequal power relation was eminently transferable, of course, to the inter-human domain, as many have noted, including critical theorist Theodor Adorno who wrote that 'the constantly encountered assertion that savages, blacks, Japanese are like animals, monkeys for example, is the key to the pogrom'.[11] More generally, as Max Horkheimer put it, 'the history of man's efforts to subjugate nature is also the history of man's subjugation by man'.[12]

The hardening of human identity was supported and reinforced by an historical 'clinging with fanatical tenacity to the specialness of man'.[13] Yet the precarity of responding with indifference (or even hilarity) to another's suffering made such a heartless response tenuous – and promises to be its undoing. Roman philosopher Pliny the Elder reported an event illustrating the point. What happened involved enslaved elephants which were being subjected to some agony-unto-death in Pompeii's arena in 55 BC. Pliny the Elder wrote the story down some decades later, but the event was well-known by contemporaries and had apparently been retold innumerable times.[14]

> When … the elephants in the exhibition given by Pompeius had lost all hope of escaping, they implored the compassion of the multitude by

attitudes which surpass all description, and with a kind of lamentation bewailed their unhappy fate. So greatly were the people affected by that scene, that, forgetting the general altogether, and the munificence which had been at such pains to do them honour, the whole assembly rose up in tears, and showered curses on Pompeius . . .[15]

By breaking the frame of spectacle with their face-to-face entreaty to the assembled, the elephants opened a space of lucidity and a recognition of kinship. Their gesture could not immediately negate the doubly false reality under construction: degrading the dignity and integrity of animals and manufacturing human callousness towards that degradation. Nevertheless, the event was of the order of revelation and was therefore inscribed into historical memory, capable of invoking the same tears over two millennia later. Looking into the mirror of the animal is a shape-shifting experience: it uplifts and presences human beings in ways that sometimes can be worded and sometimes are ineffable. The profound reflection between human and animal, 'through the grace of its advents and the melancholy of its departures . . . leads you to that You in which the lines of relation, though parallel, intersect'.[16]

Yet even a broken mirror is a looking-glass, albeit one reflecting a fractured face. When entertainment was foisted on the masses as eviscerations, beheadings and the slaughtering of animals and barbarians, and acrid sights, smells and sounds reverberated within a communal space, a gateway was opened to something that for lack of a better word we can call 'the demonic'. The demonic is a dimension of its own. With the irruption of that dimension into human reality, human beings did not 'fall'; nor did they become 'evil'. Rather, human beings became capable of living in the fallen state of tolerating some degree of evil, as well as of inventing strategies to avoid looking at evil's repulsive visage. Why does the public, for example, not only tolerate how farm animals are treated in industrial systems but even eat food made through animal abjection and suffering? When civilisation put the human on a pedestal, and ruptured the human mirroring with the plenum of living beings cohabiting the planet, the ensuing trauma morphed into conceding the demonic a degree of legitimacy in the world of affairs. In the case of factory farms – since they cannot be countenanced without extreme revulsion – windowless quarters and 'ag-gag' laws (prohibiting filming or photography in factory farms) are installed to manufacture a charade of invisibility.

Looking at the subjugation of the animal still promulgated by global civilisation, we can recognise that it is underpinned by a long-standing worldview that separated and elevated the human. No aspect of this supremacy is inborn to human nature; rather, its ideology is lodged into the collective through social conditioning that starts at infancy and continues throughout the span of a human lifetime.[17] This conditioning is all the more powerful for its numerous historical layers and discourses, reaching back (to rehearse some milestones) to the epic of Gilgamesh's triumphant deforestation, Aristotle's invention of the Great Chain of Being, the Bible's creation story and Descartes' mephitic implantation of doubt regarding animals' subjectivity and awake awareness.

A decisive culmination of the human–animal rupture is defaunation in our time, founded on 'Differential Imperative' narratives that have spread and taken root in human societies.[18] Ethically, politically, theologically and in daily practice, the human was constituted above and against the animal. Stories about Big differences between human and animal long posed as narratives of knowledge, insight and science. The animal has instinct; the human reason. The animal is mute; the human has language. The animal is without morality; the human has ethics. The animal lives in the now; the human in temporal extension. The animal perishes; the human dies. The animal is without contract; the human has politics. The animal was made on the fifth day; the God-like human on the sixth. The animal is for using; the human has dominion. The animal can be a means to an end; the human never. As geographer Stuart Elden notes, 'a distinction from animals becomes a way of ordering, regulating, controlling and exploiting them'.[19] Thus, by early modernity, animals became explicitly constructed as 'natural resources' or threats thereof: livestock, game, fisheries, vermin, pests or protein. Implacably, threading through a long history into the present, the animal has become banally killable.

The ascendancy of the distinguished human drove the annihilation of animals for centuries. The long-standing entrenchment of a supremacist belief-system, coupled with the expansion of formidable physical factors (which that belief system, in good part, gave permission to swell) – factors such as twenty-four/seven global trade, a huge and growing human population, amoral technological advancement and spread, and escalating consumption of food, water, energy and materials – has transmuted the obliteration of wild animals into global defaunation.[20] The whole planet has gone into a rapidly declining ecological baseline, both driven by and driving the deterioration of wild animal life.

Defaunation in Our Time

Etymologically, holocaust means everything set on fire. Holocaust describes what is happening and experienced by many wild animals as populations and as species. Killing and agriculture are the principal drivers.[21] Large herbivores, large carnivores and large fish are on the front line.[22] Yet fish, reptiles, amphibians and invertebrates of rivers, lakes and wetlands are also afflicted by extinctions and massive declines.[23] Moreover, many birds, such as seabirds, migrating birds and parrots, are dwindling in numbers and threatened with extinction.[24] Amphibians and bats are losing out to invasive pathogens. Insects are disappearing owing to industrial agriculture, and so are the animals who eat the insects; 40 per cent of insect species are in decline and one-third are endangered.[25] Tropical deforestation is the leading cause of species extinction.[26] If deforestation trends continue in Southeast Asia, for example, the region will lose 75 per cent of its forests and half its biodiversity by 2100.[27] Industrial fishing has demolished marine animal life into a faint echo of what it once was.[28] Climate change is altering ecologies too rapidly for animals to adapt; and, given widespread habitat fragmentation, wild animals are hard-pressed to move and survive.

With such a multi-scale, multi-causal onslaught on wildlife, it is no wonder that numbers have declined immensely – an average 60 per cent loss in the last fifty years.[29] The greatest losses have occurred in Central and South America, where 89 per cent of animal populations vanished in that time-period. Freshwater species have suffered severe global declines of 83 per cent since 1970.[30] Defaunation is this holocaust of animals. The wild ones are in retreat, their numbers plummeting, their ranges collapsing, many becoming nocturnal as a hiding tactic, others experiencing mass mortality events, while untold numbers of species are annihilated daily with an extinction rate estimated at 1,000 times faster than the fossil record.[31]

This holocaust is occurring because of the scope and scale of impact. It is purposeful: filling forests with snares and oceans with longlines.[32] It is deliberate: stalking elephants, rhinos, big cats, pangolins and others for their body parts. It is masculinist: the spectacles/spectres of trophy-hunting, shark- and coyote-killing contests, or shooting wolves from aircraft. It is depraved: catching turtles, tortoises, lizards, birds, seahorses and other critters for the 'pet trade'. It is collateral: climate change altering the hydrological conditions of amphibians and reptiles, favouring dangerous pathogens, warping the synchronisation of birds' fledgling feeding with their food base, reducing the lichen that reindeer feed on, starving polar bears and so on. It is a way of life: plastic in the ocean kills an estimated 100 million animals a year – whales are beaching dead with stomachs full of plastic, while every sampled sea turtle corpse has had plastic in its gut. It is puerile: killing poisonous snakes from hate and fear. It is conventional: industrial fishing vacuuming the ocean of its living abundance, and this being regarded as 'normal'. It is gluttonous: bushmeat for wealthy markets, shark fins for tasteless but prestigious soup, bluefin tuna for sushi. It is traditional: hunting. It is institutional: the so-called Wildlife Services of the United States killing millions of animals every year so as to serve agricultural and other economic interests.[33] It is irresistible: the amounts of money to be made from selling pangolin scales or rhino horn. It is a conflagration: eliminating endemic rainforest animals for soy, palm oil or beef. And it is inexorable: agriculture, human settlements, forestry and other land-uses now occupy three-quarters of the Earth's ice-free land and continue to expand.

Empty world syndrome is a world emptied of wild animals and the expansiveness of the places they inhabit and contribute to creating. In a different sense, though, the world is far from empty: the biomass of livestock and humans now comprises 96 per cent of the vertebrate biomass, leaving just 4 per cent to wild big animals. Farmed poultry accounts for 70 per cent of all bird biomass.[34] These figures nonetheless convey defaunation, conveying it by weight. In that context, the world is emptied of wild animals' physical presence. But it is also emptied of their signs – trails, dens, tracks, nests, burrows, lodges, cries and songs. A lush world inscribed by wild animals is a world moulded, designed and enriched by their inner lives: by their intentions, desires, instincts, plans, exuberances and engineering. It is a world filled not only with their bodies but with animal minds.

Defaunation thus empties the world of animal forms and whittles down the manifestations of animal consciousness that shape and ornament surroundings. Animals' landscaping, as well as their peregrinations and migrations, which once filled the ecosphere, were vibrant mindscapes, not simply biologically moulded matter. Alongside destroying biological kinds, natural habitats and animal populations, humanity is now diminishing Earth's wild noosphere, elaborated especially through animal emotions, intentions, understandings, perceptions and experiences – through varieties of awareness sculpting and adorning the living world.[35] The world becomes de-animated, disenchanted, more predictable, less lively and more static and prosaic. Large animals, the ones in decline, contribute disproportionately to the distribution of nutrients across landscapes.[36] Thus, the decline of wild animals affects the world of plants: the soil that feeds the plants is less fertilised and less tilled, while plants' seeds, fruits and pollen are less widely dispersed. The plants experience the absence of their animal kin, but the dying away of plants is slower, while of plant suffering most of us know nothing. 'As we kill our fellow Earth creatures,' wrote Deborah Bird Rose, 'we make ourselves and the whole world more lonely, more empty than when we started.'[37]

Facets of Humanisation

The humanisation of the planet is not a straightforward phenomenon; it is multilayered. Importantly, to speak of Earth's humanisation is not a misanthropic diagnosis, for humanisation constitutes a world impoverishment that is abhorrent not only for non-humans but also to the full potential of human life – spiritual, experiential, aesthetic, relational and physical. At the coarsest layer, humanisation is about the seizure of land and seas, imposing formations of conquest inimical to life's diversity – industrial agriculture, industrial forestry, industrial fishing, burgeoning settlements, lethal incursions into wild natural areas, and sprawling technological systems and infrastructures.

At a more subtle layer, humanisation is about all the aforementioned impositions foregrounded into the perceptual and experiential field, while what is left of free nature becomes marginalised and backgrounded. When Martin Heidegger invited a comparison between the bridge and the dam on the Rhine, the politics of aesthetic experience is precisely what he was pointing to.[38] On the one hand, the bridge is integrated with the river and it enjoins the human to participate with the river's being. On the other, the dam is imposed on the river, politically decreeing that the river has been subjugated as a resource and aesthetically relegating the river's being as the dam's background. The bridge is about participation; the dam is about using. The bridge can be an ornament of the river; the dam is a show of mastery over it. Not coincidentally, the bridge does not afflict the river's beings (except during the building of it), but the dam afflicts the river and its beings in perpetuity.

At a biological level, Earth's humanisation produces a peculiar monoculture. Which non-humans live and survive, at some level of abundance, are those who humans favour (for example, domestic animals), those who can eke out a living at the interstices or expense of human life (for example, ticks or certain nocturnal mesopredators) and those who are omnivorous, versatile and otherwise 'generalist' (i.e. able to prosper under a range of conditions, for example rats). Other animals are geographically constricted, denied mobility, incarcerated in zoos and parks, reduced to low numbers, reconfigured as 'protein' (wild fish), facilely extinguished (especially if they are anonymous and still-undiscovered) and left at the mercy of the collateral damage of plastic, agricultural or industrial pollution and (increasingly) climate change.

Deeper yet, humanisation entrains the silencing of multitudinous signs of diverse others, with the manifestations of their consciousness erased. The landscapes and seascapes that were once numinous – animal-moulded fusions of mind and matter – are divested of that quality. The world remade as less self-illuminated better conforms to the dominant materialistic metaphysics, wherein being appears 'a cosmic accident, meaningless and mechanical'.[39] However, as philosopher Erazim Kohák understood and endeavoured to convey, the human-as-master becomes himself bereft, alongside the world deprived of its self-created luminous being. 'When we assume the posture of masters', Kohák wrote, 'proudly conquering the world, that posture ... is our crushing burden, condemning us to loneliness in a world reduced to meaninglessness.'[40]

At the level of phenomenology, Earth's humanisation ushers in the disenchantment of the world on physical and mental planes, through erasing or stripping down the great variety of wild non-human forms, minds and phenomena that *precisely* fashion an enchanted world. Disenchantment bolsters (and is subsequently reinforced by) the killjoy cosmology of a mechanical, purposeless universe in which existence is a random and pointless event. On the other hand, enchanted cosmologies, such as the animistic perspectives of indigenous peoples, were nourished in witnessing bewildering tapestries of physical forms and forms of consciousness, as well as in the regularity of unexpected occurrences arising within such a plenum. Humanisation profoundly undermines the experiential grounding of enchanted cosmologies, thereby delivering them to unreality and sentencing them to appear obsolete, naïve, romantic, fantastic and unsubstantiated. Cosmologies in which everything brims with life force and personhood are, by the lights of a modern-rationalist perspective, literary and/or ignorant fabrications. Yet the 'arid wisdom' of the modern rationalist wherein there is 'nothing new under the sun' is utterly unreflexive about the man-made existential grounding of its own assessment – namely, a world impoverished through humanisation.[41] Moreover, animist cosmologies were and remain true, vested with the authority of the plenum.[42]

The humanisation of the world produces a false consciousness of the Earth and of the human. The supremacist human shapes the Earth's ontology as human-owned, and then assumes and inhabits that ontology as though it were normal, desirable, stable or just the way things are. Parallel to normalising the humanisation of the world, the supremacist identity that forged that ontology is reified – that is, the human conqueror appears as the 'natural human'. This constitutes a double danger for humanity – the danger of being swallowed up by a false consciousness of Earth and of itself. Defaunation is pivotal to this twin alienation, because an abundance of wild animals shapes a completely different planet while also making abundantly visible the reality of diverse minds. Wiping out wild animals secures Earth's hostile takeover and instals the consciousness of the conqueror into uncontested dominance. Thus, opposing defaunation by unmasking the human imperialism that sponsors it while simultaneously supporting eco-restoration, rewilding and wild animal reintroduction initiatives are not only acts of justice on behalf of Earth's non-human citizens[43]; they are also acts of resistance to the oblivion into which humanity is in danger of descending by misconstruing a humanised Earth and a naturalised conqueror as ontological realities, rather than socio-historically constructed realities.[44]

Reanimating and Re-enchanting Earth

We can aspire anew for a world of reciprocity, communion and complementarity between humans and all other animals. A first step is to think *politically* about defaunation. Defaunation is a present-day epiphany of having represented animals (and all non-humans for that matter) as 'inferior'. That historical construction served as a bedrock for perpetual encroachments upon the natural world under the guise of being normal. Politicising the ordinariness of invading nature is to recognise nature's invasion as colonisation. While humanity has largely rejected the colonising project with respect to fellow humans, the occupation of non-human nature constitutes civilisation's last bastion of 'normal' colonialism.[45] A new humanity is bound sooner or later to recognise and overthrow a colonialism of 'nature', embracing a universal norm of multispecies justice.[46]

Freeing the non-human world from subjugation and freeing human identity from being a subjugator go together. We do not live in the 'Anthropocene'; we live in a time where the destiny of the natural world, and who humans are destined to become, hang together in the balance.

Redressing defaunation and, more broadly, Earth's plight calls for willingly limiting ourselves in order to inaugurate a new human–Earth relationship. Over time, this will enable both the restoration of a biodiverse ecosphere and the emergence of a virtuous human civilisation.[47] Embracing limitations means scaling down the human presence on demographic and economic fronts, by means of an ethos and policies that honour justice for all people. Embracing limitations further mandates pulling back from vast expanses of the natural world, thus letting the lavishness of wild (free) nature rule Earth again.[48] 'Wildness is the patterning power', wrote naturalist Scott Russell Sanders, of 'lavish production: it is orderly, extravagant, inventive. Wildness coils the molecules of DNA; it spirals the chambered nautilus and the nebulae; it shapes the whorls on a fingertip, the grain in wood, the planes of cleavage in stone; it regulates the waves breaking on a beach and the beating of a heart; it designs the amoeba's flowing form, the zebra's stripes, the dance of the honeybee.'[49]

Wild nature's patterning creates a profusion of material and spiritual gifts. It creates an abundance that humanity can inhabit by means of downscaling our physical presence and shrinking our geographical reach, for the sake of belonging with our Earth family. Letting wild animals flourish again is key to unleashing nature's bounty and to re-enchanting landscapes and seascapes.

Notes

1. Val Plumwood, *The Eye of the Crocodile* [ed. Lorraine Shannon] (Acton: ANU E Press, 2012), p.79.
2. Eileen Crist, 'Ecocide and the Extinction of Animal Minds' in Marc Bekoff (ed.), *Ignoring Nature No More: The Case for Compassionate Conservation* (Chicago: University of Chicago Press, 2013), pp.45–61.
3. Charles Darwin, 'A Posthumous Essay on Instinct' in George John Romanes, *Mental Evolution in Animals* (New York: AMS Press, 1883), pp.355–84; W. L. G. Joerg (ed.), *Bering's Voyages. Volume II: Steller's Journal of the Sea Voyage from Kamchatka to America and Return on the Second Expedition 1741–1742* (New York: Octagon Books, 1968).
4. Barbara Smuts 'Encounters with Animal Minds', *Journal of Consciousness Studies* 8(5–7) (2001), 293–309 (p.302).
5. Ibid.
6. World Wide Fund for Nature, 'Asian Elephants' (2019), wwf.panda.org/discover/knowledge_hub/endangered_species/elephants/asian_elephants/.
7. Marlee A. Tucker et al., 'Moving in the Anthropocene: Global Reductions in Terrestrial Mammalian Movements', *Science* 359(6374) (2018), 466–9.

8. Will Steffen et al., 'The Trajectory of the Anthropocene: The Great Acceleration', *The Anthropocene Review* 2(1) (2015), 81–98.

9. Michael MacKinnon, 'Supplying Exotic Animals for the Roman Amphitheatre Games: New Reconstructions Combining Archeological, Ancient Textual, Historical and Ethnographic Data', *Mouseion* 6 (2006), 1–25.

10. Matthew Calarco, 'Identity, Difference, Indistinction', *The New Centennial Review* 11 (2012), 41–60.

11. Theodor Adorno, *Minima Moralia: Reflections from Damaged Life* (London: Verso, 1978), p.105.

12. Max Horkheimer, *The Eclipse of Reason* (New York: Continuum, 1974), p.105.

13. Daniel Quinn, *Ishmael: An Adventure of the Mind and Spirit* (New York: A Bantam/Turner Books, 1992), p.146.

14. See Linda Kalof and Amy Fitzgerald (eds.), *The Animal Reader: The Essential Classic and Contemporary Writings* (Oxford: Berg, 2007), p.195.

15. Pliny the Elder, 'Combats of Elephants' [AD 75], in Kalof and Fitzgerald, *The Animal Reader*, pp.195–6 (p.196).

16. Martin Buber, *I and Thou* (New York: Touchstone, 1970), p.84.

17. Eileen Crist, *Abundant Earth: Toward an Ecological Civilization* (Chicago: University of Chicago Press, 2019).

18. John Rodman, 'Paradigm Change in Political Science: An Ecological Perspective', *American Behavioral Scientist* 24(1) (1980), 49–78; Crist, *Abundant Earth*.

19. Stuart Elden, 'Heidegger's Animals', *Continental Philosophy Review* 39 (2006), 273–91 (p.284).

20. Rodolfo Dirzo et al., 'Defaunation in the Anthropocene', *Science* 345(6195) (2014), 401–6; William Ripple et al., 'Bushmeat Hunting and Extinction Risk to the World's Mammals', *Royal Society Open Science* 3 (2016), 160498.

21. Sean Maxwell et al., 'The Ravages of Guns, Nets and Bulldozers', *Nature* 536(7615) (2016), 143–5.

22. William Ripple et al., 'Status and Ecological Effects of the World's Largest Carnivores', *Science* 343(6167) (2014); William Ripple et al., 'Collapse of the World's Largest Herbivores', *Science Advances* 1(4) (2015); Christopher Wolf and William Ripple, 'Rewilding the World's Large Carnivores', *Royal Society Open Science* 5(3) (2018); Ransom Myers and Boris Worm, 'Extinction, Survival or Recovery of Large Predatory Fishes', *Philosophical Transactions of the Royal Society B* 360(1453) (2005), 13–20.

23. David Dudgeon et al., 'Freshwater Biodiversity: Importance, Threats, Status and Conservation Challenges', *Biological Review* 81 (2006), 163–82.

24. BirdLife International, *State of the World's Birds: Taking the Pulse of the Planet* (Cambridge, UK: BirdLife International, 2018).

25. Damian Carrington, 'Plummeting Insect Numbers "Threaten Collapse of Nature"', *The Guardian* (10 February 2019); Freya Mathews, 'Planet Beehive', *Australian Humanities Review* 50 (2011), 159–78; Francisco Sánchez-Bayo and

Kris A. G. Wyckhuys, 'Worldwide Decline of the Entomofauna: A Review of Its Drivers', *Biological Conservation* 232 (2019), 8–27.

26. Alexander Lees and Stuart Pimm, 'Species, Extinct before We Know Them?', *Current Biology* 25(5) (2015), 177–80.

27. Ripple et al., "Collapse of the World's Largest Herbivores', p.5.

28. Callum Roberts, *The Unnatural History of the Sea* (Washington, DC: Island Press, 2007); Jeremy Jackson, 'Ecological Extinction and Evolution in the Brave New Ocean', *PNAS* 105(1) (2008), 11458–65; Douglas J. McCauley et al., 'Marine Defaunation: Animal Loss in the Global Ocean', *Science* 347(6219) (2015).

29. Damian Carrington, 'Humanity Has Wiped Out 60% of Animal Populations since 1970, Report Finds', *The Guardian* (29 October 2018).

30. Michael Gross, 'Can Vanishing Wildlife Evolve Back?', *Current Biology* 28(22) (2018), R1283–R1295.

31. Carl Safina, 'In Defense of Biodiversity: Why Protecting Species from Extinction Matters' (2018), e360.yale.edu; Gerardo Ceballos et al., 'Accelerated Modern Human-Induced Species Losses: Entering the Sixth Mass Extinction', *Science Advances* 1(5) (2015).

32. Thomas Gray et al., 'The Wildlife Snaring Crisis: An Insidious and Pervasive Threat to Biodiversity in Southeast Asia', *Biodiversity Conservation* 27 (2018), 1031–7; Ted Danson, *Oceana: Our Endangered Ocean and What We Can Do to Save It* (New York: Rodale, 2011).

33. Ashley Curtin, 'US Department of Agriculture's Wildlife Services Becomes Multi-Million Dollar Federal Wildlife-Killing Program' (2018), nationofchange.org.

34. Gross, 'Can Vanishing Wildlife Evolve Back?', p.R1284.

35. see Bernie Kraus, *The Great Animal Orchestra: Finding the Origins of Music in the World's Wild Places* (London: Profile Books, 2012).

36. Ripple, 'Collapse of the World's Largest Herbivores'; Gross, 'Can Vanishing Wildlife Evolve Back?'

37. Deborah Bird Rose, *Wild Dog Dreaming: Love and Extinction* (Charlottesville: University of Virginia Press, 2011), p.41.

38. Martin Heidegger, 'On the Question Concerning Technology' in *The Question Concerning Technology and Other Essays* (New York: Harper & Row, 1977), pp.3–35.

39. Erazim Kohák, *The Ember and the Stars: A Philosophical Inquiry into the Moral Sense of Nature* (Chicago: University of Chicago Press, 1987), p.183.

40. Ibid., p.81.

41. Max Horkheimer and Theodor Adorno, *Dialectic of Enlightenment* (New York: Continuum, 1972), p.12.

42. Graham Harvey, *Animism: Respecting the Living World* (New York: Columbia University Press, 2006); Jerry Mander and Victoria Tauli-Corpuz (eds.), *Paradigm Wars: Indigenous People's Resistance to Globalization* (San Francisco: Sierra Club Books, 2006).

43. Philip Seddon et al., 'Reversing Defaunation: Restoring Species in a Changing World', *Science* 345(6195) (2014), 406–12; Callum Roberts et al.,

'Marine Reserves Can Mitigate and Promote Adaptation to Climate Change', *PNAS* 114(24) (2017), 6167–75; Eric Dinerstein et al., 'An Ecoregion-Based Approach to Protecting Half the Terrestrial Realm', *BioScience* 67(6) (2017), 534–45; Christopher Wolf and William Ripple, 'Prey Depletion as a Threat to the World's Large Carnivores', *Royal Society Open Science* 3(8) (2016).

44. Helen Kopnina et al., 'The "Future of Conservation" Debate: Defending Ecocentrism and the Nature Needs Half Movement', *Biological Conservation* 217 (2018), 140–8; Crist, *Abundant Earth*.

45. Tom Butler, 'Protected Areas and the Long Arc toward Justice' in George Wuerthner, Eileen Crist and Tom Butler (eds.), *Protecting the Wild: Parks and Wilderness, the Foundation for Conservation* (Washington, DC: Island Press, 2015), pp.ix–xxvii.

46. A. Treves, F. J. Santiago-Ávila and W. S. Lynn, 'Just Preservation', *Biological Conservation* 229 (2019), 134–41.

47. Crist, *Abundant Earth*.

48. Harvey Locke, 'Nature Need Half: A Necessary and Hopeful New Agenda for Protected Areas', *Parks* 19(2) (2013), 13–22; E. O. Wilson, *Half Earth: Our Planet's Fight for Life* (New York: W. W. Norton, 2016).

49. Cited, Tom Butler, 'Rewilding Ourselves, Rewilding the Land', *Wild Earth* (1999), 7–8 (p.7).

CHAPTER 12

Humans

Hannes Bergthaller

The Anthropocene as Paradox

One of the most frequently rehearsed lines of critique regarding the Anthropocene is that the concept reinforces a dangerous sense of human superiority. Eileen Crist has argued that it affirms a 'Promethean' self-image of Homo sapiens as 'a genius if unruly species, distinguishing itself from the background of merely-living life, whose unstoppable and in many ways glorious history ... has yielded an "I" on a par with Nature's own tremendous forces'.[1] While this critique applies to some versions of the Anthropocene concept, it overlooks another, equally salient aspect – that humans are hardly the first species in the history of our planet to have attained the status of a geological force. About 3.5 billion years ago, cyanobacteria figured out how to use sunlight, water and carbon dioxide in order to synthesise carbohydrates. The oxygen which resulted as a waste product of photosynthesis poisoned the atmosphere for most fellow microbes; it also removed methane from the atmosphere, weakening the greenhouse effect and plunging the Earth into an ice age which lasted for 300 million years.[2] About 3.25 billion years later, a species of microbe known as methanosarcina took the opposite route, ratcheting up the greenhouse effect to such an extent that about 90 per cent of all species were wiped out.[3] In other words, there is nothing special about life forms dabbling in large-scale terraforming experiments, or in those experiments turning out badly.

So if there is something that sets Homo sapiens apart from other terraforming species, and that would therefore distinguish the Anthropocene from all preceding geological epochs, it is not that we have acquired the ability to transform the Earth system but rather that our species has come to *recognise* what it is doing. This entails an epistemological conundrum which underlies much of the irritation that geologists have expressed about the Anthropocene concept.[4] As scientists, geologists aim at an *objective* description of the world. Objectivity, in the words of Heinz von Foerster, 'requires that the properties of the observer be left out of any descriptions of his observations'.[5] The problem with the concept of the Anthropocene is that it makes it manifestly impossible to quarantine the observer like this. The insight that human actions have geological consequences will surely change how humans act – or at least change the meaning of their inaction. What we *believe* the Anthropocene to be will change what the Anthropocene *is*. Indeed, for many scholars, that is precisely the point: they champion the term because of its capacity for political mobilisation. But this also implies that *the concept of the Anthropocene is itself an element of that which it names.*

This, however, is a paradox. Like every true paradox, it instals ambiguity at the heart of the matter. The Anthropocene proposes that humans act as a geological force; but insofar as they form a *concept* of themselves *as* a geological force, they are also fundamentally unlike any other such force. This suggests that the Anthropocene is not just another geological epoch but rather an event which, as Gisli Palson et al. have argued, 'potentially changes the very nature of the geological by clearly marking it as a domain that includes intentionality and meaning'.[6] This formulation preserves the ambiguity: it joins intentionality and meaning, those quintessential properties of the human as it is traditionally understood, with the domain of geology, that is, of blind natural forces – without subsuming one under the other. The idea of the Anthropocene contains both possibilities: that human meaning-making is revealed as another aspect of geological process, *or* that geological process is incorporated into human meaning-making.

In this chapter, I will argue that this paradox is of crucial importance for the stories we tell about the Anthropocene, and that it finds poignant expression in a structural element of such stories that, with reference to Aristotelian poetics, I will refer to as *Anthropocene anagnorisis*. For Aristotle, *anagnorisis* (or 'recognition') marks 'a change from ignorance to knowledge, producing love or hate between the persons destined by the poet for good or bad fortune'.[7] It is the hallmark of good plots that they pivot on moments of recognition, which ideally should coincide with *peripeteia*, that is, a dramatic reversal of fortunes. Aristotle's prime example is Sophocles' *Oedipus the King*, whose action converges on the moment when it is revealed to Oedipus that, by killing his father and marrying his mother, he himself brought destruction upon the city of Thebes.

Oedipus the King is pertinent here because Anthropocene anagnorisis also involves a moment of *self*-recognition – albeit a paradoxical self-recognition which entails a doubling of the human, because the human which recognises itself as a geological force *both is and is not* that geological force, and, like Oedipus, is revealed as both innocent and guilty. What critiques of the Anthropocene concept as an expression of human hubris fail to acknowledge is precisely the way in which the Anthropocene fractures our understanding of the human. In an important sense, conceiving of the human as a geological force entails a debasement of our species rather than an apotheosis. Paraphrasing Crist, one might say that 'our glorious history' has yielded not an 'I' but a monstrous *it*.[8] After all, in most instances we experience this new geological force not as something proper to us but as something that impinges on us from outside. The anthropogenic transformation of the Earth system may be an outcome of human efforts to control our environments, but, insofar as it now threatens to make the planet uninhabitable for humans, it suggests that we are unable to contain our own powers of control. The Anthropocene is not the direct outcome of purposeful actions but the cumulative effect of individual behaviour multiplied by billions. The human as a force of nature thus radically negates the human as understood by traditional humanism, that is, of the human as the master of its own fate, a rational, self-determined being, or as the subject of a universal history of emancipation. To recognise the human as a geological force is to see ourselves as on the same level with the cyanobacteria and methanosarcina. We encounter ourselves as an alien force.

Homo *and* Anthropos

The Anthropocene entails, therefore, a split between two opposing conceptions of the human. Dipesh Chakrabarty has described this as a doubling of the figure of the human into a 'human-human' and a 'nonhuman-human'.[9] More recently, he has designated these as *homo* and *anthropos*. *Homo* describes the human as a being which acts purposefully, with reference to goals expressed and contested in language, a being concerned with 'issues of justice' and which can thus be blamed, praised or admonished.[10] This is the human of traditional humanism as well as of the contemporary humanities insofar as they conceive of humans as historical creatures differentiated by culture, economic status, gender or race, but at the same time as unified in terms of an abstract equality based on some notion of universal rights. *Anthropos*, on the other hand, describes the human as a geohistorical force – a force which acts blindly, not in terms of consciously held purposes but by way of cumulative effects and, as it were, behind the back of *homo*.[11]

Anthropocene anagnorisis involves a recognition of this doubleness – a recognition which determines the relationship between *homo* and *anthropos* in a particular way and thus brings about a reversal of fortunes. Anthropocene narratives unfold or explicate the paradox by distinguishing among different versions of the human and arranging them into a temporal sequence, thus generating stories that tell people how to act. There are as many ways of doing this as there are stories about the Anthropocene. Broadly speaking, however, such narratives tend to fall into two large categories which cut across all genres and apply equally well to fiction, non-fiction or scholarly texts.

On the one hand, there are stories in which rational *homo* subdues the wayward *anthropos*, such that the blind force of our species is transformed into a power that can be wielded with purpose. A version of this narrative was already implied in the earliest formulations of the Anthropocene concept,[12] and has been explicitly articulated by writers such as Erle Ellis, Mark Lynas or Emma Marris, and especially by the self-declared 'eco-modernists' associated with the Californian Breakthrough Institute (discussed in this collection by Higgins and Somervell, in Chapter 10).[13] This *eco-modernist narrative* is the one that Crist denounces as 'Promethean'.

On the other hand, there is the kind of story in which it was the arrogance of *homo* that got us into the present mess. This is the *ecological posthumanist narrative*.[14] In this story, humans recognise that they must renounce delusions of grandeur and learn to view themselves as just one other biological species. *Homo* is chastened and abdicates to *anthropos*. Amitav Ghosh opens *The Great Derangement* with an example of this type of anagnorisis: the scene from *The Empire Strikes Back* 'in which Han Solo lands the Millennium Falcon on what he takes to be an asteroid – but only to discover that he has entered the gullet of a sleeping space monster'.[15] Ghosh speculates that for future humans this scene will have lost all shock value because they will 'surely understand, knowing what they presumably will know about the history of their forebears on Earth, that only in one, very brief era, lasting less than three centuries, did a significant number of their kind believe that planets and asteroids are inert'.[16] This is *anthropos*, looking back at poor deluded *homo*. Ghosh links the anecdote explicitly to Aristotle's anagnorisis, but emphasises the recognition of non-human agency – the Anthropocene, in his telling, forces us to 'become aware of the urgent proximity of nonhuman presences' which may have their 'own purposes of which we know nothing'.[17] Nevertheless, his story, too, converges on a moment of *self*-recognition, because to understand the agency of the non-human is at the same time to reconceive *human* agency: 'The knowledge that results from recognition . . . is not of the same kind as the discovery of something new: it arises rather from a renewed reckoning with a potentiality that lies within oneself.'[18] For Ghosh, Anthropocene anagnorisis is about recovering a sense of kinship with the 'lost other' which Western modernity had denied.[19]

Among ecocritics, this narrative is by far the more popular. It is the story that Bruno Latour has been telling since *We Have Never Been Modern*, which casts modernity as a strange historical interlude where those in its thrall convinced themselves of their privileged position in a universe devoid of purpose.[20] It is also the story that underpins Donna Haraway's *Staying with the Trouble* when she criticises the Anthropocene concept for its myopic focus on the human and celebrates the ways in which human agency is inhabited and enabled by the agency of non-human others.[21] In all its variants, this version of Anthropocene anagnorisis entails the recognition that the human is not what we believed it was – not the self-conscious, self-identical actor limned in the humanist tradition but, rather, one that is historically variable, acting within 'interspecies relationships' or as a node in a complex assemblage of material agents. In this view, the new geological epoch demands stories in which (post-)humans recognise the agency of the non-human world, renounce the project of mastering it and hopefully bring about a reversal of fortunes.

Weird Tales for the Anthropocene: Jeff Vandermeer's *Southern Reach* Trilogy

The genre that has become most closely associated with this set of ideas is weird fiction. A literary hybrid splicing together elements from the Gothic tradition, fantasy, science fiction and the modernist avant-garde, weird fiction began to find wider recognition as a distinctive genre only around the turn of the last century, in no small measure owing to prominent protagonists such as China Miéville or Jeff VanderMeer.[22] More recently, it has become something of a critical commonplace to see weird fiction, from H. P. Lovecraft onwards, as prefiguring and articulating the onto-logical shock of the Anthropocene.[23] VanderMeer's *Southern Reach* trilogy (*Annihilation*, *Authority*, and *Acceptance*, all published in 2014) has, in particular, been widely hailed as an exceptionally powerful literary response to the new geological age.[24] Usually, this is understood to mean that the novels present a version of the ecological posthumanist narrative. As

Siobhan Carroll writes, they tell a story about 'the return of our repressed
awareness of humanity's implication in a natural world' and the surrender
of 'human pretensions of environmental power'.[25] I will argue here that
such readings tend to overlook the profound ambiguity of the novels. The
trilogy, I suggest, dramatises moments of Anthropocene anagnorisis but
keeps the underlying paradox in suspense, refusing to resolve it in favour of
either *anthropos* or *homo*.

The novels revolve around Area X, a mysterious zone somewhere on the
coast of Florida which, about thirty years before the diegetic present, was
suddenly sealed off from the surrounding world by an invisible, imperme-
able boundary, leaving only a single entry-point. Officially, Area X is
declared an environmental disaster area; in reality, a secret government
organisation, the Southern Reach, has been tasked with investigating the
phenomenon. After sending expedition after failed expedition through the
gate in futile attempts to determine the nature of Area X, they have learned
very little. The zone appears to be cleansing itself of toxic pollutants and
other traces of human inhabitation, but most of the few expedition
members who actually return are mentally blank and die from cancer in
a matter of months.

The first novel, *Annihilation*, takes the form of a journal by one member
of the twelfth and last expedition, a female biologist distinguished by
antisocial tendencies and her love of wild nature. In the opening pages,
she painstakingly lists the precautions which have been taken by expedition
members to ensure that their accounts of Area X are objective. In what
amounts to a caricature of the scientific method, they are stripped of their
proper names, referring to each other only by their functions (surveyor,
psychologist, anthropologist, etc.).[26] However, we do learn that the biologist's motives for joining the group are deeply personal: her husband
disappeared with the previous expedition. Her goal, if not to find him, is
at least to share his fate.

The separation of the observer from the observed and the pretence of
impersonality begin to break down almost immediately. In the first
chapter, the expedition descends into a kind of well which the biologist,
for reasons she does not understand, feels compelled to think of as
a 'tower' (p.6). They find the walls covered with 'sparkling green vines'
(p.23) which spell out a vaguely biblical incantation. As the biologist
leans in closer – 'like someone ... tricked into thinking that words
should be read' (p.25) – spores rise from the letters and enter her nose.
From this moment onwards, her perception of the environment is
changed: during their ascent, she is overwhelmed by the intuition

(soon to be confirmed) that they are 'inside the gullet of a beast' (p.27), and her subsequent description of events is overshadowed by a sense that her mind and body are gradually changing. A 'brightness' that has lodged itself inside of her (p.83) endows the biologist with a preternatural sensitivity to her wild surroundings: 'The wind picked up, and it began to rain. I saw each drop fall as a perfect, faceted, liquid diamond ... The wind was like something alive; it entered every pore of me ... I remembered that just a day ago, I had been someone else' (p.74).

As Carroll has pointed out, *Annihilation* reverses the trajectory of the classic exploration narrative, a genre in which the modern project of mastering nature found paradigmatic expression. Rather than 'opening up' an unknown environment, the biologist is mastered and transformed by it: 'the brightness washed over me in unending waves and connected me to the earth, the water, the trees, the air, as I opened up and kept opening up' (p.161). This transformation is not just a psychological or a figurative one: analysing samples from the various creatures she encounters, the biologist realises that they consist of human tissue. Area X is literally assimilating those who have entered it, reassembling them into human-animal hybrids and creating replicas which, we later learn, are sent to the outside to take the place of their originals. By the end of the novel, the biologist comes to understand that what is happening to her may be a harbinger of the future, and that the mysterious presence inside Area X is on the verge of breaching its boundary and engulfing the larger world. She is uncertain whether to fear or welcome this prospect: 'the terrible thing ... is that I can no longer say with conviction that this is a bad thing. Not when looking at the pristine nature of Area X and then the world beyond, which we have altered so much' (p.192). She has given up not only on the epistemic drive that constituted her professional identity – 'observing' the changes around her, she writes, 'has quelled the last ashes of the burning compulsion I had to know everything' – but even on her own humanness: 'the thought of continually doing harm to myself to remain human seems somehow pathetic' (p.194). In the immediate terms of the biologist's narrative, the last sentence refers to the fact that physical injuries (which she had allowed others to inflict on her) appear to slow down the process of transformation that she is undergoing. Within the wider set of concerns raised by the novel, however, this suggests that the forms of subjectivity which are commonly understood to constitute the 'human' are predicated on a kind of ontological self-mutilation – a constriction of the possibilities that open up when humans are viewed not as separate from but rather as connected to the non-human world.

Many commentators have read Area X and the transformation of the human which it heralds as a positive metaphor for the entangled, 'posthuman' way of being championed by Ghosh, Latour, Haraway and others. Gry Ulstein, for example, suggests that Area X represents the 'revenge of Gaia . . .', rendering poetic and ecological justice by 'striking back and colonizing the human world in the same way that humans have possessed and exploited nature'.[27] Ulstein views Ghost Bird – the copy of the biologist whom Area X sends back to the outside world in *Authority*, and who returns to Area X in the trilogy's final instalment in order to solve the riddle of her origin – as a spokesperson for the non-human world, an 'enhanced' version of Homo sapiens whose increased capacity for 'empathy or connectedness with other organisms' marks its superiority over the older model.[28] Similarly, Siobhan Carroll reads the conclusion of the trilogy as hopeful. In the final chapters of *Acceptance*, Ghost Bird returns to the 'tower' with Control, a character who in *Authority* is dispatched to the Southern Reach in a futile bid to restore order at the institution. At the bottom of the stairwell, they encounter the 'Crawler', the strange organism whose inscriptions the biologist saw at the beginning of *Annihilation*, and which appears to be the primary agent of metamorphosis in Area X. As the Crawler takes over his body, Control experiences an 'overwhelming feeling of connection' and, already in the shape of a hare, 'elongate[s] down the final stairs' and 'jump[s] into the light.'[29] For Carroll, this is a moment of positive 'transcendence' and 'the novel's most hopeful assertion of humanity's ability to change in response to the challenges of phenomena such as climate change'. In surrendering their humanity, the characters also renounce the pernicious 'Nature–Society binary' and humanity's 'pretensions of environmental management'.[30]

The Posthuman Leviathan

Such readings interpret the narrative of the *Southern Reach* trilogy as an ascendancy of *anthropos* over *homo*. However, they gloss over the profound ambivalence of the transformation which the novels describe. After all, Area X is clearly not 'Gaia' – it is gradually revealed to be the product of an extraterrestrial organism who has fled to Earth after the destruction of its home-world by an unknown cause; an organism, moreover, who was able to take hold on Earth only because it received unwitting assistance from yet another secret government agency.[31] Ulstein is surely right to describe its efforts to transform the planet as resembling human efforts to take possession of the Earth – but rather than signifying the moment when nature turns the tables on our species, it can equally well be taken to suggest that the anthropogenic transformation of the Earth should itself be seen as 'natural' – that is, as a process in which a tendency inherent in the natural world plays itself out, outside the conscious control of human individuals, and to which they have no choice but to resign themselves. The dissolution of the 'Nature–Society binary' leaves one not with a society at peace with nature but, rather, with a bewildering paradox that confounds our understanding of both these terms. It can imply that 'nature' has properties that were formerly viewed as a privilege of the social, such as intentionality, purpose or moral value; but it can also imply that the social is characterised by qualities formerly associated with nature, and driven by blind forces which are fundamentally amoral and beyond human control.

Indeed, the several instances in the novels of what one could call 'desemanticised' language, that is, language that somehow operates outside the domain of meaning, can be understood as gesturing at this latter possibility. Language is the privileged medium in which *homo* asserts itself – the medium of conceptual thought and moral judgement, the medium in which cultural traditions and identities are articulated. The strange organic lettering which the Crawler leaves on the walls of the 'tower' is only the first example, in the novels, of language which puts this understanding into question. The words are endowed with an agency that is camouflaged by their overt meaning. One of the first effects that the 'brightness' has on the biologist is that she becomes impervious to the hypnotic suggestions of the psychologist – simple phrases such as 'no *reward in the risk*' which have been imprinted on the expedition members to induce unquestioning obedience.[32] What another character will later say about the Crawler's lettering also applies to these hypnotic commands: 'The words aren't important but what's channeled through them is.'[33]

Leaving the tower behind and pressing onwards into Area X to search for her husband, the biologist, in *Annihilation*, reaches a lighthouse – the place where, we later discover, the alien organism first made landfall. Its basement is brimming with 'a moldering pile' of journals such as the one in which she is recording her experiences (pp.111–12). The sheer volume of these 'ripples and hillocks of paper' (p.111) baffles her – the journals are filled with a 'bewildering confusion' (p.113) of writings marked by a 'hypnotic, trancelike quality' (p.114) and do not add up to a coherent picture of what actually occurred in Area X. Here, too, we are dealing with writing whose significance, like that of the archaeological remains of prehistoric cultures, lies not so much in its barely decipherable semantic content but rather in its stratigraphic layering. It testifies to the power of

Area X to assimilate and erase the human: 'Slowly the history of exploring Area X could be said to be turning into Area X' (p.111).

All these episodes play with the idea that the systems of meaning by which humans make sense of the world possess an agency which is itself not subordinate to human purpose. Language here is not primarily the meaningful expression of an individual consciousness but rather the material instrument of a larger, inhuman force – or perhaps, as Ghost Bird speculates about the Crawler's marks, merely an incidental 'pattern' irrelevant to the 'purpose' of the underlying dynamic.[34] Together, these passages begin to suggest what it might mean to think of language not as the defining property of *homo* but rather as an attribute of *anthropos*. Thus, Area X stands not only for the 'lost other' which rescues humans from a destructively narrow conception of themselves but also for the *anthropos* as that aspect of the human which eludes conceptual thought. There is a scene towards the end of *Annihilation* which, though not explicitly concerned with Area X, lucidly articulates this possibility. The biologist recalls how, during her fieldwork in a tidal pool on the northwest coast, she encountered a 'colossal starfish' belonging to a species colloquially known as 'destroyer of worlds':

> It was covered in thick spines, and along the edges I could see, fringed with emerald green, the most delicate transparent cilia, thousands of them, propelling it along upon its appointed route as it searched for its prey: other, lesser starfish. [T]he longer I stared at it, the less comprehensible the creature became. The more it became something alien to me, the more I had a sense that I knew nothing at all – about nature, about ecosystems. [. . .] And if I kept looking, I knew that ultimately I would have to admit I knew less than nothing about myself as well . . . (p.175)

Both its name and its physical appearance mark this creature as a premonitory type of the Crawler – but the biologist's final admission that she may know 'less than nothing about myself' also turns it into a metaphor for the *anthropos*, for that aspect of the human which is consuming the planet. That a starfish can serve as a figure for the human also suggests that the anthropogenic transformation of the Earth may, after all, be a mark not of humanity's *alienation* from nature but, on the contrary, of its *naturalness*, the expression of a self-destructive tendency inherent in the natural world itself. The biologist's encounter with the starfish is a moment of self-recognition wherein the human is dispersed into two contradictory aspects which are, at the same time, identified with each other – a conscious human individual reflecting on the enigma of its own nature, and a blind natural force.

A similar dynamic plays out in one of the most dazzling scenes of the entire trilogy. This passage occurs after Ghost Bird has returned to Area X to solve the riddle of her own identity. She finds the island where the biologist spent the remainder of her human existence. As she is reading the biologist's journal, the biologist herself suddenly makes a personal appearance, seeking her own double. It turns out that she has metamorphosed into a kind of hyper-dimensional Leviathan, a being that could equally well be described as a geomorphic beast or a theriomorphic landscape:

> The mountain that was the biologist came up almost to the windowsill, so close she could have jumped down onto what served as its back. The suggestion of a flat, broad head plunging directly into torso. The suggestion, far to the east ..., of a vast curve and curl of the mouth, and the flanks carved by dark ridges like a whale's ... The green-and-white stars of barnacles on its back in the hundreds of miniature craters, of tidal pools from time spent motionless in deep water, time lost inside that enormous brain. ... It had many, many glowing eyes that were also like flowers or sea anemones spread open, the blossoming of many eyes ... all across its body, a living constellation ripped from the sky. Her eyes, Ghost Bird's eyes. Staring up at her in a vast and unblinking array. ... In the multiplicity of that regard, Ghost Bird saw what they saw. She saw herself, standing there, looking down. She saw that the biologist now existed across locations and landscapes, those other horizons gathering in a blurred and rising wave. ... She understood the biologist in that moment ... She might be stranded on a planet far from home. She might be observing an incarnation of herself she could not quite comprehend, and yet ... there was connection, there was recognition.[35]

The confusion of pronouns in the final sentences of this passage is not incidental but indicative of the paradoxical unity of *homo* and *anthropos* that is disclosed in moments of Anthropocene anagnorisis. In this instance, the paradox is compounded by the fact that it is Ghost Bird, the artificial duplicate of the biologist created by Area X, who occupies the 'human-human' standpoint, and who seeks to grasp the strangely dispersed, non-local existence of the 'nonhuman-human' that her original has become. Timothy Clark has described the geological agency of humankind as a kind of psychopathic revenant of Thomas Hobbes's Leviathan: whereas the latter instituted a political order that protects humans from the vicissitudes of the state of nature, the new 'planetary giant would not seem to have the supposedly definitive human characteristics of foresight and restraint, but it would be a self-destructive and self-deluding figure'.[36] VanderMeer's biologist presents a different vision of this planetary Leviathan – one which, terrifying and destructive as it may appear to the human mind, also harbours an unfathomable generative power.

Composing the Human

In the *Southern Reach* trilogy, anagnorisis does not engender 'love and hatred' but a far more ambiguous emotional state hovering between attraction and repulsion, fascination and horror. This is the affect of the 'weird' that, according to Mark Fisher, characterises VanderMeer's chosen genre.[37] It is also, I believe, an appropriate stance in the face of our own geohistorical present. The 'global weirding' of our life-worlds throws a wrench into the narrative machinery which in the past helped us to process humanity's paradoxical relationship with nature.[38] Humans are both *a part* of nature and *apart* from it; they are evolved biological beings that, unlike all other such beings, must have stories to tell them what they are, creatures who have used their capacity to act purposefully in a manner that defeats all the purposes they might possibly aspire to. Eco-modernist and ecological posthumanist narratives both resolve this paradox, but in doing so also evade it. Eco-modernism cannot explain why this time should be different – why the effort to bend nature to human ends would be any less blind and self-destructive than it always turned out to be in the past, now that it is to be applied at a planetary scale. There really is no reason to think that *homo* could step away from its own shadow. Ecological posthumanism, on the other hand, often deals in flattering images of an *anthropos* who miraculously retains all those features of *homo* that are most dear to us – an egalitarian *anthropos* who, with his penchant for diversity and cultural pluralism, looks suspiciously like an avatar of the 'American cultural left'.[39] Naturally, the writings in which this improved version of the human is disseminated are nothing like those of VanderMeer's Crawler. Therefore, they fall back on the same rhetorical tricks that have served since time immemorial to coax human beings into proper behaviour. They cannot help but appeal to the very same property of Homo sapiens that served Aristotle in defining our species: the idea that humans can be reasoned with.

Finola Prendergast has argued that *Annihilation* employs the poetic licence afforded by weird fiction in order to show what it would mean to adopt an environmental ethic based on posthumanist theories, and how it remains possible to act in spite of the radical uncertainty which such theories entail.[40] I would amend this to suggest that the measure of the trilogy's success is that it shows us not how to act but, rather, in keeping the paradoxical unity of *homo* and *anthropos* in suspense, how to come to terms with the irreducible ambiguity of human agency. This is not to relinquish the human but to learn how 'to give in but not give up', as Saul the lighthouse keeper, the first person infected by Area X, puts it to himself.[41] Half of the time, the novels' characters barely know whether their thoughts and actions are truly their own, whether they are still human or already something else, acting or being acted upon. And yet, for all its emphasis on the agency of the non-human, the trilogy remains preoccupied with individual human beings puzzling over their singular fates, writing their own faltering stories, and in this manner composing themselves in the face of a world that, as the psychologist writes in her undelivered love letter to Saul, with which the last novel closes, has become 'unimaginably difficult' (p.338). This, it seems to me, is a pretty good brief for literature in the Anthropocene.

Notes

1. Eileen Crist, 'On the Poverty of Our Nomenclature', *Environmental Humanities* 3 (2013), 129–47 (p.131).
2. Robert E. Kopp et al., 'The Paleoproterozoic Snowball Earth: A Climate Disaster Triggered by the Evolution of Oxygenic Photosynthesis', *PNAS* 102(32) (2005), 11131–6.
3. Daniel H. Rothman et al., 'Methanogenic Burst in the End-Permian Carbon Cycle', *PNAS* 111(15) (2014), 5462–7.
4. See, for example, Stanley C. Finney and Lucy E. Edwards, 'The "Anthropocene" Epoch: Scientific Decision or Political Statement?', *GSA Today* 26(3–4) (2016), 4–10.
5. Heinz von Foerster, *Understanding Understanding: Essays on Cybernetics and Cognition* (Berlin: Springer, 2003), p.293.
6. Gisli Palson et al., 'Reconceptualizing the "Anthropos" in the Anthropocene: Integrating the Social Sciences and Humanities in Global Environmental Change Research', *Environmental Science and Policy* 28 (2013), 3–13 (p.8).
7. *The Poetics of Aristotle* [trans. Samuel H. Butcher] (London: Macmillan, 1902), p.41.
8. Crist, 'On the Poverty', p.131.
9. Dipesh Chakrabarty, 'Postcolonial Studies and the Challenge of Climate Change', *New Literary History* 43(1) (2012), 1–18 (p.11).
10. Dipesh Chakrabarty, *The Human Condition in the Anthropocene*, Tanner Lectures on Human Values (2015), tannerlectures.utah.edu.
11. Eva Horn and Hannes Bergthaller, *The Anthropocene* (London: Routledge, 2020), p.70.

12. Paul J. Crutzen, 'Geology of Mankind', *Nature* 415(6867) (2002), 23.

13. Erle C. Ellis, 'The Planet of No Return: Human Resilience on an Artificial Earth', *Breakthrough Journal* 2 (2012), 39–44; Mark Lynas, *The God Species: Saving the Planet in the Age of Humans* (London: National Geographic, 2011); Emma Marris, *Rambunctious Garden: Saving Nature in a Post-Wild World* (New York: Bloomsbury, 2013). See also John Asafu-Adjaye et al., 'An Ecomodernist Manifesto' (2015), ecomodernistmanifesto.squarespace.com.

14. The distinction between ecomodernism and ecological posthumanism as different ways of dealing with the relation between *homo* and *anthropos* is further developed in Horn and Bergthaller, *Anthropocene*, pp.70–4.

15. Amitav Ghosh, *The Great Derangement: Climate Change and the Unthinkable* (Chicago: University of Chicago Press, 2016), p.3.

16. Ibid.

17. Ibid., p.5.

18. Ibid.

19. Ibid.

20. Bruno Latour, *We Have Never Been Modern* [trans. Catherine Porter] (Cambridge, MA: Harvard University Press, 1993).

21. Donna Haraway, *Staying with the Trouble: Making Kin in the Chthulucene* (Durham, NC: Duke University Press, 2016).

22. Anne VanderMeer and Jeff VanderMeer (eds.), *The Weird: A Compendium of Strange and Dark Stories* (New York: Tor, 2011); China Miéville, 'Weird Fiction' in Mark Bould (ed.), *The Routledge Companion to Science Fiction* (London: Routledge, 2009), pp.510–17.

23. Brad Tabas, 'Dark Places: Ecology, Place, and the Metaphysics of Horror Fiction', *Miranda* 11 (2015), journals.openedition.org/miranda; Elvia Wilk, 'Toward a Theory of the New Weird', *Literary Hub* (2019), lithub.com.

24. David Tompkins, 'Weird Ecology: On the Southern Reach Trilogy', *Los Angeles Review of Books* (30 September 2014).

25. Siobhan Carroll, 'The Terror and the Terroir: The Ecological Uncanny in New Weird Exploration Narratives', *Paradoxa* 28 (2016), 67–89 (pp.67, 81).

26. Jeff VanderMeer, *Annihilation* (New York: Farrar, Straus, and Giroux, 2014), p.9.

27. Gry Ulstein, 'Brave New Weird: Anthropocene Monsters in Jeff VanderMeer's The Southern Reach', *Concentric* 43(5) (2017), 71–96 (p.86).

28. Ibid., 87.

29. Jeff VanderMeer, *Acceptance* (New York: Farrar, Straus, and Giroux, 2014), pp.310, 312.

30. Carroll, 'Terror and the Terroir', pp.81–2.

31. VanderMeer, *Acceptance*, pp.295–7.

32. VanderMeer, *Annihilation*, p.40.

33. VanderMeer, *Acceptance*, p.333.

34. Ibid., p.189.

35. VanderMeer, *Acceptance*, pp.195–6.

36. Timothy Clark, *Ecocriticism on the Edge: The Anthropocene as a Threshold Concept* (London: Bloomsbury, 2015), p.15.
37. Mark Fisher, *The Weird and the Eerie* (London: Repeater, 2016).
38. Horn and Bergthaller, *Anthropocene*, p.100.
39. Jedediah Britton-Purdy, 'The Mushroom That Explains the World: An Anthropologist Tries to Understand Capitalism by Studying a Japanese Delicacy', *The New Republic* (8 October 2015).
40. Finola Ann Prendergast, 'Revising Nonhuman Ethics in Jeff VanderMeer's *Annihilation*', *Contemporary Literature* 58(3) (2017), 333–60.
41. VanderMeer, *Acceptance*, p.326.

CHAPTER 13

Fossil Fuel

Sam Solnick

Ella Hickson's 2016 play *Oil* opens on a bitingly cold Cornwall smallholding in the late nineteenth century. Amidst frostbite and foul weather, the Singer family struggle to split logs to fire an inadequate solid-fuel range. Into this grim depiction of historical fuel poverty steps William Whitcomb, an American oil importer keen to purchase their land for storage and distribution. His demonstration of this new energy source floods a previously gloomy stage with light:

> *WW Lights a kerosene lamp. The lamp flame roars. The light lights the room in a way we haven't previously seen [. . .] We see parts of the room – dirt – corners – which we've never seen before. MAY takes a step toward the light – she reaches out to it*
>
> MA SINGER: God almighty.
> *MAY holds her hand out to the flame*
> MAY: It's warm. It's/
> *MAY eyes alight with wonder*
> WW: /This here miracle is kerosene – it comes right out of the ground – just
> like the birds and the bees, the trees and the rivers – it's natural.
> JOSS: We got light.
> WW: It creates much more heat than whale lamps or wood, it's hotter than
> coal – and you saw how easy it was to light.
> THOMAS: It's expensive, I guess?
> WW: Cheaper by half than whale [. . .]
> WW: There are millions of years, right there on the end of your finger[1]

Incorporating the language of divinity and miracles, this *fiat lux* moment of theatrical illumination captures the sudden phenomenological shift emerging from what J. R. McNeill describes as a transition from a 'somatic energy regime' associated with the muscular labour of humans and other animals, to a 'much more complex set of arrangements that one might call the "exosomatic regime"' based on fossil fuels and their associated technologies and infrastructure.² The excerpt also contains, in miniature, many of the features associated with the oil economy that fuel the concerns of Hickson's drama: the materiality and distribution of a 'natural' resource, with a geological history far longer than the Anthropocene-epoch repercussions of its extraction; the populations coerced, displaced or damaged by the production and distribution of this commodity that underpins modernity; and the power of new fuels to drive economic, ecological and technological transformation.

These are also thematic concerns that have come to typify the ever-expanding body of contemporary literature that deals directly with oil. What Graeme Macdonald says about 'petrofiction' holds for the main preoccupations of oil-focused poetry and drama too. Features of 'petroliterature' include

> extraction narratives, local and transnational stories of oil's development, and its dramatic transformation of space, place, and lifestyle. To these we can add tales of corporate corruption and petro-despotism, spill and disaster, the conflict between oil capital and labor, and even the "drama" of barrel prices and fictive petro-capital enacted across international territories.³

For Macdonald, a comprehensive analysis of oil in literature must go beyond such narratives of drills, spills and resource conflicts to examine the relations between 'the oblique and surface world of fuel', not least the ways in which 'petroculture' enables 'a world of electronic gadgets, just-in-time goods, and financial transactions reliant on oil consumption but abstracted from the backstage forms of its conversion, extraction, refining, and delivery'.⁴ Consequently, reading oil (in) literature means combining critical awareness with affective responses. As Patricia Yaeger reminds us, 'energy sources also enter texts as fields of force that have causalities outside (or in addition to) class conflicts and commodity wars', not least the phenomenological transformations we see tracked in moments like Hickson's scene that render the 'touch-a-switch-and-it's-light magic of electrical [or kerosene] power'.⁵

Examining *Oil* alongside Jennifer Haigh's 2016 oil and fracking novel *Heat and Light* and Juliana Spahr's 2015 poem about Deepwater Horizon 'Dynamic Positioning', this chapter suggests that contemporary literature of oil (and its intimately related fossil fuel, natural gas) is at its most interesting when it tries to find a formal response – whether through stagecraft or metaphor or metre – that negotiates this duality of fossil fuels as both volatile substances and abstract commodities. This means being able to move forward and back between mutually affecting scales, between surface extraction and oblique consumption, taking in the corporeal as well as the climactic, the affective as well as the abstract, the deep-time of geology alongside a rapidly changing geopolitics, to show the vibrant materiality of this fossilised sunlight and its violent economy and ecology on a changing planet.

Fuelling Domesticity and Desire in Ella Hickson's *Oil*

The transition from locally sourced fuel to international energy supply in *Oil*'s opening scene also inaugurates the play's concern with the ways the fossil-fuel economy extends the impact of the domestic sphere across unfamiliar spatial and temporal scales. Fuel, Karen Pinkus explains, derives from the Old English *feuel*, itself derived from the old French *foaile* used in the fourteenth century to refer to a bundle of firewood – not dissimilar to that cut by Joss to warm his pregnant wife May in Hickson's opening. *Foaile* comes from 'the Latin legal term *focalia*, meaning the right to demand material for making fire' and *focalia* itself comes from '*focalis*, pertaining to the hearth, from focus, or hearth'. The hearth, Pinkus goes on to point out, 'is related to protection, the *oikos* (origin of both "economy" and "ecology"), home, family'.[6]

Hickson captures the oil-fuelled transition from domestic *oikos* to global *Oikonomia* in the structure of her play as it ranges across continents and into a speculative future via the lives of her main characters – May and her daughter Amy – who age far slower than history. (As in Caryl Churchill's *Cloud 9*, which employs a similar device, this impossible temporal disjunction between setting and character is not explained or indeed really commented upon.[7]) Through a series of self-contained episodes, the play moves through what Frederick Buell calls the twin motifs of oil in culture, a transition from 'exuberance' (the surplus energy of a new fuel creating optimism and possibility) to 'catastrophe' (dependency on a limited resource and the problems arising from scarcity, pollution, extractive violence, etc.).[8] The second scene sees May working as a servant in Tehran nine years after she first leaves the farm seeking the better life that oil might bring, and by scene three she is a middle-aged oil executive caught in the beginnings of the 1970s energy crisis. After moving through Kirkuk in 2021 (ravaged by another Iraq War), the final scene sees Amy caring for an older May back in Cornwall in 2051; no longer able to fire their own hearth but now dependent on an unreliable grid and the promise of the post-oil technologies of Chinese energy corporations.

The stretching of slow-ageing characters across time provides an onstage embodiment of how petro-modernity extends the material ramifications of past lives.[9] Hickson's time frames draw out the different temporalities of oil, the ultimate lubricant for the increasing efficiency, immediacy and velocity of life the play shows developing across the twentieth and twenty-first centuries and which Hickson offsets against the far slower geological accumulation of the substance over millions of years. Between geological accumulation and the post-oil future that closes the play, Hickson's final lines refer to the 'age of oil', where oil fuels the creation (and fall) of institutions, regimes and empires. As 1970s May explains to a Libyan government officer:

MAY: When has land ever belonged to anyone for any other reason than someone marching in and taking it? The earth wasn't created with little dotted lines with scissor symbols all over it. It takes a hundred and fifty million years to make oil – Saudi Arabia has existed for forty years; the German Democratic Republic is only marginally older than my daughter – taking national boundaries too seriously in the distribution of global resources is short-sighted.
FAROUK: Well right now – under our government – we declare it Libyan property and we will fight to see the end of Western Companies operating in our country.[10]

Hickson's depictions of resource conflicts in the Middle East and North Africa that show the international human cost of domestic fossil fuel use are supplemented by an awareness that the hard-won social improvements in equality that Amy and May enjoy as the play progresses are themselves dependent on the petroleum industry that exports negative impacts elsewhere. As May reminds the 1970 rebellious teenage version of Amy (and her environmentalist boyfriend Nate), oil seeps into those activities that idealistic youth see as private and individual, corporeal rather than corporate.

MAY: Durex – lubricant – KY Jelly and even Vaseline if you're on a budget and – actually – now I come to think of it, the contraceptive pill.
NATE: It's important to be safe.
MAY: All made of oil.

The personal is not just political, it's petroleum.

Oil's search for ways of embodying the different temporalities and material incarnations of the fossil economy speaks to the challenge facing theatre – an art form that by its nature is normally orientated around the human scales of characters and actors – when it has had to adapt to the scales of oil or, in plays tackling climate change directly, carbon emissions more generally. Hickson's attempt to show the hydrocarbon infrastructure that now subtends even sex – both as recreation and, more commonly (given children create the ultimate carbon footprint), as procreation – is a motif that emerges frequently in post-

2000 plays concerned with energy, emissions or climate. These include productions as varied as computational scientist Steve Emmott's play-cum-lecture *10 Billion* (2013) and Steve Waters' political satire and flood drama *The Contingency Plan* (2009). In such plays, playwrights and directors find a way of capturing the link between the individual/domestic sphere and energy through staging, dialogue and plot. Significant examples include Duncan Macmillan's *Lungs*, where director Katy Mitchell's 2014 production saw pedal-powered lighting illuming a love story about the carbon consequences of conception; the oil pouring through the scenery of a dinnertime conversation about children in Matt Hartley and Kristy Housley's *Myth* (2017); and the deterioration of a fracking executive's house and relationships as he clashes with his ursine-costumed child in *F*ck the Polar Bears* (2015). Theatre about energy and climate change, particularly when it tends towards naturalism, has to find new strategies to negotiate the multiple scales of the Anthropocene; comparable challenges face the realist novel when authors try to incorporate both place and planet.

Heat and Light: Embodying Submerged Dependencies

In Haigh's *Heat and Light*, children are positioned not so much as inheritors of a potentially disastrous, climate-changed future-to-come but as victims of environmental injustice in the present. Anthropocene transformations are written both into the landscape's geology and on its inhabitants' bodies. Central to the novel's interwoven plots surrounding the Pennsylvania energy industry is the sickness of Olivia Devlin, probably caused by the gas rig drilled on her father Rich's property contaminating the water supply. The Devlin's pastor, Wes – whom we first meet as a child in 1979 – develops cancer in later life having been exposed to radiation as a child during the Three Mile Island nuclear incident. Olivia is treated at the 'miners hospital' itself built for workers suffering from black-lung associated with the coal industry that previously sustained the town of Bakerton where *Heat and Light* is set. (Bakerton Coal was the subject of a previous Haigh novel, *Baker Towers*.) Across both novels Haigh shows how energy sources transform people, place and social formations: landscapes are prospected and their mineral wealth extracted; associated institutions – schools, hospitals, unions, environmental campaign groups – spring up alongside new mining practices; industrial accidents and business opportunities emerge from the shifts of energy economics, driven as they are by technological innovation, international geopolitics and environmental awareness. Haigh shuttles across different scales to find ways of linking the individual and domestic to the multiple interlocking aspects of the fossil-fuel ecology and economy. In doing so Haigh not only establishes a series of metonyms for the depredations of the fossil economy but also uses the sickened and, crucially, addicted bodies of Bakerton's inhabitants as a powerful metaphor for Anthropocene changes wrought on both landscapes and populations.

Heat and Light's opening and closing sections repeat the phrase 'More than most places, Pennsylvania is what lies beneath'.[11] The words speak to petro-literature's dual incursions: the geological/vertical (drilling into deep time for a fossil-fuel reward) and the horizontal/geographical (the repercussions of these fuels pumping across different economies and territories). The closing section continues:

> Accidents of geology, larger than history, older than scripture: continents colliding, seas encroaching and receding, peat bogs incubating their treasures like a vast subterranean kiln. In the time before recorded time, Pennsylvania was booby trapped.[12]

Here we have two important images for oil in culture: fossil fuels as gift or treasure (natural resource) and as 'resource curse', a concept encapsulating the negative effects of oil on resource-rich territories. The energy firm Dark Elephant ('elephant' being industry slang for a giant oil or gas field) uses the language of treasure to convince the Devlins to part with the mineral rights to their farm, describing the underlying fossil resources as 'a sea of riches, nature's self-deposit box, its treasures locked away like insurance for the future. Now, at last, American ingenuity has found the key'.[13] Inevitably, the get-rich-quick scheme turns out to be something of a Trojan elephant.

Exploring the oil and gas industry through the specific tribulations of the Devlins and their neighbours enables Haigh to map the tendrils of a petrochemical network: the subcontractor's massive rigs and machines that enter the neighbourhood; the chain of debt-fuelled speculation, dependent on the vagaries of the market; the earth-shaking seismic testing; the deforestation for digger access. Once Olivia sickens, the focus shifts towards legal obfuscations and corporate evasions related to the pollution arising from Bakerton's transformation into a new hydrocarbon frontier. As the Devlin's neighbour Rena discovers, the new fossil-fuel boost to Bakerton's economy brings with it the attendant problems of what Rob Nixon famously terms 'slow violence', environmental injustice written upon the bodies and landscapes of the poor or marginalised:[14]

"The disinfectants react with bromides in the frackwater and give you brominated trihalomethane, which are known carcinogens . . . A few years ago there was a big discharge into the Monongahela. That's where half of Pittsburgh gets its drinking water"
"That's *legal*?" says Rena[15]

The surprising legality of petro-industry contamination arises, a *Silent Spring*-reading geologist informs Rena, from the so-called 'Halliburton Loophole'. This 2005 bill (the subject of Josh Fox's Emmy Award-winning documentary *Gasland* (2010)) 'exempts fracking fluid from the Clean Water Act', not just with implications for the health of Pennsylvania ecosystems and citizens but with broader geopolitical and environmental ramifications:

"You've seen those billboards, right? *Clean Energy for America's Future*? The industry wants you to believe that natural gas is better for the environment than coal or oil. And it is, on paper. But when you factor in all the emissions from thousands of truck trips, the methane that's vented or lost from gas lines—"
   He goes on this way for nearly an hour. At first Rena takes diligent notes: names of congressmen, senators, pieces of legislation. After a while she simply watches . . .[16]

Haigh tracks not just the daunting challenge of rendering apprehensible the social, economic, political, environmental and technological facets of fossil fuels, from local toxicities to greenhouse gases. She also nods towards those moments where the layperson can no longer refine their understanding, where these interlocking systems become too complex, disempowering or daunting to process and we face what Robert MacFarlane, drawing on the work of Sianne Ngai, describes as an Anthropocene 'stuplime', the 'aesthetic experience in which astonishment [that one might associate with the sublime] is united with boredom, such that we overload on anxiety to the point of outrage-outage'.[17]
   Through their imbrication in both the polluting materiality of the local fracking economy and its global, abstract commodity flows, the private space of the Devlin's homestead is turned inside out by the movement both vertically into the cursed treasure of the Marcellus geology and horizontally across the petro-industry's geography. As in *Oil*, the family farm, with its dream of self-sufficiency (Rich Devlin wants the mineral lease to fund a dairy business), is undermined by the fuel that subtends the property. *Heat and Light* sees the domestic *Oikos*, that which should be protected, contaminated by the toxic spills of energy production, be they carcinogenic

trihalomethane or radioactive Cesium-137. These materials are not inert. They open out into different temporalities and spatialities, with half-lives and after-effects that transform cells, landscapes, labour practices and foreign policy.

Both the events and the materials associated with the fossil-fuel economy have afterlives. One of the novel's epigraphs is taken from the eponymous section of Jimmy Carter's famous 1977 'moral equivalent of war' speech that warns of the USA's dangerous dependency on foreign oil. The challenges of Carter's presidency are interwoven into the events of the novel – it is the Iranian hostage crisis and its effect on the oil industry that drives the rise of the (pointedly named) Kip Oliphant, CEO of Dark Elephant; and, of course, US fracking is itself intimately related to a desired independence from oil imports. But Carter's warning is also related to key thematic and metaphorical concerns: addiction on both an individual and an industry/national scale.

Olivia's uncle Darren is one of several addicts in the novel – depressing realism given the ongoing challenges with substance abuse faced in the sorts of rural Pennsylvanian communities described in the novel, particularly in coal-mining areas.[18] The boom and bust of the fossil-fuel industry not only causes addiction but is described as an addiction. Kip Oliphant, we are told, '*is* an addict. He's addicted to drilling.' Likewise, campaigning geologist Lorne Trexler tells his corporate equivalent Amy Rubin that 'Drilling the Marcellus is costing billions. If we invested *half* that much in renewables, we'd have a permanent solution to this mess instead of swapping one fossil fuel addiction for another. Gas is no more sustainable than coal or oil.'[19]

As Gerry Canavan has detailed, Carter's concerns have been voiced by other politicians who, significantly, have used the language of 'addiction' (and the associated concept 'dependence') to describe the relationship of the US economy to oil. From Richard Nixon, who said that by 1980 'the United States will not be dependent on any other country for the energy we need', to George H. W. Bush's 'there is no security for the United States in further dependence on foreign oil', to John Kerry:[20]

> it results in a massive, continuous transfer of American wealth to oil exporting nations, and leaves us vulnerable to price and supply shocks. But the true cost of our addiction extends far beyond what we pay at the pump: Its revenues empower and sustain despots and dictators. And it obliges our military to defend our energy supply in volatile regions at great expense.[21]

As Canavan shows, the figuration of fossil fuels as addiction permeates some classic energy literature and film. This is particularly obvious in depictions of the individual victims of oil wealth – particularly alcoholics such as the Native American Chief Leatherneck in Upton Sinclair's *Oil!* (1927), James Dean's disgraced oil entrepreneur Jett in the 1956 film *Giant* and his '2007 counterpart Daniel Plainview from Paul Thomas Anderson's *There Will be Blood*. But oil is also figured as an (inter)national dependency, as in sci-fi classic *Dune* (1965), where the key resource 'Spice', the perception-altering drug which makes space travel possible, is, tellingly, only found on a desert planet 'populated by religious fundamentalists who ultimately unleash an intergalactic "jihad"'.[22]

Canavan uses the American Psychiatric Association's definitions of substance dependence to highlight some untapped resources of the oil-as-addiction metaphor. Perhaps the most striking descriptor for *Heat and Light*, and many other petro-literature texts, is the one stating that 'substance use is continued despite knowledge of having a persistent physical or psychological problem that is likely to have been caused or exacerbated by the substance'.[23] This is a particularly troubling lens through which to view Pennsylvania's oil addiction: sickened children, poisoned landscapes, failing economies, debt chains, rampant inequalities, foreign resource wars.

The interplay between the literal and the figurative renderings of oil and addiction finds an interesting manifestation in the two narcotics most important to the novel. Darren Devlin is a recovering heroin addict; heroin being a substance that is mixed with water and injected, therefore bearing an uncanny resemblance to hydraulic fracking. Another of the novel's subplots involves the theft of anhydrous ammonia, one of the key products of the petrochemical industry but also used in the production of methamphetamine. It is not for nothing that the name of the 'meth head' who targets 'two fertilizer tanks' which hold enough ammonia to 'make a mountain of methamphetamine, enough to get all of Bakerton high' is Rich Devlin's old school-friend 'Booby Marstellar', the sort of booby caught by the 'booby trap' of Pennsylvania's resource curse where collective petro-addiction breeds individual addicts.

Juliana Spahr's Iambic Petrometer: Sounding-Out Oil

The final paragraph of *Heat and Light* sees Rich Devlin recollecting his teenage navy stint in the Persian Gulf on the SS *Roosevelt* – nicknamed 'the big stick' (an acknowledgement of Roosevelt's infamous description of US diplomacy). The final words of the novel are 'We are all sailors', yet another instance where *Heat and Light* highlights that readers whose lifestyles rely on the petro-economy cannot ignore their complicity with it and with the violence that emerges at different oil frontiers.[24] Whether in the Persian Gulf, Pennsylvania or the extraction-ravaged Niger Delta explored by writers such as Ogaga Ifowodo, Helon Habila and Ben Okri, the realities of the fossil economy in many resource-cursed territories exemplifies frontier capitalism with social and environmental injustices emerging through a version of contemporary enclosure.[25] Sites of extraction may give rise to states of exception where indigenous communities and environmental campaigners are subject to potentially deadly slow violence (via disease, effect on livelihood) and the more conventional 'fast' violence (unregulated militaries and militias, political killing) tied to both corporations and governments; the execution of Nigerian author-activist Ken Saro-Wiwa being one of the most egregious examples. When, as so often with addiction, oil dependency necessitates searching for a dirtier or riskier hit, then new sorts of frontiers open up, such as the previously unreachable deep-sea oil reserves in the Gulf of Mexico addressed in Spahr's long poem 'Dynamic Positioning'.

As Michael Watts points out, the blowout and sinking of the Deepwater Horizon rig in 2010, and the massive oil spill that followed, emerged from the combination of a

> technologically risky resource frontier (the deepwater continental shelf in the Gulf), with the production of what one can call neoliberalized risk, a lethal product of cutthroat corporate cost-cutting, the collapse of government oversight and regulatory authority, and the deepening financialization and securitization of the oil market.[26]

'Dynamic Positioning' explores the opening of this sort of petro-frontier. Across 152 lines of iambic pentameter, the poem drills down into the depths before rising explosively up again. Spahr draws on the terminology of extractive engineering to take the reader through the technologies of deep-sea drilling (from 'wellheads' to 'float shoe'), through the levels of ocean (the 'mesopelagic' and the 'bathypelagic'), and down more than another 'thirteen thousand feet' to a hydrocarbon 'pay zone'. The risky extraction is compounded by inadequate corporate diligence ('An environmental/Impact and blowout plan declared to be/not necessary'). The second half of the poem moves to the specific events of 20 April 2010: the moment when 'hydrocarbons enter the bot-/Tom of the well undetected'; the mounting pressure before 'ten o'clock when mud/Then shoots up through the derrick'; the explosions, the mayday call and the (initial) human cost: 'Deepwater Horizon gutted stern/To stern. What happens next ends with eleven/Dead'.[27]

The 'dynamic positioning' of Spahr's title refers to the computer-controlled system that keeps rigs such as Deepwater Horizon in their drilling position on what the poem calls 'this ever moving sea'. But the technology of dynamic positioning finds a counterpoint in poetic *technique*: the striking decision to structure the exploration of drilling into oil's deep-time and the explosive industrial event in tick-tock couplets of iambic pentameter; a startling departure for an avant-garde poet hardly known for using traditional forms and for a collection – *That Winter the Wolf Came* – mainly constituted by long lines, Whitmanian accumulations and prose poems.

'Brent Crude', an earlier poem in that collection, foregrounds the genesis of 'Dynamic Positioning':

> All the while the Brent Crude Oil Spot price moves from 112.11 down to 106.97 back to 115.61.
>
> I start writing a poem about oil extraction in iambic pentameter because Cara emails me and asks me this: "how can we, as poets, take care of ourselves, our creative work, and the larger planetary body on which we depend?" She wants, she says, to "call attention to the material life of the artist, as person, who, in addition to being creator/conspirator to a body of work, possesses a physical body, and real financial, medical and social needs."[28]

The shifting spot price, which appears throughout 'Brent Crude', turns substance into abstract commodity, highlighting a disjunction between economic and corporeal realities. 'Dynamic Positioning' resists such abstraction, detailing the materials and the technologies of oil extraction alongside its human cost, choosing regular metrics as the formal response to Cara's desire for a poetics of 'care' (as in concern for and awareness of) that will draw together personal and planetary bodies. (As with the other texts in this chapter, Cara's email is itself another gesture towards the importance of Anthropocene artworks finding ways to negotiate different spatial and temporal scales.)

Both parallel instances of technological control via dynamic positioning buckle under pressure: the blowout overcomes the rig; words refuse to fit the metre. The strictures of the iambic pentameter engender lexical and syntactical distortions with enjambments becoming more frequent and pronounced as the poem moves towards disaster, complicating the relationship between line and sentence, sound and sense.

> At ten o'clock, diverter shut so that
> The gas and drilling fluid could be routed
>
> To the baffle plates, the poorboy degass-
> Er, then the lower annual prev-

Enter is activated. The drill press-
Ure, the volumes of gases, fluids, drill-

Ing mud, seawater, then is steadily in-
Creasing. And it begins again. Or be-

Gins some more. First as mud. A mud that roar-
Ing, rained. Then the gas as it discharge-

Ing, hissing, the poorboy degasser fill-
Ing. Next the first gas alarm then the oth-

Ers. It was then almost close to ten o'
Clock, still when next a roaring noise, a vib-

Ration, engines began rapid increase-
Ing as also the drill pipe pressure rap-

Idly increasing as the rig then los-
Ing power, shut down processes then fail-

Ing. First explosion on five seconds aft-
Er. Then explosion again, ten sec-

Onds later. It was not yet ten
O'clock when the mayday call was first made.[29]

For Nicola M. Merola, the parallel failure of the rig's dynamic positioning as a synecdoche for risky resource extraction and the lexical fracturing emerging from the impossibility of metrical adherence is supplemented by the way the body is brought into the reading experience. As words are broken and enjambed, these 'visual stutter steps' correlate 'with uneven ragged breathing and reading' where the breath sounds are further emphasised through

> the use of consonantal echo ("degasser," "pressure," "increasing," "discharging," "hissing," "process") via which Spahr forces the reader into a form of becoming-well: the hissing sound the reader makes underlines complicity with the well; the hissing sound here relays from body to carbon emissions generated by fossil fuel consumption and back.[30]

It is striking that the increasing corporeal awareness, where the conscientious reader articulating these sibilant syllables hisses as they follow materials back up the drill pipe, occurs at the moment in the poem immediately before it switches focus from subterranean materials and drilling technologies to those killed in the explosion. The sonic 'becoming-well' is, on another level, matched by a reminder of complicity. Spahr lists the dead and insists on remembering our relationship to their fate:

> I will not tell
> You their lives, their loves, their young children their
>
> Relationship to oil. Our oil. The well
> Exploded. They then died. Some swam away.[31]

Merola argues that the preceding section's fractured words 'deform into non-sense, their meaninglessness further emphasised by the futile practice of capitalising whatever starts each line in an attempt to pry meaning back into the fissured word'.[32] However, it seems to me that the capitalisation actually encourages a reading strategy that asks readers to pay attention to phonemes and lines as discrete units as well as within the full sentence. Lines such as 'Ration, engines begin rapid increase-' or 'Idly increasing as the rig then los-' function as ominous soundbites speaking to the unthinking excesses and growth demands of the fossil economy in the face of scarcity and carbon-fuelled climate change: these are the twin poles of exuberance and catastrophe.

It is worth paying attention to Spahr's careful patterning of specific phonemes at the start of the line. Across nine couplets, the phoneme 'Ing' appears six times and 'Er/Ers' three. Annunciating 'Ing' functions as a kind of anaphoric alarm bell. But the relentless repetition of the phoneme both retards the sense of these fractured words and complicates the temporality of the lyric. The fracturing of the 'Ing' suffix leaves these enjambed words hovering between present participles driving the poem towards incipient disaster and more static gerunds belonging to a disaster that has already happened, and which has already been transformed from event to spectacle: remediated into news report, and later poetry, graphic novel, Hollywood blockbuster.[33]

'Er/Ers' has a different function. To err is all-too-human; but whose error is this? The poem which started with the non-human – technologies, sediments, gasses – ends with a roll-call of names. Spahr lists not only the dead but also the corporate executives who, like the speaker, watch ecological disaster from the safety of the domestic *oikos* on a 'flatscreen'. In the multi-billion-dollar blame game following the disaster, BP (who chartered the rig to explore the Macondo Well), Transocean (the rig operator) and Halliburton (subcontractors on aspects of the well) were all deemed legally culpable. But the charge of heat and light that wrecks the rig means that not only had someone blundered but some*things* too. This system error that caused the largest accidental oil spill in history emerges not only from corporate malfeasance but from what Jane Bennett would call the political ecology of things: the emergent non-human agencies of technologies, and the vibrant materials of extractive capitalism.[34]

A Smoking Mirror

Haigh takes her second epigraph to *Heat and Light* from a text that can be read as an older instance of petro-literature, capturing many of the tropes and concerns of this chapter: Muriel Rukeyser's poem 'Murmurs from the earth of this land'. The reasons for Haigh's choice are clear. The excerpt she chooses speaks of 'murmurs from the earth' and the 'watercourses of our dragon childhood', chiming with the novel's concern with place, the subterranean and the connectivity and contamination of water. The submerged sense of children breathing fire is particularly ominous coming from a poet whose *The Book of the Dead* famously documented the impact of mining on the lungs of the poor. But, as the earlier quote from Yaeger suggests, tracking the ways energy sources enter texts means an attentiveness to affect and phenomenology, to 'fields of force' that go beyond merely highlighting environmental and economic injustice.

> You know the murmurs. They come from your own throat.
> You are the bridges to the city and the blazing food-plant green;
> The sun of plants speaks in your voice, and the infinite shells of
>   accretions
> A beach of dream before the smoking mirror.[35]

In the Anthropocene, the earth's murmurs are ours: humanity's discourses and dreams, and the policies and programmes to which they give rise, will leave a mark in the geological record; not least thanks to the fossil capital that is extracted and burnt. Like the other texts in this chapter, Rukeyser insists on the materiality of the abstract commodity, where the geological deep-time of oil that emerges from the 'accretions' of fossilised sea-creatures' 'shells' over aeons is juxtaposed with the corporeal, the poem drawing together body, society, technology and (industrialised) land. Rukeyser holds a 'smoking mirror' up to smoking nature.

The most interesting emergent petro-literature finds formal mechanisms to bring together body, substance and Earth, whether it's Hickson staging the phenomenological shifts related to fuel transformations, Haigh figuring the bodies of populations residing at hydrocarbon frontiers, both metonym and metaphor for oil dependency, or Spahr encouraging an embodied reading technique to render and interrogate the human and non-human interrelations of the Deepwater disaster. Reading and writing our fossil economy means drawing on both the intellectual and the affective responses to oil; negotiating the relations between the embodied hydrocarbon encounter and its often-unseen infrastructure, between the immediacy of domesticity and mediated disaster elsewhere, between geological deep-time and (slow or spectacular) geopolitical violence. In doing so we can explore how the fuels that fire our hearths power the past, present and potential futures of the Anthropocene.

Notes

1. Ella Hickson, *Oil* (London: Nick Hern Books, 2016), pp.17–18.
2. J. R. McNeill, *Something New under the Sun: An Environmental History of the Twentieth-Century World* (New York: W. W. Norton & Co., 2000), p.11.
3. Graeme Macdonald, 'The Resources of Culture', *Reviews in Cultural Theory* 4 (2) (2013), 1–24 (p.13).
4. Graeme Macdonald, 'Fiction' in Imre Szeman, Jennifer Wenzel and Patricia Yaeger (eds.), *Fueling Culture: 101 Words for Energy and Environment* (New York: Fordham University Press, 2017), 162–5 (p.164).
5. Laurie Shannon et al., 'Editor's Column: Literature in the Ages of Wood, Tallow, Coal, Whale Oil, Gasoline, Atomic Power, and Other Energy Sources', *PMLA* 126(2) (2011), 305–26 (p.309).
6. Karen Pinkus, *Fuel: A Speculative Dictionary* (Minneapolis: University of Minnesota Press, 2016), p.12.
7. Hickson discusses how this device speaks to intergenerational relations in her interview with Michael Dunwell, '"Our Freedom Is Based on Something Finite": Ella Hickson on "Oil"', *Transition Network*, 2017, transitionnetwork.org.
8. Frederick Buell, 'A Short History of Oil Cultures: Or, the Marriage of Catastrophe and Exuberance', *Journal of American Studies* 46(2) (2012), 273–93.
9. See Andreas Malm, *Fossil Capital: The Rise of Steam-Power and the Roots of Global Warming* (London and New York: Verso, 2015), p.9.
10. Hickson, pp.72, 59.
11. Jennifer Haigh, *Heat and Light* (New York: Ecco, 2016), pp.4, 426.
12. Haigh, p.426.
13. Ibid., p.10.
14. Rob Nixon, *Slow Violence and the Environmentalism of the Poor* (Cambridge, MA: Harvard University Press, 2011).
15. Ibid., p.224.
16. Haigh, p.224.
17. Robert Macfarlane, 'Generation Anthropocene: How Humans Have Altered the Planet for Ever', *The Guardian* (1 April 2016).

18. Christina Simeone, Theodora Okiro and Bennett DeShaun, *Reimagining Pennsylvania's Coal Communities* (Philadelphia: Kleinman Center for Energy Policy, University of Pennsylvania, 2018).

19. Haigh, pp.402, 375.

20. Gerry Canavan, 'Addiction', in Imre Szeman, Jennifer Wenzel and Patricia Yaeger (eds.), *Fueling Culture: 101 Words for Energy and Environment* (New York: Fordham University Press, 2017), 25–7 (p.25).

21. John Kerry, Remarks at Jimmy Carter's Testimony to US Senate on Energy Policy, 12 May 2009, www.cartercenter.org.

22. Canavan, 'Addiction', p.26.

23. Ibid.

24. Haigh, p.427.

25. See Stephanie LeMenager, *Living Oil: Petroleum Culture in the American Century* (New York: Oxford University Press, 2014), chapter 3.

26. Michael Watts, 'Oil Frontiers: The Niger Delta and the Gulf of Mexico' in Ross Barrett and Daniel Worden (eds.), *Oil Culture* (Minneapolis: University of Minnesota Press, 2014), 189–210 (p.196).

27. Juliana Spahr, *That Winter the Wolf Came* (Oakland, CA: Commune Editions, 2015), pp.46–50.

28. Ibid., pp.22, 45.

29. Ibid., pp.48–9.

30. Nicole M. Merola, '"What Do We Do but Keep Breathing as Best We Can This / Minute Atmosphere": Juliana Spahr and Anthropocene Anxiety', in Kyle Bladow and Jennifer Ladino (eds.), *Affective Ecocriticism: Emotion, Embodiment, Environment* (Lincoln: University of Nebraska Press, 2018), 25–49 (p.38).

31. Spahr, p.51.

32. Merola, '"What Do We Do . . ."', pp.37–8.

33. Steve Duin and Shannon Wheeler, *Oil and Water* (Seattle: Fantagraphics Books, 2011); Peter Berg (dir.), *Deepwater Horizon*, 2016.

34. Jane Bennett, *Vibrant Matter: A Political Ecology of Things* (Durham, NC: Duke University Press, 2010).

35. Muriel Rukeyser, 'Murmurs from the Earth of This Land' in *The Collected Poems of Muriel Rukeyser* [eds. Janet E. Kaufman, Anne F. Herzog and Jan Heller Levi] (Pittsburgh: University of Pittsburgh Press, 2006), p.378.

CHAPTER 14

Warming

Andreas Malm

What is life like inside the human-built walls that trap heat from the sun? In *Men in the Sun*, Ghassan Kanafani's iconic 1962 novella, three refugees cross a border seeking employment. They have been expelled from Palestine and hope to make a living in Kuwait's booming economy. Two physical forces shape their journey: oil and heat. They travel around pipelines, on an asphalt road, behind a roaring engine, eyes set on a kingdom whose promise of a decent living wage shimmers in the ubiquitous sun; oil itself drips into the text. They travel farther into the heat. On the very first page, Kanafani lays down the parameters of the men's passage: from the homeland – now just the object of hallucinatory dreams – where rain was plentiful, ground damp, water cold and fresh, into a world where there is 'nothing but scorching heat and dust'.[1] Back home, one of the men, Abu Qais, had trees that showered him in olives every spring, but a friend working as a driver in Kuwait tells him what to expect. No trees in the kingdom of oil.

Near the border, in the Iraqi city of Basra, Abu Qais and his fellow travellers Assad and Marwan meet a fourth man in the sun, another Palestinian refugee, Abul Khaizuran. Removed from their homeland, these human filings are pulled to the magnetic force of oil-based circuits of accumulation, to which Abul Khaizuran has been attached for some time. He makes money by driving the water tank of a rich merchant back and forth across the border. A chaperon into the kingdom of oil, he has internalised its ethos: 'Shall I tell you the truth? I want more money, more money, much more. And I find it difficult to accumulate money honestly.'[2] Always looking for extra cash, Abul Khaizuran offers to smuggle his compatriots.

A plan emerges. When they approach a border station, Abu Qais, Assad and Marwan – stateless and paperless – will climb into the empty water tank. Abul Khaizuran will lock it, get his papers stamped in the office and return to the wheel. The three have misgivings: 'In heat like this, who could sit in a closed water tank?' Their smuggler taunts them to try walking through the desert with no water as far as the eye can see. Bowing to his argument, they accept the plan and take their seats. On the road, 'the sun was pouring its inferno down on them without any respite'; however much the driver wipes it, sweat flows down his face: relentlessly, Kanafani hammers home the soaring temperatures. 'Come on!', Abul Khaizuran yells, close to the first border station, a callous tone in his voice: 'I'll open the cover of the tank for you. Ha! The climate will be like the next world inside there.'[3] Indeed, Assad, first to enter the tank, reports: 'This is hell. It's on fire.'

The three are locked up. Abul Khaizuran makes it through the first border station, opens the tank after six minutes and helps the panting men out. They continue their journey, on to the next station:

> The lorry, a small world, black as night, made its way across the desert like a heavy drop of oil on a burning sheet of tin. The sun hung high above their heads, round, blazing, and blindingly bright. None of them bothered to dry their sweat any longer. . . . The lorry travelled on over the burning earth, its engine roaring remorselessly.

Like an incantation, Kanafani repeats the words 'the lorry travelled on over the burning earth', and repeats them again.[4]

Heat

There is an absolute limit to the heat the human body can withstand. Scientists use 'wet-bulb temperature', a combined measure of temperature and humidity – mugginess – to specify that limit. Above a wet-bulb temperature of 35°C, the human body can no longer cool itself by sweating (i.e. evaporating heat) or ventilating (exchanging heat with the air); after six hours or so, even the fittest body will expire. That threshold is never reached under current climatic conditions. In February 2016, however, Pal and Eltahir projected that unabated global warming will create regular wet-bulb temperatures of 35°C in at least one region: the Persian Gulf. In the second half of this century, the threshold will be crossed frequently; in Kuwait City, sheer temperatures – humidity uncounted – may well exceed 60°C. The region is prone to developing conditions beyond tolerance limits because it is close to shallow water, uncovered by clouds in summertime and exposed to the sun: it is on a course towards uninhabitability. Even the most basic outdoor activities might become impossible.[5]

The authors could not fail to note a certain irony: the region that has given the world so much oil will receive some of its most extreme heat. Fossil fuels from the Gulf, poured on fires across the globe, will return, via the atmospheric concentration of CO_2, to implement a particularly stark form of the general predicament. The future could be felt already in the second decade of the twenty-first century. In summer the heat reached levels unfamiliar even here, drawing Egypt, Jordan, Palestine, southern Iran into the oven; eventually, this future will extend to other parts of the planet.

Heat Death

The lorry travels on. As the men get closer to the Kuwaiti border station, they contemplate their next course of action. Surrendering himself to these overwhelming forces, Abu Qais confirms his resolution to carry on towards Kuwait: he must take the 'plunge into the frying pan with the rest of humanity'. Abul Khaizuran reiterates his own credo to himself: 'Let the dead bury the dead. I only want more money now, more money.' Wiping his sweat in vain, cursing weather more awful than any he has seen before, he murmurs: 'This is the Hell that I have heard of.'[6] Yet he shoves his passengers back into the tank. This time the paperwork drags on, the bureaucrats deciding to hold him up.

Abul Khaizuran, it is important to note, is no simple crook; the most complex character in *Men in the Sun*, he had been a freedom fighter in Palestine until a roadside bomb ripped off his genitals and drained him of all spirit. Embodying his people's fate, he has fallen from the path of struggle into a spiral of jaded money-making. But he still retains some sympathy for his countrymen. Knowing fully well that time is running out, his heart seems to beat ever more loudly inside the office. He has advised the men to take their shirts off, but nevertheless the clock ticks.[7] The customs officers fiddle around. They enjoy themselves, taunting the driver and making obscene jokes. They seem unbothered by anything other than banal routine.

When he finally receives his papers, Abul Khaizuran rushes to the lorry, looks at the tank and is struck by 'the impression that the metal was about to melt under that fearful sun'. Full throttle, he drives a minute and a half out of sight and then hits the brakes, opens the tank and shouts out the men's names. There is no reply. He slides his hands into the tank, and they fall on still bodies:

> Abul Khaizuran had a choking sensation. His body had begun to run with sweat at such an amazing rate that he felt he was coated in thick oil, and he

couldn't tell whether he was trembling because of this oil covering his chest and back or whether it was caused by fear.

Dazed, he continues to a rubbish dump. Before leaving the corpses among the garbage, he robs them of their money and valuables – and then cries out in despair: 'Why didn't they knock on the sides of the tank?' A further incantation, Kanafani repeats the words at the very end of the text: 'Why didn't you knock on the sides of the tank? Why didn't you bang on the sides of the tank? Why? Why? Why?'[8]

Anthropocene Stories

The Anthropocene calls for compelling stories that will echo the alarm bells from science. The first assessment reports of the Intergovernmental Panel on Climate Change in the 1990s are when the basics of climate science became common knowledge – a precondition for the emergence of 'climate fiction', or 'cli-fi'. One of the most noticeable cultural responses to the crisis, cli-fi has, however, failed on one score. Rarely if ever does it broach the cause of the problem. Most cli-fi novels are set in the future, in ravaged post-apocalyptic landscapes where effects can be amply represented, but where causes – notably the extraction and combustion of fossil fuels – tend to be as invisible as in any other literature.[9] The catastrophe is detached from what normal life used to be. It has irrupted after a caesura in time, and enveloped the globe in soot and deserts and rising seas, with no narrative relation to the actions of characters. First was the good life, then came the bad; in neither do we see the actual history of the fossil economy – this, crudely, is the half-blind temporal vision that cli-fi has given us.

The roots of global warming do run, of course, further back, before our awareness of its by-products. Cli-fi is only the providential tip of the iceberg: the fossil economy must have made impressions and appearances in literature much earlier. To borrow a metaphor from Allen MacDuffie: just as ice cores drilled from deep within Antarctica contain traces of the late spike in CO_2 concentrations, so literature written close to the fireplace might encapsulate experiences of how our current epoch has unfolded.[10] It might teach us what is missing in cli-fi, not least because most of the latter comes from advanced capitalist countries.

While we wait for new writers to connect the dots, we might, then, turn to some past literature. The purpose, in Walter Benjamin's words, would be 'to discover in the analysis of the individual moment the crystal of the total event'. A work of art or even just a fragment of one can be read as an object – more precisely, a monad – 'into which all the forces and interests of history enter on a reduced scale'.[11] It can be retrieved as a *dialectical image*, whose import may be fully recognised only now that we stand on the precipice of catastrophe on a biospheric scale. In this afterlife, the image leaves behind the intentions of its creator and, 'flashes up at the moment of its recognizability'.[12] History, says Benjamin, is a 'constellation of dangers', and if people in the present discern danger coming towards them, they have to return to a 'prehistory' to grasp the true nature of that danger.[13] Between these points in time, a bond suddenly surfaces; only from the vantage point of the contemporary emergency can the underlying image become legible. It is a process much like waking from a dream. A dialectical image is 'manifest, on each occasion, only to quite a specific epoch – namely, the one in which humanity, rubbing its eyes, recognizes just this particular dream image as such'.[14] With this method to hand, we might approach images from Palestinian literature to see how the present might awaken to aspects of itself.

Allegories of Warming

There is no more famous scene in Palestinian literature than the three men perishing in *Men in the Sun*. Can there likewise be a more powerful image of the fate of subaltern people in a warming world? The book has long been recognised as an intensely allegorical text, in the basic sense of the literal drama, the persons and events standing in for a higher order of signification.[15] Thus the desert has been read as a symbol of the tribulations of Palestinian refugees, a space devoid of meaning, a vast nothingness in which the traces of the wanderers disappear.[16] The sun of the title is the 'light of truth' whose rays the sorry characters cannot withstand.[17] Reading *Men in the Sun* in a warming world, however, some pressing realities begin to reconfigure the allegory. The material components of the text now insist on being taken literally – the desert on being read *as desert*, the sun *as sun*. The desolate, overheated landscape of Kanafani's novella is no longer an allegory but a *type of landscape* that is now widely recognisable. Likewise, the empty water tank appears as a more accurate metonym than 'the greenhouse', with its connotations of fecundity and moistness. When Abul Khaizuran opens up the tank, he almost literally invites the three workers into the furnace of fossil capital.[18] The spiral pulling them into the heat is the accumulation of money through the production of oil; the journey from wet soil to parched sand adumbrates the business-as-usual trajectory of the twenty-first-century Earth; the forward movement of the lorry is inexorable, impervious to the obvious dangers. The officials waste time on petty details. All these images now strike the reader as thoroughly dialectical. They draw their force from having been dreamed up long before the 1990s.

Men in the Sun sets the historical record of the Anthropocene straight. Standard narratives of the epoch slip, all too easily, into depicting humanity as a monolithic entity, a species marching in unison towards mastery of the Earth, as though humans per se have wrecked the planet. To pick just one instance, Timothy Clark conceives of the *Anthropos* as a Leviathan, 'enormous and dense tectonic plates of humanity'.[19] Climate change, he argues, is the outcome of the most humdrum activities, undertaken by more or less everyone to enhance their welfare: poverty reduction, food production or wider distribution of medical support have all sent global emissions soaring.[20] Reading Kanafani via Benjamin yields the opposite result. If we see in *Men in the Sun* the crystal of a total event created by the forces and interests of the fossil economy – 'a small world, black as night, made its way across the desert like a heavy drop of oil' – then we learn something else about our epoch. The poor masses are locked inside a tank being driven into a warming world. Their lives are constricted from all sides. The significant decisions were not theirs to make, and, against a forward motion propelled by fossil fuels, their fate has carried no weight.

Oil, Nature and Palestinian Literature

If this were just one book, it could perhaps be brushed aside. But far beyond its most famous single work, Palestinian literature fractures the unitary structure of Anthropocene narratives breaking up the before/after-temporality of cli-fi: in its pages, the end of the world has always already happened. The catastrophe of ethnic cleansing in Palestine in 1948, the *nakba*, is the event around which everything else revolves.[21] How do Palestinian writers describe this end of their world? In *The Ship*, Jabra Ibrahim Jabra, who himself left Palestine for Iraq in 1948, remembers a land overflowing with 'rivers and waterfalls' and laments the expulsion of his people into 'flaming deserts and screaming oil-producing cities'.[22] The same route is retraced in his poem 'In the deserts of exile':

> Our Palestine, green land of ours [. . .]
>
> March adorns its hills [. . .]
>
> April bursts open in its plains [. . .]
>
> They crushed the flowers on the hills around us,
> Destroyed the houses over our heads,

Scattered our torn remains,
Then unfolded the desert before us [. . .]

Our land is an emerald,
But in the deserts of exile,
Spring after spring,
Only the dust hisses in our face.[23]

Both Jabra and Kanafani associated oil with heat because expelled
Palestinians who finished up in the Gulf went from a land with
a Mediterranean climate, ample precipitation in winter and lush greenery
in spring, to a hotter, drier place, where oil was the king of commodities.
A political history superimposed on a geological accident generated
a sequence of dialectical images. However, exile in the Gulf was not the
first Palestinian encounter with the fossil economy.

In November 1840, four British steamboats pulverised the city of Akka
burning their supplies of coal in the process. The Empire had never before
deployed steamboats in a major engagement; now it marvelled at their
prowess. After this war's conclusion, with a string of coastal towns reduced
to rubble, the British Empire made its first attempt to transplant Jewish
colonies into Palestine.[24] From the beginning, therefore, modern Palestine
unfolded in the shadow of the country that gave the world the spiral of
ever-growing fires. However, when Britain occupied Palestine and set
about implementing its vision of a 'national home for the Jewish people',
the state-of-the-art fossil fuel was no longer coal but oil. Promising deposits
had been located in countries bordering the Persian Gulf. The central
industrial project of the Mandate came to be the pipeline that brought
crude oil all the way from Iraq, across the northern West Bank and the
Galilee, to the refinery in Haifa. When, in April 1936, the Palestinians rose
in their great revolt against British occupation and Zionist colonisation
(incidentally the month Ghassan Kanafani was born, in Akka), much of
the revolt centred on the pipeline. The rebels tore it apart at some point
almost every night. They blew it up with bombs, set it on fire, punctured it
with potshots and dug into it along sections where it was buried
underground.

After two years of incessant strikes, boycotts, guerrilla war and sabotage,
deprived of its main source of revenue and energy, the Mandate set up
Special Night Squads to quell the revolt and defend the pipeline. Captain
Orde Wingate, a fanatical supporter of the Zionist enterprise, drilled
fighters from Jewish colonies in old-new counterinsurgency methods,
such as 'decimation', or the killing of every eighth or tenth male villager

as punishment for a failure to produce rifles or intelligence. Along the pipeline, in the hills between Jenin and Haifa, Wingate established further practices. According to recently uncovered testimonies, after sabotage attacks the Special Night Squads would gather all the Palestinian men from the nearest village, order them to open their mouths and then shove down earth soaked in oil; or they'd fling male villagers into pools of burnt oil.[25]

Yet with regard to the decades before the *nakba*, Palestinian life appears in other ways too. A sumptuous sourcebook, Elias Sanbar's *The Palestinians: Photographs of a Land and Its People from 1839 to the Present Day* covers an era that began with British landfall.[26] Many of these pictures are distorted by the perspectives of European cameramen into preconceptions of Palestine: as Biblical territory, desolate ruin, spiritual source or empty land – each flayed by Sanbar in acerbic comments. Nonetheless, the realities shine through; and before 1948, the Palestinians cannot be kept out of the pictures.

We see fishermen tending their nets; boatloads of fruit leaving the port of Jaffa; a man placing ladders so he can reach the highest olives; women returning from harvest with enormous bales on their heads. A young mother carries her infant, bites a corner of her veil and smiles flirtatiously. An elegantly dressed woman rests on four pillows puffing on an *arghileh*. Farmers crop wheat below the walls of Jerusalem; stonecutters display their picks and axes; a merchant walks imperiously ahead of a man in ragged clothes carrying his burden on his back. Street vendors offer tomatoes, potatoes, bread and carpets to passers-by. The River Jordan almost overflows with water. Tiberias is a collection of houses around the central mosque, between the mountains and the lake, green and blue on all sides; hills around Jerusalem extend towards the horizon; half a picture of Nazareth is filled by a foreground of flowers. Haifa rests calmly on the turquoise coast. A turbaned sheikh squats in snow at the top of Mount Hermon; dancers perform *dabke* in front of a monastery.

And now look at them there, the Palestinian villagers who come to life in Sanbar's photographs, standing in line, not knowing if they will survive, sympathetic with the rebels but ignorant of the details of the latest sabotage, shaking, as the British and Zionist soldiers press petroleum into their bodies. Or imagine them thrown into a big pool of black oil. That would be an image as close as any to the essence of this epoch: subaltern masses having fossil fuels and their residues physically forced onto them.

After the revolt had been quenched in 1939, the Palestinians were disarmed. Their movement was shattered; the road to catastrophe lay clear. Sanbar names this moment 'the drowning': 'In 1948 a country disappeared, drowned. Within a few weeks, it was exile. Absence swallowed up the thousands who left their homes on foot or aboard trucks, boats, or other makeshift means of transportation.'[27] Palestinian writers of fiction rarely describe this end of the world in terms of water and sea; more often, they choose images of nature obliterated by fire and smoke.

No Palestinian novelist has matched the global bestseller status of Susan Abulhawa, whose *Mornings in Jenin* and *The Blue between Sky and Water* brought the Palestinian experience into the mainstream book market. Each novel follows the same tripartite structure: a prelude on the lifeworld of Palestine; the end of that world; the travails of the protagonists after. In *Mornings*, the prelude pivots on the harvesting of olives; in *The Blue*, on bee-keeping, practised since time immemorial in a village where the river – 'brimming with God's assortment of fish and flora' – carried away the gossip and prayers of the peasants and meandered to the rhythms of their life. Then came the Haganah 'with their mechanized weaponry and fighter planes'. The village was engulfed in flames. 'Clouds of smoke hovered low, painting the world black, settling on the dead like dark shrouds and invading the lungs of the living, who heaved and convulsed as they sought refuge.'[28]

In the Palestinian experience this moment of ending recurs endlessly: Abulhawa refers to 1948 as 'an infinite mist of one moment in history'; Mahmoud Darwish calls it 'the year without end'; not only are the refugees blocked from returning but the initial act of destroying their houses is repeated again and again.[29] In *A Balcony over the Fakihani*, Liyana Badr describes one of these eternal recurrences, in Beirut in 1982, but her words could fit any:

> I saw piles of concrete, stones, torn clothes scattered about, shattered glass, little pieces of cotton wool, fragments of metal, buildings destroyed or leaning crazily ... White dust smothered the district, and through the gray of the smoke loomed the gutted shells of blocks and the debris of houses razed to the earth ... Everything there was mixed up together. Cars were upside down, papers whirling in the sky. Fire. And smoke. The end of the world.[30]

To read Palestinian literature in the Anthropocene is to 'explode the homogeneity of the epoch, interspersing it with ruins – that is, with the present'. For Benjamin: 'The tradition of the oppressed teaches us that the "state of emergency" in which we live is not the exception but the rule.'[31] Dialectical images can be recovered 'to bring the present into a critical state'.[32]

Literature and the Palestinian Catastrophe

Marwan Darwish is one writer who believes that Palestine can stand in for, or communicate with, any number of catastrophes. In his long 1992 poem 'The penultimate speech of the "Red Indian" to the white man', Darwish merges the idiom of the native populations of America – honouring the 'seventy million hearts' killed at the dawn of the epoch – with that of Palestine. The effect is a universal *j'accuse* for the Capitalocene, the White (M)Anthropocene or whatever else one calls it:

> What the stranger says is truly strange.
> He digs a well deep in the earth to bury the sky [. . .]
>
> Don't dig any deeper!
> Don't pierce the shell of the turtle that carries our grandmother the earth on
>   its back!
> Don't bruise the earth, don't smash
> the smooth mirror of her orchard.[33]

Le Trio Joubran's Nazarene *ouds*, mournful and infuriated, likewise offer a soundtrack to this view of life. Their latest record *The Long March* opens with the voice of Darwish booming the most compelling stanzas from 'The penultimate speech' in Arabic:

> We will face the long march, but first,
> we will defend the trees we wear.
> We will defend the bell of the night and the hanging moon over our huts,
> we will defend the leaping dear and the clay of our pots,
> and the eagle feathers in the wings of our final songs.
> But soon you will erect your world on our remains,
> you will pave over the sacred places to open a road
> for the satellite moon.
> This is the age of industry,
> the age of coal and fossils to fuel your thirst for fine wine [. . .]
> Where, oh white master, are you taking my people [. . .] and yours?[34]

The truth of this age might have been – may still be – invisible to those enjoying fine wine and champagne, but for those on the underside, catastrophe is to be expected *as long as things go on like this*.

Global Palestine/Literatures of Resistance

Less an exception, anomaly or leftover from a colonial past, this country should, John Collins argues in *Global Palestine*, be seen as a monad. Forces operating worldwide come together in Palestine, which works as a laboratory or 'prophetic index', holding clues to the future that others will face. 'Are we all becoming Palestinians?', Collins asks; a list of global tendencies – the proliferation of walls, rise of drone warfare, accelerating technologies of repression – tempts him to answer 'yes'. Collins mentions the destruction of the natural environment, or 'war on the milieu',[35] and in her Edward Said lecture from 2016, Naomi Klein likewise suggests that the Palestinian experience of displacement and homesickness undergoes universalisation in a warming world.

> The state of longing for a radically altered homeland – a home that may not even exist any longer – is something that is being rapidly, and tragically, globalised. . . . If we don't demand radical change we are headed for a whole world of people searching for a home that no longer exists.[36]

Millions will move along a Palestinian axis. There'll be deserts, heat, fire, smoke, debris and drowning, first for masses of fisherfolk, labourers, peasants, street vendors, stone-cutters and mothers working in their homes, and then, if the warming proceeds unmitigated, for almost everyone else. As in *The Ship*, they will scramble onboard boats that can only cruise and circle between shores. There will be no solid ground on which to disembark.

But if Palestine is the paradigm, another possibility opens up: resistance. As long as the catastrophe is cut off from its causes and the stories voided of conflict, resistance remains hard to visualise. Without intra-human antagonism conditioning the trajectory, there can be no exit: the human species will be caught up in 'an impersonal dynamic it cannot command', a victim of faults inherent to humans per se.[37] Yet once you have some people benefiting and others locked inside the tank, you also have the possibility – hypothetical, counterfactual, but logical – of breaking out; the pipeline might be blown up. This is what Kanafani aimed at with *Men in the Sun*. He composed his novella in a moment of utter bleakness, when organised resistance had yet to be relaunched. The lack of a collective effort by the Palestinian people to take destiny in their own hands represented to Kanafani, whose Popular Front for the Liberation of Palestine would be formed five years later, a suicidal paralysis: 'Assad spread his shirt over his head, bent his legs, and let the sun roast him without resistance.'[38] *Men in the Sun* was conceived as an indictment of passivity, and as a subtle, if profoundly pessimistic, clarion call for resistance. One wonders then what future readers will think about when they reach those final sentences. Will anyone have banged on the sides of the tank?

Hope of redemption rests, writes Benjamin, on widening 'the tiny fissure in the continuous catastrophe'.[39] The simile suggests a closed compartment. A feeling of claustrophobia has been associated with the current geological epoch, when, for the first time, the planet appears to be a sealed space, with no wild and free exteriors – and throbs through Palestinian literature, as it swings between experiences of captivity and dispersion, extremely crammed enclaves and a vaporous diaspora. No one has charted this experience as exquisitely as Elias Khoury, the Lebanese author and chronicler of the *nakba*. His latest masterpiece *My Name Is Adam: Children of the Ghetto*, the first instalment of a planned trilogy, follows the inhabitants of Lydda as they are first trapped behind barbed-wire and then scattered to the ends of the Earth. His storytelling coils and twists like endless calligraphy around the central catastrophe. Fittingly, the novel's prelude mirrors *Men in the Sun*. Khoury has a poet hiding inside a coffer in his lover's room. Eventually his rival the caliph finds out about him and buries the coffer and its living content deep in the grounds of the palace. The poet expires, in analogy with the people of Lydda and the men in the sun, giving Khoury an excuse to comment on Kanafani: banging on the tank would have been 'meaningless' as it would have 'been impossible for the Kuwaiti border officials, barricaded inside their offices, their ears deafened by the air conditioners, to hear anything'. The apparent reproach of the question – why didn't you bang on the sides of the tank? – should be read as a call not for resistance but for empathy. 'The real question' would not be 'the silence of the Palestinians but the deafness of the world to their cries'.[40]

For all Khoury's greatness, this must be a misreading. The banging requested *ex post facto* by Abul Khaizuran would not have been addressed to the border officials but to him. *He* would have heard the bangs. Ever the Leninist, Kanafani arranged him in relation to the masses, those inside the tank, so that resistance *could* have been activated on two conditions: self-activity from the inside; responsiveness and guidance from the erstwhile freedom fighter. The division of our species runs through Abul Khaizuran. He personifies both the crisis and the collapse of leadership. Resigned to the forces of accumulation, he knowingly exposes his countrymen to lethal dangers. At the same time, the former cadre, with a deep memory of battles fought and lost, most likely stretching back to the great revolt of 1936–9, holds the key to liberation. His 'why?' is also a cry for his own salvation: if only the men had banged on the tank, he would have been compelled to act and return to the path of struggle. As Bashir Abu-Manneh has recently demonstrated in his excellent *The Palestinian Novel: From 1948 to the Present*, the greatest works of Palestinian literature – *Men in the Sun*, *The Ship*, Khoury's *Gate of the Sun* – have all been written in pungent ink from the latest defeat.[41] But each author's remembrance of the struggle has also passed forward the possibility of breaking the spiral. Even in defeat, resistance, if remembered, contains the promise of a resurgence in the next moment of danger.

Hope in the Anthropocene

Optimism, it follows, is not the standpoint of Palestinian resistance. Rarely if ever have illusions about imminent victory been harboured. Emerging from constantly renewed catastrophic defeat, resistance has always been conscious of the enormity of forces stacked against it and – under the current balance of power – the slim to non-existent chances of liberating the land. But one day this *might* change and pressure must be maintained. Central to this is Palestine itself. The land is still there, as are the people. 'We're here', shouts a voice in *A Balcony over the Fakihani*, 'we're still here! The world hasn't come to an end yet!'[42] This is the first principle of the storied Palestinian *sumud*, roughly 'steadfastness' – the land itself as a partner. 'This land will rise again' – not the people, but *al-ard* itself, says the refrain of Abulhawa's *The Blue between Sky and Water*.[43]

Hence Palestinian literature is filled with paeans to the persistence and beauty of the land. In her short but still unsurpassed study *Giving Voice to Stones: Place and Identity in Palestinian Literature*, Barbara McKean Parmenter shows that writers rarely articulated an attachment to the land before 1948, since it was the matter of everyday life. After the catastrophe, they had no more urgent mission. Hence the ubiquitous, obsessive references to olive trees – surviving on sparse rainfall, able to grow in confined places, reaching an age of many hundreds of years – and rocks – fixed, immobile – to give proof of the unbreakable bond between people and land. What remains of nature itself becomes the foundation for freedom. 'Authors enlist nature in general, and the land in particular, as their last and strongest ally.'[44] Between the water tank of *Men in the Sun* and the coffer of *My Name Is Adam*, there is thus the cave of *Gate of the Sun*: a naturally formed and not entirely sealed cabin, in which the hero *fedai* hides and meets his love, during the high point of the armed struggle, when Palestine seemed within reach.[45] The light and heat of the cave represent an opening, not a closure or death sentence. Listen, likewise, to the poet Layla Allush describing travel along the newly built highway from her native Jerusalem to Haifa:

> Along the amazing road drawn from the throat of recent dates,
> The trees were smiling at me with Arab affection.
> In the earth there was an apology for my father's wounds [. . .]
>
> Everything is Arab despite the change of tongue,
> Despite the trucks, the cars and the car lights,
> Despite all the hybrid green and blue signs.
> All the poplars and my ancestors' solemn orchards
> Were, I swear, smiling at me with Arab affection.
> Despite all that had been eliminated and coordinated and the 'modern'
>   sounds,
> Despite all the propaganda that slaps the traveller,
> Despite the seas of light and technology [. . .]
> The earth continued to sing out with Arab affection.[46]

As the particularities of the Palestinian experience are globalised, are there analogous strata in the biosphere, somewhere beneath the change of climate, in which similar hopes of redemption can be invested?

'I'm an optimist because we have a mammoth task in front of us that has to be completed', says Wadi. '"What task is that?" The task? It's everything. Palestine. The future. Freedom.'[47] Following Christian existentialist Gabriel Marcel, this is what Terry Eagleton calls 'fundamental hope'. It is a hope that acknowledges the immensity of the defeats and the desolation. Yet it refuses to capitulate.

Notes

1. Ghassan Kanafani, *Men in the Sun and Other Palestinian Stories* (Boulder, CO: Lynne Rienner, 1999), p.21.
2. Ibid., p.56.
3. Ibid., pp.49, 52, 56.
4. Ibid., pp.57, 63–4.
5. Jeremy S. Pal and Elfatih A. B. Eltahir, 'Future Temperature in Southwest Asia Projected to Exceed a Threshold for Human Adaptability', *Nature Climate Change* 6 (2016), 197–200.
6. Kanafani, *Men in the Sun*, pp.64–5.
7. Ibid., p.57.
8. Ibid., pp.70–1, 74.

9. See Adam Trexler, *Anthropocene Fictions: The Novel in a Time of Climate Change* (Charlottesville: University of Virginia Press, 2015), pp.79, 82, 118, 236.

10. Allen MacDuffie, *Victorian Literature, Energy, and the Ecological Imagination* (Cambridge: Cambridge University Press, 2014), p.11.

11. Walter Benjamin, *The Arcades Project* (Cambridge, MA: Harvard University Press, 1999), pp.461, 475.

12. Walter Benjamin, *Selected Writings, Volume 4: 1938–1940* (Cambridge, MA: Harvard University Press, 2003), p.390; on leaving intentions behind, cf. Walter Benjamin, *Selected Writings, Volume 3: 1935–1938* (Cambridge, MA: Harvard University Press, 2002), p.262.

13. Benjamin, *Arcades*, pp.470, 474.

14. Ibid., p.464.

15. For example Barbara Harlow, *After Lives: Legacies of Revolutionary Writing* (London: Verso, 1996), p.48; Muhammad Siddiq, *Man Is a Cause: Political Consciousness and the Fiction of Ghassan Kanafani* (Seattle: University of Washington Press, 1984), pp.11, 14.

16. Ilan Pappe, 'A Text in the Eye of the Beholder: Four Theatrical Interpretations of Kanafani's *Men in the Sun*', *Contemporary Theatre Review* 3 (1995), p.162; Hilary Kilpatrick, 'Tradition and Innovation in the Fiction of Ghassan Kanafani', *Journal of Arabic Literature* 7 (1976), pp.58–9; Barbara McKean Parmenter, *Giving Voice to Stones: Place and Identity in Palestinian Literature* (Austin: University of Texas Press, 1994), pp.54–9. The last author, however, has an unusually keen eye for the physicality of the desert.

17. Siddiq, *Man Is a Cause*, p.13.

18. See Ellen McLarney, '"Empire of the Machine": Oil in the Arabic Novel', *Boundary 2* 36(2) (2009), 177–98 (p.187). On the concept of fossil capital, see Andreas Malm, *Fossil Capital: The Rise of Steam-Power and the Roots of Global Warming* (London and New York: Verso, 2016).

19. Timothy Clark, *Ecocriticism on the Edge: The Anthropocene as a Threshold Concept* (London: Bloomsbury, 2015), pp.4, 14.

20. Ibid., p.111.

21. See Ihab Saloul, *Catastrophe and Exile in the Modern Palestinian Imagination* (New York: Palgrave Macmillan, 2012).

22. Jabra Ibrahim Jabra, *The Ship* (Boulder, CO: Lynne Rienner, 1985), p.25.

23. A. M. Elmessiri, *The Palestinian Wedding: A Bilingual Anthology of Contemporary Palestinian Resistance Poetry* (Washington, DC: Three Continents Press, 1982), pp.69–71.

24. For a synopsis, see Andreas Malm, 'The Walls of the Tank: On Palestinian Resistance', *Salvage* 4 (2017), 21–56 (pp.26–30).

25. Matthew Hughes, 'Terror in Galilee: British-Jewish Collaboration and the Special Night Squads in Palestine during the Arab Revolt, 1938–9', *The Journal of Imperial and Commonwealth History* 43 (2015), pp.590–610.

26. Elias Sanbar, *The Palestinians: Photographs of a Land and Its People from 1839 to the Present Day* (New Haven, CT: Yale University Press/Hazan, 2014).

27. Ibid., p.286.

28. Susan Abulhawa, *The Blue between Sky and Water* (London: Bloomsbury, 2015), pp.7, 27, 31.
29. Susan Abulhawa, *Mornings in Jenin* (New York: Bloomsbury, 2010), p.35; Darwish in Elmessiri, *The Palestinian Wedding*, p.203; cf. Saloul, *Catastrophe and Exile*, pp.53–4.
30. Liyana Badr, *A Balcony over the Fakihani* (New York: Interlink Books, 2002), pp.73–81. On this overlooked novel, see Saloul, *Catastrophe and Exile*, chapter 2.
31. Clark, *Ecocriticism*, p.48; Benjamin, *Selected Writings*, vol. 4, p.392.
32. Benjamin, *Arcades*, pp.474, 471.
33. Mahmud Darwish, *The Adam of Two Edens: Selected Poems* [trans. Sargon Boulos] (Syracuse: Syracuse University Press, 2000), p.136.
34. Le Trio Joubran, *The Long March*, Randana, 2018.
35. John Collins, *Global Palestine* (London: Hurst, 2011), pp.2, 115, 137.
36. Naomi Klein, 'Let Them Drown: The Violence of Othering in a Warming World', *London Review of Books* (2 June 2016).
37. Clark, *Ecocriticism*, p.149; see also pp.30, 90.
38. Kanafani, *Men in the Sun*, p.63.
39. Benjamin, *Selected Writings*, vol. 4, p.185.
40. Elias Khoury, *My Name Is Adam: Children of the Ghetto: Volume 1* [trans. Humphrey Davies] (London: MacLehose, 2018), pp.30–1.
41. Bashir Abu-Manneh, *The Palestinian Novel: From 1948 to the Present* (Cambridge: Cambridge University Press, 2016), pp.165–8.
42. Badr, *Balcony*, p.70.
43. Ibid., pp.24, 275, 286.
44. Parmenter, *Giving Voice to Stones*, p.79; cf. Saloul, *Catastrophe and Exile*, pp.40, 51.
45. Elias Khoury, *Gate of the Sun* (London: Harvill Secker, 2005).
46. Elmessiri, *The Palestinian Wedding*, pp.173–5.
47. Jabra, *Ship*, pp.103–4.

CHAPTER 15

Ethics

Zainor Izat Zainal

Moralising about the Anthropocene is inevitable. As Maldonado has pointed out, 'we have no choice but to live in *an* Anthropocene, the choice we make now will have some influence on the shape of the future, so that, to some extent, we can choose *which* Anthropocene is it going to be'.[1] Recent works on ethics in the Anthropocene have underscored many normative approaches and perspectives. Willis Jenkins proposes a 'theocentric pragmatism' in which religious communities play a role by uniting in identifying common ground, building trust and learning to take action together.[2] Seeing the Anthropocene as both phenomenon and discourse, Joanna Zylinska in her 2014 book *Minimal Ethics* asserts that responses to the Anthropocene should first be ethical, implying that we have the responsibility to look at inequalities of power and understand how diverse groups of people exert power in different ways with different consequences. This responsibility, according to Zylinska, is a shared one.[3] Curren and Metzger focus on sustainability which they argue should revolve around 'long term preservation of opportunity to live well into the future',[4] which requires the cultivation of shared norms, fair cooperation and aligned institutions. Drawing on virtue ethics, Williston posits that virtues of justice, truth and hope are needed in one's character to persevere in the age of the Anthropocene.[5] Schmidt, Brown and Orr likewise assert that ethics remains relevant but must adapt to the novel circumstances of the Anthropocene.[6] They appeal to a conventional ethical tradition – the ethics of virtue – that emphasises the (good) character of human beings.[7]

These decisive points imply that ethics and the Anthropocene need to be actively engaged with each other in order to facilitate our sense of what responsibilities we hold. To this end, I shall engage here with stories as they 'have served as the cultural origins and conditions of the Anthropocene',[8] and 'often [provoke] literary experimentation as writers seek forms appropriate to the subject matter',[9] bearing in mind that we live in a world of diverse cultures 'highly differentiated in both experience of and contribution to these [Anthropocene] impacts'.[10]

Ethics and Literature

Literature and ethics have long been interrelated. McGinn asserts that literature 'invites moral appraisal' as 'questions of ethics intersect with artistic and literary questions'.[11] Moreover, according to Eskin, our moral education is inextricably linked to the myriad fictions that permeate our lives: 'Nursery rhymes, stories, plays, verbal and filmic narratives perused from early childhood have been supposed to ensure, more or less successfully, the formation of the variously conceived good person.'[12] Ethical criticism was largely shunned in literary criticism, however, especially with the advent of literary theory in the 1960s, when studies of literature and ethics became 'separate discourses'.[13] Nonetheless, the ethical dimension in critical literary undertakings has been addressed commendably by scholars from the 1980s onwards, with the publication of Wayne Booth's *The Company We Keep* (1988), Barbara Herrnstein Smith's *Contingencies of Value: Alternative Perspectives for Critical Theory* (1988), Tobin Siebers' *The Ethics of Criticism* (1988), Andrew Newton's *Narrative Ethics* (1995), Hadfield, Rainsford and Woods's *The Ethics in Literature* (1999) and Louis Pojman's *The Moral Life: An Introductory Reader in Ethics and Literature* (1999), to name but a few.

The starting point of this essay is the issue of human responsibility in the age of the Anthropocene. I analyse this in three contemporary Malaysian novels that delve into environmental degradation: Keris Mas's *Jungle of Hope* (2009), Zakaria Ali's *The Dam* (2009) and Chuah Guat Eng's *Days of Change* (2010). *Jungle of Hope* offers a critical account of the environmental issues brought about by colonial capitalist industrialisation. Set in the 1920s–30s in colonial Malaya, it traces the life of a Malay rice farmer, Pak Kia, who is forced to move from his land in Ketari to the jungle of Janda Baik when disastrous floods and the conversion of Ketari and its adjacent areas into a sledge tin mine by the British threaten his livelihood. Set in the late 1980s, *The Dam* delves into J's efforts to bring awareness to his village folks about the unsustainable construction of a dam that is fast demolishing the river and forest in his village. *Days of Change*, spanning several decades from colonial times to the early 2000s, revolves around the life of Hafiz, a fifty-five-year-old self-made Malay man who is suffering from amnesia. He uses the I Ching, the Chinese 'book of changes', which results in eight notebooks in which he records memories of his life, including his battle with his friends against a major corporation bent on appropriating his land at Ulu Banir. The common thread in these works is grassroots struggles against land threatened by development projects. Broadly speaking, environmental degradation in Malaysia comes in many forms such as water and toxic pollution, climate change and extinction of species, but a major factor is the loss of forest cover,[14] usually owing to economic development plans.

Through these texts, I will examine the ways in which writers and characters understand and attempt to cope with the destruction of the environment. This will be informed by three areas of ethical enquiry in the Anthropocene: reassessing present norms, raising novel concerns and rethinking traditional concerns.[15] According to Schmidt, Brown and Orr, reassessing present norms involves recognising how individuals and organisations perceive and plan actions to tackle long-term environmental challenges; raising novel concerns entails understanding how individual actions can affect others through non-linear relationships; and rethinking traditional concerns requires repositioning diverse cultural and traditional views concerning fairness and environmental ethics.[16] I will then establish the model of environmental ethics promoted by the writers under discussion.

The Green Movement in Malaysia

Environmental degradation in Malaysia has its roots in British colonial administration, which was preoccupied with capitalising land endowed with plenty of natural resources in order to fulfil the needs of industrialising Europe. Indeed, colonial control brought about a great deal of socioecological transformation in Malaysia, especially that which involved land use and people's relationships with it. As late as the middle of the nineteenth century, prior to British colonisation, 95per cent of the land area of Malaysia was still forested.[17] This was attested to by early European travellers, who described the Malaysian landscape they saw as 'ranges of hill and valley everywhere covered with interminable forest, with glistening rivers winding among them'.[18]

The implementation of unjust forest or land laws triggered protests among the Malays, whose livelihood in the forest was threatened. Tok Bahaman's 1891–5 rebellion in Pahang exemplified these protests.[19] Haji Abdul Rahman from Terengganu, who represented forty-three peasants who refused to bow to the British system of getting permits to plant hill paddy, contested the British notion of land use at the Land Office.[20]

Discontentment over land rights grew, which culminated in a Malay peasant uprising in Terengganu in 1928, led by To' Janggut. However, this resistance was quashed 'swiftly and ruthlessly by British guns'.[21]

The contemporary green movement has become quite a formidable force in Malaysian civil society. Largely made up of non-governmental organisations (NGOs), grassroots campaigns and community-driven protest groups, it has made tremendous progress since the early 1970s, despite operating under 'testing semi-authoritarian conditions, suffering from restrictions over registration of organisations, as well as fears of state intimidation and coercion'.[22] In Malaysia, the green movement exists within what Neher calls semi-democracy.[23] A semi-democracy is characterised by liberal democracy (such as competitive elections, citizen participation and civil liberties) coupled with authoritarian rule (dominant ruling parties and strong interventionist states).[24] In Malaysia, a general election is held every five years, out of which a government is formed based on the majority political party in Parliament. Barisan Nasional (National Front), a coalition predominantly made up of three major race-based political parties, had been Malaysia's ruling political coalition since independence in 1957, until it was defeated in the 2018 general election.

The Barisan Nasional regime believed that economic development would increase the people's quality of life, which in turn would lead to political stability. Development, therefore, became its overriding priority and ideology, implemented mainly through economic and political measures such as the National Economic Policy (NEP), which, designed as a social restructuring programme, covered a period of twenty years (1970–90). The NEP aimed to eradicate poverty and eliminate the association of ethnicity with economic function on the basis that creating conducive socio-economic conditions was seen as crucial to political stability and national unity. The period when the NEP was fully enforced became the most important in the country's development. Malaysia's economy accelerated tremendously in this period. In the 1970s and 1980s, it was the world's largest producer and exporter of tin, timber, rubber and palm oil. By the 1990s, Malaysia had significantly expanded its economy to include the manufacturing sector and experienced rapid economic growth, equitable distribution of income and dramatic improvements in human welfare.

Development is, then, largely state-led and state-facilitated.[25] The Barisan Nasional regime enforced legislation that worked in favour of implementing development policies, including the Internal Security Act (1960) (later replaced with the Security Offences (Special Measures) Act

(2012)), which gave the government and the police absolute power to arrest and detain without trial anyone they think is a threat to national security. Though two regimes have taken over since 2018, it remains to be seen whether these legislations will be repealed or improved.

I have argued elsewhere that, taking into account grassroots environmental protests that began during colonial rule, the phases of the Malaysian green movement are divided into: Hard Times (1824–1957), Growing Awareness (1970–90), Environmental Movement Was Born (1990–2000) and Marching Forward (2000 onwards).[26] Hard Times was the period when locals struggled against unjust laws that threatened their livelihood and dependence on the forests. Growing Awareness saw environmental laws introduced, environmental NGOs (ENGOs) founded to promote environmental awareness, justice and sustainability, and grassroots activism proliferate. Environmental Movement Was Born saw massive degradation of the environment as well as the rise of an environmentalism in civil society that became more assertive and critical and less race-based. Marching Forward is the phase from 2000 onwards when globalisation and information communication technologies (ICTs) are further accelerating environmental awareness, co-operation and lobbying. While I commend the progress of the green movement, I want to suggest that we can also learn about environmental activism and ethics from Malaysian literature in English, and in particular the novels under discussion.

Green Malaysian Literature in English

Malaysia has a rich and diverse literary tradition which includes writing in Malay, English, Chinese and Indian. Literature in English is a particularly vibrant tradition that continues to expand in multiple directions. Since its establishment in the 1940s, the Malaysian English literary tradition has become considerably more progressive, evident from the array of writers who have earned substantial recognition and literary prizes locally and internationally. Over a span of more or less six decades, the thematic trends in the Malaysian English literary tradition are plenty and diverse, reflecting the nation's multi-ethnic, multireligious and multicultural background. Themes such as poverty, destitution, class distinction, nation formation, gender hierarchy, victimisation of women, and race relations have occupied writers.[27] Ng argues that Malaysian writers writing in English are 'more interested in the people who make up this imagined [Malaysian] community – their day-to-day struggles, their personal embrace of cultures, and their private religious beliefs'.[28] In a recent anthology of six decades of Malaysian short stories in English, Vethamani asserts that stories are presented 'in a variety of styles from social realism to supernatural and horror subgenres, and the tone of the stories range from the serious to the humorous'.[29] The varied and diverse multicultural voices of Malaysia in the anthology address issues related to patriarchal families; inter-racial relations; identity and belonging; superstition; horror and the supernatural; and modern-day familial relationships.[30] However, while Trexler and Johns-Putra argue that climate fiction in the form of science fiction, thriller and dystopian novels has become predominant in twenty-first-century literature,[31] this is not the case with Malaysian literature in English. In fact, Malaysian writers rarely delve into these genres or 'green' concerns.

This is not to say that the environment has been completely absent. The Malaysian environmental setting and culture are often reconstructed and reflected in Malaysian literary texts written in English. The treatment of environmental themes, however, has been lacking, and even if an environmental theme becomes the main focus of the work, this is more prevalent in poetry than in other genres. Poets like Muhammad Haji Salleh, Ee Tiang Hong, Shirley Lim and Cecil Rajendra, to name but a few, have indeed written and explored varied aspects of the environment in their works. The treatment of these distinctive aspects of the environment in general, however, does not appear to have explicitly green concerns.[32]

Recent criticism highlights, then, the need for a more direct engagement with questions related to the environment in Malaysian literature in English. This could happen through the idea of the Anthropocene. Yeow has dealt with place, race, identity and their relations to the environment in Malaysian poetry in English.[33] My own ecocritical thesis on environmental attitudes in Malaysian novels in English has delineated four pertinent environmental issues in Malaysia: alienation from nature, politics of the environment, capitalist-based development, and ethics.[34] Other work has delved into environmental ethics as promoted in Malaysian novels.[35] However, these critical endeavours have not considered, in detail, the representation of grassroots activism – how this functions in literature, what this teaches us about activism, and how it provides a lens to ethical questions involving the environment and the Anthropocene.

Ethics of Activism: From Individualised to Collective Activism

How individuals perceive and plan actions to tackle environmental challenges is exemplified in *Jungle of Hope*, which illuminates the environmental damage produced by colonialism, specifically the alienation of Malay peasants from their land. In *Jungle of Hope*, although restrictive new laws and regulations regarding the land were enforced, and tin mining and rubber plantation become the order of the day, Pak Kia still works religiously on his rice field; continuing the traditional lifestyle. In contrast, most of the villagers around him have opted to grow rubber. Enticed by the material progress that came with the new economy, some 'had money and some had property'.[36] Pak Kia, on the other hand, continues to resist the vicious imposition of capitalist forces and works even harder in the rice field.[37] His resistance is echoed by a number of Malays in his village, like Jusuh, who refuse to 'work as coolies', 'clinging even more firmly to their old way of life', to 'their original rice fields and village', which 'they felt, were their last bastion'.[38] This form of resistance has typically been condemned in colonialist discourse, resulting in Malays being accused of being indolent, lazy and unproductive.[39] Adas, however, sees this resistance as a typical avoidance protest in pre-colonial and colonial Southeast Asia, by which dissatisfied peasants seek to attenuate their hardships and express their discontent through flight, sectarian withdrawal or other activities that minimise challenges to or clashes with those whom they view as their oppressors.[40] Throughout *Jungle of Hope*, Keris evaluates this resistance, delineating the strong relationship the Malays have with the natural world around them.

Through Pak Kia's struggle to begin a new life in the jungle of Ketari, Keris reveals how capitalist progress and development brought about by the British are fast replacing the rural Malays' traditions, as well as inducing the displacement of the Malays from their land. He also foregrounds the restrictions involved in activism during colonial times. The people in Ketari are divided into two groups: those who refuse to grow rubber and choose to relocate to the forests; and those who willingly embrace the plantation economy, and thus obstruct a unified resistance against the impending destruction of the land. Keris presents this image through two antagonistic characters, Pak Kia and his brother Zaidi. Zaidi realises that the traditional way of life, relying solely on the rice fields, has become almost impossible to maintain. He sees the need for the Malays to compete in the new capitalism. He tries to make Pak Kia see this, knowing that the Malays will be lagging behind economically if they do not adapt to the economic changes happening around them: 'This country will have bigger schools, roads surfaced with tarmac, bigger hospitals and government offices. And where will we be? In the jungle.'[41] Zaidi's argument, however, cannot sway Pak Kia's stand.

The break-up of the people in Ketari presents a reverse image of the sense of community among (traditional) Malays. Wilson has emphasised the 'kinship ties' that people in *kampongs* (villages) practise, even though they are not related by blood.[42] It is this 'kinship' that becomes the unifying force in Malay villages, so much so that individualistic social behaviour is disdained.[43] The break-up of the village in Ketari alludes to the adverse effects of capitalist modernity on traditional Malay spirit and values of co-operation and helpfulness that characterise traditional, rural village life and which could, potentially, draw individuals in the direction of collective activism.

Whilst *Jungle of Hope* delineates the onset of the Malays' resistance to environmental changes, *The Dam* illuminates the construction of a dam in the 1980s that is demolishing the river and forest in a remote village. J, who returns to his village after many years studying abroad, tries to stop the hazardous construction, which the village leaders seem to have a stake in. Villagers are not allowed to go anywhere near the construction site, and heavy fines and physical punishment are imposed on villagers who do so. For this, J is brought to trial by the clan leaders, who warn him that his right to stay in the village could be forfeited. Mostly alone in his fight to raise awareness, J does a survey of the villagers' opinions. He finds that many want the project to stop. However, many others support the project because it is advantageous to them for reasons that range from job opportunities to the benefits of having electricity. Careful, J stresses that development should not come at a price the villagers can ill-afford to pay. J's efforts to bring awareness to the village folks are met with contempt, however, when his car is set on fire. He is also poisoned. Undefeated, J again tries to fight for justice by questioning Nira Hitam about whether compensation is paid to those affected by the development. His mission is complicated by the fact that some of the villagers are given grants during British rule but some people living on ancestral lands possess no grants. The latter are most vulnerable since Nira Hitam is 'buying over' these people by taking their land. Daun Nadim, who has always been J's staunch supporter, also falls victim to Nira Hitam's schemes. J's efforts to salvage the land from Nira Hitam fail, though, when the dam bursts, 'wip[ing] the Village of the Swamps from the face of the earth'.[44]

Like Keris, Zakaria highlights the decay of a spirit of co-operation and helpfulness in Malay villages by depicting how J is treated when he starts questioning and investigating the construction of the dam. J's village is pretty much still conservative, in the sense that the villagers still practise traditional beliefs, tradition and *adat* (Malay customs) and espouse 'the traditional Malay mind/mentality [which] is steeped in a conglomeration of tribal mores and lore and feudalistic *adat* that demands subservience to a leader or council of elders as in the tribal communities or to a single individual as in an absolute monarchy'.[45] J's bold actions garner hatred and respect from the people. To some, he is the man responsible for championing the mountain folks adversely affected by the construction of the dam, but to others, especially village leaders like Nira Hitam, he is an insolent 'phony white man' who defies the *adat* by violating rules set by the leaders and by inciting rebellion.[46] J seems to have gone against 'the Malay [traditional] social code [which] encourages indirect ways of communicating'[47] by being too direct and forthright when dealing with the leaders. His words and actions are perceived as insensitive, rude and disrespectful towards them. To some village leaders, and folks whose minds have been shaped and conditioned by these values, J is a nuisance. This gives us a sense of the acute hierarchical impediment involved in striving for solidarity to save a village. It also alludes to the disintegration of Malay values developed out of a history of communal living and co-operation.

Chuah's *Days of Change* illuminates the struggle of Hafiz and his friends in their efforts to protect the ordinary citizens of Ulu Banir against injustices perpetrated by politically connected companies. Before a fall that causes him to lose his memory, Hafiz is a successful, wealthy property developer whose life is nevertheless filled with hatred, revenge, a loss of faith, and meaninglessness. His outlook and attitude towards land is one of indifference. He has had his share of building condominiums, reaping profit from commoditising land. Even the initial meeting he attends, which gathers his friends from different professional backgrounds and concerns bent on protesting the proposed theme park at Ulu Banir where he grew up, does not really affect him. However, subsequent threats that follow after he is approached by Abu Bakar, the CEO of Hartindah (a property developer), make Hafiz wonder how many people are threatened and yet helpless and not able to fend for themselves.

The threat facing Banir Valley and its people fosters solidarity among Hafiz and his friends. This solidarity, however, is initially built on Hafiz's doubts and scepticism about the point of protesting. Instead of worrying about the cause, Hafiz is more worried about the ramifications of the protest, about what it would do to the protesters rather than what it might achieve for the land as a whole:

> I didn't see much point in a protest. To whom would they protest? To whom could they protest? I ran through in my mind what the protestors

were likely to do: hold meetings, pass resolutions, write protest letters, and then hope the press would be courageous enough to run their story. Things like that could work, but only temporarily. They were more likely to land the more vocal activists in indefinite detention under the Internal Security Act ... I decided to attend the meeting to see if there were any firebrands who needed to be held in check – for their own sake.[48]

This 'culture of fear' – fear of being detained for protesting – has been indoctrinated into the people for many decades. Chuah captures this through Hafiz's fear of the ramifications of protesting. Hafiz's scepticism mirrors common attitudes towards power relations in Malaysia, whereby attempts to resist are often slighted and accorded an implicit and reducible role in view of the immense possibility of being detained under repressive laws such as the ISA, which have operated long enough to maintain the state's power, thus denying and discouraging people from exercising their rights to coexist with the land and participate in land-related issues and decision-making.

Hafiz's multiracial friends – Yew Chuan, Dr. Mohini, Faridah, Hector Wong, a journalist attached to a regional newsmagazine based in Hong Kong, and Sundram, an engineer who works with the Waterworks Department and is chairman of the local branch of the Malaysian Nature Society – lobby through their expertise and knowledge. They take it as their duty to do what is right for Banir Valley, at a time when its sustainability is becoming increasingly uncertain. Giving different perspectives on the catastrophe that awaits the Valley, the group displays the sensitivity and responsibility of keeping a special eye out for local environments and environmental issues. It is this sensitivity that creates deep caring on the part of the group and promotes activism, which is played out collectively in the public sphere to stop the proposed project. Months of intense lobbying by Yew Chuan's group pays off when, a few months later, the project is shelved by the state until a thorough environmental impact assessment is made.

Engaged in various lobbying actions, Hafiz's group's fight against Hartindah's proposed project demonstrates the result of claiming participatory rights in environmental problems and striving for solidarity among different individuals, regardless of race and religion. After decades of progress in economy and education, Hafiz and his friends are convinced of their right to participate in issues that concern the land. The community-based group proves to be a formidable player in the controversial project, challenging the moral character of the state and business corporations. The larger community beyond the Valley learn about the history of the place they are exposed to, recognise past relationships that have enabled the Valley to prosper, and begin to see through empathetic eyes the ways in which development could influence environmental and human futures. Chuah demonstrates that activism begins with the actions of citizens politically advocating their rights, and then claiming their participatory right to information, decision-making and justice in the form of collective action organised through grassroots movements.

These three novels illustrate the strong relation the Malaysian people have with the environment around them, and by extension their moral response to the Anthropocene. All of the protagonists' fights to protect the environment begin as soon as they and/or the community around them are threatened by displacement from their land owing to either capitalist or state-backed development projects. Pak Kia and J are given the ultimate responsibility to do this, which seems to encourage an individualised project of environmental activism. Hafiz and his knowledgeable, environmentally motivated friends, on the other hand, work together and take measures such as gathering relevant information, getting the message out, forming alliances and lobbying extensively in the media, proving that activism is best when it becomes a shared norm, a co-ordinated effort and a collective political participation in decisions related to projects that would have an impact on the land and community. For instance, Faridah, a psychologist, drums up public interest in the issue by highlighting the sociological and psychological impact of displacing people from their land. Faridah's activism demonstrates that the role of knowledge, backed by scientific research and evidence, is crucial in advancing more powerful arguments about risky environmental projects and the need for a more discriminating approach to development.

Harnessing the power and influence of a group seems too big a task for Pak Kia and J, leaving them alone in their quest to seek environmental justice and fairness. However, taking into account the socio-political contexts of *Jungle of Hope* and *The Dam*, individualised activism seems inevitable. *Jungle of Hope* (set in the 1920s–30s) takes place in Hard Times, the period when locals struggled, usually in vain, against unjust laws that threatened their livelihood and dependence on the forest. *The Dam* is set in the late 1980s, the period of Growing Awareness when environmental laws were only just being introduced and grassroots activism was only just beginning to proliferate. *Days of Change*, on the other hand, where some of the settings are in the period post-2000, reflects the Marching Forward phase, when environmental awareness, co-operation and lobbying are on the rise. Chuah seems to build upon the idea of solidarity and collective activism in the public sphere to secure political leverage. So even though development in Malaysia is largely state-led and state-facilitated, collective activism as demonstrated in *Days of Change* helps to ensure that the state adheres to the rules of checks and balances. Activism could now stop, change or shape decisions related to development and/or environmental sustainability.

Overall, however, efforts to protect the environment – whether individual or public – to ensure sustainability are the basis of the ethics of activism promoted in these novels. This is a reflection of the writers' sense of a deepseated responsibility to the land, which attests to the tensions involved in developing a semi-democratic country while maintaining and protecting the environment. The Anthropocene seems to demand a strengthening of the traditional Malaysian values of fighting to coexist peacefully with the environment, mediated through the multiple sense of cultural worth, survival and sustainability. Past normative thinking has not left us wholly unprepared to tackle ethical questions. In fact, as *Jungle of Hope* and *The Dam* have illuminated, the absence, or rather the decay, of the traditional value of 'kinship ties', which used to bring unity in Malay villages, could sensitise us to the importance of solidarity. This traditional camaraderie is reconstructed in *Days of Change*, re-emphasising that traditional ethical thinking and values have a place but need to be developed into a more modern, practical environmental ethics that incorporates grassroots activism, participation and collective action, media strategies, and research and evidence. The ethics of activism here bears affinities with some ethical principles in moral reasoning about the environment, namely solidarity and participation. As Warner explains, the principle of solidarity invites us to consider how we as a community could act for the well-being of others whereas the principle of participation extends this idea of solidarity and makes it practical by giving all parties access to information and decision-making.[49] Hafiz and his friends' tireless solidarity to save Banir Valley also demonstrates that the challenge lies in how to draw on the diversity of Malaysian society and culture, leaving behind race-based politics, in order to strengthen activism and foster more rigorous and innovative measures to ensure that environmental issues are treated as a fundamental ethical issue in the Anthropocene.

Conclusion

A central moral position regarding the Anthropocene, as suggested by these writers, is an ethics of activism. The ethics of activism delineated in these novels seems to revolve around the profound idea that responsibility to the environment is a shared one, that activism needs to be more assertive, that the future of the environment hinges on actions, knowledge and lobbying, and that action develops from claiming rights to participate, question and lobby for environmental issues. While individualised effort, race-based politics and state and capitalist control may be the nation's Achilles heel, in terms of activism, Malaysians have all the leverage that they need through ICTs that have brought about platforms, opportunities and paradigm shifts in mobilising grassroots environmental movements. These writers' treatment of ethics offers a lens that seeks to distil from Malaysian culture those values and attitudes that govern and develop humanity's judgement about its moral relationship and interconnection with the environment in the age of the Anthropocene.

Notes

1. Manuel Arias-Maldonado, *Environment and Society: Socionatural Relations in the Anthropocene* (Cham: Springer, 2015), p.85.
2. Willis Jenkins, *The Future of Ethics: Sustainability, Social Justice, and Religious Creativity* (Washington, DC: Georgetown University Press, 2013), p.43.
3. Joanna Zylinska, *Minimal Ethics for the Anthropocene* (London: Open Humanities Press, 2014).
4. Randall Curren and Ellen Metzger, *Living Well Now and in the Future: Why Sustainability Matters* (Cambridge, MA: MIT Press, 2017), p.xvii.
5. Byron Williston, *The Anthropocene Project: Virtue in the Age of Climate Change* (Oxford: Oxford University Press, 2015), p.14.
6. Jeremy J. Schmidt, Peter G. Brown and Christopher J. Orr, 'Ethics in the Anthropocene: A Research Agenda', *The Anthropocene Review* 3(3) (2016): 188–200.
7. Ibid., p.13.
8. Christophe Bonneuil, 'The Geological Turn: Narratives of the Anthropocene' in Clive Hamilton et al. (eds.), *The Anthropocene and the Global Environmental Crisis: Rethinking Modernity in a New Epoch* (London: Routledge, 2015), pp.17–31.
9. Diletta De Cristofaro and Daniel Cordle, 'Introduction: The Literature of the Anthropocene', *C21 Literature: Journal of 21st-Century Writings* 6 (2018): 1–6.
10. Bruce Erickson, 'Anthropocene Futures: Linking Colonialism and Environmentalism in an Age of Crisis', *Environment and Planning D: Society and Space* 38(1) (2018), 111–28.
11. Collin McGinn, *Ethics, Evil, and Fiction* (Oxford: Oxford University Press, 2003), pp.2–3.

12. Michael Eskin, quoted in Barbara Arizti and Silvia Martínez-Falquina, *On the Turn: The Ethics of Fiction in Contemporary Narrative in English* (Newcastle: Cambridge Scholars Publishing, 2007), pp.ix–xxiii.

13. Jil Larson, *Ethics and Narrative in the English Novel, 1880–1914* (Cambridge: Cambridge University Press, 2001), pp.ix–xxiii.

14. J. R. Vincent and Rozali Mohamed Ali, *Managing Natural Wealth: Environment and Development in Malaysia* (Washington, DC and London: Institute of Southeast Asian Studies, 2005), pp.366–7.

15. Schmidt, Brown and Orr, 'Ethics in the Anthropocene'.

16. Ibid.

17. Harold Brookfield, Lesley Potter and Yvonne Byron, *In Place of the Forest: Environmental and Socio-economic Transformation in Borneo and the Eastern Malay Peninsula* (Tokyo and New York: United Nations University Press, 1995), p.23.

18. Alfred Russel Wallace, *The Malay Archipelago: The Land of the Orang-Utan and the Bird of Paradise: A Narrative of Travel with Studies of Man and Nature* (London: Macmillan, 1869), p.25.

19. Jeyamala Kathirithamby-Wells, *Nature and Nation: Forest and Development in Peninsular Malaysia* (Copenhagen: Nordic Institute of Asian Studies, 2005), p.128.

20. Shahridan Faiez Mohideen, 'How Culture Determines Land Use Relationships: Revisiting an Old Land Conflict' in Consumers' Association of Penang (ed.), *Tanah Air Ku: Land Issues in Malaysia* (Penang: Consumers' Association of Penang, 2000), pp.238–49.

21. S. M. Mohamed Idris, 'Foreword', in Consumers' Association of Penang (ed.), *Tanah Air Ku: Land Issues in Malaysia* (Penang: Consumers' Association of Penang, 2000), p.7.

22. Wei Lit Yew and Azmil Tayeb, 'Malaysia's Green Movement: Old Continuities and New Possibilities', in Sophie Lemière (ed.), *Illusions of Democracy: Malaysian Politics and People* (Amsterdam: Amsterdam University Press, 2018), 243–60 (p.244).

23. Clark D. Neher, 'Asian Style Democracy', *Asian Survey* 34 (1994), 949–61.

24. Ibid., p.949.

25. Sandra Smeltzer, 'The Message Is the Market: Selling Biotechnology and Nation in Malaysia' in Joseph Nevins and Nancy Lee (eds.), *Taking Southeast Asia to Market: Commodities, Nature, and People in the Neoliberal Age* (Ithaca, NY: Cornell University Press, 2009), pp.191–205; K. S. Jomo and Chong Hui Wee, 'Lessons from Post-Colonial Malaysian Economic Development' in Augustine K. Fosu (ed.), *Achieving Development Success: Strategies and Lessons from the Developing World* (Oxford: Oxford University Press, 2013), pp.50–71.

26. Zainor Izat Zainal, 'Environmentalism in the Realm of Malaysian Novels in English' in Scott Slovic, Swarnalatha Rangarajan and Vidya Sarveswaran (eds.), *Routledge Handbook of Ecocriticism and Environmental Communication* (London: Routledge, 2019), pp.339–50. For an alternative model, see Yew and Tayeb, 'Malaysia's Green Movement', pp.245–55.

27. Mohammad A. Quayum, *One Sky, Many Horizons: Studies in Malaysian Literature in English* (Singapore: Marshall Cavendish (Malaysia) Sdn. Bhd., 2007), pp.62–9.

28. Andrew Ng Hock Soon, *Intimating the Sacred: Religion in English Language Malaysian Fiction* (Hong Kong: Hong Kong University Press, 2011), pp.2–13.

29. Malachi Edwin Vethamani, *Ronggeng-Ronggeng: Malaysian Short Stories* (Selangor, Malaysia: Maya Press Sdn. Bhd., 2020), p.xii.

30. Ibid., p.xv.

31. Axel Goodbody, 'Telling the Story of Climate Change: The German Novel in the Anthropocene' in Caroline Schaumann and Heather I. Sullivan (eds.), *German Ecocriticism in the Anthropocene* (New York: Palgrave Macmillan, 2017), p.297.

32. Agnes S. K. Yeow, 'Visions of Eco-Apocalypse in Selected Malaysian Poetry in English: Cecil Rajendra and Muhammad Haji Salleh'. International Conference on Literature and the Environment (November 2008), Wuhan, China, 1.

33. Ibid.

34. Zainor Izat Zainal, 'Environmental Attitudes in Selected Contemporary Malaysian Novels in English: An Eco-Marxist Perspective', PhD thesis, University of Malaya (2016).

35. Zainor Izat Zainal, 'Environmental Ethics in KS Maniam's *Between Lives* and Yang-May Ooi's *The Flame Tree*', *South East Asia Research* 25 (2017), 1–17.

36. Keris Mas, *Jungle of Hope* [trans. Adibah Amin] (Kuala Lumpur: Institut Terjemahan Negara Malaysia Berhad, 2009), p.7.

37. Ibid., p.8.

38. Ibid., pp.62–5.

39. Syed Hussein Alatas, *The Myth of the Lazy Native* (London: Cass, 1977), p.95.

40. Michael Adas, 'From Avoidance to Confrontation: Peasant Protest in Precolonial and Colonial Southeast Asia', *Comparative Studies in Society and History* 23(2) (1981), 217–47 (p.217).

41. Mas, *Jungle of Hope*, p.58.

42. Peter J. Wilson, quoted in Anthony Milner, *The Malays* (Chichester: Wiley-Blackwell, 2011), p.195.

43. Milner, ibid., p.194.

44. Zakaria Ali, *The Dam* (Kuala Lumpur: Institut Terjemahan Negara Berhad, 2009), p.107.

45. M. G. Nasarudin, 'The Intriguing Mentality of Malays', *New Straits Times* (16 March 2019).

46. Ali, *The Dam*, pp.27–8.

47. J. C. Kennedy, 'Leadership in Malaysia: Traditional Values, International Outlook', *Academy of Management Executive* 16 (2002), 15–26.

48. Chuah Guat Eng, *Days of Change* (Chuah Guat Eng, 2010), p.33.

49. Keith Warner, 'Using Ethical Principles in Moral Reasoning about the Environment', charterforcompassion.org.

CHAPTER 16

Interspecies

Heather Alberro

Though it is increasingly undeniable that we are living in times of severe socio-ecological precarity, this fact bears remembrance lest one might think that the 'Now' as presently constituted is ethically acceptable. In the Anthropocene epoch, our climate system is in disarray owing to the highest atmospheric CO_2 concentrations seen over the last 800,000 years, portending severe socio-ecological breakdown without urgent political action and fundamental structural transformations on a global scale.[1] Others have documented a twofold decline in plant biomass – through deforestation for agricultural expansion and timber extraction, for instance – since the start of human civilisation.[2] Perhaps most worrying is the onset of an era of biological annihilation characterising the planet's sixth mass extinction event since life's three-and-a-half-billion-year tenure on earth, wherein we've lost a near incomprehensible 68 per cent of monitored vertebrate species over the last fifty years.[3] As discussed in Eileen Crist's Chapter 11 in this volume, these are beings prematurely – and many would argue immorally – cast into the abyss of non-existence at rates many times higher than those of previous extinction events.[4] This does not even include the deaths of more than fifty-five billion land-based animals per year in industrial factory farming.[5] The Anthropocene is laden with paradoxes on the one hand characterised by a ubiquitous and destabilising human agency that leaves increasingly fewer spaces not thoroughly (and disastrously) altered while, on the other, severe ecological perturbations resulting from such disturbance threaten human as well as non-human life on earth. These ecological perturbations can be conceived as 'protests by recalcitrant entities' – hurricanes, floods, droughts, infectious diseases, etc. – who, no longer consenting to being treated as mere inert objects for furthering human *ends*, pose formidable challenges to long-standing notions of humans as the only earth-movers.[6] Of course, the 'Anthropos' of the 'Anthropocene' conceals a considerable degree of historical, cultural, geographic and socio-economic variation in terms of culpability for the present predicament. Consider the wildly disproportionate ecological footprints of the globe's plutocratic elite in comparison with those of the poorest 3.8 billion.[7]

Nevertheless, one can speak of species culpability while still emphasising a politics of 'common but differentiated responsibility'.[8] Many have designated, in particular, Western-capitalist modes of subsisting and perceiving the natural world and other species, which are predicated on ceaseless growth, the exploitation and commodification of humans and particularly non-humans for fuelling ever intensifying production and consumption, as ecologically and ethically deficient.[9] The aforementioned is further facilitated by dominant Western-anthropocentric worldviews which deploy a logic of dualism that construes non-human otherness antagonistically in relation to the 'Master' human identity,[10] thereby avowing the purported separateness and superiority of humans and their right to exploit non-humans at will. Thus, this chapter employs utopianism as an overarching theoretical framework for the critical analysis of substantially better modes of being and relating to earth others. The utopian imaginary in its myriad manifestations, for instance, whether as literary or social movement, often surfaces during times of crisis and from concrete experiences of lack and deprivation. Today, these abound as extreme socio-economic inequality, and the looming prospects of environmental breakdown cast a haze of uncertainty over our futures. The enduring value of utopianism lies in its insightful critiques of the limitations of present structures and modes of being, and, crucially, in its imaginative proposals of alternatives which shatter the perceived immutability of the 'Now', thus demonstrating that other worlds are possible. Green utopianism, or ecotopianism, deploys critiques of industrial-capitalism from an ecological standpoint and generally seeks to envision ecologically harmonious modes of human–animal–nature relationality.[11] This chapter considers critical assessments of these relationships as depicted in four canonical ecotopian literary texts: Aldous Huxley's *Island* (2009), Marge Piercy's *Woman on the Edge of Time* (1976), Kim Stanley Robinson's *Pacific Edge* (1990) and Ursula K. Le Guin's *Always Coming Home* (1985). I give particular emphasis to depictions of humans in relation to non-human species and the wider natural world through the lens of post-anthropocentric and posthumanist scholarship, specifically Val Plumwood's theory of ecological animalism for assessing the commensurability of consumption and the use of others with ethical modes of relationality.[12] The chapter concludes with ruminations on potentially ethical modes of relationship that move beyond hierarchical and antagon-istic structurings of 'otherness'[13] and incorporate reverence and respect for irreducible animal alterity.

Towards Socio-ecological Resilience

Conceptualisations surrounding socio-ecological resilience and in particu-lar appropriate levels of 'human intervention' in 'natural processes' and the lives of other species are multifarious, long-standing and contested. At one end of the spectrum lies the 'hands off' or 'let it be' approach advocated by certain strands of the radical environmental movement and seen within conservationist calls for the setting aside of vast swaths of natural habitat.[14] This amounts for some, such as biologist E. O. Wilson, to up to half of the earth's land surface for the flourishing of other species.[15] These spaces would be devoid of socio-economic development, or even all modes of human intervention, a point that I will return to subsequently. At the other end lie arguably undesirable anthropocentric feats of geo-engineering, as seen in attempts to control climate change by enhancing the Albedo effect – the phenomenon wherein light surfaces reflect more heat than dark sur-faces – via stratospheric sulphur injections.[16] Such debates surrounding the relative desirability of certain modes of human–animal–nature interaction feature prominently in ecotopian literary works, as they are engaged in the crucial task of exploring the intricacies of more resilient socio-ecological alternatives. In Ernest Callenbach's genre-defining work *Ecotopia* there are attempts at embracing inter-being entanglement by eroding conceptual-physical barriers and 'bringing nature inside'.[17] For example, the trains in the ecotopian society depicted are filled with plant species of various sorts.[18] Similarly, architectural design in Kim Stanley Robinson's *Pacific Edge*, rather than eradicating plant and animal communities in order to make room for ever-expanding human development, incorporates them into human homes, where all-encompassing glass walls obfuscate distinctions between a building's 'inside' and 'outside'.[19] In the era of biological annihilation, approaches that preserve rather than further extinguish non-human life are especially paramount.

Rewilding, though not explicitly mentioned as an approach in the ecotopian texts under consideration, features implicitly in imaginings of socio-ecological configurations that make room for the flourishing of more-than-human life. The term 'rewilding' was first utilised in the 1980s by radical environmental group Earth First!'s co-founder Dave Foreman, and emerged as an established concept in environmental conservation in the late 1990s.[20] The prefix 're' connotes 'back to', a notoriously nebulous concept. Human alterations of natural systems and landscapes have been occurring for thousands of years, rendering conceptualisations of a pre-civilisational, pristine state of natural equilibrium more mythical than factual. Indeed, many proponents of rewilding are well aware of the conceptual baggage attached to traditional notions of 'wilderness' as denoting an ontologically 'pure' nature preceding and separate from a destructive humanity.[21] Nevertheless, unprecedented alterations can be detected after the industrial revolution and associated large-scale extraction of atmosphere-altering fossil fuels from the earth, and especially after the post-1945 'great acceleration' period of near exponential productive and consumptive activity.[22] Crucially, then, much discourse around rewilding appears future-oriented, marked by a striving not for the resurrection of pristine wilderness but for the proliferation of *wildness*, conceived as 'unbounded, limitless life with incalculable potential for "creative" complexity'.[23] An overarching aim is not only to halt present rates of loss but to 'replenish, restore, reforest, and recreate' through, for instance, reintroducing large predators and other keystone fauna in order to increase ecosystem diversity and resilience.[24] Beyond such reintroduction, though, excessive or unnecessary human intervention would be kept to a minimum, as a core tenet of rewilding is leaving natural processes to self-regulate.

For conservation initiatives like rewilding, as in most ecotopian literary works, a core objective from an ethical as well as an ecological standpoint is to 'scale back' the human enterprise and establish a principle of non-interference or the negative duty of not excessively or unnecessarily thwarting the lifeways of other organisms.[25] As the ecotopian denizen Ben in *Ecotopia* recounts to protagonist Will during their visit to an abandoned whaling station, subsequently transformed into a museum:

> Americans and their technology had been in the forefront of this tragic and irreversible process. And indeed I hadn't realized how far it has gone: it is a horrible story. Our role in it was heavy, and thousands of marvellous creatures that once inhabited this earth have now vanished from the universe forever. We have gobbled them up in our relentless increase. There are now 40 times more weight of humans on the earth than of all the wild mammals together![26]

What the inhabitants of Ecotopia have achieved is a steady-state socio-ecological system that has checked humanity's 'relentless increase'. However, the 'hands off' approach of non-interference denoted earlier warrants greater reflection as it risks subtly perpetuating traditional human/nature and human/animal dualisms by presupposing that humans and 'nature' are separate entities that can be disentangled. If everything is indeed interconnected, then there is no background or foreground, no humans over here and nature 'over yonder'; we drive and fly 'using crushed and liquefied dinosaur bones. You are walking on top of hills and mountains of fossilized animal bits. Most of your house dust is your skin.'[27] To a significant extent, the purportedly sovereign 'Self' is always already a 'We'; we are constituted by the microorganisms in our gut that aid digestion and compose part of our skin as the very barrier differentiating the inside (*oikos*) of the 'human subject' from the outside, as well as the hundreds of thousands of fragments of ancient viral DNA mixed with our own.[28] Or, as Will similarly comes to realise after spending some time in Ecotopia, 'I am part of systems; no one, not even myself, can separate me off as an individual being.'[29] Initiatives such as rewilding can certainly be worthwhile – and indeed necessary – endeavours, but perhaps not in the form of 'animal' reserves in one area and 'human' settlements situated elsewhere, as if the two could ever be so neatly segregated. The goal, rather, should be careful integration and multispecies co-habitation wherever possible, so that we might learn to live respectfully with our co-evolutionary kin, in whose lives we are always implicated to varying degrees as they are in ours.[30]

Deconstructing Anthropocentric Human–Animal–Nature Relations

Classic utopian works such as More's *Utopia* (1516) and Bellamy's *Looking Backward* (1888) have traditionally focused on societal reconfigurations largely for ushering improvements in *human* well-being. Though nonhuman animals are featured in often more harmonious relations with humans, they nevertheless still exist largely for human ends. In *Utopia*, for example, nonhuman animals are deemed possessors of immortal souls along with their human counterparts, though 'not comparable to ours in dignity or destined to equal felicity'.[31] Anti-hierarchical, non-instrumental human–animal relations tend to feature far more centrally, therefore, in ecotopian texts. However, like the hubristic geoengineering approaches described earlier, in Mattapoisett, the ecotopian society depicted in Marge Piercy's *Woman on the Edge of Time*, insect life deemed 'irritating' to humans, such as mosquitoes, has been eliminated.[32] A similar idea appears in H. G. Wells's rather eco-dystopian novel *Men Like Gods*, where the 'utopian' society depicted has actually engaged in a 'systematic extermination of tiresome and mischievous species'.[33] Before doing so, and subsequently in relation to any other beings further encountered, the utopians ask of each organism, 'What good is it [*to humans*]? What harm does it do [*to humans*]? How can it be exterminated [*for the overriding benefit of human society*]?' (p.76). For those species lucky (or rather unlucky) enough to win the favour of the world's human inhabitants, careful genetic engineering has ensured that any characteristics potentially harmful to humans have been bred out. The disastrous ecological impacts of such callous and arrogant manipulation of the biosphere are not lost on one visitor to the society, who laments that owing to the extermination of the majority of utopia's insect life, there were 'no swallows to be seen in Utopia because there were no gnats nor midges' (p.75). Such willingness to eradicate species deemed either useless or threatening in *Woman on the Edge of Time* is curiously juxtaposed with an aversion to technological manipulation of the climate owing to the potential dangers resulting from feedback loops (p.101). Consider the following telling exchange between Connie (the visitor) and Luciente, inhabitant of the ecotopian society of Mattapoisett:

> CONNIE: 'All over Mattapoisett I see patches of woods, meadows, swamps, marshes. You could clear a lot more land'.
> LUCIENTE: 'We have far more land growing food than you did. But, Connie, aside from the water table, think of every patch of woods as a bank of wild genes. In your time thousands of species were disappearing. We need that wild genetic material to breed with ....'
> (p.298)

This constitutes a poignant example of the utopian method of estrangement, wherein an undesired characteristic or mode of thought associated with the society under critique – for example, industrial-capitalism and the underlying logic of ceaseless economic expansion – is juxtaposed with an arguably better alternative, that of preserving natural systems and keeping other species intact. However, still implicit within Luciente's response is an instrumental concern with the preservation of woodland primarily for *human* need rather than because countless other species, their needs and well-being might be ends-in-themselves. Similarly, problematic is the reductive framing of woodlands as mere 'banks of wild genes', as though such complex ecosystems constitute nothing more than 'standing reserves'[34] for human harvest rather than intricate and intrinsically valuable assemblages of living and non-living entities. In such aforementioned characterisations, one can detect the reproduction of the arrogant denial of non-human agency, and the Cartesian reduction of non-human animals to things acted upon, as not *seeing* but merely 'seen' by purportedly superior human observers.[35] However, somewhat paradoxically the novel, more often than not, articulates a decidedly deep ecological[36] ethos and alludes to the presence of dialogical interactions and partnerships predicated on negotiation rather than domination:[37] 'You might say our – you'd say, religion? – ideas make us see ourselves as *partners* with water, air, birds, fish, trees' (p.132); and 'We're part of the web of nature' (p.303). Perhaps more accurately, the partnership in this instance predominantly includes beings that are either innocuous or directly beneficial to humans. Though traces of anthropocentrism haven't been entirely eradicated, the novel features modes of human–animal–nature relationality that are more or less non-hierarchical and non-binary. Devoid of possessive relations between 'self' and 'other', rudimentary forms of non-verbal communication with non-human animals are commonplace and companion animals are depicted as subjects of a life.

Le Guin's singular work *Always Coming Home* likewise features decidedly non-hierarchical human–non-human interactions.[38] The Kesh, the novel's ecotopian community who inhabit an area known as the Valley, exhibit a vital materialist cosmological system wherein even stones and other non-living components of the natural world are imbued with agency. On an expedition through a forest as part of a rite of passage into adulthood, protagonist Stone Telling remarks: 'It was a long way I went before a spring let me find it' (p.20). Here, crucially, the notion of the human subject as the only active agent navigating a world of mute objects is dismantled, with the human resituated in a world brimming with other agentic entities who must be negotiated and reckoned with. The Kesh's seemingly anti-hierarchical and non-dualistic ontology features 'Nine Houses of Being':

> The beings or creatures that are said to live in the Five Houses of Earth and are called Earth People include the earth itself, rocks and dirt and geological formations, the moon, all springs, streams, and lakes of fresh water, all human beings currently alive, game animals, domestic animals, individual animals, domestic and ground-dwelling birds, and all plants that are gathered, planted, or used by human beings . . .

> The people of the Sky, called Four-House People, Sky People, Rainbow People, include the sun and stars, the oceans, wild animals not hunted as game, all animals, plants, and persons considered as the species rather than as an individual, human beings considered as a tribe, people, or species, all

people and beings in dreams, visions, and stories, most kinds of birds, the dead, and the unborn. (p.44)

Kesh cosmology thus characterises not only all living and non-living entities as beings on equal ontological footing 'dancing the same dance' but also non-corporeal entities such as 'beings in stories or dreams' (p.47). As those familiar with Bruno Latour will know, he grants all 'actants' the equal capacity to affect and be affected by others, wherein none enjoy special ontological status in terms of the ability to engage in meaningful actions. Latour's theory of the actant thus constitutes one of the most powerful and thorough intellectual critiques of human exceptionalism. Reality is re-conceived as a vast, pluralistic and horizontal network of ever-shifting alliances between various actants who gain as well as lose power through such alliances, indeed *are* their alliances, and wherein humans are thoroughly dependent on other actants for their existence.[39] The following quote from *Always Coming Home* reveals, however, conflicting sentiments:

> Thinking human people and other animals, the plants, the rocks and stars, all the beings that think or are thought, that are seen or see, that hold or are held, all of us are beings of the Nine Houses of Being, dancing the same dance. (p.307)

Despite the quote's ending, traces of the Cartesian subject–object divide re-emerge when certain beings are posited as *either* seen *or* seeing, thinking *or* thought. Presumably at least, most animals can be *both* seen *and* seeing, thinking *and* thought to varying degrees, and not merely one or the other. overall the novel contains trenchant criticisms of the possessive ('having') orientations characteristic of Western-industrial-capitalism, that is, the desire to acquire, consume and dominate.[40] The Kesh's strong aversion to the concept of ownership, and the vibrant animism which pervades their language, have led them to substitute the word 'pet', which has 'patronizing and condescending overtones', with the word *commensal*, which denotes 'people living together' (p.419). Thus, traditional human–animal hierarchies are critiqued and dismantled to a considerable degree, while human modes of being in relation to other species become marked by egalitarianism, reverence and respect.

In Robinson's *Pacific Edge*, in a manner akin to the Kesh's ecocentric relations with the wider non-human world, protagonist Kevin evinces an intimate knowledge of and connectedness to the landscape of El Modena, the novel's ecotopian society, and its non-human inhabitants: 'He knew the configuration of every dark tree he passed, every turn in the path, and for a long moment rushing along he felt spread out in it all, interpenetrated, the smell of the plants part of him, his body a piece of the hills …' (p.32). In this passage as well as in other instances throughout the novel, Kevin articulates an ecocentric identity or 'ecological self', a term first coined by eco-philosopher Arne Naess to denote an expansive sense of self that extends beyond the individual 'self' construct in its identification with wider ecosystems and their inhabitants.[41] The 'ecological self' and associated processes of cognitive and perceptual identification in turn yield a deep sense of empathic connectedness and emotional resonance with others, particularly when they are perceived to be under threat. This is perhaps why Kevin becomes a key figure in the battle to protect Rattlesnake Hill – one of the last areas of intact wilderness in El Modena – from pro-development forces within the community. Though there is the risk with this mode of identification that the 'other' merely gets subsumed within the expanded 'Self' rather than acknowledged as a singular and irreducible entity, the 'ecological self' nevertheless holds promise as a source of environmentally responsible behaviour, and as a way to help promote empathic engagement with the lived experiences of other beings.[42]

Despite constituting notable strides towards non-exploitative and non-oppressive human–animal–nature relations, animal agriculture, hunting and the use of animals to meet human needs and desires persist in these novels. In *Ecotopia*, though trees are often referred to as 'brother tree' and cattle roam freely throughout the countryside, rather than being confined within the sunless abysses of factory farms, the latter are still unquestioningly regarded as food for human consumption. In Huxley's *Island*, numerous animal species live in and amongst human homes and settlements, so that intimate and largely egalitarian interactions between them are the norm. Moreover, the very concept of animal ownership is undermined by such statements as 'The mynahs [a local bird species] are like the electric light … they don't belong to anyone' (p.15). Yet still, animals such as chickens and fish that have been traditionally categorised as 'food' remain as such. Similarly, in *Woman on the Edge of Time*, although a palpable yet inconsistent bioegalitarian ethos pervades the work, and though industrial-scale animal agriculture appears to have been eradicated, various species are still bred and reared for human consumption (although plant-based foods constitute the primary source of nourishment for Mattapoisett's inhabitants). Lastly, in *Always Coming Home*, deer and quail are hunted and domestic animals such as sheep are featured in festivals, while 'sheepskin and wool [are] used for various leather goods and such' (p.414). However, though sheep are utilised for various human purposes, they are also 'not a symbol of passive stupidity and blind obedience as it is to us, but rather . . . regarded with a kind of affectionate awe, as an intrinsically mysterious being' (p.415). Thus, non-humans appear as respected commensals *as well as* sources of warmth and nourishment. This alludes to a contentious issue that warrants further discussion: are post-anthropocentric human–animal relations compatible with human consumption and the use of other species for food and the like, or does such use remain inherently exploitative and therefore ethically unacceptable?

Against Reductive Use: Plumwood's Theory of Ecological Animalism

Late feminist eco-philosopher Val Plumwood's contextual theory of ecological animalism seeks to dismantle human supremacy in the form of the traditional oppression and exploitation of animal others by simultaneously resituating humans in ecological terms *and* more-than-human species in cultural and ethical terms. This is done by affirming a universe wherein animals *as well as humans* are equally available for mutual and *respectful* use.[43] Plumwood refers to an unyielding opposition to consumption or use of any kind as a moral wrong in and of itself – rather than by virtue of its mode and extent – as ontological veganism. An ontological vegan might argue that it is inherently wrong for humans to consume animals, that the nature of animals' being should exempt them in absolute terms from consumption. However, for Plumwood such a position subtly reinforces and reproduces human/animal and nature/culture dualisms in a similar manner to the separatist 'let it be' approach in some conceptualisations of rewilding. For example, ontological veganism denies ecological embeddedness and reproduces an exclusionary logic in framing only beings within tenuously delineated bounds of ethical consideration as inedible. Rigid boundaries between sentience/non-sentience or animal/plant are underscored in order to justify claims for exempting certain beings from wider food webs, a move that is ontologically problematic because ecosystems and wider inter-actant interactions don't conform to such methodical categorisations. Moreover, ontological veganism risks demonising predation more generally by positing it as a morally unacceptable wrong, a position that can only be maintained by redeploying yet another binary: 'Nature/Culture'. Herein, humans as the sole 'cultural' beings are deemed capable of abstaining from consumption of others while non-human predators are consigned to the 'Natural' realm of necessity. Yet, ecosystems are characterised by a multiplicity of complex and ever-shifting relationships, the consumption of others being a particularly crucial one: orcas prey upon fish, seals and even other cetaceans; we must consume vegetable matter, at least, in order to subsist; when we die, we become food for a host of microorganisms, nourishing them in turn. In *Ecotopia*, Callenbach evokes a similar notion:

> There's a lot of change going on – plants growing, other plants dying, bacteria decomposing them, mice eating seeds, hawks eating mice, a tree or two beginning to grow up and shade the grasses. But the meadow sustains itself on a steady-state basis – unless men come along and mess it up.[44]

Use and consumption, which are essential for the continuity of life, are not *inherently* exploitative or reductive. Consider mutualistic forms of 'use' between plants and pollinating insects, or among sea anemones, anemonefishes and zooxanthellae.[45] Conversely, the immeasurable cruelty, violent denial of animal subjectivity, reduction of animals to saleable commodities, and disastrous ecological impacts of industrial factory farming call for its eradication or at least radical reconfiguration. These all-too-common phenomena constitute the exact opposite of mutuality and respect. Rather, they are so thoroughly degrading and profoundly inimical to the formation of ethical interactions with our co-evolutionary kin that, as Vijaya, inhabitant of the ecotopian society Pala in *Island*, observes: 'For animals everywhere else, Satan, quite obviously, is Homo sapiens.'[46] We have poisoned waterways, razed forest homes, so altered the climate as to create new generations of non-human climate migrants, and systematically exterminated them to the extent that our biomass and that of our enslaved, factory-farmed kin now exceeds that of all other vertebrates apart from fish.[47] In 'gobbling them up in our relentless increase',[48] we have effectively stolen other animals' abilities to flourish in the present as well as into futurity. Alluding to the theme of ownership, often a figure of criticism in these ecotopian works, Plumwood problematises instrumental and reductive forms of use and modes of relationality characterised by Fromm's 'having' orientation. Here, the overarching objective is to acquire and possess rather than *be*, a key impediment to the construction of more ethical modes of human–animal–nature relationality.[49] Conversely, the following poignant excerpt from *Always Coming Home* wonderfully illustrates Plumwood's theory of ecological animalism:

Come among the unsown grasses bearing richly, the oaks heavy with
    acorns, the sweet roots in unplowed earth.
Come among the deer on the hill, the fish in the river, the quail in the
    meadows. You can take them, you can eat them,
Like you they are food.
They are with you, not for you [emphasis added].
Who are their owners?
This is the puma's range,
this hill is the vixen's
this is the owl's tree,
this is the mouse's run,
this is the minnow's pool:
it is all one place. Come take your place.
No fences here, but sanctions. No war here, but dying; there is dying
    here. Come hunt, it is yourself you hunt. Come gather yourself
    from the grass, the branch, the earth.
Walk here, sleep well, on ground that is not yours, but is yourself.

(pp.76–7)

The notion that the ground 'is not yours, but is yourself' recalls the disavowal of ownership of earth others in *Island* and *Woman on the Edge of Time*, as well as Kevin's intimation of an 'ecological self' when he sensed his body as 'a piece of the hills'. From the standpoint of building more compassionate relations with 'more-than-human' life and the wider biosphere, perhaps Plumwood's approach, evinced forcefully in the passage here, appears as the truly post-anthropocentric one. Non-human others are *with us*, not *for us*; if humans are indeed animals who differ from other species only by degrees rather than kind, as actants on equal ontological footing, then surely, like them, we are food – as well as so much more. Such a view depicts human and non-human animals as commensals and as deserving of respect on that basis. No beings may be extricated from biospheric interconnectivity or elevated to a position of superiority. Living well and ethically with earth, others, particularly amid the turbulent Anthropocene, demands a recognition that they are not ours to do with as we please, and that they are more than *mere* means, but ends in themselves.[50]

Ecotopia: Valuing Irreducible Alterity

'Ecotopian' modes of human–animal–nature relationality would perhaps adopt an approach to difference that does not subsume the other within the same 'Self' but rather affirms difference and recognises a 'deep zoe-egalitarianism between humans and animals'.[51] In this vein, our language warrants a critical rethink as with Le Guin's substitution of the word 'pet' with the more inclusive 'commensal'. Homogenising terms such as 'human' and 'animal' conceals their intermingling and mutual constitution while the latter reduces millions of singular beings moulded by all manner of unique experiences and interrelations into one woefully inadequate term that fails to capture complexity.[52] Derrida's apt reference to (animal) others as unsubstitutible singularities reminds us that they always regard us, as we do them, from the point of view of an 'absolute other' that is never completely accessible, although ethics demands that we try to understand and empathise with them.[53] These unsubstitutible singularities, co-evolutionary kin with whom we share a common terrestrial dwelling-place, can no longer be conceived as *unseeing* things merely *seen* by detached human subjects; they possess agency and subjectivity that, though distinct, is not 'less than' ours. This is the very nature of alterity as articulated by Plumwood, an approach to otherness and singularity that moves beyond rigid binaries of self/other, human/animal, male/female, culture/nature, etc. and wherein, crucially, difference does not equate to 'less than'.[54] From this standpoint, we can begin to construct ways of being wherein other species are with us, not for us, and wherein none are treated as mere means.

Despite occasional contradictions and limited focus on the lived experiences of non-humans, the ecotopian works discussed in this chapter attempt, to varying degrees, to delineate such ways of being: *Ecotopia* in its ecocentric vision where trees are kin; *Island* and *Woman on the Edge of Time* in foregrounding non-possessive relations between humans and non-humans; *Pacific Edge* in its inklings of an ecological self-construct that sees itself as thoroughly entwined with, rather than isolated from, earth others; and, most especially, *Always Coming Home*'s portrayal of a vibrant world brimming with non-human agency. Such examples demonstrate that substantially better ways of relating to our co-evolutionary kin are well within the bounds of possibility.

Notes

1. Rebecca Lindsey, 'Climate Change: Atmospheric Carbon Dioxide' (2018), www.climate.gov.
2. Yinon M. Bar-On, Rob Phillips and Ron Milo, 'The Biomass Distribution on Earth', *PNAS* 115(25) (2018), 6506–11.

3. World Wildlife Fund (WWF), 'Living Planet Report 2020: Bending the Curve of Biodiversity Loss' [eds. R. E. A Almond, M. Grooten and T. Petersen, https://www.worldwildlife.org/publications/living-planet-report-2020

4. E. O. Wilson, *Half-Earth: Our Planet's Fight for Life* (New York: W.W. Norton & Co., 2016).

5. Compassion in World Farming (CIWF), 'Strategic Plan 2013–2017 for Kinder, Fairer Farming Worldwide', www.ciwf.org.uk/research/policy-economics/strategic-plan-2013-2017/.

6. Bruno Latour, *The Politics of Nature: How to Bring the Sciences into Democracy* (Cambridge, MA: Harvard University Press, 2004).

7. Oxfam International, '5 Shocking Facts about Extreme Global Inequality and How to Even It Up' (2019), www.oxfam.org/en/5-shocking-facts-about-extreme-global-inequality-and-how-even-it.

8. Dipesh Chakrabarty, 'The Climate of History: Four Theses', *Critical Inquiry* 35(2) (2009), 197–222 (p.218).

9. See, for example, Jason W. Moore, 'The Capitalocene, Part I: On the Nature and Origins of Our Ecological Crisis', *The Journal of Peasant Studies* 44(3) (2017), 594–630.

10. Val Plumwood, *Feminism and the Mastery of Nature* (London: Routledge, 2002).

11. Lisa Garforth, *Green Utopias: Environmental Hope Before and After Nature* (Cambridge: Polity, 2018).

12. See, respectively, Francesca Ferrando, 'The Party of the Anthropocene: Post-Humanism, Environmentalism and the Post-Anthropocentric Paradigm Shift', *Relations* 4(2) (2016), 159–73 (p.159); Nik Taylor, 'Animals, Mess, Method: Post-Humanism, Sociology and Animal Studies', *Crossing Boundaries* (2012), 37–50; Val Plumwood, 'Animals and Ecology: Towards a Better Integration' (2003), https://openresearch-repository.anu.edu.au/handle/1885/41767.

13. Murray Bookchin, *The Ecology of Freedom: The Emergence and Dissolution of Hierarchy* (Edinburgh: AK Press, 2005).

14. Timothy Morton, 'Thinking Ecology: The Mesh, the Strange Stranger, and the Beautiful Soul', *Collapse* 6 (2010), 265–93.

15. Wilson, *Half-Earth*, p.209.

16. Victor Brovkin et al., 'Geoengineering Climate by Stratospheric Sulfur Injections: Earth System Vulnerability to Technological Failure', *Climatic Change* 92(3–4) (2009), 243–59.

17. Ernest Callenbach, *Ecotopia: The Novel of Your Future* (New York: Bantam, 1975).

18. Ibid., p.8.

19. Kim Stanley Robinson, *Pacific Edge: Three Californias* (London: HarperCollins, 1995).

20. Michael Soulé and Reed Noss, 'Rewilding and Biodiversity: Complementary Goals for Continental Conservation', *Wild Earth* 8 (1998), 18–28.

21. Andrea R. Gammon, 'The Many Meanings of Rewilding: An Introduction and the Case for a Broad Conceptualisation', *Environmental Values* 27(4) (2018), 331–50.

22. Will Steffen et al., 'The Trajectory of the Anthropocene: The Great Acceleration', *The Anthropocene Review* 2(1) (2015), 81–98.

23. Robert L. Chapman, 'Ecological Restoration Restored', *Environmental Values* 15(4) (2006), 463–78 (p.468).

24. Richard T. Corlett, 'Restoration, Reintroduction, and Rewilding in a Changing World', *Trends in Ecology & Evolution* 31(6) (2016), 453–62.

25. Philip Cafaro et al., 'If We Want a Whole Earth, Nature Needs Half: A Response to Büscher et al.', *Oryx* 51(3) (2016), 400.

26. Callenbach, *Ecotopia*, p.76.

27. Morton, *Thinking Ecology*, p.269.

28. Michael Emerman and Harmit S. Malik, 'Paleovirology—Modern Consequences of Ancient Viruses', *PLoS Biology* 8(2) (2010), 1.

29. Callenbach, *Ecotopia*, p.88.

30. Tom Van Dooren, *Flight Ways: Life and Loss at the Edge of Extinction* (New York: Columbia University Press, 2014).

31. Thomas More, *Utopia* (New York: Penguin, 1965), p.223.

32. Marge Piercy, *Woman on the Edge of Time* (London: Penguin Random House, 2016).

33. H. G. Wells, *Men Like Gods* (New York: Macmillan, 1923), p.76.

34. Martin Heidegger, 'The Question Concerning Technology' in Heidegger, *The Question Concerning Technology and Other Essays* [trans. William Lovitt] (New York: Harper, 1977), pp.3–35.

35. Jacques Derrida and David Wills, 'The Animal That Therefore I Am (More to Follow)', *Critical Inquiry* 28(2) (2002), 369–418 (p.383).

36. Arne Naess, 'The Shallow and the Deep, Long-Range Ecology Movement: A Summary', *Inquiry* 16(1–4) (1973), pp.95–100.

37. Val Plumwood, 'Nature in the Active Voice', *Climate Change and Philosophy: Transformational Possibilities* (2010) 113–29 (p.123).

38. Ursula K. Le Guin, *Always Coming Home* (London: Gateway, 2016).

39. That is, power not in the Machiavellian sense but as in the capacity to do and to make things happen.

40. See Erich Fromm, *To Have or To Be?* (London: Bloomsbury Academic, 2013).

41. See Arne Naess, 'Identification as a Source of Deep Ecological Attitudes' in Michael Tobias (ed.), *Deep Ecology* (San Diego: Avant Books, 1985), pp.256–70; and Abraham Maslow, *Toward a Psychology of Being* [2nd ed.] (Princeton, NJ: D. Van Nostrand Co., 1968).

42. Elizabeth A. Bragg, 'Towards Ecological Self: Deep Ecology Meets Constructionist Self-Theory', *Journal of Environmental Psychology* 16(2) (1999), 93–108.

43. Plumwood, *Animals and Ecology*, p.2.

44. Callenbach, *Ecotopia*, p.34.

45. Philip F. P. Schmiege, Cassidy C. D'Aloia and Peter M. Buston, 'Anemonefish Personalities Influence the Strength of Mutualistic Interactions with Host Sea Anemones', *Marine Biology* 164(1) (2017), p.24.
46. Aldous Huxley, *Island* (London: Vintage, 2005), p.186.
47. See Samantha Noll, 'Nonhuman Climate Refugees: The Role that Urban Communities Should Play in Ensuring Ecological Resilience', *Environmental Ethics* 40(2) (2018), 119–34; Bar-On et al., *The Biomass Distribution on Earth*.
48. Callenbach, Ecotopia, p.76.
49. Fromm, *To Have or to Be?*
50. See Immanuel Kant and J. B. Schneewind, *Groundwork for the Metaphysics of Morals* (New Haven, CT: Yale University Press, 2002).
51. Lucy Sargisson, 'Green Utopias of Self and Other', *Critical Review of International Social and Political Philosophy* 3(2–3) (2000), 140–56; Rosi Braidotti, *The Posthuman* (Cambridge: Polity, 2013).
52. Morton, *Thinking Ecology*, p.277; Derrida and Wills, 'The Animal That Therefore I Am', p.378.
53. Ibid., p.381.
54. Plumwood, *Feminism and the Mastery of Nature*.

CHAPTER 17

Deep Time Visible

Pippa Marland

In accounts of the Anthropocene, the assertion that human culture is ill-equipped to respond to the epoch's spatio-temporal dimensions has become something of a commonplace: Timothy Clark identifies irreconcilable 'derangements of scale' in our thinking as we try to move between individual and planetary considerations; Bruno Latour states that it is 'easy for us to agree' that people lack 'the mental and emotional repertoire to deal with such a vast scale of events'; and Timothy Morton describes the emergence of uncanny 'hyperobjects' that defy comprehension, either through their massive distribution in time and space or through their resistance to organic processes of decay.[1] It seems, then, that the crisis of the environmental imagination identified by Lawrence Buell in an early articulation of ecocriticism has only deepened further in the twenty-first century.[2] Adam Trexler, like Buell two decades earlier, calls for a '*cultural transformation*' that can address the ongoing crisis, and asks, 'What tropes are necessary to comprehend climate change or to articulate the possible futures faced by humanity? What longer, historical forms aid this imagination?'[3] Clark, more radically, questions whether 'certain limits of the human imagination, artistic representation and the capacity of understanding [are] now being reached'.[4]

If this encounter with cognitive and imaginative limits is the case with any form of artistic representation, however innovative, then what hope might arguably more traditional forms of literature, such as prose nature writing, have of responding in any useful way? As early as 2003, the American scholar Dana Phillips argued against what he saw as ecocriticism's rehabilitation of mimesis, challenging Buell's championing of the nature writing of Henry David Thoreau and seeking to divert attention away from 'one of literature's more pedestrian, least artful aspects'.[5] Likewise, Morton has critiqued the notion of 'ecomimesis' in nature writing – the idea that the genre can offer unmediated access to nature through its reliance on a sense of situatedness and authenticity of

experience.[6] Tellingly, in framing his enquiry into Anthropocene literature, Trexler omits to mention prose nature writing at all, listing fiction,
poetry and drama before settling on the climate change novel as his
primary focus. In the midst of this crisis of representation, and in
a world that exists 'post-nature' (with no area of the planet's surface
escaping anthropogenic activity), what role can nature writing hope to
fulfil?

Yet, recent years have seen a popular resurgence of the genre. While the
term 'New Nature Writing' remains an area of contention, not least
around its 'newness', these texts are nevertheless increasingly characterised
by a growing apprehension of the plight of the environment and an
awareness of the contingency of conceptualisations of 'nature'.
Moreover, in Graham Huggan's view, nature writing is now, and has
been throughout its modern incarnation, 'as much an interrogation as
a performance of mimesis'.[7] A genre marked by anxieties and tensions such
as these might be regarded as evincing a usefully fractured quality, one
potentially open to new light.

The very notion of the 'Anthropocene' inevitably raises questions of
subjectivity and the place of the human on Earth – elements that might be
seen as central to modern nature writing. While Terry Gifford and Anna
Stenning note that the 'personal epiphanies' associated with nature writing
are perhaps most prevalent in British and American traditions, rather than
other areas of the world, broadly speaking they see the genre as hinging on,
and enriched by, a 'subjective appreciation' of nature.[8] Semantically speaking, the Anthropocene places *anthropos* centre-stage, not in a celebratory
fashion, but rather in what Don McKay identifies as a form of 'negative
recognition', of naming and 'owning' an atrocity.[9] Thus, Latour argues,
the time for objective natural science has passed; he cites Michel Serres,
who says of the Earth, 'Now it *has a subject once again*.'[10] This is not the
historical, transcendent human subject but one utterly enmeshed with the
world, and with whom the non-human world is likewise inescapably
enmeshed. 'To be a subject', writes Latour, 'is not to act autonomously
in front of an objective background, but to share *agency with other subjects
that have also lost their autonomy*.'[11] It is a moot point, perhaps, as to
whether the Earth *has* lost its autonomy, given that one of the greatest
ironies of the Anthropocene is that while its naming recognises anthropogenic effects on a planetary scale, humans are ultimately powerless to
predict or manage its course. But insofar as this refers to the Earth's post-
natural state, then it also indicates a shared subjectivity for all planetary life.
To borrow and paraphrase Morton's term, if the Anthropocene is

a hyperobject, the Earth itself might be regarded as a 'hypersubject': an assemblage of animacies and agencies brought together in a complex multispecies entanglement.

With its tendency towards subjective reflection and its increasing preoccupation with navigating the territory of damage, New Nature Writing might yet provide a site of witness to the Anthropocene as it unfolds. This chapter explores, therefore, the ways in which the genre offers insights in relation to both the term's stratigraphic frame of reference and its more discursive and affective aspects. In doing so, I hope to challenge an assumption prevalent in contemporary literary criticism: that the Anthropocene is 'ungraspable' – cognitively and imaginatively – by the kinds of situated, descriptive and autobiographical registers that operate within prose nature writing. I also highlight a strand of New Nature Writing particularly relevant to this enquiry. A prominent feature of much of the genre's recent output in the British Isles is its attraction to the peripheries of the archipelago and its attendant interest in rich histories and far-reaching interconnections obscured by the dominant narratives of centralised power.[12] This archipelagic orientation is certainly significant in relation to the Scottish islands, which feature powerfully (among other locations) in the work of established nature writers such as Kathleen Jamie, Adam Nicolson and Robert Macfarlane, as well as that of newer voices including Amy Liptrot and David Gange.[13]

This chapter is divided into four sections. In the first two sections, I offer examples of the ways in which these authors' Scottish island-themed writings speak to the cognitive and imaginative challenges of the Anthropocene's geological and planetary scales. The topographies encountered in these works set the human within a massively more-than-human context, bringing deep time into view and facilitating the contemplation of global interconnections through the presence of birds and marine mammals whose migrations trace lines across the globe. In the third section, I explore the manner in which these texts enable us to think through other, more elusive elements of the epoch, by registering phenomena that are, as it were, *hiding in plain sight* in these terrains – species decline and the effects of plastic pollution, both of which speak to complex forms of human and non-human entanglement. Finally, in the last section, I reflect on the ways in which these encounters foster an Anthropocene imaginary for the future, enabling us not just to see ourselves as spectres of epochs to come but also, in the shorter term, to imagine alternative human possibilities based on 'routes as yet untravelled'.[14]

On Ancient Rocks

Jeremy Davies suggests that 'the world of the early twenty-first century is undergoing changes that can be grasped only by switching to timescales of tens of thousands or even millions of years'.[15] Thinking in these scales is, as already noted, problematic for humans, especially given that we measure our own lives in scores and tens of years, and our existence as a species in hundreds of thousands. Caspar Henderson writes: 'Even if we accept the idea of deep time as a reality, it is still hard to *understand* because its dimensions are so far outside our normal cognitive range.'[16] Rather than looking for conceptual analogies to explain this (he gives the example, '[I]f all Earth history is a 24 hour day then humans emerged around 3 seconds before midnight'), Henderson argues that a better way to feel deep time is 'a walking meditation among ancient rocks'.[17] Such a meditation informs the island texts discussed here. The very pedestrian quality that Phillips disparages takes literal form; these writers walk (or in the case of David Gange walk and kayak) and this kinetic methodology opens them to embodied insight. On these outcrops in the Atlantic, ancient rocks are an inescapable feature of island life; here we find geologies laid bare, deep time made visible.

In *The Outrun*, Amy Liptrot chronicles her retreat from a life of addiction in London to her childhood home on the Orkney Islands, so beginning her gradual and hard-won recovery. In a process of recuperative re-grounding, she discovers that the islands put her in touch with scales of time and space that dwarf the urban hub she has left behind. Walking around Papay [Papa Westray], she observes,

> it is hard not to start thinking about how the land itself was formed ... Layers of rock are clearly visible on the cliffs, like the pages of a book. These layers on different islands once met up when the archipelago was one continuous landmass but have been worn away by the action of sea and ice over millennia ... Most of Orkney is formed from Caithness flagstone ... dating back to the Devonian period 400 million years ago.[18]

She sees the landscape as textual, as 'storied matter', to use the discourse of material ecocriticism, in a way that both productively shrinks the human subject and demonstrates archipelagic, geological connections that reach outward spatially from the local while travelling millions of years back in time.[19]

A similar contextualising effect can be seen in historian David Gange's hybrid work *The Frayed Atlantic Edge: A Historian's Journey from Shetland to the Channel*, which combines historiography with travel memoir and nature writing.²⁰ His methodology involves navigating the British and Irish Atlantic littoral by kayak and on foot, developing an archive formed through 'slow travel'.²¹ This approach affords new insights gained when the islands are viewed from the seas that surround them, not least the apprehension of histories massively predating the human. The Shetland Islands inspire a sustained meditation on deep time in which Gange traces their history back three thousand million years to before the formation of the Caledonian mountains. Gazing up at the cliffs, he observes: 'I was staring through cross-sections of those ancient hills, with an access to the distant past that is rarely possible from land.'²² It is a perspective that brings the passage of thousands and millions of years into view, giving a glimpse of the very strata that form the Earth's geological record and are already beginning to mark the accelerated passage of the Holocene into the Anthropocene. Jos Smith notes insightfully that one of the qualities of the New Nature Writing is the way in which, in the face of environmental uncertainty, it simultaneously encompasses both 'the intensely local and ... the globally interconnected'.²³ The additional information that Gange offers – that these specific 'drowned mountains' once 'stretched from what is now Norway to the present day United States' – draws disparate parts of the globe together conceptually in a way that troubles ideas of nationhood, a perception that may prove increasingly valuable as climate breakdown results in ever greater displacement of human populations.²⁴

If the visibility of deep time is one notable 'island effect', then another is the apparent instability of linear time in these sites, such that the past remains a powerfully tangible presence. In *The Old Ways: A Journey on Foot*, Robert Macfarlane encounters on the coast of Lewis a deep time that still seems fresh and vital underfoot:

> The peat thinned as I gained height and rock began to show through the heather: Lewisian gneiss, the most ancient surface rock in Europe – 3.1 billion years old, zebra-striped, scarred and smoothed by multiple glaciations. The Pleistocene felt only a few weeks gone, the ice just recently retreated.²⁵

The same is true for ancient human history (which, of course, enters Earth history relatively late in the day): earlier human occupation remains extraordinarily legible on the islands, again giving a sense of strands of island time that weave together and coalesce rather than replacing each other in linear fashion. The effect leads to a strong sense of continuity and community with the past. On Mainland Orkney, Liptrot, repairing drystone dykes after a particularly savage storm, writes: 'I start to think in decades and centuries rather than days and months. I think about the people who built the original dykes.'[26] Jamie, whose two essay collections *Findings* and *Sightlines* see her frequently gravitating to the Scottish islands, visits the Neolithic village of Skara Brae, also on Mainland Orkney, and comments:

> There, you can marvel at the domestic normality, that Late Stone Age people had beds and cupboards and neighbours and beads. You can feel both their presence, their day-to-day lives, and their utter absence. It's a good place to go. It re-calibrates your sense of time.[27]

This interplay of presence and absence enables a sense of personal, affective and phenomenological involvement in both deep and (relatively) recent time, offering a foothold for an Anthropocene temporal imagination that ultimately requires us to understand what humans *have been* in order to negotiate what we *might become*. As such, it begins to answer Trexler's question about the longer historical forms that might aid cultural transformation.

Deep time's spatial corollary is, of course, the cosmos. On the Scottish islands, planetary effects make their presence felt, and as a result alter perceptions and recalibrate attention. After a few weeks on Papay, Liptrot notices that she is 'always pretty much aware of the height of the tide, the direction of the wind, the time of sunrise and sunset, and the phase of the moon'.[28] Thinking of how these phenomena are related, she goes on:

> The tide is influenced not just by the earth's rotation and the positions of the moon and the sun, but also the moon's altitude above the equator and the topography of the seabed – or bathymetry – and the complicated way water moves between islands. I think about the earth's rotation, and realise that it's not the tide that is going out or the moon rising: rather, I am moving away from them.[29]

It is a subtle form of reorientation that unmoors ideas of the fixed self and the static Earth and sets them afloat in a cosmic ocean. If the Anthropocene planet is a hypersubject, these reflections put some of its constituent parts in dialogue, extending our cognition of planetary interconnections that might otherwise elude our understanding.

'The Palm of the World's Hand'

It is not only through direct contact with the mineral evidence of deep time and with the phases of the moon and the tides that the temporal and spatial imaginations are expanded in these accounts. Some of the animals inhabiting these islands also provide tangible evidence of deep time, as well as being extraordinary navigators of the globe. Adam Nicolson, in *Sea Room*, his 'love letter' to the Shiants, writes of one of these islands' bird species: 'The oldest shag, identical to its modern descendants, has been found in rocks laid down sixty million years ago.'[30] The Scottish islands have long been a site in which the navigational attributes of the avian world have been recognised. Martin Martin, considering the properties of the solan goose (or gannet) in his 1698 volume *A Late Voyage to St Kilda*, describes the way in which 'the inhabitants [of the islands] take their measures from the flight of those fowls, when the heavens are not clear, as from a sure compass'.[31] The Western ecological imagination is perhaps only just beginning to recover this pre-Enlightenment respect for avian abilities, as we learn ever more about the astonishing trajectories of bird migration.

New Nature Writing, with its combination of natural history and reflective, autobiographical content, might be seen as the ideal genre in which to explore the gradual reassessments of thought and belief that arise from such knowledge. Gange's hybrid history from the 'outside in' involves a recovery of the interweaving of human and animal lives that has been in evidence since the islands were populated, but has been lost in the urban- and anthropocentric narratives that have dominated post-Enlightenment historical discourse. He writes that 'seabirds, fish and species of seaweed play roles as significant in this book as politicians or their institutions: they had as great an effect on past shoreline lives'.[32] Echoing Martin Martin's late-seventeenth-century sentiments, Macfarlane, describing the importance of the invisible but highly travelled sea routes around the Scottish archipelago, notes that the first sea-road mariners would have used navigation aids such as watching 'the direction of flight at dusk of land-roosting birds like fulmars, petrels or gannets'.[33] Moving into a larger geographical frame, Nicolson's description of the migratory passage of Barnacle geese marks a growing, global-ecological sensibility. He sees them tracing an arc 'from the west coast of Ireland, across to the Inner Hebrides, up past the Shiants to Rona and Sula Sgeir, on to the Faeroes, Iceland and Greenland', their flight imagined beautifully as 'a line creased into the palm of the world's hand'.[34]

For Nicolson, our increasing knowledge of avian lives offers an opportunity to apprehend something of their *umwelten* – the world as it is experienced through their species-specific subjectivities.[35] There is certainly a sense of expanded understanding in Jamie's account of finding the body of a Leach's storm petrel on the island of North Rona. The bird has been ringed at some point in an ornithological survey, and after sending off its tag, Jamie receives a letter telling her this happened 'twenty-four years previously, not on Rona ... but 170 miles northeast of there, on the island of Yell'.[36] As she reads this, 'a connection shot between them [Rona and Yell]. Suddenly they were linked by a flight-path, straight as an arrow. I thought I knew my maps, but not as the storm petrel does.'[37] The information instils in her a new sense of non-human waymaking, of 'mappings' unrelated to human geographical and geopolitical understandings. In Liptrot's account of her conservation work with the RSPB (Royal Society for the Protection of Birds), monitoring corncrake populations on the Orkney Islands, she likewise reveals a process of entering into the bird's world, while it in turn infiltrates hers: 'Somehow this bird has become my thing. I am hallucinating a *Crex crex* call in the background music on the radio and at night I dream of corncrakes.'[38]

'The Fundamental Earth Is Trembling'

All of these accounts bring out a sense of timescales, connections and vibrant non-human lives that, without the tangible markers of rock and flesh on the islands, might be difficult to grasp. Some of the authors' reflections also prepare us for the notion of flux, establishing the idea that the landmasses and oceans of the Earth have seen massive changes over the aeons, whether by slow accretions or sporadic accelerations. These are not Anthropocene effects, but merely a feature of the Earth's long history. Liptrot writes: 'I hear that Europe and America are gradually getting further apart, as lava bubbles up into the gap between the tectonic plates in Iceland.'[39] The islands themselves are dynamic forms; Gange notes: 'Shetland may have sunk as much as nine metres in 5,000 years ... This scale of change, over so short a time – the absence of a "million" in the number is not an error – explains some of the extraordinary transitoriness of this coastline.'[40] Animal species also morph and fluctuate; bird numbers plummet and rise again according to global cycles and patterns of wind and weather, and on some of the islands unique evolutionary effects can be seen in biologically isolated populations. Gange discovers on Shetland that several species, including wrens, voles, moths and mosses, 'have evolved along unique trajectories'.[41] He concludes: 'There is as much social change in nature, and as little permanence, as there is among people.'[42]

While such reflections bring out the notion that the universe is itself a process not a static being, these works also begin to differentiate between flux and the anthropogenically influenced changes making their presence felt as the Anthropocene begins to gather pace. In a sense, the time for cognitive and imaginative readjustments around time and space, while still a necessary component of our understanding, has already passed. Instead we are faced with an 'existential crisis' in which, to use Serres' phrase, 'the fundamental Earth is trembling'.[43] How is the New Nature Writing responding to such an intensification of crisis? Again, just as these island texts speak to ideas of deep time and planetary connection, so do they also register the epoch's affective, existential impacts, along with an increasingly complex understanding of the entanglement of human and non-human life. For example, where the celebratory tone of Nicolson's *Sea Room* revelled in the Shiant Islands as a hub for 'millions of birds and animal lives',[44] *The Seabird's Cry*, coming nearly two decades later, documents the drastic decline in their numbers. The title can be seen as referring not just to the seabirds' vocalisation but also to an inter-species, Earth-wide cry of anguish: the 'hypersubject' keening for the lost.[45] Nicolson draws heavily on the latest research into seabird lives, but, in an echo of Latour's sense of the belatedness of objective science – or perhaps its inadequacy when not combined with subjective soul searching and broader cultural understanding – he writes that 'science is coming to understand the seabirds just as they are dying. By one measure, in the last sixty years they have declined across the world ocean by about two-thirds'; climate change, pollution and the effects of industrialised fishing 'ripple through the seabird community like songs to be sung at the apocalypse'.[46]

Nicolson also brings out his sense that the loss of these animals represents a reduction in what it means to be human. In introducing his subject, he cites Seamus Heaney's poem 'Set questions for the ghost of W.B.': 'What came first, the seabird's cry or the soul/ Imagined in the dawn cold when it cried?'[47] Human soul and seabird's cry are seen here as coexistent from the beginning. In Nicolson's view, the birds have been integral to the development of the myths and legends that humans have created in order to understand ourselves, and yet 'it looks as though we are now destroying them'.[48] As the ecocritic and nature writer Michael Malay argues: 'Animals have worked their way into the very fabric of our imagination, and into the nature of our being. They have shaped what it means to be human.'[49] It is perhaps the perception of this interweaving that restores Liptrot's commitment when, '[o]n tough nights', she begins to entertain doubts about her work with the corncrake: 'And then I learn that, in 1977, corncrake remains were excavated from the Pictish and Viking Age site at Buckquoy, in Orkney's West Mainland.'[50] The knowledge that the birds have been the islanders' companions for millennia and yet have now been all but wiped out by human activity shocks Liptrot and reinvigorates her dedication to monitoring and protecting them: '[I]t seems right that we should take responsibility to conserve the last few.'[51] Associating species decline with human diminishment is undoubtedly an anthropocentric perspective, but it also fruitfully generates in both Nicolson and Liptrot a heightened sense of human responsibility – one that resonates with Donna Haraway's *Chthulucene*, in which we are tasked with 'learning to stay with the trouble of living and dying in response-ability on a damaged earth'.[52] Their insights into the ways in which animals constitute the human, combined with their recognition of human culpability and our corollary duty to conserve non-human life, gesture towards just such 'response-ability'.

It is not enough, though, to recognise the interweaving of animal lives with our own, along with our culpability as a species, albeit markedly unequal across the globe; as Haraway has long indicated, the notion of the 'human' itself must be investigated. This is an area that one might assume to lie beyond the scope of nature writing, but, in registering the more uncanny phenomena that come to light in these terrains, the texts in question evince at times a haunting and haunted quality that gestures towards just such an enquiry. Plastic waste is a case in point – items washing up on the shores of long-uninhabited islands bring a troubling sense of matter out of place. Landing on the Monach Islands, Jamie finds the sand dunes 'choked with plastic' including a doll's head, a discovery that stimulates a meditation on the human tendency to value 'that which endures'.[53] She questions whether this feature 'is still a virtue, when we have invented plastic, and the dolls head with her tufts of hair and rolling eyes may well persist after our own have cleaned back down to the bone'.[54] The episode brings out both a need to rethink human 'values' and an uncomfortable recognition of plastic items as uncanny objects that, though we might think of them as dead or inert matter, will outlive us by hundreds of years or more, continuing in their environmental effects long after their creators are gone. Liptrot's account of Papay fisherman Douglas's stories of seeing 'gannets flying, trailing plastic necklaces – they had dived straight through the holes in plastic drinks can packaging' conjures a similar feeling of disjunction.[55] The metaphor of the necklace makes the image all the more mortifying – birds encumbered and restricted, sometimes fatally, by an item that resembles a human form of decoration. But, what is more eerie and perhaps more profoundly unsettling is when the plastic is present but not visible. Nicolson writes: 'It is a literal truth that every albatross and fulmar has eaten plastic and it is reliably predicted that by 2050, about 99.8 percent of all seabird species will have plastic in their stomachs.'[56] The observation reveals that it is not just the geological record but the hidden fleshy strata of the planet's creatures – including, of course, the human – that evidence the Anthropocene. The rupture of structural integrity represented by this 'trans-corporeality'[57] brings Latour's concept of an overarching loss of autonomy more sharply into focus, with a clear sense of *Anthropos* both as the author of that loss and as integrally and inescapably compromised by it.

Anthropocene Futures

Macfarlane argues that the Anthropocene 'compels us to think forward in deep time', and to imagine ourselves as 'ancestors'.[58] Again, these island texts seem to heighten opportunities for such reflection, in their ability both to think forward to the lives of human generations to come and, ultimately, to imagine a time when the human species will no longer exist. As Gange kayaks around the Orkney islands, he witnesses geological 'freaks of deep time' which, he notes, in the manner of W. G. Sebald, 'felt like the imaginary future ruins of a civilisation lost to the rising seas of the Anthropocene'.[59] His perception involves thinking towards a distant future which is looking back to the point (still in the future from our perspective) at which human civilisation (or at least an element thereof) will have been engulfed by the ocean. A similar perspective figures in Jamie's consideration of the human abandonment of Rona. She uses the island's history as a model for two potential future scenarios. In the first, expressed in a piece written for *The Guardian* newspaper, she imagines

> [a] remote, changed future, when more once-inhabited places will be abandoned. We can see beginning already floods here, drought there. We may need such images as Rona provides to help us imagine the world to come, because beneath the surf and birds' calls you can hear the long withdrawing roar of human occupation.[60]

Here, the abandoned landscape of Rona is seen as prefiguring other future abandonments as humanity recedes in the face of climate breakdown. For Gange, there is almost something to be relished in that long withdrawing roar, particularly, when it is accompanied by a re-encroachment of the natural world. Though registering the tragedy implicit in abandoned places that were once full of human life, he feels, given the propensity of humans for violence, against both each other and the natural world, that 'it might be heartening to see the agency of animals reshaping realms to which humans are, more than ever, peripheral'.[61]

Jamie's second futuristic vision, from the *Sightlines* essay 'On Rona', is a little more optimistic. Contemplating the remains of a dwelling that has been inhabited, abandoned and then reinhabited over thousands of years, she imagines a possible repopulation of Rona: '[P]erhaps someday in the future, when unimaginable change has come to the life we know, a few acres far out in the Atlantic might be pressed into service again.'[62] Moreover, these acres may be graced with modes of human habitation that we have not yet fully explored in Western modernity. Gange likewise presents a more positive, and more politicised, scenario, finding that his 'outside-in' historical method 'shows us there are other ways to live than those practised today'[63]:

> [T]he past is not full of dead things but of unfinished business: germs of fruitful routes as yet untravelled. Every coastal ruin whose living creatures were once steamrollered by the homogenising logics of industrial capitalism is a site at which the possibilities for an escape from those logics can be entertained.[64]

There are signs that some such possibilities are even now being realised on the islands, as they show the way towards an alternative future. For example, while not necessarily departing from capitalism, the Orkney archipelago is a world leader in terms of renewable energy.[65] As Liptrot notes, describing the view from the Outrun (a large coastal field on her family's farm): 'Out at sea, bobbing on the surface, I can make out wave-energy devices being tested by engineers.'[66] Nicolson also sees potential for a new era, at times viewing the Anthropocene as an ontological threshold rather than the apocalypse he fears:

> The Anthropocene will have brought one geological moment to an end; it could now usher in the Ecozoic ... an age which has at its heart the belief that all living beings have a right to life and to the recognition that they have forms of understanding we have never shared and probably never will.[67]

In this optimistic vision, scientific advances in knowledge about non-human life can be rewoven into new ontologies able to incorporate a regard for, if not a full ability to understand or enter into, the *umwelten* of other beings.

Nature writing is often framed in terms of simple nostalgia for modes of being in the world that are passing, but Huggan has recently identified another layer of temporal complexity in the genre – the prevalence of the *future anterior*, or future perfect tense, which is oriented towards a future which is always, already looking back.[68] This is the orientation that inflects the future imaginaries cited here. As such, New Nature Writing, particularly, texts grounded in the materialities of archipelagic spaces, offers us a mode uniquely suited to the Anthropocene, the temporal frame of which requires us to conjure ourselves imaginatively, as David Farrier writes, 'as ghosts that will haunt the very deep future'.[69] However, coalescing around a crucial juncture – a time in which the implications of the Anthropocene are inexorably revealing themselves – the works discussed in this chapter, while conceding that we may not be able to reverse or control the passage of the new epoch, also recognise ourselves as 'ancestors' who must address, and who might yet mitigate, the record we leave behind for the deep future to read.

Notes

1. Timothy Clark, 'Scale', in Tom Cohen (ed.), *Telemorphosis: Theory in the Era of Climate Change* (Michigan: Open Humanities Press, 2012), vol. 1, n.p.; Bruno Latour, 'Agency at the Time of the Anthropocene', *New Literary History* 45 (2014), 1–14; Timothy Morton, *Hyperobjects: Philosophy and Ecology after the End of the World*, (Minneapolis: University of Minnesota Press, 2013).

2. Lawrence Buell, *The Environmental Imagination: Thoreau, Nature Writing and the Formation of American Culture* (Cambridge, MA and London: Harvard University Press, 1995).

3. Adam Trexler, *Anthropocene Fictions: The Novel in a Time of Climate Change* (Charlottesville, VA: University of Virginia Press, 2015).

4. Timothy Clark, *Ecocriticism on the Edge: The Anthropocene as a Threshold Concept* (London and New York: Bloomsbury, 2015), p.24.

5. Dana Phillips, *The Truth of Ecology: Nature, Culture, and Literature in America* (New York: Oxford University Press, 2003), p.8.

6. Timothy Morton, *Ecology without Nature: Rethinking Environmental Aesthetics* (Cambridge, MA and London: Harvard University Press, 2007).

7. William Abberley, Christina Alt, David Higgins, Graham Huggan and Pippa Marland, *Modern British Nature Writing, 1789–2020*: Land Lines. (Cambridge: Cambridge University Press, forthcoming).

8. Terry Gifford and Anna Stenning, 'Introduction: European New Nature Writing', *Ecozon@* 6(1) (2015), 1–6.

9. Don McKay, 'Ediacaran and Anthropocene: Poetry as a Reader of Deep Time', in Elizabeth Ellsworth and Jamie Kruse (eds.), *Making the Geologic Now: Responses to Material Conditions of Contemporary Life* (New York: punctum books, 2012).

10. Latour, 'Agency', p.4.

11. Ibid.

12. Jos Smith proposed the term 'archipelagic literature' in preference to New Nature Writing (see 'An Archipelagic Literature: Re-framing "The New Nature Writing"', *Green Letters: Studies in Ecocriticism* 17(1) (2013), 5–15. He returned to the latter in *The New Nature Writing: Rethinking the Literature of Place* (London and New York: Bloomsbury, 2017), but still regards 'periphery' and 'archipelago' as key tropes.

13. For example, islands such as The Shiants, Orkney, Shetland, Sula Sgeir, Rona and St Kilda.

14. David Gange, *The Frayed Atlantic Edge: A Historian's Journey from Shetland to the Channel* (London: Harper Collins, 2019), p.114.

15. Jeremy Davies, *The Birth of the Anthropocene* (Oakland: University of California Press, 2016), p.20.

16. Caspar Henderson, *The Book of Barely Imagined Beings* (London: Granta Books, 2012), p.33.

17. Ibid.

18. Amy Liptrot, *The Outrun* (Edinburgh: Canongate Books, 2016), p.210.

19. See Serenella Iovino and Serpil Oppermann (eds.), *Material Ecocriticism* (Bloomington: Indiana University Press, 2014), p.x.

20. Gange, *Frayed Atlantic Edge*.

21. Ibid., p.x.

22. Ibid., p.33.

23. Smith, *The New Nature Writing*, p.17.

24. Gange, *Frayed Atlantic Edge*, p.33.

25. Robert Macfarlane, *The Old Ways: A Journey on Foot* (London: Hamish Hamilton, 2012), p.141.

26. Liptrot, *Outrun*, p.89.

27. Kathleen Jamie, *Findings* (London: Sort of Books, 2005), p.11.

28. Liptrot, *Outrun*, p.149.

29. Ibid.

30. Adam Nicolson, *Sea Room: An Island Life* (London: HarperCollins, 2001), p.184.

31. Martin Martin, *A Description of the Western Islands of Scotland Circa 1695* [ed. Donald Munro] (Edinburgh: Birlinn, 1999), p.239.

32. Gange, *Frayed Atlantic Edge*, p.xii.

33. Macfarlane, *Old Ways*, pp.91–2.

34. Nicolson, *Sea Room*, p.134.

35. In *The Seabird's Cry* (London: William Collins, 2018), Adam Nicolson discusses Jakob von Uexküll's development of this term, pp.17–20.

36. Kathleen Jamie, *Sightlines* (London: Sort of Books, 2012), p.215.

37. Ibid., p.216.

38. Liptrot, *Outrun*, p.130.

39. Ibid., p.218.

40. Gange, *Frayed Atlantic Edge*, p.49.

41. Ibid., p.18.

42. Ibid., p.47.
43. Michel Serres, *The Natural Contract* (Ann Arbor: University of Michigan Press, 1995), p.86.
44. Nicolson, *Sea Room*, p.13.
45. The knowledge that many species of seabird mate for life, a fact iterated several times in *The Seabird's Cry*, perhaps renders less anthropomorphic this sense of shared grief.
46. Ibid., p.15.
47. Ibid., p.3.
48. Ibid., p.15.
49. Michael Malay, Unpublished essay, 2018.
50. Liptrot, *Outrun*, p.131.
51. Ibid., p.131–2.
52. Donna Haraway, *Staying with the Trouble: Making Kin in the Chthulucene* (Durham, NC: Duke University Press, 2016), p.2.
53. Jamie, *Findings*, p.59.
54. Ibid.
55. Liptrot, *Outrun*, p.258.
56. Nicolson, *Seabird's Cry*, p.22.
57. See Stacy Alaimo, 'Trans-corporeal Feminisms and the Ethical Space of Nature' in Stacy Alaimo and Susan Hekman (eds.), *Material Feminisms* (Bloomington: Indiana University Press, 2008), pp.237–64.
58. Robert Macfarlane, *Underland* (London: Hamish Hamilton, 2019), p.77.
59. Gange, *Frayed Atlantic Edge*, p.78.
60. Kathleen Jamie, 'Island at the Edge of the World', *The Guardian*, 26 August 2006.
61. Gange, *Frayed Atlantic Edge*, p.48.
62. Jamie, *Sightlines*, p.207.
63. Gange, *Frayed Atlantic Edge*, p.114.
64. Ibid.
65. See, for example, Laura Watts, *Energy at the End of the World: An Orkney Islands Saga* (Cambridge, MA: MIT Press, 2018).
66. Liptrot, *Outrun*, p.4.
67. Nicolson, *Seabird's Cry*, pp.22–3.
68. Graham Huggan, *Colonialism, Culture, Whales: The Cetacean Quartet* (London: Bloomsbury, 2018), p.ix.
69. David Farrier, 'Deep Time's Uncanny Future Is Full of Ghostly Human Traces', *Aeon* (31 October 2016), https://aeon.co/ideas/deep-time-s-uncanny-future-is-full-of-ghostly-human-traces.

Further Reading

Anthropocene: General Introductions

Bonneuil, Christophe, and Jean-Baptiste Fressoz, *The Shock of the Anthropocene* (London: Verso, 2017).

Davies, Jeremy, *The Birth of the Anthropocene* (Oakland: University of California Press, 2016).

Haraway, Donna, 'Anthropocene, Capitalocene, Plantationocene, Chthulucene: Making Kin', *Environmental Humanities* 6 (2015), 159–65.

Horn, Eva, and Hannes Bergthaller, *The Anthropocene: Key Issues for the Humanities* (London: Routledge, 2020).

Ivakhiv, Adrian J., 'On Naming the Anthropocene' (12 June 2014), blog.uvm.edu/aivakhiv.

Moore, Jason W. (ed.), *Anthropocene or Capitalocene?: Nature, History, and the Crisis of Capitalism* (Oakland: PM Press, 2016).

Schwägerl, Christian, *Anthropocene: The Human Era and How It Shapes Our Planet* (London: Synergetic Press, 2014).

Vince, Gaia, *Adventures in the Anthropocene: A Journey to the Heart of the Planet We Made* (London: Vintage, 2014).

Wark, McKenzie, *Molecular Red: Theory for the Anthropocene* (London and New York: Verso, 2015).

Anthropocene and the Humanities

Adamson, Joni, 'Networking Networks and Constelling New Practices in the Environmental Humanities', *PMLA* 131(1) (2016), 347–55.

Adamson, Joni, and Michael Davis (eds.), *Humanities for the Environment: Integrating Knowledge, Forging New Constellations of Practice* (New York: Routledge, 2016).

Chakrabarty, Dipesh, 'The Climate of History: Four Theses', *Critical Inquiry* 35 (Winter 2009): 197–222.

Crist, Eileen, 'On the Poverty of Our Nomenclature', *Environmental Humanities* 3 (2013), 129–47.

Emmett, Robert S., and David E. Nye, *The Environmental Humanities: A Critical Introduction* (Cambridge, MA: MIT Press, 2017).

Hamilton, Clive, Christophe Bonneuil and François Gemenne (eds.), *The Anthropocene and the Global Environmental Crisis: Rethinking Modernity in a New Epoch* (London and New York: Routledge, 2015).

Heise, Ursula K., Jon Christensen and Michelle Niemann (eds.), *Routledge Companion to the Environmental Humanities* (London: Routledge, 2016).

Holm, Poul, et al., 'Humanities for the Environment—A Manifesto for Research and Action', *Humanities* 4 (2015), 977–92.

Oppermann, Serpil, and Serenella Iovino (eds.), *Environmental Humanities: Voices from the Anthropocene* (London and New York: Rowman & Littlefield, 2017).

Palsson, Gisli, et al., 'Reconceptualizing the "Anthropos" in the Anthropocene: Integrating the Social Sciences and Humanities in Global Environmental Change Research', *Environmental Science and Policy* 28 (2013), 3–13.

Simon, Zoltán Boldizsár, 'Why the Anthropocene Has No History: Facing the Unprecedented', *Anthropocene Review* 4(3) (2017), 239–45.

Anthropocene Science

Crutzen, Paul J., 'Geology of Mankind', *Nature* 415 (3 January 2002), 23.

Crutzen, Paul, and Eugene F. Stoermer, 'The Anthropocene', *IGBP* 41 (May 2000), 17–18.

Edgeworth, Matt, et al., 'The Chronostratigraphic Method Is Unsuitable for Determining the Start of the Anthropocene', *Progress in Physical Geography* 43(3) (2019), 334–44.

Lenton, Timothy M., *Earth System Science: A Very Short Introduction* (Oxford: Oxford University Press, 2016).

Rockström, Johan, et al., 'A Safe Operating Space for Humanity', *Nature* 461 (2009), 472–5.

Lewis, Simon L., and Mark A. Maslin, *The Human Planet: How We Created the Anthropocene* (New Haven: Yale University Press, 2018).

'Defining the Anthropocene', *Nature* 519 (2015), 171–80.

Ruddiman, William F., 'The Anthropogenic Greenhouse Era Began Thousands of Years Ago', *Climatic Change* 61(3) (2003), 261–93.

Steffen, Will, et al., *Global Change and the Earth System: A Planet under Pressure.* (Stockholm: IGBP Secretariat, 2004).

Zalasiewicz, Jan, *The Earth after Us: What Legacy Will Humans Leave in the Rocks?* (Oxford: Oxford University Press, 2008).

Zalasiewicz, Jan, et al., 'When Did the Anthropocene Begin? A Mid-Twentieth Century Boundary Level Is Stratigraphically Optimal', *Quaternary International* 383 (2015), 196–203.

Anthropocene: Social, Cultural, Philosophical Themes

Asafu-Adjaye, John, et al., *An Ecomodernist Manifesto* (2015), squarespace.com.

Ceballos, Gerardo, Anne Ehrlich and Paul Ehrlich, *The Annihilation of Nature: Human Extinction of Birds and Mammals* (Baltimore: Johns Hopkins University Press, 2015).

Chakrabarty, Dipesh, 'The Human Condition in the Anthropocene', Tanner Lectures on Human Values, delivered at Yale University (18–19 February 2015), https://tannerlectures.utah.edu/Chakrabarty%20manuscript.pdf.

Clark, Nigel, *Inhuman Nature: Sociable Life on a Dynamic Planet* (London: Sage, 2011).

Clover, Joshua, and Juliana Spahr, *#Misanthropocene: 24 Theses*. First presented at Curds and Whey Oakland 6.13.2014 (Oakland: Commune Editions, 2014).

Comaroff, Jean, and John L. Comaroff, 'Theory from the South: Or, How Euro-America Is Evolving toward Africa', *Anthropological Forum: A Journal of Social Anthropology and Comparative Sociology* 22(2) (2012), 113–31.

Crist, Eileen, *Abundant Earth: Toward an Ecological Civilization* (Chicago: University of Chicago Press, 2019).

Downton, Paul, *Ecopolis: Architecture and Cities for a Changing Climate* (Collingwood, AU: CSIRO, 2009).

Escobar, Arturo, 'Worlds and Knowledges Otherwise: The Latin American Modernity/Coloniality Research Program', *Cultural Studies* 21(2–3) (2007), 179–210.

Haraway, Donna, *Staying with the Trouble: Making Kin in the Chthulucene* (Durham, NC: Duke University Press, 2016).

Hulme, Mike, *Weathered: Cultures of Climate* (London: Sage, 2017).

Latour, Bruno, 'Agency at the Time of the Anthropocene', *New Literary History* 45 (2014), 1–18.

Lorimer, Jamie, *Wildlife in the Anthropocene: Conservation after Nature* (Minneapolis: University of Minnesota Press, 2015).

Malm, Andreas, *Fossil Capital: The Rise of Steam Power and the Roots of Global Warming* (London and Brooklyn, NY: Verso, 2016).

Marris, Emma, *Rambunctious Garden: Saving Nature in a Post-Wild World* (New York: Bloomsbury, 2011).

Nixon, Rob, 'The Great Acceleration and the Great Divergence: Vulnerability in the Anthropocene', *MLA Profession* (2014), profession.mla.org.

Plumwood, Val, *The Eye of the Crocodile* (ed. Lorraine Shannon) (Canberra: ANU Epress, 2003).

Rose, Deborah Bird, *Wild Dog Dreaming: Love and Extinction* (Charlottesville: University of Virginia Press, 2011).

Smith, Zadie, 'Elegy for a Country's Seasons', *New York Review of Books* (3 April 2014).

Swanson, Heather Anne, 'The Banality of the Anthropocene', *Fieldsights* (22 February 2017), culanth.org/fieldsights.

Tsing, Anna Lowenhaupt, *The Mushroom at the End of the World: On the Possibility of Life in Capitalist Ruins* (Princeton: Princeton University Press, 2015).

van Dooren, Thom, *Flight Ways: Life and Loss at the Edge of Extinction* (New York: Columbia University Press, 2014).

Weisman, Alan, *The World Without Us* (Toronto: HarperCollins, 2010).

Yusoff, Kathryn, *A Billion Black Anthropocenes or None* (Minneapolis: University of Minnesota Press, 2018).

Zylinska, Joanna, *Minimal Ethics for the Anthropocene* (London: Open Humanities Press, 2014).

Forms and Genres

Bracke, Astrid, *Climate Crisis and the 21st-Century British Novel* (London: Bloomsbury Academic, 2018).

Bristow, Tom, *The Anthropocene Lyric: An Affective Geography of Poetry, Person, Place* (Basingstoke: Palgrave Macmillan, 2015).

Chang, Alenda Y., *Playing Nature: Ecology in Video Games* (Minneapolis: University of Minnesota Press, 2019).

Dürbeck, Gabriele, 'Narratives of the Anthropocene in Interdisciplinary Perspective' in Gina Comos and Caroline Rosenthal (eds.), *Anglophone Literature and Culture in the Anthropocene* (Newcastle-upon-Tyne: Cambridge Scholars Publishing, 2019), pp.23–45.

Farrier, David, *Anthropocene Poetics: Deep Time, Sacrifice Zones, and Extinction* (Minneapolis: University of Minnesota Press, 2019).

'Animal Detectives and "Anthropocene Noir" in Chloe Hooper's *A Child's Book of True Crime*', *Textual Practice* 32(5) (2018), 875–93.

Garforth, Lisa, *Green Utopias: Environmental Hope before and after Nature* (Cambridge: Polity, 2018).

Graulund, Rune, 'Writing Travel in the Anthropocene: Disastrous Life at the End of the Arctic', *Studies in Travel Writing* 20(3) (2016), 285–95.

Johns-Putra, Adeline, *Climate Change and the Contemporary Novel* (Cambridge: Cambridge University Press, 2019).

'The Rest Is Silence: Postmodern and Postcolonial Possibilities in Climate Change Fiction', *Studies in the Novel* 50(1) (2018), 26–42.

LeMenager, Stephanie, 'Climate Change and the Struggle of Genre' in Tobias Menely and Jesse Oak Taylor (eds.), *Anthropocene Reading: Literary History in Geologic Times* (University Park: Pennsylvania State University Press, 2017), pp.220–38.

'The Humanities after the Anthropocene' in Ursula K. Heise, Jon Christensen and Michelle Niemann (eds.), *Routledge Companion to the Environmental Humanities* (London: Routledge, 2016), pp.473–81.

Nersessian, Anahid, 'Two Gardens: An Experiment in Calamity Form', *Modern Language Quarterly* 74(3) (2013), 307–28.

Parikka, Jussi, *A Geology of Media* (Minneapolis: University of Minnesota Press, 2015).

Rochester, Rachel, '*We're Alive*: The Resurrection of the Audio Drama in the Anthropocene', *Philological Quarterly* 93(3) (2014), 361–81.

Rose, Deborah Bird, 'Anthropocene Noir', *Arena* 41–2 (2013–14), 206–19.

Ruffino, Paolo, 'Nonhuman Games: Playing in the Post-Anthropocene' in Matt Coward-Gibbs (ed.), *Death, Culture and Leisure: Playing Dead* (Bingley, UK: Emerald Publishing, 2020), pp.11–26.

Solnick, Sam, *Poetry and the Anthropocene: Ecology, Biology and Technology in Contemporary British and Irish Poetry* (London: Routledge, 2017).

Swanson, Heather Anne, Nils Bubandt and Anna Tsing, 'Less Than One but More than Many: Anthropocene as Science Fiction and Scholarship-in-the-Making', *Environment and Society: Advances in Research* 6 (2015), 149–66.

Taylor, Jesse Oak, 'The Novel after Nature, Nature after the Novel: Richard Jefferies's Anthropocene Romance', *Studies in the Novel* 50(1) (2018), 108–33.

Trexler, Adam, *Anthropocene Fictions: The Novel in a Time of Climate Change* (Charlottesville: University of Virginia Press, 2015).

van Dooren, Thom, 'Nature in the Anthropocene? A Reflection on a Photograph', *Yearbook of Comparative Literature* 58 (2012), 228–34.

Weik von Mossner, Alexa, 'Imagining Geological Agency: Storytelling in the Anthropocene' in Robert Emmett and Thomas Lekan (eds.), Special Issue: 'Whose Anthropocene? Revisiting Dipesh Chakrabarty's "Four Theses"', *RCC Perspectives: Transformations in Environment and Society*, 2 (2016), 83–8.

Literature and the Anthropocene

Boes, Tobias, and Kate Marshall, 'Writing the Anthropocene: An Introduction', *Minnesota Review* 83 (2014), 60–72.

Clark, Timothy, *Ecocriticism on the Edge: The Anthropocene as a Threshold Concept* (London: Bloomsbury, 2015).

(ed.), Special Issue: 'Deconstruction in the Anthropocene', *Oxford Literary Review* 34(2) (2012).

De Cristofaro, Diletta, and Daniel Cordle, 'Introduction: The Literature of the Anthropocene', *C21 Literature: Journal of 21st-Century Writings* 6(1) (2018), 1–6.

DeLoughrey, Elizabeth M., *Allegories of the Anthropocene* (Durham, NC: Duke University Press, 2019).

Ghosh, Amitav, *The Great Derangement* (Chicago: University of Chicago Press, 2016).

Menely, Tobias, and Jesse Oak Taylor, *Anthropocene Reading: Literary History in Geologic Times* (University Park: Pennsylvania State University Press, 2017).

Mentz, Steve, *Shipwreck Modernity: Ecologies of Globalization, 1550–1719* (Minneapolis: University of Minnesota Press, 2015).

Rigby, Kate, *Dancing with Disaster: Environmental Histories, Narratives, and Ethics in Perilous Times* (Charlottesville: University of Virginia Press, 2015).

Shannon, Laurie, et al., 'Editor's Column: Literature in the Ages of Wood, Tallow, Coal, Whale Oil, Gasoline, Atomic Power, and Other Energy Sources', *PMLA* 126(2) (2011), 305–26.

Woods, Derek, 'Scale Critique for the Anthropocene', *Minnesota Review* 83 (2014), 133–42.

Texts, Authors, Traditions

Caminero-Santangelo, Byron, *Different Shades of Green: African Literature, Environmental Justice, and Political Ecology* (Charlottesville: University of Virginia Press, 2014).

Comos, Gina, and Caroline Rosenthal (eds.), *Anglophone Literature and Culture in the Anthropocene* (Newcastle-upon-Tyne: Cambridge Scholars Publishing, 2019).

Huang, Hsinya, 'Radiation Ecologies in Gerald Vizenor's Hiroshima Bugi', *Neohelicon* 44 (2017), 417–30.

Iheka, Cajetan, *Naturalizing Africa: Ecological Violence, Agency, and Postcolonial Resistance* (Cambridge: Cambridge University Press, 2018).

Keller, Lynn, *Recomposing Ecopoetics: North American Poetry of the Self-Conscious Anthropocene* (Charlottesville and London: University of Virginia Press, 2017).

Marcone, Jorge, 'The Stone Guests: Buen Vivir and Popular Environmentalisms in the Andes and Amazonia' in Ursula K. Heise, Jon Christensen and Michelle Niemann (eds.), *Routledge Companion to the Environmental Humanities* (London: Routledge, 2016), pp.227–35.

Marland, Pippa, *Ecocriticism and the Island: Readings from the British-Irish Archipelago* (London: Rowman & Littlefield, in press).

Niblett, Michael, 'World-Economy, World-Ecology, World Literature', *Green Letters: Studies in Ecocriticism* 16 (2012), 15–30.

Pirzadeh, Saba, 'Postcolonial Development, Socio-Ecological Degradation, and Slow Violence in Pakistani Fiction' in Scott Slovic, Swarnalatha Rangarajan and Vidya Sarveswaran (eds.), *Routledge Handbook of Ecocriticism and Environmental Communication* (London: Routledge, 2019).

Ronda, Margaret, *Remainders: American Poetry at Nature's End* (Stanford, CA: Stanford University Press, 2018).

Schaumann, Caroline, and Heather Sullivan (eds.), *German Ecocriticism in the Anthropocene* (New York: Palgrave Macmillan, 2017).

Taylor, Jesse Oak, *The Sky of Our Manufacture: The London Fog in British Fiction from Dickens to Woolf* (Charlottesville: University of Virginia Press, 2016).

Thornber, Karen L., 'Literature, Asia, and the Anthropocene: Possibilities for Asian Studies and the Environmental Humanities', *Journal of Asian Studies* 73(4) (2014), 989–1000.

Wilke, Sabine, and Japhet Johnstone (eds.), *Readings in the Anthropocene: Environmental Humanities, German Studies, and Beyond* (Rochester, NY: Bloomsbury, 2017).

Zainal, Zainor Izat, 'Environmental Ethics in K. S. Maniam's *Between Lives* and Yang-May Ooi's *The Flame Tree*', *South East Asia Research* 25(4) (2017), 342–58.

Index

Cambridge Companions To . . .

AUTHORS